Theoretical Aspects of Reasoning About Knowledge

Proceedings of the Third Conference (TARK 1990)

Edited by

ROHIT PARIKH
Brooklyn College of CUNY
and CUNY Graduate Center

MARCH 4–7, 1990
PACIFIC GROVE, CALIFORNIA

Sponsored by
IBM RESEARCH, ALMADEN RESEARCH CENTER
and supported by the
AMERICAN ASSOCIATION FOR ARTIFICIAL INTELLIGENCE
and the
AIRFORCE OFFICE OF SCIENTIFIC RESEARCH

President and Editor *Michael B. Morgan*
Production Managers *Shirley Jowell and Sharon E. Montooth*
Cover Designer *Beverly Kennon-Kelley*

Library of Congress Cataloging-in-Publication Data

Theoretical aspects of reasoning about knowledge : proceedings of the third conference (TARK 1990) March 4-7, 1990, Pacific Grove, California / edited by Rohit Parikh : sponsored by IBM Research, Almaden Research Center and supported by the American Association for Artificial Intelligence and the AirForce Office of Scientific Research.
p. cm.
Selected papers presented to the 3rd Conference on the Theoretical Aspects of Reasoning About Knowledge.
Includes bibliographical references.
ISBN 1-55880-105-8
1. Artificial intelligence--Congresses. 2. Knowledge, Theory of--Congresses. 3. Logic, Symbolic and mathematical--Congresses. I. Parikh, Rohit, 1936- . II. Conference on the Theoretical Aspects of Reasoning about Knowledge (3rd : 1990 : Pacific Grove, Calif.) III. Almaden Research Center (IBM Research)
Q334.T48 1990
006.3--dc20 90-5435
CIP

Morgan Kaufmann Publishers, Inc.
San Mateo, California

93 92 91 90 5 4 3 2 1

CONTENTS

SESSION 5

SESSION 6

SESSION 7

PREFACE

The nineteen contributed papers in this volume were selected from 79 papers submitted to the Third Conference on the Theoretical Aspects of Reasoning About Knowledge. The program committee consisted of Nicholas Asher, Cristina Bicchieri, Fred Dretske, Jon Doyle, Ronald Fagin, Mike Fischer, Haim Gaifman, John Geanakoplos, Shafi Goldwasser, Kurt Konolige, Isaac Levi, Rohit Parikh, and Robert Stalnaker; a good mix of computer scientists, philosophers, and mathematical economists. We met in New York City for two days in October of 1989 and the program was compiled after a lively but amicable discussion.

Because of time constraints, we could not select all of the good papers submitted. Also, the papers cannot be regarded as being formally refereed, though each paper received the close attention of at least three and usually five members of the committee. It was decided to include four tutorials and an invited talk in addition to the contributed papers in order to give some background that would help the reader better appreciate the contributed papers.

It is clear that this subject has become quite a central interdisciplinary area, and it is gratifiying to find that it has borne fruit. There are several papers in this volume where the area of the paper and the formal departmental affiliation of the author(s) are different, and I would like to suggest that previous meetings of TARK have somthing to do with this.

The conference was sponsored by the IBM Almaden Research Center and supported in part by the American Association for Artificial Intelligence and the Air Force Office of Scientific Research (under proposal AFOSR-89-NM-678). We thank them all. The organizing committee of the conference consisted of Joseph Halpern, Rohit Parikh, and Moshe Vardi. The conference chair was Moshe Vardi and I thank him personally for all his hard work and help.

Rohit Parikh
Program Chair

NONMONOTONIC REASONING

Kurt Konolige
SRI International
Menlo Park, California 94025/USA

In this talk I will give an overview of nonmonotonic reasoning as background, and then address the question of its relevance and importance for theoretical issues in reasoning about knowledge and belief. In the past few years the area of nonmonotonic reasoning has grown tremendously, as witnessed by the increase in submitted and accepted papers to conferences such as this one. It would be impossible to give detailed accounts of the major formalisms and their application domains, so instead I will present very short overviews of the basic ideas, and then recount the issues that are currently being addressed, and their relevance for future research, especially regarding knowledge and belief. This should give a framework for understanding the significance of the papers presented at this conference.

Broadly speaking, there are two classes of nonmonotonic formalisms, consistency-based and model-based. Among the former are default logic, autoepistemic logic, and various types of inheritance and argument systems. The most prevalent model-based account is circumscription in several different forms, along with systems that have a model preference semantics, such as conditional logics. I will point out some of the major strengths and weaknesses of these approaches. In general the consistency-based logics, especially autoepistemic logic, have a strong relation to standard epistemic modal logics, and I will concentrate on these systems. Most of the nonmonotonic reasoning papers in this conference are influenced by this connection.

The nonmonotonic formalisms are meant to characterize certain forms of reasoning. I will discuss three general forms of reasoning: default or prototypical reasoning, reasoning about closure, and abductive and diagnostic reasoning. All of these, especially the last two, are important modes of reasoning either for an agent who has beliefs, or when reasoning about an agent's beliefs. I will show how nonmonotonic formalisms have been used for this purpose, and point out future directions.

RECENT ISSUES IN REASONING ABOUT KNOWLEDGE[1]

Rohit Parikh[2]

INTRODUCTION:

It is by now common knowledge that the recent period of intense activity in reasoning about knowledge begins with two books, both by philosophers: *Knowledge and Belief* by Hintikka [Hi], and *Convention* by David Lewis [Lew]. Since then there has been much talk about muddy children and non-coperating generals, but the field has actually grown to be quite wide and interesting and we will try and give an overview of some of the work that has been done and some of the issues that are still of concern.

It should be said at the outset that most of the work that has been done concerns itself with information rather than with knowledge. A familiar example from [FHV] goes "Dean doesn't know whether Nixon knows that Dean knows that Nixon knows about the Watergate break-in". Now it is likely in the case of Dean and Nixon that if they had the relevant information then they also had the knowledge, but of another, more recent president, it is easier to believe that he might have had the requisite information about the Iran-Contra affair and simply failed to make the necessary deduction which would lead to *knowledge*. This split between information and knowledge is one that almost all workers in the field have come to be aware of, but the issue is not resolved. More of this later.

It is customary to introduce a language for studying knowledge by starting with some base level "object" language, say propositional logic, and augmenting it with operators K_i where i is the name of some individual or knower and $K_i(A)$ stands for "i knows or has the information that A". One can then study the resulting language in terms of an abstract model theory and consider issues of satisfiability, validity and the computational complexity of the set of valid formulae.

The most common semantics used for this purpose is Kripke semantics where a set W of possible worlds is stipulated. There are some basic statements P_j, whose truth value is specified at each of these possible worlds, and some binary relations R_i, one for each knower i, are also specified. Roughly speaking, if s and t are two possible worlds (elements of W), then sR_it means that worlds s and t are indistinguishable to i, i.e. furnish the same evidence to i. Then the formula $K_i(A)$ holds at a world s iff A holds at each world t such that sR_it.

In the most common case, the relations R_i considered are equivalence relations, and if the base language is the propositional calculus, then the logic is S5-like, and the validity

[1]This paper should be regarded as a working draft towards a more comprehensive survey of recent work in reasoning about knowledge. If we have ignored important work, or misrepresented any position, we apologise in advance and welcome comments. When there are several references to the same result, we have tried to follow a *chronological* order.

[2]Department of Computer and Information Science, Brooklyn College of CUNY and Departments of Computer Science, Mathematics and Philosophy, CUNY Graduate Center, 33 W 42nd Street, New York, NY 10036. Email: RIPBC@CUNYVM.bitnet, Research supported in part by NSF grant CCR-8803409

problem is decidable, shown to be in DEXPTIME in [Pa] but is in fact in PSPACE. See [HV] for a survey of complexity results. A complete axiomatisation is also available, essentially along the lines of S5, see [Ma], [Pa].

While the Kripke style model theory is elegant and simple, it has two defects. One is that the notion of possible world as used there *includes* the psychological states of the knowers. Two worlds s and t may agree on all *facts*, but may be different because some knowers know different things in them. If this is the case, then the notion of possible world as in the Kripke models is *complex* and needs to be analysed. Another reason for dissatisfaction is that while the Kripke semantics yields a finite model property, it is in fact true, as shown by [FHV], that the state of total ignorance, where no one knows anything, can only be represented by an infinite Kripke model.

[FHV], as also [MZ],[3] therefore propose another model theory, where a possible world is represented as a tower of levels, the bottom level being facts, the next level being the individuals' knowledge of these facts, the next one specifying the individuals' knowledge of other individuals' knowledge, and so on. [FHV] prove that their version is equivalent to Kripke semantics and that the models are inter-translatable in a natural way.

The semantics that we have considered so far is abstract; an application, say to distributed computing, must give us some way of going from a described protocol to the relevant Kripke model, and the most common proposal, due independently to [PR], [CM] and [HM2], is to use the distinction between local runs and global runs as the basis for the relations R_i. Specifically, when processes co-operate in a computation, then each process has certain events happening locally as well as messages received from and sent to other processes. If A is a property of global states and process i has gone through a sequence r_i of local events (including sends and receives if any), then i *knows* A iff A is true in all global states compatible with r_i. [HV] point out that there are many choices that may be made in such models, whether time is synchronous or asynchronous, whether the processes have finite or infinite memory, etc., and they show that the complexity of the resulting logics can vary from PSPACE to Π^1_1-complete.

There have been some specific applications of knowledge in distributed computing. [PR] contains some preliminary results, but there are other, more substantial applications; e.g. in [HZ] to the sequence transmission problem, in [DM] to Byzantine failures and in [Maz] to the problem of recovery from crashes. See also [MT].

COMMON KNOWLEDGE:

Common knowledge as an issue in knowledge theory was introduced independently by Lewis [Lew] and Schiffer [Sch]. What they pointed out was that co-ordinated action, or proper communication, requires infinitely many levels of knowledge in the following sense: if, say, i and j are the two individuals involved, then there is in these situations some proposition

[3] The two models differ a little in that the [MZ] model includes probabilities, but we shall not go into this here.

A such that the infinitely many propositions $K_i(A)$, $K_j(A)$, $K_i(K_j(A))$,... must all be true for some co-ordinated action to take place, or respectively, some reference to be made successfully from i to j. [CM2] contains a series of amusing examples about a Marx Brothers movie to substantiate this claim.

The problem with common (or mutual) knowledge is that it seems difficult to attain. [HM] show that it cannot be attained in asynchronous systems and [CM2] give informal arguments why it cannot be attained in ordinary social situations, thus turning the whole business into something of a paradox.

Barwise [Bar] takes the stance that we really have *three* notions here: (i) the infinite iteration mentioned above, (ii) a fixed point B defined by $B = A \wedge K_i(B) \wedge K_j(B)$, and (iii) the existence of a situation s such that s implies A *and* that both i and j see s.[4] Certainly, many situations where we would attribute common knowledge *are* such as described in (iii). E.g. where both i and j are in the presence of a card which is lying face up on the table. However, common knowledge of *abstract* facts, needed to make use of the concrete facts, seems harder to explain this way.

Anyway, Barwise seems to be arguing that common knowledge may imply a transfinite iteration in certain cases, a point of view which receives some support from a result proved in [Pa4] that some facts can be learned only through transfinite dialogues and cannot be learned at any finite stage. However, a willingness to take a risk, no matter how small, reduces the needed time to a finite value. Perhaps this explains why we might, in practice, make do without actual common knowledge. A dance requires common knowledge between partners, but only approximate common knowledge is in fact present, and an occasional stubbed toe is the price that most of us are willing to pay for the pleasure.

Common Knowledge of a fact is in some sense the highest level at which a group might know it. The lowest level (barring implicit knowledge) is where the fact is known to *just one* of the individuals in question. [Pa2] considers the question of what intermediate levels there might be and shows[5] that they correspond precisely to a family of regular languages in the alphabet $\{K_1, ..., K_n\}$ where $\{1, ..., n\}$ are the individuals involved.

However, is there only *one* level of common knowledge? Suppose, for example, that a young man sitting next to a girl moves his knee so that it touches hers. This fact will then be common knowledge between them even if she ignores it. If, however, she says: "Excuse me, but your knee is touching mine", then the dynamics between them will change and whether he removes his knee or not, the action will have a different significance than if she had not spoken. A similar situation will arise if country A masses troups on the border of country B. If it is common knowledge that country B has a good espionage system, then this massing of troups will be common knowledge between A and B. The situation will nonetheless change if the prime minister of country B summons the ambassador of country

[4] Barwise suggests that the correct representation of cases (ii) and (iii) requires us to resort to non-well founded sets in the sense of Aczel [Ac].

[5] This result is joint with P. Krasucki.

A and mentions the massing of troups. The common knowledge will rise to a "higher" level and some action will now become necessary.

This seems to indicate that what we call common knowledge may actually stand for a game-theoretic situation, that such situations may differ from each other, and may neither imply nor require common knowledge as we *usually* understand it. This is already implicit in [Lew], but clearly there is a great deal of subtlety here.

STARTING FROM IGNORANCE:

Suppose I tell you that $0 < a < b$ and that $a \cdot b = 6$, then you know that $a = 2$ and $b = 3$. If, however, I had told you instead that $a \cdot b = 12$, then you would not know what a and b are. It turns out that your ignorance in the second case cannot be proved in a monotonic logic, since it will not survive the additional (and consistent) information that a is even. The point is that your ignorance is due to the implicit assumption that what you have been told about a and b is *all* you know about them. McCarthy has suggested that this kind of default reasoning be formalised using the inference rule

$$\frac{\Gamma \nvdash K_i(A)}{\Gamma \vdash \neg K_i(A)}$$

This rule, however, does have its problems. For example, the formula $C = K_i(A) \vee K_i(B)$ does not imply $K_i(A)$ nor $K_i(B)$ and hence implies their negations by McCarthy's rule. These, however, together imply the negation of the original formula. A more subtle argument shows that even the empty set Γ is inconsistent under McCarthy's rule. This problem is tackled in [Pa] where a model theory and a completeness theorem for McCarthy's rule are given. Roughly, the idea is that larger Kripke models represent more possibilities and hence less knowledge. Hence a state of maximum ignorance, compatible with certain given facts, is represented by a largest Kripke model, and the existence of such a model is equivalent to consistency under certain normal applications of McCarthy's rule. When consistency does obtain, then all formulae true in the largest Kripke model can be proved through normal[6] applications of McCarthy's rule. In particular, the formula C above *is* inconsistent, it has no largest model, but the empty set (thank heavens!) turns out to be just fine.

Normal deducibility from consistent formulae can be shown to be in PSPACE, but, as Joe Halpern has pointed out, the existence of a largest Kripke model for a given formula A may be non-elementary.[7]

---

[6] An application of McCarthy's rule to $K_i(A)$ is *normal* if all subformlae of A, to which the rule could be applied, have been dealt with first.

[7] In particular, while the completeness theorem, as implied by Theorem 8(i) of [Pa], is correct, there are subtle errors in the proofs of parts (ii) and (iii), and all we can say is that the consistency problem is decidable and, at worst, of the same complexity as the system WS1S.

THE PROBLEM OF LOGICAL OMNISCIENCE:

One of the principal diffferences between knowledge and mere information shows up in the fact that if we have information that A and information that $A \rightarrow B$, then we also have information that B. Moreover, if B is logically true, then it requires no information in the first place. If an individual's knowledge *does* happen to have these closure properties, then we call that individual logically omniscient. Nonetheless, it does happen in fact that we are not logically omniscient and that we often fail to know B, either because the computation is intractable, or because we happen not to think of the justification for B, or, as Doyle [Doy] points out, we are not actually interested in B.

One area where this issue becomes important is public key cryptography, where the cypher-text does contain the same information that the plain-text does, but, lacking the key, the computation of the plain-text from the cypher-text is intractable. Thus a theory of knowledge which avoids assuming logical omniscience is crucial.

There have been several attempts to deal with this problem by developing logics in which knowledge is not closed under all logical inferences. Some examples include [FH], [Mos] and [FZ]. These papers all attempt to develop logics of knowledge which allow for limited reasoning powers. However, the analysis of why the systems proposed are the right ones is not completely convincing and the logics go only part way towards the heart of the logical omniscience problem. By contrast, the papers [Doy] and [Pa3] contain informal analyses of the problem and give us some insight into it, but there are no formal systems proposed that one could use to formalise actual, limited, knowledge. Indeed, [Doy] argues that formal systems are bound to be distortions, since they do not take into account the *goals* of the reasoning agent or the fact that resources, while bounded, may change with time.

It is worth mentioning the beautiful results in [Va] where Vardi analyses the logical omniscience problem from a pure complexity point of view and shows that the complexity of deducing logical conclusions stems from the ability to put together two distinct known facts. In other words, it is the *binary* rules of inference which are computationally expensive and, perhaps, account for why we don't know as much as we should.

A related, interesting problem is that of formalising the logical *goals* of a public key cryptographic system or of a zero knowledge proof system. What the standard literature gives us is the implementations of the goals, "I should convince you that I can factorise n without actually giving you the factors", but we do not have a formal language for stating the specifications. [BAN] contains a formal language that represents a beginning in this direction, but it would be nice to have a clean language whose formal semantics corresponds to our intuitions about what the logical issues are and which allows us to separate the complexity issues from the logical ones.

THE SYNTACTIC APPROACH:

In his "Three Grades of Modal Involvement", [Q], Quine proposed that modalities might apply to sentences rather than to propositions. This can of course also be done with knowledge operators and then this device neatly bypasses the issue of referential opacity. For now it is easy to see why I might know the sentence $\ulcorner A \urcorner$ and fail to know the sentence $\ulcorner B \urcorner$, even though the propositions A and B are logically equivalent.

Unfortunately, this approach has its limitations. Thomason [Th] showed, using techniques adapted from Montague, that very reasonable systems following this approach and containing a certain amount of arithmetic, are inconsistent. There is more recent work in this direction, by Asher and Kamp [AK], using techniques of Herzberger and Gupta and an abstract version of the basic problem by Koons [Koo]. While these approaches do not lead to any definitive logics, this line is still a promising one.

THE PROBLEM OF IDENTITY:

When one uses an ATM to withdraw money, the screen sometimes contains reference to an entity identified as "I". One could ask here whether this "I" is the terminal, the central computer that drives it, or perhaps the bank itself. We don't ask, since we do usually get the money and that is all that matters, but it is worth remembering that in a distributed computing situation, the *individuals* i who do the knowing are stipulated by us. [HM] refer to knowledge jointly held by several individuals as implicit knowledge. Thus if I know A and you know $A \rightarrow B$, then together, we implicitly know B. But this distinction between implicit and explicit knowledge presupposes that we know who the individuals are.

To consider one example, while we usually think of a Turing machine as an individual which attempts to compute (say) in polynomial time, we could also think of it as a *system* consisting of infinitely many tape squares together with one head, which have implicit (or distributed) knowledge whether the given string x is in the stipulated language L, but communication is needed to concentrate this implicit knowledge at a single node so that it can be used. If this is the case, then we should not regard all forms of implicit knowledge as equal, but differentiate between them according to how much communication is necessary to make it explicit. In this context one could well regard Yao's theory [Y] as a study of implicit knowledge.

FINAL REMARKS:

There are many issues that we have not been able to touch on here. Auto-epistemic reasoning is one. Applications to Mathematical Economics is another. There is also a large body of strictly philosophical literature dealing with the nature of knowledge and beliefs and the general issue of propositional attitudes. Hopefully some of these will be addressed by some of the other tutorials.

REFERENCES:

[Ac] P. Aczel, *Non Well-founded Sets.* CSLI Lecture note 14, 1988.

[AK] N. Asher and H. Kamp, The Knowers Paradox and Representational Theories of Attitudes, in *TARK-I*, Ed. J. Halpern, Morgan Kaufmann 1986, pp. 131-148.

[BAN] M. Burrows, M. Abadi and R. Needham, Authentication: A Practical Study in Belief and Action, in *TARK-2*, Ed. M. Vardi, Morgan Kaufmann 1988, pp. 325-342.
[Bar] J. Barwise, Three Views of Common Knowledge, in *TARK-2*, Ed. M. Vardi, Morgan Kaufmann 1988, pp. 369-380.
[CM] M. Chandy and J. Misra, How Processes Learn, *Distributed Computing* **1**:1, 1986, pp. 40-52.
[CM2] H. H. Clark and C. R. Marshall, Definite Reference and Mutual Knowledge, in *Elements of Discourse Understanding*, Ed. Joshi, Webber and Sag, Cambridge U. Press, 1981.
[DM] C. Dwork and Y. Moses, Knowledge and Common Knowledge in a Byzantine Environment, *TARK-I*, Ed. J. Halpern, Morgan Kaufmann 1986, pp. 149-170.
[Doy] J. Doyle, Knowledge, Representation and Rational Self-Government, in *TARK-2*, Ed. M. Vardi, Morgan Kaufmann 1988, pp. 345-354.
[FHV] R. Fagin, J. Halpern and M. Vardi, A Model-Theoretic Analysis of Knowledge (research report), RJ 6461, IBM 1988.
[FZ] M. Fischer and L. Zuck, Relative Knowledge and Belief, Research report YALEU/DCS/TR-589, 1987.
[Hi] J. Hintikka, *Knowledge and Belief*, Cornell U. Press, 1962.
[HM] J. Halpern and Y. Moses, Knowledge and Commmon Knowledge in a Distributed Environment, *Proc. 3rd ACM Symposium on Distributed Computing* 1984 pp. 50-61
[HM2] J. Halpern and Y. Moses, A Guide to the Modal Logics of Knowledge and Belief, *Ninth IJCAI*, 1985, pp. 480-490.
[HV] J. Halpern and M. Vardi, The Complexity of Reasoning about Knowledge and Time, *JCSS* **38** (1989) pp. 195-237.
[HZ] J. Halpern and L. Zuck, A Little Knowledge goes a Long Way, *Proc. 6th PODC*, 1987, pp. 269-280.
[Koo] R. Koons, Doxastic Paradoxes without Self-Reference, in *TARK-2*, Ed. M. Vardi, Morgan Kaufmann 1988, pp. 29-42.
[Lew] D. Lewis, *Convention, a Philosophical Study*, Harvard U. Press, 1969.
[Ma] D. Makinson, On Some Completeness Theorems in Modal Logic, *Zeit. f. Math. Logik* **12**, 1966, pp. 379-384.
[Maz] M. Mazer, A Knowledge Theoretic Account of Recovery in Distributed Systems, *TARK-2*, Ed. M. Vardi, Morgan Kaufmann 1988, pp. 309-324.
[Mos] Y. Moses, Resource-Bounded Knowledge, in *TARK-2*, Ed. M. Vardi, Morgan Kaufmann 1988, pp. 261-276.
[MT] Y. Moses and M. Tuttle, Programming Simultaneous Actions using Common Knowledge, Research Report MIT/LCS/TR-369 (1987)
[MZ] J. Mertens and S. Zamir, Formulation of Bayesian Analysis in Games with Incomplete Information, *Int. J. of Game Theory* **14** (1985) pp. 1-29.
[Pa] R. Parikh, Logics of Knowledge, Games and Dynamic Logic, *FST-TCS* 1984, Springer LNCS 181, pp. 202-222.
[Pa2] R. Parikh, Levels of Knowledge in Distributed Computing, *IEEE LICS Symposium*,

1986, pp. 314-321.
[Pa3] R. Parikh, Knowledge and the Problem of Logical Omniscience, *ISMIS-87*, North Holland, pp. 432-439.
[Pa4] R. Parikh, Finite and Infinite Dialogues, to appear in the Proceedings of a Workshop on Logic and Computer Science, MSRI, November 1989.
[PR] R. Parikh and R. Ramanujam, Distributed Computing and the Logic of Knowledge, *Logics of Programs* 1985, Springer LNCS 193, 256-268.
[Q] W. V. Quine, Three Grades of Modal Involvement, in *the Ways of Paradox*, Harvard U. Press, 1975. (Originally published in 1953).
[Sa] M. Sato, A Study of Kripke-type Models for Some Modal Logics, Research report, Kyoto University, 1976.
[Sch] S. Schiffer, *Meaning*, Oxford U. Press, 1972.
[Th] R. Thomason, A Note on Syntactic Treatments of Modality, *Synthese* **44** (1980), pp. 391-395.
[Va] M. Vardi, On the Complexity of Epistemic Reasoning, *4th IEEE-LICS Symposium*, 1989, pp. 243-252.
[Y] A. Yao, Some Complexity Questions Related to Distributed Computing, *Proc. 11th ACM-STOC*, (1979), pp. 209-213.

INTENTIONAL PARADOXES AND AN INDUCTIVE THEORY OF PROPOSITIONAL QUANTIFICATION

Nicholas Asher
The University of Texas at Austin and IMS, Stuttgart
Universitaet Stuttgart
17 Keplerstrasse
7000 Stuttgart 1, West Germany

ABSTRACT

Quantification over propositions is a necessary component of any theory of attitudes capable of providing a semantics of attitude ascriptions and a sophisticated system of reasoning about attitudes. There appear to be two general approaches to propositional quantification. One is developed within a first order quantificational language, the other in the language of higher order logic. The first order theory is described in Asher & Kamp (1986), Asher (1988), Asher and Kamp (1989). This paper concentrates on propositional quantification in a higher order framework, the simple theory of types. I propose a method of resolving difficulties noticed by Prior and Thomason with propositional quantification. The method borrows from Kripke's (1975) defintition of truth and results in a partial logic, which I call the *simple theory of partial types* (SPT). SPT offers a tractable, complete logic (with respect to general models) that includes propositional quantification, accomodates a semantics of the attitudes that avoids logical omniscience, and allows for some self-reference.

1. Introduction

Consider the following examples in which there is apparent quantification over propositions.[1]

(1.a) Everything Mary believes is true.

(1.b) Every fact you discover may be relevant.

(1.c) Nothing you have said convinces me.

The question I would like to pose here is a familiar one from analytic philosophy since the turn of the century:[2] what is the logical form underlying this apparent reference and quantification over abstract

---

[1] I would like to thank Rich Thomason for comments on an earlier version of this paper read at the Logic and Linguistics Meetings in Tuscon AZ 1989.

[2] See for instance Russell's (1903) arguments in *The Principles of Mathematics.* The concern with abstract entities and their logic remained a concern throughout Russell's life.

entities? Two general theories emerge, one a first order theory, the other a higher order theory of quantification.[1] The difficult task for such theories is to develop a coherent theory of quantification over abstract objects that are suitably descriminated to be objects of attitudes. The task is difficult because many attempts to do so have led to paradoxes concerning abstract entities. These paradoxes have bedeviled philosophers and logicians since ancient times.

There are two generally recognized families of paradoxes. One contains paradoxes having to do with sentences and direct quotation contexts like the Liar. Then there are paradoxes of application like the property version of Russell's paradox and the family of associated set theoretic paradoxes (Burali-Forti, Russell, etc). Arthur Prior (1961) and more recently Rich Thomason (1982) have argued that there is a third family of paradoxes, the so called "paradoxes of indirect discourse," which have to do with the nature of propositions or other abstract entities. The category of paradoxes of indirect discourse is potentially very varied. The defining characteristic of a paradox of indirect discourse is that it does not directly involve a quotational context.[2] Here is an example of such a paradox originally due to Jean Buridan, embellished by Prior and Thomason: Suppose Prior is thinking to himself,

(2) Either everything that I am thinking at the present moment or everything that Tarski will think in the next instant, but not both, is false.

Suppose that at the present moment Prior thinks nothing else and at the next moment Tarski thinks that snow is white and nothing else. I'll call this the *Prior situation.* By reasoning that is valid in the simple theory of types, we conclude that Tarski was not able to think that snow is white, a bizarre and unwanted consequence of a logic for belief.

The two theories of quantification dictate two approaches to such intentional paradoxes. Beginning with a representationalist's view of attitudes and abstract entities, one can arrive at a natural formulation in a first order language of what Prior is thinking to himself. This is a congenial perspective to someone committed to a representational theory of attitudes. By exploiting the inductive or semi-inductive techniques used by Kripke (1975), Herzberger (1982) and Gupta (1982) to define truth, one can build a families of models and develop a variety of logics for knowledge and belief.[3] Such a framework assimilates a treatment

---

[1] Many people have been suggesting a first order theory of abstract entities in the past few years-- for instance Bealer (1982), Turner (1987), (1989), Aczel (1989). Higher order theories have found advocates like Russell (1901) (1911), Ramsey (1926), Prior (1960) e.g., and others like Fine, Cocchiarella, and Thomason (1980.b), and Menzel. I will use Turner and Thomason as my main sources here, but that is not because I have made a detailed survey of all the proposals.

[2] Other ways of constructing paradoxes of indirect discourse do not depend on direct discourse at all. There are paradoxes of intention (similar to Newcomb's Problem and explored recently by Gaifman) that resemble at least semantic paradoxes. Gaifman's puzzle gives a *prima facie* plausible example of a very odd, but desirable goal. By having the intention to reach the goal, you in effect have the intention of not getting it, because you know that if you have the intention to reach the goal you won't reach it. Conversely, by having the intention not to reach the goal, you have the intention of reaching it. This supposition results in a diagonal intention of achieving φ iff you don't intend to achieve φ. This diagonalized intention appears to yield similar difficulties for the logic of intention. Yet it has nothing to do with direct quotation at least on the face of it; they appear to be properly classified as paradoxes of indirect discourse.

[3] Hans Kamp have investigated a proposal along these lines in Asher & Kamp (1986), Asher(1988), Asher & Kamp (1989).

of the Prior situation to a treatment of various paradoxes of direct discourse. But that approach also has certain drawbacks. A theorem of Asher & Kamp (1989) shows that the full logic of reasoning about belief or knowledge in such a framework is not axiomatizable. Moreover, it remains unclear how to weaken systems in that framework without making certain stipulations on the models that in effect rule out semantic self-reference (see theorem 14 of Asher and Kamp (1989)).

Somewhat surprisingly, a modification of the higher order approach to propositional quantification yields an axiomatizable theory (when we consider general structures) while nevertheless permitting significant possibilities for self-reference. But to get a viable theory of propositional quantification I must give a satisfactory solution to the problem posed by the Prior situation and another general difficulty afflicting higher order theories of propositional quantification. This general difficulty, noticed originally by Russell (1903), is that the simple theory of types is too liberal in what it countenances as propositions and propositional functions, and this forces unintuitive consequences upon the theory. For example, we are forced to say as a truth of logic that there are two propositional functions p and q such that an agent must believe that p = q even though p and q are not coextensive. The core of my proposal is an inductive definition for the propositional quantifiers. This appears to solve both the paradox of the Prior situation and Russell's difficulty.

2. The Language of Higher Order Propositional Quantification and the Intentional, Simple Theory of Types

The first order framework here entails that variables of quantification only occur in argument positions to relational symbols; there are no variables occuring in predicate positions. In particular variables do not occur in 0-place predicate positions-- i.e., in the positions of sentences or formulas. So propositions are quantified over in such a theory, only insofar as they are arguments to properties.

We could, however, quantify also over relations and properties, considering propositions to be 0-place properties. Quantification over predicate positions is the syntactic criterion for a higher order logic. The expressive power of higher order logic is quite attractive when thinking about mathematical theories.[1] There is also evidence in natural language of at least an indirect sort that we do directly quantify over higher order objects, and not just their first order correlates that some have assumed to be the denotions of sentential and verbal nominals. But I won't go into that here.

---

[1] When we think of a theory like standard set theory or arithmetic we think of a certain canonical structure. We find the Lowenheim Skolem Tarski theorems surprising, even paradoxical when applied to theories of these structures (as we think of them naively) Higher order logic can describe these structures up to isomorphism, and the Lowenheim Skolem Tarski theorems don't hold for higher order theories. For a very good defense of the view that second order logic underlies mathematical practice see Shapiro (1985).

This train of thought leads to a different theory of propositional quantification, the one that Thomason and Prior had in mind.[1] Syntactically, propositional variables and constants are 0-place property variables and constants. The language of propositional quantification, L_2, is thus a second order language. However, I shall consider a natural extension, L_ω, the language of the theory of simple types.[2] Formulas are constructed in the usual manner from the truth functional connectives and quantifiers. L_ω is a language containing individual and temporal constants and variables for all finite types formed from the basic primitive types-- P (the set of propositions), E (the set of individuals) and T (the set of truth values {0, 1}). Formulas are defined for each type using λ-abstraction and functional application. So for instance, if ζ is a formula of type τ and x is a variable of type τ', then $\lambda x \zeta$ is a formula of type $\tau \rightarrow \tau'$, and if ψ is of type $\tau \rightarrow \tau'$ and β is of type τ, then $\psi(\beta)$ is of type τ'.

L_ω has extensional and intentional versions of the connectives and quantifiers. $\forall$, $\exists$, &, $\vee$, $\rightarrow$, $\neg$ will be the truth functional operators and quantifiers, while Π, Σ, $\cap$, $\cup$, $\Rightarrow$ and $\sim$ will be the intensional correlates. Extensional identity, =, also has an intentional correlate, $\approx$. I shall also assume that in the language there is also a function constant $^\vee$ from propositions to their truth values as in Thomason (1980) (manuscript). Note that $^\vee p$ is not considered to be a proposition!

We insure a homomorphism between extensional and intensional correlates if we take the following as axioms:

(HOM)

for all p, q:	$^\vee[p \cap q] = {}^\vee p \,\&\, {}^\vee q$	$^\vee[p \cup q] = {}^\vee p \vee q$	$^\vee[p \Rightarrow q] = {}^\vee p \rightarrow {}^\vee q$
for all ζ:	$^\vee[\Pi x^\tau \zeta] = \forall x^{\tau\vee} \zeta$	$^\vee[\Sigma x^\tau \zeta] = \exists x^{\tau\vee} \zeta$	
for all p:	$^\vee[\sim p] = \neg {}^\vee p$		
for all t, t':	$^\vee[t \approx t'] = {}^\vee[t = t']$		

To get a complete freedom in choosing one's intentional logic for the attitudes, it is better to give for each usual extensional quantifier and connective an intentional operator. But for the statement of various truth definitions, it is very tiresome to read recursive clauses for each quantifier and connective; so in what follows I shall illustrate the various definitions by just exploiting the connectives, quantifiers and operators in the first column of the above table. The rest of the cases are always entirely obvious, and the interested reader may easily fill them in.

Once variables range over sentence denotations, it no longer make sense to take these to be truth values a la Frege, Carnap and Montague, if we wish to justice to propositional attitudes and other intensional

---

[1]There are arguments for getting rid of the types in doing natural language semantics. But I want to sidestep those here, as they usually revolve around a treatment of properties (with one or more argument places!) and this would lead us too far afield here.
[2]It is interesting to note that some difficulties such as those in the last section of the paper arise in full type theory but not simple quantification over propositions and properties in intentional logic. This seems to cast doubt on the equivalence in intentional logic between second order and full type theory. This equivalence is a fact of extensional, higher order logic.

contexts. Rather, we must take the denotations of sentences to be propositions. A sentence will be true iff the proposition it denotes is true. Thus, (1.a) expresses the proposition,

(3) Πp (believe(mary, p) $\Rightarrow$ p).

(3) is a formula of L_ω; in L_ω 'believe' is a second order predicate of individuals and propositions. By the correspondence rules in (HOM) (7) and hence (1.a) are true just in case,

$\forall p$ ($^\vee$believe(mary, p) $\rightarrow$ $^\vee$p), where p ranges over the domain of propositions.

A *standard intentional model* with times of L_ω consists of a quadruple $<\underline{E}, [\![\,]\!], f, \mathcal{F}>$. $\underline{E}$ is an inductively defined set of domains of various types, with non-empty sets E_O, E_P, E_I and E_T (of individuals, propositions, times and truth values respectively) as the basic types of objects. Other types are constructed from basic types as functions from types to types. In a standard model, if $\tau_1, \ldots \tau_n$ are types, then the set of all objects of type $< \tau_1, \ldots, \tau_n>$, $E(< \tau_1, \ldots, \tau_n>)$, $= \wp(E(\tau_1) \times E(\tau_2) \times \ldots \times E(\tau_n))$. The interpretation of expressions of the other types are the functions constructible from these basic types. I shall also assume that types are closed under functional application.

(FA)

If ν is of type $\tau \rightarrow \tau'$ and ζ of type τ, then $\nu(\zeta) \in E_{\tau'}$

$[\![\,]\!]$ assigns an (intentional) interpretation to each expression of type τ; the interpretation is some element of $E(\tau)$. The interpretation function of an intentional model respects λ abstraction and application in its assignments. That is, we have for any term α of type τ and any term $\lambda x\ \beta$ of type $\tau \rightarrow \tau'$,

(ABS)

$[\![\lambda x \beta]\!]([\![\alpha]\!]) = [\![\beta(x/\alpha]\!]$.

Our theory is intentional; so the objects assigned to predicates of a language by $[\![\,]\!]$ are properties and relations, not sets. Since sets are useful in the truth definition, however, intentional models have a function f that assigns to each object in a type a certain extension. Let [] be the extension of $[\![\,]\!]$ and f to include the assignment of denotations to complex terms of the form $^\vee\varphi$. Then $\mathcal{F}$ is a function from $P \times I$ into $T = \{0, 1\}$ such that:

i. $\mathcal{F}_t(G(a_1, \ldots a_n)) = 1$ iff $<[\![a_1]\!], \ldots, [\![a_n]\!]> \in f([\![G]\!])$

ii. $\mathcal{F}_t(p \cap q) = 1$ iff $\mathcal{F}_t(p) = \mathcal{F}_t(q) = 1$

iii. $\mathcal{F}_t(\sim q) = 1 - \mathcal{F}_t(q)$

iv. $\mathcal{F}_t(\Pi x^\tau \zeta) = 1$ iff $\mathcal{F}_t(\zeta(a)) = 1$ for all objects a of type τ

v. $\mathcal{F}_t(\alpha \approx \beta) = 1$ iff $[\alpha]_t = [\beta]_t$

(similarly for the other operators)

If $[\![\varphi]\!]$ is a proposition, $^\vee\varphi$ is a singular term denoting in $\mathcal{M}$ the truth value of $[\![\varphi]\!]$ in $\mathcal{M}$. It requires a special interpretation. Further these singular terms may combine with truth functional operators and quantifiers, which will have the usual recursive, semantic clauses. Let us write $[A]_{t, M} = 1$ if A denotes in M truth at t; $[A]_{t, M} = 0$ otherwise.

a. If A is of the form ${}^{\vee}\varphi$ where $[\![\varphi]\!]_{\mathcal{M}}$ is a proposition, then $[A]_{t, M} = \mathcal{F}(\varphi)$

b. If A is of the form $B \ \&\ C$, then $[A]_{t, M} = 1$ iff $[A]_{t, M} = 1$ and $[A]_{t, M} = 1$.

c. If A is of the form $\neg B$, then $[A]_{t, M} = 1$ iff $[A]_{t, M} = 0$.

d. If A is of the form $\forall x^{\tau}\, \zeta$, $[A]_{t, M} = 1$ iff $[\zeta(a/x)]_{t, M} = 1$ for all a of type τ.

e. If A is of the form ${}^{\vee}[\alpha = \beta]$, $[A]_{t, M} = \mathcal{F}_t(\alpha \approx \beta)$.

f. If A is of the form $at({}^{\vee}\varphi, t)$, $[A]_{t, M} = \mathcal{F}_t(\varphi)$.

(similarly for the other operators)

Let T_0 be the theory consisting of the axioms of quantification generalized to higher types, the usual axioms for identity, and the rule of β conversion, closed under the rule modus ponens. Given my definition of intentional models, every intentional model $\mathcal{M}$ for L_{ω} verifies (HOM) as well as the usual rules of predicate logic and β-conversion in T_0. The models for L_{ω} impose a structure on P.[1] P is closed under the operations $\cap, \sim, \cup$ and $\Rightarrow$; Π, Σ must be functions from PF $\rightarrow$ P, where PF is the set of propositional functions $\{f \mid f: E \cup P \rightarrow P\}$. I will take P to be an algebra whose atoms are given by the atomic sentences of L_{ω}.

Let's now formulate the intentional paradoxes or paradoxes of indirect discourse within this theory. I'll assume some standard addition of constants for times and set of times in the models for $L\omega$. The proposition denoted by (2) is easily expressed in L_{ω}, and it is true just in case (4) holds.

$$(4)\ (\forall p\, ({}^{\vee}B(prior, p, t_0) \rightarrow \neg at({}^{\vee}p\ t_0) \vee \forall p\, ({}^{\vee}B(tarski, p, t_1) \rightarrow \neg at({}^{\vee}p, t_0))) \ \&$$
$$(\exists p\, ({}^{\vee}B(tarski, p, t_0) \ \&\ at({}^{\vee}p, t_0)) \vee \exists p\, ({}^{\vee}B(prior, p, t_1) \ \&\ at({}^{\vee}p, t_0)))$$

Prior's informal argument now can be stated as follows:

Proposition 1: There is no intentional model for L_{ω} $\mathcal{M}$ such that Prior thinks (4) at t_0 in $\mathcal{M}$, Tarski thinks that snow is white at t_1 in $\mathcal{M}$ and 'snow is white' is true at t_1 in $\mathcal{M}$.

The paradox of the Prior situation differs from the semantic paradoxes like the Liar and paradoxes of application and comprehension like Russell's predicative paradox. There is no question of inconsistency in the theory T_0 or HOM; and the simple intentional theory of types is after all a highly restricted framework (in comparison, for instance, to ZF). Nevertheless, Prior's thought experiment yields entirely unsatisfactory results.

3. A Semi-Inductive Definition of Propositional Quantification

---

[1]A couple of facts about ${}^{\vee}$ are immediate once we realize it is a function constant from propositions into truth values. First of all, ${}^{\vee}$ does not iterate; so ${}^{\vee\vee}\varphi$ isn't well-defined. Thus any identity statement like $p = {}^{\vee}[\sim p]$ is false in every model! So if we formalize the Liar as such an identity, the Liar is just necessarily false. We might also symbolize the Liar as ${}^{\vee}p \leftrightarrow \neg{}^{\vee}p$. But this sentence too is false in every model; it is a simple contradiction. Thus, the liar does not pose any problems in this higher order logic. Higher order logic says that the liar is false in every model. Note also that the strong liar, which says that the Liar is false, is logically true in this theory!

The reason why this theory of propositional quantification gets into difficulties is not hard to discover, if we contrast the higher order theory of propositions with the more familiar first order theory of propositional quantification. As the translations for (1.a) and (2) in higher order logic make evident, the truth predicate has disappeared into the theory of propositional quantification. The higher order theory of quantification (as Ramsey and Prior might naturally have suggested) yields a "pro-sentential theory of truth," on which the truth predicate in English is just an anaphor, or perhaps even more simply a dummy or redundant predicate needed because of the limitations of natural language syntax. The theory of quantification has in effect swallowed up the truth predicate. To fix the sort of difficulties that Priorean thought experiments like (2) give rise to, then, the natural suggestion is to do for quantification what Kripke and Gupta-Herzberger have done for predicates like truth. Just as truth is defined inductively or semi-inductively mirroring the restrictions of the Tarskian hierarchy, so too is quantification to be similarly bounded by types until the construction is finished. My proposal complicates the connection between propositions and their truth values in intentional models by using either semi-inductive or inductive definitions for the domains of quantification.

Let me make the suggestion a bit more precise by looking at the semi-inductive case first. Let $\mathcal{M}_0$ be a standard intentional model for type-theory. I distinguish a subset of $P_{\mathcal{M}}$, P_0, which contains just those propositions not containing propositional variables. We now define a *revision sequence* of models $\mathcal{M}_{QH}{}^{\alpha}$ as follows. Let $\mathcal{M}_{QH}{}^{\alpha} = \langle \underline{\mathbf{E}}, [\![\,]\!], f, \mathcal{F}^{\alpha} \rangle$. We now define a recursion for $\mathcal{F}^{\alpha}$ on the ordinals. $\mathcal{F}^0 = \mathcal{F}\!\upharpoonright\! P_0 \cup (P\text{-}P_0 \times \{0\})$. All the definitions for $\mathcal{F}$ and the assignment of truth values to terms of the form ${}^{\vee}\varphi$ largely the same as before with the exception of the quantified clauses:

i. $\mathcal{F}_t{}^{\alpha}(G(a_1, \ldots a_n)) = 1$ iff $\langle [\![a_1]\!], \ldots, [\![a_n]\!] \rangle \in f([\![G]\!])$

ii. $\mathcal{F}_t{}^{\alpha}(p \cap q) = 1$ iff $\mathcal{F}_t{}^{\alpha}(p) = \mathcal{F}_t{}^{\alpha}(q) = 1$

iii. $\mathcal{F}_t{}^{\alpha}(\sim q) = 1 - \mathcal{F}_t{}^{\alpha}(q)$

iv. $\mathcal{F}_t{}^{\alpha+1}(\Pi x^{\tau} \zeta) = 1$ iff $\mathcal{F}_t{}^{\alpha}(\zeta(a)) = 1$ for all a of type $\tau \neq P$.

v. $\mathcal{F}_t{}^{\alpha}(\alpha \approx \beta) = 1$ iff $[\alpha]_{\mathcal{M}^{\alpha}} = [\beta]_{\mathcal{M}^{\alpha}}$

vi. If A is of the form ${}^{\vee}\varphi$ where $[\![\varphi]\!]_{\mathcal{M}}$ is a proposition, then $[A]_{\mathcal{M}^{\alpha}} = \mathcal{F}_t{}^{\alpha}(\varphi)$

vii. If A is of the form B & C, then $[A]_{t, \mathcal{M}^{\alpha}} = 1$ iff $[B]_{t, \mathcal{M}^{\alpha}} = 1$ and $[C]_{t, \mathcal{M}^{\alpha}} = 1$.

viii. If A is of the form $\neg B$, then $[A]_{t, \mathcal{M}^{\alpha}} = 1$ iff $[B]_{t, \mathcal{M}^{\alpha}} = 0$.

ix. If A is of the form $\forall x^{\tau} \zeta$, $[A]_{t, \mathcal{M}^{\alpha}} = 1$ iff $[\zeta(a^{\tau}/x)]\delta t, = 1$ for all a^{τ} $\tau \neq P$.

x. If A is of the form ${}^{\vee}[\alpha = \beta]$, $[A]_{t, \mathcal{M}^{\alpha}} = \mathcal{F}_t{}^{\alpha}(\alpha \approx \beta)$.

(similarly for the other operators and non-propositional quantifiers)

The clauses for the propositional quantifiers must be defined relative to previous models in the sequence. We need a pair of clauses for successor and limit ordinal cases.

xi.a. $\mathcal{F}_t^{\alpha+1}(\Pi x^P \zeta) = 1$ iff $\mathcal{F}_t^{\alpha}(\zeta(t^P)) = 1$ for all t^P.

xii.a If A is of the form $\forall x^P \zeta$, $[A]_{t, \mathcal{M}^{\alpha+1}} = 1$ iff $[\zeta(t^P/x)]_{t, \mathcal{M}^{\alpha}} = 1$ for all t^P.

xi.b. $\mathcal{F}_t^{\lambda}(\Pi x^P \zeta) = 1$ iff $\exists\beta\, \forall\alpha\, (\beta \leq \alpha < \lambda \rightarrow \mathcal{F}_t^{\alpha}(\Pi x^P \varphi) = 1)$.

xii.b If A is of the form $\forall x^P \zeta$, $[A]_{t, \mathcal{M}^{\lambda}} = 1$ iff $\exists\beta\, \forall\alpha\, (\beta \leq \alpha < \lambda \rightarrow [A]_{t, \mathcal{M}^{\alpha}} = 1$.

(similarly for Σx^P)

The first stage of our model revision procedure now may have a quantificational incoherence in there. For instance, a quantificational proposition of the form $\pi x^P \varphi$ will be false in $\mathcal{M}^0$ even though all it's instances may be true. But this incoherence is erased once the revision procedure gets started. We can still show that every model $\mathcal{M}^{\alpha}_{QH}$ in the revision sequence defined verifies (HOM).

Our model revision procedure now yields eventually a *higher order semistable* model, as all sentences with a string of propositional quantifiers of a given depth that will stabilize eventually do so. $\mathcal{M}^{\delta}$ is a *higher order semistable* model just in case δ is a perfect stabilization ordinal for $\mathcal{M}$ with respect to the revision sequence above and $\mathcal{F}$.[1] Let $\mathcal{M}^{\gamma}$ be such a model. Prior's belief, (4), is false at $\mathcal{M}^{\gamma}$, if Tarski's belief is true. Moreover, the truth of Tarski's belief, if it is a simple proposition, does not depend upon Prior's thinking (4) or not thinking (4). So far so good. But a rather surprising result is in store for us:

Proposition 2: There is no semi-inductive model such that such that (i) Prior thinks (4) at t_0 in $\mathcal{M}$ and nothing else, (ii) Tarski thinks that snow is white at t_1 in $\mathcal{M}$ and nothing else, (iii) 'snow is white' is true at t_1 in $\mathcal{M}$, and (iv) $\mathcal{M}$ is a model of T_0.

The proof proceeds by an examination of cases. We observe that on such a theory (4) also has a 2 cycle interpretation. Any $\mathcal{M}^0$ cannot be a model of T_0, because the T_0 theorem $\varphi(c^P) \rightarrow \exists x^P \varphi(x^P)$ is false at $\mathcal{M}^0$, where c^P is a propositional term. Successor states $\mathcal{M}^{\gamma+1}$ either fail to verify $\forall x^P \psi(x^P) \rightarrow \psi(c^P/x^P)$, where ψ is either the subformula

$${}^{\vee}B(\text{prior}, p, t_0) \rightarrow \neg at({}^{\vee}p\ t_0)$$

or

$${}^{\vee}B(\text{tarski}, p, t_1) \rightarrow \neg at({}^{\vee}p, t_0)$$

of (4); or they share the following difficulty with limit stages $\mathcal{M}^{\lambda}$. $\mathcal{M}^{\lambda} \models (4)$ iff $\mathcal{M}^{\lambda} \models \forall x^P\ ({}^{\vee}B(a, x^P, t_0) \rightarrow \neg{}^{\vee} x^P)$ iff $\exists\beta\, \forall\gamma\, (\beta \leq \gamma < \lambda \rightarrow \mathcal{M}^{\gamma} \models \forall x^P\ ({}^{\vee}B(a, x^P, t_0) \rightarrow \neg{}^{\vee}x^P)$. So $\mathcal{M}^{\lambda} \models \neg(4)$. But then by ordinary quantificational logic, $\mathcal{M}^{\lambda} \models \neg(4)$ iff $\mathcal{M}^{\lambda} \models \exists x^P\ ({}^{\vee}B(a, x^P, t_0)\ \&\ {}^{\vee} x^P)$. But by the constraint (i), $\mathcal{M}^{\lambda} \models \neg(4)$ iff $\mathcal{M}^{\lambda} \models (4)$.

[1] Call γ a *perfect stabilization ordinal for* $\mathcal{M}$ with respect to the revision scheme and $\mathcal{F}$ just in case every proposition that comes to have a stable truth value assignment from $\mathcal{F}$ in the revision scheme does so before or at γ and further $\mathcal{F}^{\gamma}(\varphi) = 1$ in iff $\exists\beta \leq \gamma\ \mathcal{F}^{\alpha}(\varphi) = 1$ for all $\alpha \geq \beta$.

4. An Inductive Definition of Propositional Quantification

A more satisfactory construction is available with an inductive definition like the one used by Kripke (1975). Let $\mathcal{M}$ be any standard intentional model for L_ω satisfying (FA) and (ABS). Recall that the distinguished subset of $P_\mathcal{M}$, P_0, contains just those propositions not containing propositional variables. An inductive revision sequence is defined by setting $\mathcal{F}^0 = \mathcal{A}P_0$ and the *base partial model* $\mathcal{M}_{QK}{}^0 = <\underline{E}, [\![]\!], f, \mathcal{F}^0>$, $\mathcal{M}_{QK}{}^\alpha = <\underline{E}, [\![]\!], f, \mathcal{F}^\alpha>$, and then requiring the following constraint on $\mathcal{F}$ (which I call the *partial model constraint* PMC):

(PMC)

1. $\mathcal{F}^\alpha$ and $[]_{\mathcal{M}^\alpha}$ are closed under the usual semantical rules for a strong Kleene interpretation of the truth functional connectives and non-propositional quantifiers.
2. All $\mathcal{M}_{QK}{}^\alpha$ verify identity statements of the form $\beta = \beta$, where β is any term. Otherwise,

   $\mathcal{M}_{QK}{}^\alpha \models \beta = \beta'$ iff $[\beta] = [\beta']$ and both $[\beta]$ and $[\beta']$ are defined in $\mathcal{M}_{QK}{}^\alpha$

   $\mathcal{M}_{QK}{}^\alpha$ $\beta = \beta'$ iff $[\beta] \neq [\beta']$ and both $[\beta]$ and $[\beta']$ are defined in $\mathcal{M}_{QK}{}^\alpha$
3. For propositional quantifiers (Again I illustrate only for Πx^P, the case for Σx^P is entirely analogous)

   A. With regard to the successor case:

   i.a. $\mathcal{F}^{\alpha+1}(\Pi x^P \zeta) = 1$ if $\mathcal{F}^\alpha(\zeta(t^P)) = 1$ for all t^P

   i.b. $\mathcal{F}^{\alpha+1}(\Pi x^P \zeta) = 0$ if $\mathcal{F}^\alpha(\zeta(t^P)) = 0$ for some t^P.

   i.c. $\mathcal{F}^{\alpha+1}(\Pi x^P \zeta)$ undefined otherwise.

   ii. If A is of the form $\forall x^P \zeta$,

   a. $[A]_{\mathcal{M}\alpha+1} = 1$ if $[\zeta(t^P/x)]_{\mathcal{M}^\alpha} = 1$ for all t^P.

   b. $[A]_{\mathcal{M}\alpha+1} = 0$ if $[\zeta(t^P/x)]_{\mathcal{M}^\alpha} = 1$ for some t^P

   c. $[A]_{\mathcal{M}\alpha+1}$ = undefined otherwise.

   B. The limit case may defined quite simply.

   a. $\mathcal{F}^\lambda = \cup_{\beta < \lambda} \mathcal{F}^\beta$

   b. $[]_{\mathcal{M}\lambda} = \cup_{\beta < \lambda} []_{\mathcal{M}\beta}$

The QK sequence of models builds up inductively the values of the partial function $\mathcal{F}_\alpha$ and the extensional definition [] for each α. In $\mathcal{M}_{QK}{}^0$ no propositionally quantified statements are given truth values. $\mathcal{A}P_0$, however, does assign every atom in the propositional algebra a truth value. After the first application of the inductive definition $\mathcal{M}_{QK}{}^1$ now verifies many propositions that quantify over propositions-- e.g. $\exists p\, p$. But notice that (4) will not get a value in $\mathcal{M}_{QK}{}^1$. In fact (4) will not get a value throughout the QK sequence. I will call the models in the QK sequence *standard partial models* for L_ω.

Standard partial models are not models of (HOM) as it stands. But they are models for a closely related theory. We must make two changes to (HOM). First, we must define correspondences for each pair of intensional and extensional connectives, and second we must replace the identities in (HOM) with the corresponding rule equivalences (e.g, replace $^\vee[p \cap q] = {}^\vee p \mathbin{\&} {}^\vee q$ with

$$\frac{^\vee[p \cap q]}{^\vee p \mathbin{\&} {}^\vee q}$$

and so on. The rule equivalences in (HOM') form a weaker theory from (HOM) to be sure. We only have a partial homomorphism from propositions to truth values respecting the propositional and truth functional connectives and quantifiers. But we can still prove the following with it. Define a L_ω formula φ' in $^\vee$ *normal form* such that $^\vee$ occurs only in front of atomic formulas. The rules in (HOM') allow us to prove

Proposition 3: Let φ be a formula of L_ω. Then given (HOM'), there is a formula φ' in $^\vee$- normal form such that φ ⊢ φ'.

Because the QK sequence of models is inductively defined and there is a fixed set of propositions, one can show by the standard argument that the sequence reaches a fixed point. I'll call any $\mathcal{M}_{QK}{}^\gamma$ model that is a fixed point of the definition a *standard fixed point* model for L_ω. Let R_1 be the following set of rules (corresponding to the strong Kleene interpretation of the connectives and quantifiers):

1. The usual introduction and elimination rules for ∃ ∀ & and ∨.
2. The equivalences

$$\frac{\neg\neg A}{A} \qquad \frac{\neg(A \mathbin{\&} B)}{\neg A \vee \neg B} \qquad \frac{\neg(A \vee B)}{\neg A \mathbin{\&} \neg B}$$

3. The rule $\psi \mathbin{\&} \neg\psi \vdash \varphi$
4. Suppose φ(ψ) is a positive context (ψ is a constituent that is not under the scope of any negations or relation symbols in prenex disjunctive form). Then if $\psi_1 \vdash \psi_2$, $\varphi(\psi_1) \vdash \varphi(\psi_2)$.
5. The axioms
   a. $\beta = \beta$
   b. $\lambda x^\tau A(\beta) = A(\beta/x)$
6. If α and α' are of type τ → τ' and β, β' of type τ', then $\alpha = \alpha' \mathbin{\&} \beta = \beta' \vdash \alpha(\beta) = \alpha'(\beta')$
7. $\forall u\, \lambda x\, \varphi(u) = \lambda x\, \varphi'(u) \vdash \lambda x\, \varphi = \lambda x\, \varphi'$.
8. The rules in (HOM')

Proposition 4: if $\mathcal{M}_{QK}{}^\alpha$ is a fixed point of the QK sequence, then if φ ⊢ ψ is a rule of R_1, then if $\mathcal{M}_{QK}{}^\alpha \models \varphi$, then $\mathcal{M}_{QK}{}^\alpha \models \psi$.

To illustrate, let us take one of the quantifier rules, the universal exploitation rule $\forall x\, \varphi \vdash \varphi\,(t/x)$. Suppose $\mathcal{M}_{QK}{}^\alpha \models \forall x\, \varphi$. If x is of other than propositional type, then by the constraints on $\mathcal{F}$ given by the strong

Kleene interpretation of the truth functional connectives and non-propositional quantifiers, $\mathcal{M}_{QK^\alpha} \models \varphi(t/x)$ for any suitable term t. Now suppose that x is of propositional type. By the construction of the sequence QK $\forall x\varphi$ will be true only if all its instances are verified at some previous stage, if α is a successor or limit ordinal. In either case, since the construction is inductive, this assures that $\mathcal{M}_{QK^\alpha} \models \varphi(t/x)$.

Let $\vdash_{R_1}$ be the derivation relation defined by the rules in R_1. A standard argument will now prove the soundness of R_1 at fixed points of model sequences QK. Let $\Vdash$ be the consequence relation defined over the class of fixed point models of QK model sequences. Then,

Proposition 5: For a set of sentences Γ, if $\Gamma \vdash_{R_1} \varphi$, then $\Gamma \Vdash \varphi$.

It appears that if we loosen the notion of a standard partial model for L_ω to get *general partial models* L_ω, we may also be able to prove a completness result about R_1. A *general model* for L_ω from Henkin (1950) is a model in which the domains of propositions, truth values, and individuals are as before and where if $\tau_1, \ldots \tau_n$ are types, then the interpretation of a type $<\tau_1, \ldots, \tau_n>$ is a *subset* of $\wp(\llbracket\tau_1\rrbracket \times \llbracket\tau_2\rrbracket \times \ldots \times \llbracket\tau_n\rrbracket)$; in a standard model $\llbracket<\tau_1, \ldots, \tau_n>\rrbracket = \wp(\llbracket\tau_1\rrbracket \times \llbracket\tau_2\rrbracket \times \ldots \times \llbracket\tau_n\rrbracket)$. Let $\Vdash_G$ be the consequence relation defined over general, fixed point models-- those fixed points that come from the jump operation being applied to general models.

Proposition 6: For a set of sentences Γ, if $\Gamma \Vdash_G \varphi$, then $\Gamma \vdash_{R_1} \varphi$.

An outline of the proof is given in the appendix. Proposition 6 establishes a logic for partial fixed point models of propositional quantification, a logic which I'll call *partial, simple theory of types* (SPT). But it does so by using general models. If we define first and order logic by means of the model theoretic properties of their *standard* models rather than by their syntax, the use of general models for SPT essentially convert higher order logic to first order logic. But in this SPT is no different from the standard simple theory of types (ST); with respect to standard partial intentional models SPT is sound just as with respect to standard intentional models, (ST) is sound. By the completeness proof, logical consequence for SPT relative to the class of general partial models is Σ_1 definable, just as (ST) is Σ_1 definable relative to general models; with respect to standard models, consequence in SPT (and in ST) is not axiomatizable.[1]

5. Russell's Problem with the Theory of Types

Thomason's paper discusses another problem for the simple theory of types, mentioned in an appendix to Russell's *Principles of Mathematics.* It motivates Thomason's proposal for dealing with the intentional paradoxes, which uses a free logic for the propositional quantifiers. My proposal solves this difficulty too, though in a manner different from Thomason's proposal.

The difficulty, due originally to Russell (1903), is that the simple theory of types is too liberal in what it countenances as propositions and propositional functions. For example in L_ω the term

---

[1]The proof of this claim would follow the lines of that given by Van Bentham and Doets (1984).

(5) $\lambda x^p \exists f^{<p,p>} ({}^\vee Ff = x \ \& \ \neg {}^\vee fx)$

denotes a property of propositions,[1] for any given F. Let's call the property of propositions in (5) w. Then assuming ${}^\vee w(Fw) \vee \neg {}^\vee w(Fw)$, we get the following disturbing result.[2]

(6) $\exists f^{<p,p>} \exists g^{<p,p>} ({}^\vee[Ff = Fg] \ \& \ \neg \forall x^p ({}^\vee fx \leftrightarrow {}^\vee gx))$

Since (6) holds for arbitrary F (underlying it is a simple cardinality argument),[3] it holds for the particular definition of F in (7)

(7) $F = \lambda g^{<p,p>} \forall x^p ({}^\vee gx \rightarrow {}^\vee x)$

By the principles of identity (6) and (7) have worrisome consequences for the theory of attitudes formulated within the simple theory of types. One such consequence is (8):

(8) $\exists f^{<p,p>} \exists g^{<p,p>} (\Box \forall x^o \Box ({}^\vee Bel(x, Ff) \leftrightarrow {}^\vee Bel(x, Fg)) \ \& \ \neg \forall x^p ({}^\vee fx \leftrightarrow {}^\vee gx))$

Thomason (1982) points out correctly that by limiting what expressions denote higher order objects in the models and by employing a free logic, one can avoid this difficulty. Thomason's proposal won't work in the partial logic for propositional quantifiers as I have defined it. It is a valid principle of the partial logic SPT that

(9) $\exists p \ {}^\vee[p = \varphi]$

This partial logic for the theory of types is no different from the classical theory of types in this respect. But Thomason's proposal also leads, as he points out, to unintuitive consequences when dealing with the Intentional Paradoxes: it implies among other things that the existence of propositions is a context dependent, speaker relative matter. This collides with our intuitions about propositions. (9) also appears to

---

[1]The superscripts in the formulas (5)-(8) are there to make clear the types of variables involved.

[2]The proof is as follows:
Dropping carrots we have
1) $w(Fw) \vee \neg w(Fw)$
Now suppose that
2) $w(Fw)$
and that
3) $\forall g \forall h (F(g) = F(h) \rightarrow \forall y(g(y) \leftrightarrow h(y)))$
Then by 2) and the definition of w,
4) $\exists f(F(f) = F(w) \ \& \ \neg f(F(w)))$
So for some f_0
4) $F(f_0) = F(w) \ \& \ \neg f_0(F(w))$
By (3) and (5),
6) $\forall y(f_0(y) \leftrightarrow w(y))$
By (2) and (6),
7) $f_0(F(w))$
which is a contradiction. So now suppose
8) $\neg w(Fw)$
By the definition of w again, and 8)
9) $\forall f(F(f) = F(w) \rightarrow f(F(w)))$
So by the laws of identity,
10) $w(F(w))$
Again this is a contradiction. Note that this proof is valid in T_0.

[3]If one thinks of how propositional functions might operate compositionally with propositions in a standard model, cardinality arguments would dictate that the function from a tuple consisting of a propositional function and its arguments to propositions could not be 1-1; (6) then is simply a special case of a much more general argument.

be a needed principle in the analysis of propositional anaphora in natural language. Even though propositions are paradoxical or non-sensical, we may refer to them anaphorically. Imagine the following dialogue:

(10) Cretan: Everything I say is false.

Socrates: I don't believe that.

According to the free logic proposal, the Cretan did not manage to express a proposition in the circumstance in which the first sentence of (10) is the only sentence he manages to utter. But then it appears that Socrates doesn't manage to have a belief-- or express a belief-- about what the Cretan said. The analysis of anaphora in (10) is a semantic mystery, unless we assume there is some proposition the Cretan expresses.

Russell's argument culminating with (6) is not valid in SPT for the simple reason that it relies on the excluded middle. So that motivation for introducing type-free logic for higher order quantification dissolves. It's also not clear, however, that (8) is such a bizarre consequence for a theory of simple types to countenance. The real difficulty hinges on what one takes to be the criterion of identity for types. Our models say little about what identity of types should amount to. One could have criteria of type identity such that $\psi(\beta) = \psi(\beta')$ but $\beta \neq \beta'$.[1] This goes against a certain natural criterion of identity for intentional objects that one might call a *structural* criterion of identity for types (SIT):

(SIT) Let β and β' be of type τ and let ψ, ψ' be of type $\tau \rightarrow \tau'$. Then $\psi(\beta) = \psi(\beta')$ implies $\psi = \psi'$ & $\beta = \beta'$.

(SIT) together with the principle of indiscernibility of identicals contradicts (6). Thus (SIT) + the principle of indiscernibility of identicals is inconsistent with the simple theory of types (ST). There are at least trivial models of (SPT), in which (SIT) + the principle of indiscernibility of identicals are never refuted and are verified in the trivial cases of where $\alpha(\beta) = \alpha(\beta)$ (which must be true according to the constraints on $\mathcal{F}$ in models for SPT).

Russell's problem suggests a comparison of PT with Russell's own solution-- the Ramified Theory of Types (RT). In all versions of (RT), there is a function from propositions to ω that recursively assigns orders. In some versions,[2] it is defined as follows:

Ord: $Ep \rightarrow \omega$ such that:

If $\varphi \in P_0$ (a designated subset of Ep), then $Ord(\varphi) = 1$.

If $\varphi = \alpha = \beta$ then $Ord(\varphi) = Max\{Ord(\alpha), Ord(\beta)\} + 1$.

If $\varphi = \neg\psi$, then $Ord(\varphi) \leq Ord(\psi)$.

If * is a boolean two place connective and $\varphi = \alpha*\beta$, then $Ord(\varphi) \leq Max\{Ord(\alpha), Ord(\beta)\}$.

---

[1] Aczel (1989) warns that the application relation should not be taken to be structure creating for such reasons. That is, he wants to deny that $\alpha(\beta) = \alpha'(\beta') \rightarrow \alpha = \alpha'$ & $\beta = \beta'$, our principle (SIT).

[2] I folow Thomason (1989) and Church (1976) here.

If Q is a quantifier and $\varphi = Q\delta\psi$, then $\mathrm{Ord}(\varphi) = \mathrm{Max}\{\mathrm{Ord}(\delta) \text{ for } \delta \in \mathrm{Dom}(Q) \text{ in } \psi\} + 1$, where if φ is of the form $Q\delta\,(\zeta, \theta)$,Dom(Q) in ψ is just the set of objects satisfying ζ. Dom(Q) in ψ is just $E_{type(\delta)}$ otherwise.

We have in effect constructed models for certain versions of RT. But the orders of our theory are given by the semantics; they are artefacts of the models, and not part of the syntax and formation rules of the language of PT (this is different for RT). For formulas of PT, then, Ord must be a partial function, because there are many propositions in our setup that cannot be assigned an order-- Prior's proposition for instance. The definition of order above then suggests the following correlation between order and stages of revision in our model theoretic framework.

Proposition 7: Suppose φ is a proposition for which Ord is defined. Then $\mathcal{M}^n \models {}^{\vee}\varphi^*$ iff $\mathrm{Ord}(\varphi) \leq n$, where ${}^{\vee}\varphi^*$ is ${}^{\vee}\alpha = {}^{\vee}\beta$, if φ is $\alpha = \beta$ and ${}^{\vee}\varphi^* = {}^{\vee}\varphi$ otherwise.

The proof of proposition 7 is by induction on n.

To sum up then, there appear to be two solutions to the paradoxes of indirect discourse. One familiar route uses a first order theory of quantification and a truth predicate. The other uses higher order logic, in particular the intentional version presupposed by Russellians and spelled out in Thomason (1980.b) and a Pro-sentential theory of truth. By giving an inductive definition of propositional quantification, we avoid the difficulties associated with other solutions to the intentional paradoxes concerning in higher order logic. The partiality of SPT is located within what truth values propositions take on, not, as in Thomason's proposal, the existence of propositions. Surprisingly, only an inductive definition not a semi-inductive definition will do the trick.

The pro-sentential theory of truth incorporated into higher order propositional quantification appears to mitigate Liar-like paradoxes. We have no restrictions on the logic of predicates of propositions. This is responsible for the completeness proof for SPT. No such completeness proof is available to the first order theory in general.[1] Somewhat surprisingly, the system with the higher order syntax-- partial type theory-- thus turns out to have a more tractable notion of validity than that of the first order theory of propositions on which a truth predicate is used. The set of valid sentences in all metastable models or semi-stable models,[2] for instance, is clearly not r.e for interesting classes of models.

I have said little so far about logics of knowledge and belief in this theory. But it seems we may accomodate within this framework most reasonable logics for knowledge and belief in a relatively straightforward way . Now suppose our semantics for attitude predicates is such that for every agent we assign a *belief state*, a collection of propositions. We may subject this state to various closure conditions. For instance we may require of every belief state S that if the proposition $p \in S$, then $B(p) \in S$. We may

---

[1]For a case where we can prove completeness, see theorem 14 of Asher and Kamp (1989).

[2]For definitions of these model classes, See Asher and Kamp (1986), Asher and Kamp (1989).

thus encode by means of these closure conditions the usual doxastic reasoning principles and validate rules which correspond, say, to the logic presented in Thomason (1980.a).[1] SPT, however, permits a variety of logics for the attitudes which go far beyond what a possible worlds framework yields. The reason for this is simple. If our semantics for attitudes ascribes to an agent a set of propositions, then we may choose from a variety of closure conditions that cannot be expressed in a possible worlds semantics. In particular we may assume very weak closure conditions-- such as those detailed in Asher (1986). Nothing forces us in SPT to require a closure condition on S that exploits logical equivalence. In SPT it is consistent to assume that two propositions may be necessarily even logically equivalent without being identical. So SPT does not validate B(p) and $\vdash p \leftrightarrow q \Rightarrow B(q)$, an inference form that is valid in most possible worlds semantics of attitudes. Thus, SPT easily avoids problems about logical omniscience.

The guarantees we have in L_ω that eliminate possibilities of expressing a proposition corresponding to the Liar sentence (see footnote 20) do not stop us from attempting similar definitions, say, with a knowledge or belief predicate. Let 'B' be a two place predicate representing the relation of belief between individuals and propositions. Suppose we stipulate in the semantics for a propositional constant c, $[\![c]\!] = \neg B(a, c)$. Alternatively, it seems as though we could imagine a theory in our language in which:

(11) $p = \sim B(a, p)$

By our constraints on $\mathcal{F}$ it follows that in every model in which (11) is true,

(12) $^{\vee}p \not\vdash\!\dashv \neg {}^{\vee}B(a, p)$

Now suppose our semantics for attitude predicates is such that for every agent we assign a *belief state*, a collection of propositions which is subject to closure conditions validating the logic presented in Thomason (1980). We can still have such identities between propositions as in (11). But p will never get assigned a truth value, and so it will be undetermined whether a believes p. We must be careful not introduce any "essentially ungrounded" propositions with such predicates as knowledge and belief into our domain; if we do so completeness will vanish (we can no longer construct the models) and the higher order theory of propositions becomes an uninteresting variant of the first order theory, as far as I can tell at present.[2] Well, we can't have everything. SPT is one option for treating propositional quantification that has some attractions. It yields a theory of propositions with a tractable logic and that countenances some self-referential propositions, while avoiding problems of logical omniscience with the semantics of the attitudes.

---

[1]Here would be the relevant closure principles for the S4 logic of Thomason (1980.a):

$p \rightarrow q, p \in S \Rightarrow q \in S$
$p \in S \Rightarrow Bp \in S$
$p \in S$ and $p \vdash q \Rightarrow q \in S$.
$Bp \in S \Rightarrow p \in S$.

[2]Thus for instance we cannot introduce an expression relation between sentences and propositions. See Parsons (1974), Asher & Kamp (1986) for a discussion. Nevertheless, one can still in this setup have beliefs about mathematics.

Appendix: Proof of Proposition 6

The outline of the proof relies on an adaptation of the Henkin method to partial models proposed by Kamp (1984). What I shall do is show that if not $\Gamma \vdash_{R_1} \varphi$ then there is a partial model that verifies Γ but does not verify φ. So suppose not $\Gamma \vdash \varphi$. Define φ to be a positive formula just in case all negation signs in φ occur only on atomic formulae. We may show that for every φ there is a positive φ' that is R-equivalent to it (i.e. $\varphi \;\; \vdash \varphi'$).,

Using an enumeration of all positive formulae of L_ω, we build up two maximal sets Ω and Σ from Γ and $\{\varphi\}$ respectively as follows. I assume that infinitely many constants of each type do not occur in the enumeration of the positive formulae.

1. $\Omega_0 = \Gamma$; $\Sigma_0 = \{\varphi\}$
2.a. if not $(\Omega_n \cup \{\psi_{n+1}\} \vdash \Sigma_n)$ and ψ_{n+1} is not existential, then $\Omega_{n+1} = \Omega_n \cup \{\psi_{n+1}\}$; $\Sigma_{n+1} = \Sigma_n$
 b. if not $(\Omega_n \cup \{\psi_{n+1}\} \vdash \Sigma_n)$ and $\psi_{n+1} = \exists v\zeta$, then $\Omega_{n+1} = \Omega_n \cup \{\psi_{n+1}, \zeta(c_j/v)\}$ where c_j is the first individual constant not appearing in $\Omega_n \cup \Sigma_n \cup \{\psi_{n+1}\}$; $\Sigma_{n+1} = \Sigma_n$
 c. if $\Omega_n \cup \{\psi_{n+1}\} \vdash \Sigma_n$ and ψ_{n+1} is not universal, then $\Omega_{n+1} = \Omega_n$; $\Sigma_{n+1} = \Sigma_n \cup \{\psi_{n+1}\}$
 d. if $\Omega_n \cup \{\psi_{n+1}\} \vdash \Sigma_n$ and $\psi_{n+1} = \forall v\zeta$, then $\Omega_{n+1} = \Omega_n$; $\Sigma_{n+1} = \Sigma_n \cup \{\psi_{n+1}, \zeta(c_j/v)\}$ where c_j is the first individual constant not appearing in $\Omega_n \cup \Sigma_n \cup \{\psi_{n+1}\}$
3. $\Omega = \bigcup_{n \in \omega} \Omega_n$; $\Sigma = \bigcup_{n \in \omega} \Sigma_n$

The next step is to show

Lemma 6.1: not $\Omega \vdash \Sigma$
This is proved by an induction on Ω_n and Σ_n.

I now construct a base partial intentional model $\mathcal{M} = <\underline{\mathbf{E}}, [\![\,]\!], f, \mathcal{F}^0>$ from these sets. First I inductively define the type structure $\underline{\mathbf{E}}$. Let $E_{0\mathcal{M}} = \{[c^0]_\Omega$: c is an individual constant occurring in $\Omega \cup \Sigma\}$, where$[c]_\Omega = \{d : \Omega \vdash d = c\}$, and let $E_{p\,\mathcal{M}} = \{[\psi]_\Omega$: ψ is a sentence occuring in $\Omega \cup \Sigma\}$. I define E_T as the set of truth values using the sentences and their negates in Ω. $\top = \{\psi$: $\psi \in \Omega\}$; $\perp = \{\psi$: $\neg\psi \in \Omega\}$. Now assume that E_τ and $E_{\tau'}$ are already defined as equivalence classes $[\alpha]_\Omega$ and $[\beta]_\Omega$ respectively. We define $E_{\tau \to \tau'}$ to be $\{[\zeta]_\Omega$: ζ is of the form $\lambda x^\tau \gamma$ and γ occurs in $\Omega \cup \Sigma\}$. We further define for each $[\zeta]_\Omega$ in $E_{\tau \to \tau'}$ to be a function such that $[\zeta]_\Omega([\alpha]_\Omega) = [\gamma(x^\tau/\alpha)]_\Omega$ for any element $[\alpha]_\Omega$ of E_τ. We can easily check this definition by exploiting (6) and (7) of R_1 and noting that for any $\alpha_1, \alpha_2 \in [\alpha]_\Omega$ and $\lambda x\gamma_1, \lambda x\gamma_2$ in $[\zeta]_\Omega$, $\lambda x\gamma_1(\alpha_1) = \lambda x\gamma_2(\alpha_2)$. Further, if $[\zeta_1]_\Omega = [\zeta_2]_\Omega$, it follows that ζ_1 and ζ_2 agree on all arguments. So $\forall u$ $\lambda x\gamma_1(x)(u) = \lambda x\gamma_2(x)(u)$. By (7) we may conclude $\zeta_1 = \zeta_2$. The set of all types $\underline{\mathbf{E}}$ for $\mathcal{M}$ are those constructed from the basic types by this procedure, and it obeys (FA).

The second step in defining the model is to specify the interpretation function. Define $[\![\,]\!]$ as follows. If φ is a term of type τ, then $[\![\varphi]\!] = [\varphi]_\Omega \in E_\tau$. Because of my definition of the type structure and because of (5.b), $[\![\,]\!]$ obeys (ABS).

The third step is to specify extensions for intentional objects. Define f such that for $[\beta]_\Omega \in E_{<\tau_1, \ldots, \tau_n>}$ $f(x) = \{<[\alpha_1]_\Omega, \ldots, [\alpha_n]_\Omega>$: $\beta(\alpha_1, \ldots \alpha_n) \in \Omega\}$.

The final step is to assign truth values to propositions. Define $\mathcal{F}^0{}_\mathcal{M}$ to be a function from E_{P_0} to E_T such that: if φ is of the form $R(\beta_1, \ldots \beta_n)$, then $\mathcal{F}_\mathcal{M}(R(\beta_1, \ldots \beta_n)) = 1$ iff $R(\beta_1, \ldots \beta_n) \in \Omega$ and $\mathcal{F}_\mathcal{M}(R(\beta_1, \ldots \beta_n)) = 0$ iff $R(\beta_1, \ldots \beta_n) \in \Sigma$.. Given my definition of f, $\mathcal{F}^0$ is correctly defined.

Now extend $\mathcal{F}^0{}_\mathcal{M}$ to a partial function $\mathcal{F}^\alpha$ from E_P to E_T using the inductive revision procedure defined in (PMC). Let $\mathcal{M}^\alpha = <E, P, [\![\,]\!], f, \mathcal{F}^\alpha>$ be the fixed point of that revision process.

Lemma 6.2: $\mathcal{M}^\alpha$ is a partial model that verifies all of Ω and fails to verify Σ. Hence $\mathcal{M}^\alpha$ verifies Γ and fails to verify φ.

We prove this by induction on the complexity of $\vartheta \in \Omega \cup \Sigma$. Suppose that ϑ is atomic of the form $R(\beta_1, \ldots \beta_n)$ The construction of $\mathcal{F}^0$ insures that $\mathcal{M} \models \vartheta$ if $\vartheta \in \Omega$ and not $\mathcal{M} \models \vartheta$ if $\vartheta \in \Sigma$. Suppose $\vartheta = \neg\psi$ and that $\vartheta \in \Omega$. By the construction of Ω, $\psi \notin \Omega$ and ψ must be atomic. But then $\psi \in \Sigma$ and so again by the definition of $\mathcal{F}^0$, $\mathcal{M} \models \psi$ and so $\mathcal{M} \models \vartheta$. An entirely parallel argument holds if $\vartheta \in \Sigma$. The truth functional cases and ordinary quantificational cases are straightforward. Suppose $\vartheta = \lambda x\alpha(\beta) \in \Omega$. By (5.b) in R_1, α'

$= \alpha(\beta/x) \in \Omega$, and by the inductive hypothesis $\mathcal{M} \models \alpha'$ if $\alpha' \in \Omega$. So $\mathcal{M} \models \alpha'$. Since $\mathcal{M}$ obeys (FA) and (ABS) as seen above, $\mathcal{M} \models \vartheta$. A similar argument holds for the case $\vartheta \in \Sigma$.
The only non-straightforward step involves quantified statements of the form $\exists p\psi$ and $\forall p\, \psi$ where p is a propositional quantifier. Let $\vartheta = \exists p\psi$ and suppose $\vartheta \in \Omega$. By the construction of Ω, if $\exists p\psi \in \Omega$, then $\psi(cP_j/p) \in \Omega$. By the inductive hypothesis $\mathcal{M}^\alpha \models \psi(cP_j/p)$ and so $\mathcal{M}^\alpha \models \exists p\psi$, since $\mathcal{M}^\alpha$ is a fixed point. Now suppose that $\vartheta \in \Sigma$. $\vartheta \in \Sigma$ only if it implies φ or is itself φ. So by the construction procedure of Σ and Ω, every instance $\psi(cP_j/p)$ of ψ must be in Σ, since $\psi(cP_j/p) \vdash \exists p\psi$. But $\mathcal{M}^\alpha \models \exists p\psi$ iff for some proposition cP_j, $\mathcal{M}^\alpha \models \psi(cP_j/p)$, since $\mathcal{M}^\alpha$ is a fixed point. Then by the inductive hypothesis it is not the case that $\mathcal{M}^\alpha \models \psi(cP_j/p)$ for any instance $\psi(cP_j/p)$ of ψ, and so not $\mathcal{M}^\alpha \models \exists p\psi$. The arguments where $\vartheta = \forall p\psi$ are analogous to those for the existential case. Suppose $\vartheta \in \Omega$. We must show $\mathcal{M}^\alpha \models \forall p\, \psi$. By the construction procedure and the fact that $\forall p\psi \vdash \psi(cP_j/p)$, every instance $\psi(cP_j/p) \in \Omega$, and by the inductive hypothesis $\mathcal{M}^\alpha \models \psi(cP_j/p)$. So $\mathcal{M}^\alpha \models \forall p\, \psi$. Now assume that $\varphi \in \Sigma$. By the construction of Σ, an instance $\psi(cP_j/p) \in \Sigma$. By the inductive hypothesis then, not $\mathcal{M}^\alpha \models \psi(cP_j/p)$. But this suffices to show that t is not the case that $\mathcal{M}^\alpha \models \vartheta$.

From Lemma 6.2, it now immediately follows that we have a model of Ω that fails to verify φ, and the proof of proposition 6 is done.

Bibliography

Aczel, P. (1989): 'Algebraic Semantics for Intensional Logics, I' in *Properties, Types and Meaning, Volume I: Foundational Issues*, eds. Chierchia G., B. Partee and R. Turner, Dordrecht: Kluwer Academic Publishers, pp. 17-46.

Asher, N. (1986): 'Belief in Discourse Representation Theory', *Journal of Philosophical Logic*, pp. 1137-189.

Asher, N. (1988): "Reasoning about Knowledge and Belief with Self-reference and Time', *Proceedings of the Second Conference on Theoretical Aspects of Reasoning about Knowledge*, ed. M. Vardi.

Asher, N. & H. Kamp (1986): 'The Knower's Paradox and Representational Theories of Attitudes', in *Theoretical Aspects of Reasoning about Knowledge*, ed. J. Halpern. Los Angeles: Morgan Kaufmann, pp, 131-148.

Asher, N. & H. Kamp (1989): 'Self-Reference, Attitudes and Paradox', in *Properties, Types and Meaning, Volume I: Foundational Issues*, eds. Chierchia G., B. Partee and R. Turner, Dordrecht: Kluwer Academic Publishers, pp. 85-158.

Bealer, G. (1982): *Quality and Concept*, Oxford: Oxford University Press.

Gupta, A. (1982): 'Truth and Paradox,' *Journal of Philosophical Logic* 12, pp. 1-60.

Henkin, L. (1950): 'Completeness in the Theory of Types', *Journal of Symbolic Logic*, 15, pp. 81-91.

Herzberger, H. (1982): 'Notes on Naive Semantics,' *Journal of Philosophical Logic* 12, pp. 61-102.

Herzberger, H. (1982): 'Naive Semantics and the Liar Paradox,' *Journal of Philosophy* 79, pp. 479-497.

Kaplan, D. & R. Montague (1960): 'A Paradox Regained,' *Notre Dame Journal of Formal Logic* 1, pp. 79-90.

Kamp, H. (1984): 'A Scenic Tour Through The Land of Situations', manuscript.

Kripke, S. (1975): 'Outline of a New Theory of Truth,' *Journal of Philosophy* 72, pp. 690-715.

Montague, R. (1963): 'Syntactical Treatments of Modality, with Corollaries on Reflexion Principles and Finite Axiomatizability,' *Acta Philosophica Fennica* 16, pp. 153-167.

Parsons, C. (1974): The Liar Paradox, *Journal of Philosophical Logic* 3, pp.381-412.

Prior, A. (1961): 'On a Family of Paradoxes', *Notre Dame Journal of Formal Logic*, 2, pp. 16-32.

Russell, B. (1903): *The Principles of Mathematics*, London.

Ramsey, F. (1927), 'Facts and Propositions', *Proceedings of the Aristotelian Society supplementary volume* 7, pp. 153-170.

Shapiro, S. (1985), 'Second-order Languages and Mathematical Practice', *Journal of Symbolic Logic*, 50 (1985), pp. 714-742.

Thomason, R. (1982): 'Paradoxes of Intentionality?', manuscript of a paper read at the 1989 Conference on Attitudes and Logic at The University of Minnesota, Minneapolis-Saint Paul, Minnesota.

Thomason, R. (1980.a): 'A Note on Syntactical Treatments of Modality', *Synthese* 44, pp. 391-395.

Thomason, R. (1980.b): 'A Model Theory for Propositional Attitudes', *Linguistics and Philosophy* 4, pp.47-70.

Turner, R. (1986): 'Intentional Semantics', manuscript.

van Benthem, J. and Doets, K. (1984): 'Higher Order Logic' in *Handbook of Philosophical Logic* , vol. I, eds. Gabbay, D. & Guenthner G., Dordrecht: Reidel Publishing Company, 274-329.

PROPAGATING EPISTEMIC COORDINATION THROUGH MUTUAL DEFAULTS I

Richmond H. Thomason
Intelligent Systems Program
University of Pittsburgh
Pittsburgh, PA 15260
U.S.A.

ABSTRACT

A *mutual default* is a rule, capable of tolerating exceptions, that is mutually supposed by a group G: i.e., the rule is supposed by all members of the group, is supposed by all members of the group to be supposed by all members of the group, etc. A family of propositional attitudes B_i indexed for $i \in G$ (and representing, say, supposition) is *coordinated* for G if B_i applies to the same propositions for all members i of G, and is commonly supposed by the members of G to do so.

This paper is a preliminary exploration of formal postulates that ensure maintenance of coordination of a propositional attitude, representing the common ground of a conversation, in dynamic environments that allow for assertional speech acts. I present results showing that mutually supposed rules of conversation provide a mechanism for preserving coordination. If coordination can be assumed, reasoning about propositional attitudes can be greatly simplified, through collapse of iterated operators.

I also show how coordination maintenance can be secured, at least in unexceptional cases, when rules of conversation are defeasible; this relaxation of the theory is needed because plausible conversational rules are subject to exceptions.

The project of formalizing coordination maintenance using Circumscription Theory raises some interesting technical problems; to provide a finitely axiomatized theory of coordination, it is apparently necessary to quantify over intensional types of at least third order. For this purpose, Richard Montague's Intensional Logic seems to be an appropriate vehicle.

1. SHARED CONVERSATIONAL CONTEXT

Planning is certainly not all there is to discourse. But planning and plan recognition are among the most important reasoning mechanisms that come into play when language is used. Through the work of a research community including James Allen, Philip Cohen, Hector Levesque, C. Raymond Perrault, and others,[1] plan-based models of speech acts and discourse have been developed to a very sophisticated level, achieving improvements in our understanding of the phenomena and in guiding the implementation of natural language understanding systems.

Certain goals—speech act goals—play a central part in this approach, both in generating and in interpreting discourse. Allen, Cohen, Levesque, Perrault, and in fact all computational linguists who have written on this topic and whose work I am familiar with, consider the goal of an act of assertion to be the creation of a kind of belief. (For instance, in telling you that your shoelace is

[1] Some references to this work are provided in the bibliography; I haven't tried to supply a complete list.

untied I am trying to get you to believe that your shoelace is untied.) It is also generally agreed that the goal of an assertive speech act should be not merely a hearer's belief, but a *mutual* belief. (My assertive speech act will not have been successful, for instance, if you came to believe that your shoelace is untied, but I didn't also come to believe that you now believe this.) This conclusion has become generally accepted on its own merit, it seems, and also through the weight of psychological authorities like Clark and Marshall [4], and of philosophical ones like Lewis [7] and Schiffer [11].

However, it is not easy to see how to formalize this goal appropriately, if we assume that conversational agents are reasonably well informed, and are sane in the sense that they reject goals that a reasonable person would consider impracticable. The problem is that *mutual* belief involves iterated combinations of the beliefs of several agents, and even when there are only two agents, these iterations are in principle unbounded, so that a mutual belief will comprise a "conjunction" of infinitely many independent beliefs. Adding a mutual belief operator to the planning language, or even infinitary conjunctions to it, as Allen seems to do in [1], seems problematic even aside from computational considerations, if we want speech act goals to be practicable. How can I reasonably intend to create a mutual belief, any more than I can reasonably intend to write down all the natural numbers?

In Cohen and Levesque [5], this problem is dealt with by relaxing the goal. Assertive acts, according to this paper, aim not at a mutual belief in the asserted proposition, but at a hearer's belief that a certain complex belief is mutually believed. But this only seems to postpone the practicability problem: if mutual belief can't be achieved, for more or less a priori reasons, then it's hard to see why the ideal hearer shouldn't recognize the very same problem that led Cohen and Levesque to settle for less. Also the ideal speaker should realize that this is how the hearer will reason. And so, if the speaker is careful he shouldn't expect that his act will induce the hearer to believe that a genuine mutual belief has been achieved.

Reacting not to this difficulty, but to problems that he traces to the indefeasible character of Cohen and Levesque's rules, Perrault not only developed, in [10], a nonmonotonic formulation of discourse rules, but also provided a reflective mechanism for restoring mutual belief as the goal state. Perrault shows that mutual belief in the asserted proposition can be obtained by strengthening the rules of conversational dynamics so that they themselves will be mutually believed. A later reformulation of Perrault's idea in Hierarchic Autoepistemic Logic was implemented in a natural language understanding system; see Appelt and Konolige [2].

Since, like many other practical rules, discourse rules are defeasible, it is good to see how to state them in one or more of the formalisms for nonmonotonic reasoning. But Perrault's solution to the feasibility of creating mutual beliefs, by shifting the burden to mutual discourse rules and to the underlying logic of belief, seems to me to be potentially even more important, and in this paper I want to concentrate on that idea, extending and developing it.

2. THE IDEA OF COORDINATION

A slightly different model of discourse, originating, I think, in Robert Stalnaker's work, can be found in the philosophical literature; see Stalnaker [12] and later works, such as [13,14,15]. On this model, the data structures of conversation are *public,* or *shared.* Among these will be a belief-like propositional attitude that represents the common ground in a conversation, and that evolves as the conversation develops. On such a view, it is very natural to speak as if the common ground were the beliefs of a kind of transcendent agent, the conversational group.

Obviously, such an assumption has to be justified somehow in terms of underlying characteristics of the members of the group. I wish to propose, as the presupposition of this conception of publicity, a condition of *group coordination* of the relevant conversational information. The members of a coordinated discourse group must not only share the same beliefs, but mutually believe that they share the same beliefs.[2]

I will show here that Perrault's methods can be extended to provide for the maintenance of coordination in conversations; coordination will be preserved after an assertion has been made, as long as it is mutually believed that the assertion was not anomalous. To push this result through, I will have to install a much more powerful underlying logic. But this secures a far-reaching simplification in the formalization of discourse planning, since—as I will show—we can reason about coordinated belief in exactly the same way that we would reason about the beliefs of a single agent. All iterated operators collapse, and there is no need to distinguish the beliefs of one agent from those of another, or for that matter from those of the group itself. It remains to be seen if this idea is useful computationally. But at a theoretical plane, it certainly does seem to provide a considerable improvement in modeling discourse.

3. SUPPOSITION

Since beliefs are private, we can't take the public common ground that is created in the course of a conversation to consist of beliefs. But we can take it to consist of suppositions.

A supposition is like a belief, but may be temporary, ad hoc, and not taken seriously by the supposer. Beliefs themselves are constantly being changed, but it is less easy to change them at will. I can easily suppose (for the sake of argument, say) that the stock market will rise tomorrow, but I can't voluntarily create the corresponding belief as I please. Closely related to this involuntary feature is the action-guiding character of beliefs, which distinguishes them from mere suppositions. I will not want to buy stock because I've supposed for argument's sake that the market will rise; but I will have a motive to buy stock if I believe that it will rise.

Letting supposition replace belief in the theory of speech acts provides a single, well-motivated solution to swarms of objections and counterexamples that have been proposed in the philosophical and computational literature.[3] An early example of this sort is cited by Grice in the William James Lectures: when a student answers a question at an oral examination, he is not trying to get his history teacher to believe that, say, William invaded England in 1066. (Evidently, this and similar examples were much discussed at Oxford during the 1950's.) Appelt and Konolige's objection in [2] to the speech act theory of Perrault [10]—that a speaker should not be able to convince himself of something that he doesn't already believe simply by saying it—is another problem that Stalnaker's idea solves.

Also—a point that is important in relation to the axiomatization of discourse rules that I will offer later in this paper—the idea enables default rules to be formulated so that they can be adopted by reasonable agents. It doesn't seem right to assume—even as a default—that if a speaker asserts p the hearer will believe p. But it *does* seem plausible that if p is asserted, p will then, by default, become part of the things that are taken for granted in later stages in the conversation. Thus, by

[2] The idea of coordination isn't stressed in Stalnaker's work, though I think it is implicit there. Coordination is, of course, a major theme in Lewis' [7].

[3] This was first realized by Stalnaker. See the references in the bibliography of this paper, and especially [12].

using supposition-based defeasible rules, the theory that I will present in the final section of this paper provides a solution (though in a very simplified case), of the impracticability problem that I raised in Section 1.

Just as we can suppose things for the sake of argument, and in the extreme case can even temporarily suppose something that we know to be false in order to refute it, we can suppose things for the purposes of conversation. We want to think of these conversational suppositions as the product of a joint project, as the shared creations of a group. But to justify this, we have to show how conversational suppositions can be coordinated.

4. COORDINATED SUPPOSITION

Let B_x be an epistemic operator indexed by the individual variable x. For definiteness, I'll assume that B_x has **S5**-like properties (but without the alethic property that what is supposed must be true); for an axiomatization, see the logic **KD45** in Chellas [3].

Where G is a one-place predicate (representing a group of communicators) and Γ is a theory, B is *weakly G-coordinated* with respect to Γ if **(Coord Scheme 1)** and each instance of **(Coord Scheme 2)** is deducible from Γ.

(Coord Scheme 1) $\forall x\, y[[G(x) \wedge G(y)] \supset \forall q[B_x(q) \equiv B_y(q)]]$

(Coord Scheme 2) $\forall x_1 \ldots x_n\, y\, z[[G(x_1) \wedge \ldots \wedge G(x_n) \wedge G(y) \wedge G(z)] \supset B_{x_1} \ldots B_{x_n}(\forall q[B_y(q) \equiv B_z(q)])]$

Provided that an operator B_G is present in the language that can serve to represent common supposition for G, we also have a notion of *G-coordination*, in which **(Coord Scheme 1)** and **(Coord Scheme 2)** are replaced by the following axioms. (Note that **(Coord Scheme 1)** and **(Coord Axiom 1)** are identical.)

(Coord Axiom 1) $\forall x\, y[[G(x) \wedge G(y)] \supset \forall q[B_x(q) \equiv B_y(q)]]$

(Coord Axiom 2) $\forall y\, z[[G(y) \wedge G(z)] \supset B_G \forall q[B_y(q) \equiv B_z(q)]]$

Later we will be dealing with time-dependent supposition operators $B_{x,t}$ that are doubly indexed. In this case, we will need to speak of weak G-coordination with respect to Γ, and of G-coordination, *at t*.

5. LOGICAL RESOURCES

To deal with supposition, we need a modal logic. To deal with circumscription, we need a second order logic. But to cope with circumscriptive rules involving *mutual* supposition we will require an even more powerful logical engine.

The problem is that Circumscription Theory requires a finite axiomatization of the domain theory. So, since part of our domain is mutual supposition, we'll have to finitely axiomatize mutual supposition. To manage this, I don't see how to avoid quantifying over higher order intensional types—in particular, over sets of sets of propositions. Since I'll need to go this far, I'll simply go the whole distance, and adopt Montague's Intensional Logic as the background logic. This logic has the advantage of being very general and powerful, it has been well described,[4] and the formalism

[4]See Montague [9] and Gallin [6].

is relatively familiar, through its use in natural language semantics. I'll assume some familiarity with Intensional Logic in what follows.

The variable t is designated to range over times, which I assume to be individuals, i.e. to have type e; $p(t)$ is a proposition depending on t; this represents the assertion that is made at t.

Some type conventions: G always has type $\langle \mathsf{e}, \mathsf{t}\rangle$; p has type $\langle \mathsf{e}, \langle \mathsf{s}, \mathsf{t}\rangle\rangle$; x, a, and b all have type e; O has type $\langle\langle \mathsf{s}, \mathsf{t}\rangle, \mathsf{t}\rangle$; and q always has type $\langle \mathsf{s}, \mathsf{t}\rangle$. Other typed terms will be flagged with their type at their first occurrence in a formula. I will use '$O(\phi)$' as an abbreviation of Montague's '$O(\hat{}[\phi])$'; and '$O_1 \circ O_2$' as an abbreviation of '$\lambda q O_1(\hat{}O_2(q))$'.

Where η has type $\langle \mathsf{e}, \langle\langle \mathsf{s}, \mathsf{t}\rangle, \mathsf{t}\rangle\rangle$ (i.e., where η represents a propositional attitude), a *finite iteration* of η is any expression having the form $\eta_{\alpha_1} \circ \ldots \circ \eta_{\alpha_n}$, where each α_i is either a or b. (Here, 'η_a' is just an alternative notation for $\eta(a)$, a term of type $\langle\langle \mathsf{s}, \mathsf{t}\rangle, \mathsf{t}\rangle$.)

In everything that follows, I will assume for simplicity a conversational group of just two members: i.e., I'll postulate $\forall x[G(x) \equiv [x = a \vee x = b]]$.

6. WEAK COORDINATION MAINTENANCE IN A MONOTONIC SETTING

The following simple rule for conversational update serves as a good introduction to the technical issues.

(Simple Update) $\quad \forall x t[G(x) \supset \forall q[B_{x,t+1}(q) \equiv B_{x,t}(\check{}[p(t)] \supset \check{}q)]]$

According to this rule, each agent updates his conversational suppositions by adding the proposition that is asserted and its supposed consequences to them.

Obviously, this rule will not maintain coordination. After an update, agents that were coordinated at t will still in fact suppose the same things as one another. But nothing guarantees that they will suppose that they have the same suppositions. The difficulty is that, though all agents share the same update rule, they needn't suppose that they share this rule. To ensure the maintenance of coordination, then, we want to close **(Simple Update)** under iterated supposition operators.[5]

Let ϕ be an instance of the scheme **(Mutual Update Scheme)** if either ϕ has the **(Simple Update)** form

$$\forall x t[G(x) \supset \forall q[B_{x,t+1}(q) \equiv B_{x,t}(\check{}[p(t)] \supset \check{}q)]]$$

or the form

$$\forall x t[G(x) \supset O(\forall q[B_{x,t+1}(q) \equiv B_{x,t}(\check{}[p(t)] \supset \check{}q)])],$$

where O is a finite iteration of B_t.

Supposing that **(Mutual Update Scheme)** belongs to our background theory Γ, it is easy to show that if B is weakly G-coordinated at t with respect to Γ then B is weakly G-coordinated at $t+1$ with respect to Γ.

7. MUTUAL SUPPOSITION IN INTENSIONAL LOGIC

In this section I will sketch the development of a finite theory of mutual supposition in intensional logic, giving the bare elements only and without proving any theorems. I will take for granted the

[5]This is the idea of Perrault's that I described in Section 1.

logical axioms of Gallin [6]. The formalized theory will have two nonlogical axioms, **(MS1)** and **(MS2)**. We will need many definitions as well: these are numbered **(D1)** to **(D9)**.

The first axiom is our simplifying assumption about the size of the group.

(MS1) $$\forall x[G(x) \equiv [x = a \vee x = b]]$$

With our first definition, we plunge into the higher order aspects that enter into the formalization of mutuality.

(D1) $$C(P^{\langle\langle\langle s,t\rangle,t\rangle,t\rangle}, B_t) =_{df} P(B_{a,t}) \wedge P(B_{b,t}) \wedge \forall O[P(O) \supset [P(B_{a,t} \circ O) \wedge P(B_{b,t} \circ O)]]$$

Intuitively, **(D1)** characterizes the sets of propositional attitudes that contain the attitudes expressed by $B_{a,t}$ and $B_{b,t}$, and also are closed under finite iterations of B_t. We now introduce a constant FI of type $\langle\langle\langle s,t\rangle,t\rangle,\langle e,\langle\langle\langle s,t\rangle,t\rangle,t\rangle\rangle\rangle$, which is intended to pick out the *finite* iterations of an agent-indexed propositional attitude. The intention of axiom **(MS2)** is to capture this, using the usual higher order account of finite iterations. In **(MS2)**, '$FI(B_t, O)$' abbreviates '$[FI(O)](B_t)$'.

(MS2) $$C(FI, B_t) \wedge \forall X^{\langle\langle\langle s,t\rangle,t\rangle,t\rangle}[C(X, B_t) \supset \forall O[FI(B_t, O) \supset X(O)]]$$

From **(MS2)** we can prove that FI in fact singles out all the finite iterations of B_t; for instance, we can prove $FI(B_{a,t} \circ B_{b,t} \circ B_{a,t}, B_t)$.

Using FI, we now define B_G of type $\langle e,\langle\langle s,t\rangle,t\rangle\rangle$. $B_{G,t}$ represents coordinated supposition at t; $B^T_{G,t}$ represents true coordinated supposition at t.

(D2) $$B_G =_{df} \lambda t \lambda q \forall O[FI(O, B_t) \supset O(q)]$$

(D3) $$B^T_G =_{df} \lambda t \lambda q[B_{G,t}(q) \wedge {}^{\vee}q]$$

8. MUTUALLY SUPPOSED SUPPOSITION UPDATE

The next four definitions have to do with update. **(D6)** and **(D7)** characterize two fundamental notions of supposition update, represented by constants $MIASU$ and $GASU$ of type $\langle e,\langle e,t\rangle\rangle$.

(D4) $$\eta^T =_{df} \lambda q({}^{\vee}q \wedge \eta(q))$$

(D5) $$AU(O, O', t) =_{df} O' = \lambda q O({}^{\vee}[p(t)] \supset {}^{\vee}q)$$

(D6) $$MIASU(t, t') =_{df} \lambda t \lambda t' \forall x[G(x) \supset B^T_{x,t}(AU(B_{x,t}, B_{x,t'}, t))]$$

(D7) $$GASU(t, t') =_{df} B_{G,t'} = \lambda q[B_{G,t}({}^{\vee}[p(t)] \supset {}^{\vee}q)]$$

In **(D4)**, η has type $\langle\langle s,t\rangle,t\rangle$, so, for instance, $B^T_{x,t}$ represents true supposition.

AU is meant to represent a relation of "assertion based supposition update" between O and O′: the propositions satisfying O′ are the updates relative to $p(t)$ of those satisfying O. $MIASU$ stands for a relation of true, "mutually supposed, individual assertion-based supposition update." This relation holds between two times if the group mutually believes that each of its members follows the update rule in getting from the first time to the second. $GASU$ represents a relation of "group assertion-based supposition update." This relation holds between two times in case group update from the first time to the second follows the group update rule.

One of our main results is that *MIASU* induces a kind of pre-established harmony, so that it's as if there is a group that behaves like an agent, in that its suppositions evolve according to the rule for individuals. That is, we will show that *MIASU* implies *GASU*.

9. COORDINATION IN INTENSIONAL LOGIC

The suppositions of the members of a group at a time are *coordinated* if the group truly mutually believes that all members of the group suppose alike. This provides the definition of a constant *Coord* of type $\langle \mathsf{e}, \mathsf{t} \rangle$.

$$\textbf{(D8)} \qquad \mathit{Coord} \; =_{df} \; \lambda t \forall x [G(x) \supset B^{T}_{G,t}(\forall q[B_{x,t}(q) \equiv B_{G,t}(q)])]$$

Theorem **(T1)** is an *object-level* result; what is claimed when **(T1)** is stated is that a certain sentence is provable in Gallin's version of Intensional Logic from our axioms. In this presentation, I will simply state major results, without giving proofs. Thus, though if I were proceeding systematically I would have to supply, and prove, a number of lemmas about coordination, I state only one representative and fairly important example, without proof.[6]

$$\textbf{(T1)} \qquad \mathit{Coord}(t) \supset \forall O[\mathit{FI}(O, B_t) \supset [\forall x[O = B_{x,t}] \wedge [O = B_{G,t}]]]$$

Results such as **(T1)** are the support for my claim that iterated attitudes will collapse if supposition is coordinated.

10. COORDINATION MAINTENANCE WITH INDEFEASIBLE UPDATE

One of our main theorems about update in a monotonic setting is that mutually supposed individual update implies group update. Note that this is proved as a consequence in Intensional Logic of our axioms, **(MS1)** and **(MS2)**.

$$\textbf{(T2)} \qquad \forall t t' [\mathit{MIASU}(t, t') \supset \mathit{GASU}(t, t')]$$

The proof of this result is fairly complex, and depends on showing that the desired property of mutual supposition after update holds for all finite iterations of supposition after update: that is, we show

$$\mathit{MIASU}(t, t') \supset \forall O[\mathit{FI}(O', B'_t) \supset [O = \lambda q B_{G,t}(\check{}[p(t)] \supset \check{}q)]].$$

Details of the proof will be supplied in Thomason [17].

From **(T2)** it is relatively easy to prove that coordination will be preserved by true, mutually supposed individual assertion-based supposition update. Again, this is an object-level theorem in Intensional Logic.

$$\textbf{(T3)} \qquad \forall t t' [\mathit{MIASU}(t, t') \supset [\mathit{Coord}(t) \supset \mathit{Coord}(t')]]$$

---

[6] The proofs are actually fairly complex. I intend to provide the details in an appendix to a forthcoming paper, Thomason [17].

11. THE NEED FOR DEFEASIBLE RULES

We have shown that an update rule, to the effect that what is asserted is always added to the stock of beliefs, will preserve coordination if it is true and mutually supposed. That is, the following monotonic rule of update will preserve coordination:

(Indefeasible Update) $\forall t\, MIASU(t, t+1)$

In fact, this is just the following special case of **(T2)**.

(T4) $\forall t[MIASU(t, t+1) \supset [Coord(t) \supset Coord(t+1)]]$

The only trouble with such a rule is that it is not in general true (and so in general will not be supposed by reasonable agents). The simplest sort of counterexample is just the case in which the speaker's assertion hasn't been correctly identified, perhaps because it wasn't heard. Or someone may object to it, or a hearer could misidentify the speech act, or the assertion may fail to make sense in a number of ways that make the hearer suspect that conversational repairs of some sort are needed.

The texture of ways in which **(Indefeasible Update)** can fail is entirely open-ended, in that it seems to be a hopeless task to enumerate precisely the all the cases in which it can fail. This sort of open-endedness is a familiar story, one that is commonly retold when people justifify the need for a nonmonotonic formalization of domains such as planning or puzzle solving. The same sort of point has been made to motivate nonmonotonic rules of conversational update in Perrault [10] and in Appelt and Konolige [2].

12. COORDINATION MAINTENANCE WITH DEFEASIBLE UPDATE

Though there seems to be general agreement that conversational rules are an appropriate domain for the application of theories of nonmonotonic reasoning, there is lack of agreement on which theory to use. Perrault [10] uses Reiter's Default Logic, and Appelt and Konolige [2] use Hierarchic Autoepistemic Logic.

Though choice of framework may be important in applications of the theory of conversation to implemented natural language processing systems, the choice should not be very important, I think, at an abstract level where one is trying to understand the general requirements for a theory of conversational update. This is my goal in the present work—I have not yet tried to implement the ideas.

In what follows I will use McCarthy's Circumscription Theory as a means of formalizing defeasible suppositional update. This decision was based primarily on the flexibility and logical depth of this approach to nonmonotonic reasoning. A secondary motivation of the choice is the natural fit between the logical resources that are required by Circumscription Theory, which uses second order logic, and the requirements of a theory of mutual supposition, which—as we have seen—lead us to adopt a rather powerful higher order modal logic. Though you may be able to go a certain distance with schemes, as in Perrault [10] and in Section 6 of this paper, I think it could be difficult to go very far without a more explicit formalization of mutuality.

I use the presentation of Circumscription Theory in Lifschitz [8], which to my knowledge is the best developed and most sophisticated version of the theory available in print, as well as the presentation that is probably most suitable for logicians. However, the application that I will make here will not make much use of the power of the later versions of Circumscription Theory.[7] In fact, it seems from the work that has been done so far that applications to rules of conversation are relatively straightforward in terms of the demands they make on the nonmonotonic apparatus.[8] Here, I will confine myself to a case that is about as simple as it can be; it is meant only to illustrate the general idea.

We retain the constants B, G, p, and FI, which have types $\langle \mathsf{e}, \langle \mathsf{e}, \langle\langle \mathsf{s}, \mathsf{t}\rangle, \mathsf{t}\rangle\rangle\rangle$, $\langle \mathsf{e}, \mathsf{t}\rangle$, $\langle \mathsf{e}, \langle \mathsf{s}, \mathsf{t}\rangle\rangle$ and $\langle\langle\langle \mathsf{s}, \mathsf{t}\rangle, \mathsf{t}\rangle, \langle \mathsf{e}, \langle\langle\langle \mathsf{s}, \mathsf{t}\rangle, \mathsf{t}\rangle, \mathsf{t}\rangle\rangle\rangle$. We add one abnormality predicate $ab1$, of type $\langle \mathsf{e}, \mathsf{t}\rangle$. We also retain the axioms of the indefeasible theory: **(MS1)** and **(MS2)**.

The intended interpretation is now as follows. The "times" I have been speaking of are really conversational turns. At each turn the speaker means something; this proposition is represented by $p(t)$. I'm indulging in gross oversimplification; of course, when some proposition is meant there usually is a linguistic vehicle, and a process of interpretation that gets from this vehicle to one or more things that are meant. This process of interpretation has to be thoroughly public and mutual.[9] In fact, one of the purposes of the theory that I am developing here is the formalization of this process. However, I leave all that out here; $p(t)$, then, represents a proposition that is meant to be recognized as something to be added to the conversational suppositions. And it is plausible that as a matter of default p(t) *will* be added to the record; that is, the conversants will take it to be added unless some recognizable exception is noted. Moreover, it is a public or mutual matter that this default obtains.

To provide for a few exceptional cases, we allow the hearer to make any of three responses at each time: (1) the null response, which we represent as the empty proposition $\hat{}\forall x[x = x]$, (2) *What,* which can be taken to be something like "I don't understand," and *No,* which can be taken to be something like "I disagree." Either of the last two responses creates an exception to the rule of "assertional uptake." To represent this, we add six conversational axioms to our list.

(D9)	$\top \;=_{df}\; \forall x[x = x]$
(Limited Responses)	$\forall t[r(t) = \hat{}\top \vee r(t) = What \vee r(t) = No]$
(Exclusive Alternatives)	$\hat{}\top \neq What \wedge \hat{}\top \neq No \wedge What \neq No$
(Rule for 'What')	$\forall t[[r(t) = What] \supset ab1(t)]$
(Rule for 'No')	$\forall t[[r(t) = No] \supset ab1(t)]$
(Defeasible Update)	$\forall x[G(x) \supset B^{T}_{G,t}(\neg ab1(t) \supset AU(B_{x,t}, B_{x,t+1}, t))]$
(Conventionality of Normalcy)	$\forall t[B_{G,t}(\neg ab1(t)) \supset \neg ab1(t)]$

The first four of these axioms are well motivated by what has just been said about the intended interpretation. The fifth, **(Defeasible Update)**, says that it is mutually supposed of every agent

[7] As far as I can see, the generalization of the underlying logic from extensional second order logic to Intensional Logic does not create any logical difficulties, and would be trouble-free even if we wished to minimize higher order constants. However, in this application, we will only need to minimize a single first order constant.

[8] I suspect that extending the theory to take implicature into account would change this, since this phenomenon seems to draw heavily on world knowledge, and to involve many complex defaults, that may well conflict with one another in some cases.

[9] See Thomason [17] for discussion and illustrations of this point.

in the group that the agent will make an appropriate assertional update if nothing unusual occurs. This is actually a fairly straightforward adaptation of the indefeasible update rule, except that—as will be seen in a moment—it is critical that the $B^T_{G,t}$ operator is placed outside the scope of $\neg ab1(t)$. We cannot assume that abnormality will automatically be recognized when it occurs, much less that it will be mutually supposed to have occurred.

The last postulate is plausible enough if you think about the interpretation of normality. Given the public, conventional nature of conversational defaults, it can't possibly happen that a situation is conversationally abnormal if at the same time the group supposes it to be normal.

We now form a circumscriptive theory by minimizing $ab1$ relative to the axioms we have given, allowing all other parameters to vary freely. That is, in terms of Lifschitz [8], we add the following single policy axiom to the rest.

(Minimize $ab1$) $$V_{ab1,ab1}$$

It is easy to see that our axioms yield the following consequence.

(T5) $$\forall t[B_G(\neg ab1(t)) \supset MIASU(t, t+1)]$$

Putting this together with **(T3)**, we have our final theorem.

(T6) $$\forall t[B_G(\neg ab1(t)) \supset Coord(t) \supset Coord(t+1)]$$

Notice that we would not want to strengthen this result by replacing the antecedent $B_G(\neg ab1(t))$ by $ab1(t)$; it is too easy to imagine situations that are abnormal, but are not mutually supposed to be abnormal. (For instance, the hearer responds with "What?" but the speaker doesn't hear the response.) This, of course, raises the question of how things that happen prominently in a shared environment come to be mutually supposed; I have nothing new to say about this problem.

REFERENCES

[1] Allen, J., "Recognizing intentions from natural language utterances." In M. Brady and R. Berwick eds., *Computational models of discourse,* Cambridge, MA: MIT Press, 1983, pp. 107–166.

[2] Appelt, D. and K. Konolige, "A practical nonmonotonic theory for reasoning about speech acts." *26th Annual meeting of the Association for Computational Linguistics: proceedings of the conference.* Association for Computational Linguistics, 1988, pp. 170–178.

[3] Chellas, B., *Modal logic.* Cambridge, England: Cambridge University Press, 1980.

[4] Clark, H., and C. Marshall, "Definite reference and mutual knowledge." In A. Joshi, I. Sag, and B. Weber, eds., *Elements of discourse understanding,* Cambridge, England: Cambridge University Press, 1981.

[5] Cohen, P., and H. Levesque, "Speech acts and rationality." *23rd Annual meeting of the Association for Computational Linguistics: proceedings of the conference.* Association for Computational Linguistics, 1985, pp. 49–59.

[6] Gallin, D., *Intensional and higher-order modal logic.* Amsterdam: North-Holland, 1975.

[7] Lewis, D., *Convention.* Cambridge, MA: Harvard University Press, 1969.

[8] Lifschitz, V., "Circumscriptive theories." In R. Thomason, ed., *Philosophical logic and artificial intelligence,* Reidel, 1989, pp. 109–159.

[9] Montague, R., "Pragmatics and intensional logic." In R. Montague, *Formal Philosophy,* pp. 119–147. New Haven: Yale University Press, 1974.

[10] Perrault, C.R., "An application of default logic to speech act theory." In *Intentions in communication.* P. Cohen, J. Morgan, and M. Pollack, eds., Cambridge, MA: MIT Press, 1990.

[11] Schiffer, S., *Meaning.* London: Oxford University Press, 1972.

[12] Stalnaker, R., "Pragmatics." In G. Harman and D. Davidson, eds., *Semantics of natural language,* pp. 380-397. Dordrecht: D. Reidel, 1972.

[13] Stalnaker, R., "Pragmatic presuppositions." In M. Munitz and P. Unger, eds., *Semantics and philosophy,* pp. 197–213. New York: Academic Press, 1975.

[14] Stalnaker, R., "Indicative conditionals." *Philosophia* 5 (1975), pp. 269–286.

[15] Stalnaker, R., "Assertion." In P. Cole, ed., *Radical pragmatics,* pp. 315–332. New York: Academic Press, 1981.

[16] Thomason, R., "Accommodation, meaning, and implicature: interdisciplinary foundations for pragmatics." In *Intentions in communication.* P. Cohen, J. Morgan, and M. Pollack, eds., Cambridge, MA: MIT Press, 1990.

[17] Thomason, R., "Propagating epistemic coordination through mutual defaults II." Forthcoming.

A Nonstandard Approach to the Logical Omniscience Problem

Ronald Fagin
Joseph Y. Halpern
Moshe Y. Vardi

IBM Almaden Research Center
San Jose, CA 95120-6099, USA
E-mail: fagin@ibm.com, halpern@ibm.com, vardi@ibm.com

Abstract

We introduce a new approach to dealing with the well-known *logical omniscience* problem in epistemic logic. Instead of taking possible worlds where each world is a model of classical propositional logic, we take possible worlds which are models of a nonstandard propositional logic we call *NPL*, which is somewhat related to *relevance logic*. This approach gives new insights into the logic of implicit and explicit belief considered by Levesque and Lakemeyer. In particular, we show that in a precise sense agents in the structures considered by Levesque and Lakemeyer are perfect reasoners in *NPL*.

1 Introduction

The standard approach to modelling knowledge, which goes back to Hintikka [Hin62], is in terms of *possible worlds*. In this approach, an agent is said to know a fact φ if φ is true in all the worlds he considers possible. As has been frequently pointed out, this approach suffers from what Hintikka termed the *logical omniscience* problem [Hin75]: agents are so intelligent that they know all valid formulas (including all tautologies of standard propositional logic) and they know all the logical consequences of their knowledge, so that if an agent knows p and if p logically implies q, then the agent also knows q.

While logical omniscience is not a problem under some conditions (this is true in particular for interpretations of knowledge that are often appropriate for analyzing distributed systems [Hal87] and certain AI systems [RK86]), it is certainly not appropriate to the extent that we want to model resource-bounded agents. A number of different semantics for knowledge have been proposed to get around this problem. The one most relevant to our discussion here is what has been called the *impossible worlds* approach. In this approach, the standard possible worlds are augmented by "impossible worlds" (or, perhaps better, *nonstandard worlds*), where the customary rules of logic do not hold [Cre72, Cre73, Lev84, Ran82, Wan89]. It is still the case that an agent knows a fact φ if φ is true in all the worlds the agent considers possible, but since the agent may in fact consider some nonstandard worlds possible, this will affect what he knows.

What about logical omniscience? Notice that notions like "validity" and "logical consequence" (which played a prominent part in our informal description of logical omniscience) are not absolute notions; their formal definitions depend on how truth is defined and on the class of worlds being considered. Although there are nonstandard worlds in the impossible worlds approach, validity and logical consequence are taken with respect to only the standard worlds, where all the rules of standard logic hold. For example, a formula is valid exactly if it is true in all the standard worlds in every structure. The intuition here is that the nonstandard worlds serve only as epistemic alternatives; although an agent may be muddled and may consider a nonstandard world possible, we (the logicians who get to examine the situation from the outside) know that the "real world" must obey the laws of standard logic. If we consider validity and logical implication with respect to standard worlds, then it is easy to show that logical omniscience fails in "impossible worlds" structures: an agent does not know all valid formulas, nor does he know all the logical consequences here (since, in computing his knowledge, we must take the nonstandard worlds into account).

In this paper we consider an approach which, while somewhat related to the impossible worlds approach, stems from a different philosophy. We consider the implications of basing a logic of knowledge on a nonstandard logic rather than standard propositional logic. The basic motivation is the observation, implicit in [Lev84] and commented on in [FH88, Var86], that if we weaken the "logical" in "logical omniscience", then perhaps we can diminish the acuteness of the logical omniscience problem. Thus, instead of distinguishing between standard and nonstandard worlds, we take all our worlds to be models of a nonstandard logic. Some worlds in a structure may indeed be models of standard logic, but they do not have any special status for us. We consider all worlds when defining validity and logical consequence; we accept the commitment to nonstandard logic. Knowledge is still defined to be truth in all possible worlds. It thus turns out that we still have the logical omniscience problem, but this time with respect to nonstandard logic. The hope is that the logical omniscience problem can be alleviated by appropriately choosing the nonstandard logic.

Similarly to relevance logic [AB75], our starting point in choosing a nonstandard logic is the observation that there are a number of properties of implication in standard logic that seem inappropriate in certain contexts. In particular, consider a formula such as $(p \wedge \neg p) \Rightarrow q$. In standard logic this is valid; that is, from a contradiction one can deduce anything. However, consider a knowledge base into which users enter data from time to time. As Belnap points out [Bel77], it is almost certainly the case that in a large knowledge base, there will be some inconsistencies. One can imagine that at some point a user entered the fact that Bob's salary is $50,000, while at another point, perhaps a different user entered the fact that Bob's salary is $60,000. Thus, in standard logic anything can be inferred from this contradiction. One solution to this problem is to replace standard worlds by worlds (called *situations* in [Lev84, Lak87], and *set-ups* in [RR72, Bel77]) in which it is possible that a primitive proposition p is true, false, both true and false, or neither true and false. We achieve the same effect here by keeping our worlds seemingly standard and by using a device introduced in [RR72, RM73] to decouple the semantics of a formula and its negation: for every world s there is a related world s^*. A formula $\neg\varphi$ is true in s iff φ is not true in s^*. It is thus possible for both φ and $\neg\varphi$ to be true at s, and for neither to be true. Intuitively, s provides the support for positive formulas and s^* provides the support for negative formulas. (The standard worlds are now the ones where $s = s^*$; all the laws of standard propositional logic do indeed hold in such worlds.)

We call the propositional logic that results from the above semantics *nonstandard propositional logic* (NPL). Unlike standard logic, for which ψ is a logical consequence of φ exactly when $\varphi \Rightarrow \psi$ is valid, where $\varphi \Rightarrow \psi$ is defined as $\neg\varphi \vee \psi$, this is not the case in NPL. This leads us to include a connective $\hookrightarrow$ in NPL so that, among other things, we have that ψ is a logical consequence of φ iff $\varphi \hookrightarrow \psi$ is valid. Of course, $\hookrightarrow$ agrees with $\Rightarrow$ on the standard worlds, but in general it is different. Given our nonstandard semantics, $\varphi \hookrightarrow \psi$ comes closer than $\varphi \Rightarrow \psi$ to capturing the idea that "if φ is true, then ψ is true." Just as in relevance logic, formulas such as $(p \wedge \neg p) \hookrightarrow q$ are not valid, so that from a contradiction, one cannot conclude everything. In fact, we can show that if φ and ψ are *standard* propositional formulas (those formed from $\neg$ and $\wedge$, containing no occurrences of $\hookrightarrow$), then then $\varphi \hookrightarrow \psi$ is valid exactly if φ entails ψ in relevance logic. However, in formulas with nested occurrences of $\hookrightarrow$, the semantics of $\hookrightarrow$ is quite different from the relevance logic notion of entailment.

When our nonstandard semantics is applied to knowledge, it turns out that although agents in our logic are not perfect reasoners as far as standard logic goes, they *are* perfect reasoners in nonstandard logic. In particular, as we show, the complete axiomatization for the standard possible worlds interpretation of knowledge can be converted to a complete axiomatization for the nonstandard possible world interpretation of knowledge essentially by replacing the inference rules for standard propositional logic by inference rules for NPL. We need, however, to use $\hookrightarrow$ rather $\Rightarrow$ in formulating the axioms of knowledge. For example, the *distribution axiom*, valid in the standard possible worlds interpretation, says $(K_i\varphi \wedge K_i(\varphi \Rightarrow \psi)) \Rightarrow K_i\psi$. This says that an agent's knowledge is closed under logical consequence: if the agent knows φ and knows that φ implies ψ, then he also knows ψ. The analogue for this axiom holds in our nonstandard interpretation, once we replace $\Rightarrow$ by $\hookrightarrow$. This is appropriate since it is $\hookrightarrow$ that captures the intuitive notion of implication in our framework.

It is instructive to compare our approach with that of Levesque and Lakemeyer [Lev84, Lak87]. Our semantics is essentially equivalent to theirs. But while they avoid logical omniscience by giving nonstandard worlds a secondary status and defining validity only with respect to standard worlds, we accept logical omniscience, albeit with respect to nonstandard logic. Thus, our results justify and elaborate a remark made in [FH88, Var86] that agents in Levesque's model are perfect reasoners in relevance logic.

The rest of this paper is organized as follows. In the next section, we review the standard possible-worlds approach. In Section 3, we describe our nonstandard approach to possible worlds and investigate some of its properties. In Section 4, we consider the logic NPL, which results from adding $\hookrightarrow$ to the syntax, and give the complete axiomatization for the logic of knowledge using NPL as a basis rather than propositional logic. We describe a concrete application of our approach in Section 5, and relate our results to those of Levesque and Lakemeyer in Section 6.

2 Standard Possible Worlds

We review in this section the standard possible worlds approach to knowledge. The intuitive idea behind the possible worlds model is that besides the true state of affairs, there are a number of other possible states of affairs or "worlds". Given his current information, an agent may not be able to tell which of a number of possible worlds describes the actual state of affairs. An agent is then said to *know* a fact φ if φ is true at all the worlds he considers possible (given his current information).

The notion of possible worlds is formalized by means of Kripke structures. Suppose that we have n agents, named $1, \ldots, n$, and a set Φ of primitive propositions that describe basic facts about the domain of discourse. A *standard Kripke structure* M for n agents over Φ is a tuple $(S, \pi, \mathcal{K}_1, \ldots, \mathcal{K}_n)$, where S is a set of *worlds*, π associates with each world in S a truth assignment to the primitive propositions of Φ (i.e., $\pi(s) : \Phi \rightarrow \{\mathbf{true}, \mathbf{false}\}$ for each world $s \in S$), and $\mathcal{K}_i$ is a *binary relation* on S. We refer to standard Kripke structures as *standard structures* or simply as *structures.*

Intuitively, the truth assignment $\pi(s)$ tells us whether p is true or false in a world w. The binary relation $\mathcal{K}_i$ is intended to capture the possibility relation according to agent i: $(s,t) \in \mathcal{K}_i$ if agent i considers world t possible, given his information in world s. The class of all structures for n agents over Φ is denoted by $\mathcal{M}_n^\Phi$. Usually, neither n nor Φ are relevant to our discusion, so we typically write $\mathcal{M}$ instead of $\mathcal{M}_n^\Phi$.

We define the formulas of the logic by starting with the primitive propositions in Φ, and form more complicated formulas by closing off under Boolean connectives $\neg$ and $\wedge$ and the modalities $K_1, \ldots, K_n$. Thus, if φ and ψ are formulas, then so are $\neg\varphi$, $\varphi \wedge \psi$, and $K_i\varphi$, for $i = 1, \ldots, n$. We also use the connectives $\vee$ and $\Rightarrow$. They are defined as abbreviations: $\varphi \vee \psi$ for $\neg(\neg\varphi \wedge \neg\psi)$ and $\varphi \Rightarrow \psi$ for $\neg\varphi \vee \psi$. The class of all formulas for n agents over Φ is denoted by $\mathcal{L}_n^\Phi$. Again, when n and Φ are not relevant to our discussion, we write $\mathcal{L}$ instead of $\mathcal{L}_n^\Phi$. We refer to $\mathcal{L}$-formulas as *standard formulas.*

We are now ready to assign truth values to formulas. A formula will be true or false at a world in a structure. We define the notion $(M,s) \models \varphi$, which can be read as "*φ is true at* (M,s)" or "*φ holds at* (M,s)" or "(M,s) *satisfies* φ", by induction on the structure of φ.

$(M,s) \models p$ (for a primitive proposition $p \in \Phi$) iff $\pi(s)(p) = \mathbf{true}$
$(M,s) \models \neg\varphi$ iff $(M,s) \not\models \varphi$
$(M,s) \models \varphi \wedge \psi$ iff $(M,s) \models \varphi$ and $(M,s) \models \psi$
$(M,s) \models K_i\varphi$ iff $(M,t) \models \varphi$ for all t such that $(s,t) \in \mathcal{K}_i$.

The first three clauses in this definition correspond to the standard clauses in the definition of truth for propositional logic. The last clause captures the intuition that agent i knows φ in world s of structure M exactly if φ is true at all worlds that i considers possible in s.

Given a structure $M = (S, \pi, \mathcal{K}_1, \ldots, \mathcal{K}_n)$, we say that φ is *valid in* M, and write $M \models \varphi$, if $(M,s) \models \varphi$ for every world s in S, and say that φ is *satisfiable in* M if $(M,s) \models \varphi$ for some world s in S. We say that φ is *valid* in $\mathcal{M}$, and write $\mathcal{M} \models \varphi$, if it is valid in all structures of $\mathcal{M}$, and it is *satisfiable* in $\mathcal{M}$ if it is satisfiable in some structure in $\mathcal{M}$. It is easy to check that a formula φ is valid in M (resp., valid in $\mathcal{M}$) if and only if $\neg\varphi$ is not satisfiable in M (resp., not satisfiable in $\mathcal{M}$).

To get a sound and complete axiomatization for validity in $\mathcal{M}$, one starts with propositional reasoning and add to it axioms and inference rules for knowledge. By propositional reasoning we mean all sound propositional inference rules of propositional logic. An inference rule for a logic L is a statement of the form "from Σ infer σ", where $\Sigma \cup \{\sigma\}$ is a set of L-formulas. Such an inference rule is sound if for every substitution τ of L-formulas $\varphi_1, \ldots, \varphi_k$ for the primitive propositions $p_1, \ldots, p_k$ in Σ and σ, if all the formulas in $\tau[\Sigma]$ are valid in L, then $\tau[\sigma]$ is also valid in L. Modus ponens ("from φ and $\varphi \Rightarrow \psi$ infer ψ") is an example of a sound propositional inference rule. Of course, if σ is a valid propositional formula, then "from $\emptyset$ infer σ" is a sound propositional inference rule. It is easy to show that "from Σ infer σ" is a sound propositional inference rule iff σ is a propositional consequence of Σ [FHV89], which explains why the notion of inference is often confused with the notion of consequence. As we shall see later, the two notions do not coincide in our nonstandard propositional logic.

Consider the following axiom system K, which in addition to propositional reasoning consists of one axiom and one rule of inference given below:

A1. $(K_i\varphi \wedge K_i(\varphi \Rightarrow \psi)) \Rightarrow K_i\psi$ (Distribution Axiom)

PR. All sound inference rules of propositional logic

R1. From φ infer $K_i\varphi$ (Knowledge Generalization)

One should view the axioms and inference rules above as *schemes*, i.e., K actually consists of all $\mathcal{L}$-instances of the above axioms and inference rules.

Theorem 2.1: *[Che80] K is a sound and complete axiomatization for validity in $\mathcal{M}$.*

We note that PR can be replaced by any complete axiomatization of standard propositional logic that includes modus ponens as an inference rule, which is the usual way that K is presented (cf. [Che80]). We chose to present K in this unusual way in anticipation of our treatment of nonstandard logic in Section 4.

Finally, instead of trying to prove validity, one may wish to check validity algorithmically.

Theorem 2.2: *[Lad77] The problem of determining validity in $\mathcal{M}$ is PSPACE-complete.*

3 Nonstandard Possible Worlds

Although by now it is fairly well entrenched, standard propositional logic has several undesirable and counterintuitive properties. One problem is that material implication, where "$\varphi \Rightarrow \psi$" is taken to be simply an abbreviation for $\neg\varphi \vee \psi$, does not quite capture our intuition about what implication is. For example, the fact that $(p \Rightarrow q) \vee (q \Rightarrow p)$ is valid is quite counterintuitive, as p and q may be completely unrelated facts. Another problem with standard propositional logic is that it is fragile: a false statement implies everything. For example, the formula $(p \wedge \neg p) \Rightarrow q$ is valid, even if p and q are unrelated. As we observed in the introduction, one situation where this could be a serious problem occurs when we have a large knowledge base of many facts, obtained from multiple sources, and where a theorem prover is used to derive various conclusions from this knowledge base.

To deal with these problems, many alternatives to standard propositional logic have been proposed. We focus on one particular alternative here, and consider its consequences.

The idea is to allow formulas φ and $\neg\varphi$ to have "independent" truth values. Thus, rather than requiring that $\neg\varphi$ be true iff φ is not true, we wish instead to allow the possibility that $\neg\varphi$ can be either true or false, regardless of whether φ is true or false. In the case we just discussed of a knowledge base, φ being true would mean that the fact φ has been put into the knowledge base. Since it is possible for both φ and $\neg\varphi$ to have been put in the knowledge base, it is possible for both φ and $\neg\varphi$ to be true. Similarly, if neither φ nor $\neg\varphi$ has been put into the knowledge base, then this would correspond to neither φ nor $\neg\varphi$ being true.

There are several ways to capture this intuition formally (see [Dun77]). We now discuss one approach, due to [RR72, RM73]. For each world s, there is an associated world s^*, which will be used for giving semantics to negated formulas. Instead of defining $\neg\varphi$ to hold at s iff φ does not hold at s, we instead define $\neg\varphi$ to hold at s iff φ does not hold at s^*. Note that if $s = s^*$, then this gives our usual notion of negation. We are interested in the case where $\neg\neg\varphi$ has the same truth value as of φ. To do this, we require that $s^{**} = s$ (where $s^{**} = (s^*)^*$), for each world s.

A *nonstandard Kripke structure* is a tuple $(S, \pi, \mathcal{K}_1, ..., \mathcal{K}_n, ^*)$, where $(S, \pi, \mathcal{K}_1, ..., \mathcal{K}_n)$ is a (Kripke) structure, and where * is a unary function with domain and range the set S of worlds (where we write s^* for the result of applying the function * to the world s) such that $s^{**} = s$ for each $s \in S$. We refer to nonstandard Kripke structures as *nonstandard structures*. We call them nonstandard, since we think of a world where φ and $\neg\varphi$ are both true or both false as nonstandard. We denote the class of nonstandard structures for n agents over Φ by $\mathcal{NM}_n^\Phi$ (or by $\mathcal{NM}$ when Φ and n are clear from the context).

The definition of $\models$ for the language $\mathcal{L}$ for nonstandard structures is the same as for standard structures, except for the clause for negation:

$$(M, s) \models \neg\varphi \text{ iff } (M, s^*) \not\models \varphi.$$

In particular, the clause for K_i does not change at all:

$$(M, s) \models K_i\varphi \text{ iff } (M, t) \models \varphi \text{ for all } t \text{ such that } (s, t) \in \mathcal{K}_i.$$

Recall that $\varphi \vee \psi$ stands for $\neg(\neg\varphi \wedge \neg\psi)$. It can be shown that $\vee$ still behaves as disjunction, i.e., $(M, s) \models \varphi \vee \psi$ iff $(M, s) \models \varphi$ or $(M, s) \models \psi$. We still take $\varphi \Rightarrow \psi$ to be an abbreviation for $\neg\varphi \vee \psi$, but now $\Rightarrow$ does *not* behave like material implication, due to the nonstandard semantics we have given negation.

Our semantics is closely related to that of Levesque [Lev84] and Lakemeyer [Lak87]. In their semantics, they have *situations* rather than worlds. In a given situation, a primitive proposition can be either true, false, both, or neither. This gives them a way to decouple the semantics of p and $\neg p$ for a primitive proposition p. In order to decouple the semantics of $K_i\varphi$ and $\neg K_i\varphi$, Lakemeyer introduces two possibility relations, $\mathcal{K}_i^+$ and $\mathcal{K}_i^-$. There are also two versions of $\models$, denoted $\models_T$ and $\models_F$, where $\models_T$ means "supports the truth of" and $\models_F$ means "supports the falsity of".[1] We call the structures introduced by Levesque and Lakemeyer *LL structures*. Although, superficially, our semantics seems quite different from the Levesque-Lakemeyer semantics, in fact the two approaches are equivalent in the following sense. For each nonstandard structure M and world s in M, we can find an LL structure M' and world s' in M' such that for each $\mathcal{L}$-formula φ, we have that $(M, s) \models \varphi$ iff $(M', s') \models_T \varphi$ and

[1] We also remark that Levesque and Lakemeyer have two different flavors of knowledge in their papers: explicit knowledge and implicit knowledge. (Actually, they talk about belief rather than knowledge, but the distinction is irrelevant to our discussion here.) We focus here on explicit knowledge, since this is the type that avoids logical omniscience. The reader who is familiar with Levesque and Lakemeyer's work should read all our references to knowledge as "explicit knowledge".

$(M,s) \models \neg\varphi$ iff $(M',s') \models_F \varphi$. Conversely, for each LL structure M and world s in M, we can find a nonstandard structure M' and world s' in M' such that for each $\mathcal{L}$-formula φ, we have $(M,s) \models_T \varphi$ iff $(M',s') \models \varphi$, and $(M,s) \models_F \varphi$ iff $(M',s') \models \neg\varphi$. Details will be given in the full paper.

We return now to examine in detail our nonstandard semantics. Note that it is possible for neither φ nor $\neg\varphi$ to be true at world s (if $(M,s) \not\models \varphi$ and $(M,s^*) \models \varphi$) and for both φ and $\neg\varphi$ to be true at world s (if $(M,s) \models \varphi$ and $(M,s^*) \not\models \varphi$). Let us refer to a world where neither φ nor $\neg\varphi$ is true as *incomplete* (with respect to φ); otherwise, s is *complete*. The intuition behind an incomplete world is that there is not enough information to determine whether φ is true or whether $\neg\varphi$ is true. What about a world where both φ and $\neg\varphi$ are true? We call such a world *incoherent* (with respect to φ); otherwise, s is *coherent*. The intuition behind an incoherent world is that it is overdetermined: it might correspond to a situation where several people have provided mutually inconsistent information. A world s is *standard* if $s = s^*$. Note that for a standard world, the definition of the semantics of negation is equivalent to the standard definition. A standard world s is both complete and coherent: for each formula φ exactly one of φ or $\neg\varphi$ is true at s.

Validity and logical implication for $\mathcal{NM}$ are defined in the usual way: φ is valid in $\mathcal{NM}$ if it holds in every world of every structure of $\mathcal{NM}$, and φ logically implies ψ in $\mathcal{NM}$ if $(M,s) \models \varphi$ implies $(M,s) \models \psi$ for all nonstandard structures M and worlds s in M. There are many nontrivial logical implications in $\mathcal{NM}$; for example, $\neg\neg\varphi$ logically implies φ and $\varphi \wedge \psi$ logically implies φ. What are the valid formulas in $\mathcal{NM}$? It is easy to verify that certain tautologies of standard propositional logic are not valid. For example, the formula $(p \Rightarrow q) \vee (q \Rightarrow p)$, whose validity in standard propositional logic disturbed us, is not valid anymore. The formula $(p \wedge \neg p) \Rightarrow q$, which wreaked havoc in deriving consequences from a knowledge base, is not valid either. What about even simpler tautologies of standard propositional logic, such as $p \vee \neg p$? This formula, too, is not valid. How about $p \Rightarrow p$? It is not valid either, since $p \Rightarrow p$ is just an abbreviation for $\neg p \vee p$, which, as we just said, is not valid. In fact, no formula is valid with respect to nonstandard structures! Even more, there is a single counterexample that simultaneously shows that no formula is valid!

Theorem 3.1: *There is no formula of $\mathcal{L}$ that is valid in nonstandard structures. In fact, there is a nonstandard structure M and a world s of M such that every formula of $\mathcal{L}$ is false at s, and a world t of M such that every formula of $\mathcal{L}$ is true at t.*

Proof: Let $M = (S, \pi, \mathcal{K}_1, \ldots, \mathcal{K}_n, ^*)$ be a special nonstandard structure, defined as follows. Let S contain only two worlds s and t, where $t = s^*$ (and so $s = t^*$). Define π by letting $\pi(s)$ be the truth assignment where $\pi(s)(p) =$ **false** for every primitive proposition p, and letting $\pi(t)$ be the truth assignment where $\pi(t)(p) =$ **true** for every primitive proposition p. Define each $\mathcal{K}_i$ to be $\{(s,s),(t,t)\}$. By a straightforward induction on formulas, it follows that for every formula φ of $\mathcal{L}$, we have $(M,s) \not\models \varphi$ and $(M,t) \models \varphi$. In particular, every formula of $\mathcal{L}$ is false at s, and every formula of $\mathcal{L}$ is true at t. Since every formula of $\mathcal{L}$ is false at s, no formula of $\mathcal{L}$ is valid with respect to nonstandard structures. ∎

It follows from Theorem 3.1 that the validity problem with respect to nonstandard structures is *very* easy: the answer is always "No, the formula is not valid!" The reader may be puzzled why there are no valid formulas. For example, $\neg\neg\varphi$ logically implies φ, as noted earlier. Doesn't this mean that $\neg\neg\varphi \Rightarrow \varphi$ is valid? This does not follow. With *standard* structures, φ logically implies ψ iff the formula $\varphi \Rightarrow \psi$ is valid. This is not the case for *nonstandard* structures. For example, φ logically implies φ, yet $\varphi \Rightarrow \varphi$ is not valid with respect to nonstandard structures. In the next section, we define a new connective that allows us to express logical implication *in the language*, just as $\Rightarrow$ does for standard structures.

What about logical omniscience? It did not go away! If an agent knows all of the formulas in a set Σ, and if Σ logically implies the formula φ, then the agent also knows φ. Because, however, we have weakened the notion of logical implication, the problem of logical omniscience is not as acute as it was in the standard approach. For example, knowledge of valid formulas, which is one form of omniscience, is completely innocuous here, since there are no valid formulas. Also, an agent's knowledge need not be closed under material implication; an agent may know φ and $\varphi \Rightarrow \psi$ without knowing ψ, since φ and $\varphi \Rightarrow \psi$ do not logically imply ψ in $\mathcal{NM}$.

We saw that the problem of determining validity is easy (since the answer is always "No"). Validity is a special case of logical implication: a formula is valid iff it is a logical consequence of the empty set. Unfortunately, logical implication is not that easy to determine.

Theorem 3.2: *The logical implication for propositional $\mathcal{L}$-formulas in nonstandard structures is co-NP-complete, and the logical implication for $\mathcal{L}$-formulas in nonstandard structures is PSPACE-complete.*

Theorem 3.2 asserts that nonstandard logical implication is as hard as standard validity; that is, it is co-*NP*-complete for propositional formulas and *PSPACE*-complete for knowledge formulas (i.e., $\mathcal{L}$-formulas).

4 Strong Implication

Certain classic tautologies, such as $(p \Rightarrow q) \vee (q \Rightarrow p)$ made us uncomfortable. In the previous section, we introduced nonstandard structures and—lo and behold!—under this approach, these formulas are no longer valid. However, the bad news is that other formulas, such as $\varphi \Rightarrow \varphi$, that blatantly seem as if they should be valid, are not valid either (in fact, no formula is valid). It seems that we have thrown out the baby with the bath water.

Let us look more closely at why the formula $\varphi \Rightarrow \varphi$ is not valid. Our intuition about implication tells us that $\varphi_1 \Rightarrow \varphi_2$ should say "if φ_1 is true, then φ_2 is true". However, $\varphi_1 \Rightarrow \varphi_2$ is defined to be $\neg\varphi_1 \vee \varphi_2$, which says that if $\neg\varphi_1$ is false, then φ_2 is true. In standard propositional logic, these are the same, since $\neg\varphi_1$ is false in standard logic iff φ_1 is true. However, in nonstandard structures, these are not equivalent. So let us define a new propositional connective $\hookrightarrow$, which we call *strong implication*, where $\varphi_1 \hookrightarrow \varphi_2$ is defined to be true if whenever φ_1 is true, then φ_2 is true. Formally,

$$(M,s) \models \varphi_1 \hookrightarrow \varphi_2 \text{ iff (if } (M,s) \models \varphi_1, \text{ then } (M,s) \models \varphi_2).$$

That is, $(M,s) \models \varphi_1 \hookrightarrow \varphi_2$ iff either $(M,s) \not\models \varphi_1$ or $(M,s) \models \varphi_2$.

We denote by $\mathcal{L}_n^{\Phi,\hookrightarrow}$, or $\mathcal{L}^{\hookrightarrow}$ for short, the set of formulas obtained by replacing $\Rightarrow$ by $\hookrightarrow$ in formulas of $\mathcal{L}_n^{\Phi}$. We call the propositional fragment of $\mathcal{L}^{\hookrightarrow}$ and its interpretation by nonstandard structures *nonstandard propositional logic* (NPL).

Strong implication is indeed a new connective, that is, it cannot be defined using $\neg$ and $\wedge$. For, there are no valid formulas using only $\neg$ and $\wedge$, whereas by using $\hookrightarrow$, there are validities: $\varphi \hookrightarrow \varphi$ is an example, as is $\varphi_1 \hookrightarrow (\varphi_1 \vee \varphi_2)$.

Strong implication is indeed stronger than implication, in the sense that if φ_1 and φ_2 are standard formulas, and if $\varphi_1 \hookrightarrow \varphi_2$ is valid with respect to nonstandard Kripke structures, then $\varphi_1 \Rightarrow \varphi_2$ is valid with respect to standard Kripke structures. However, the converse is false, since the formula $(p \wedge \neg p) \Rightarrow q$ is valid in standard propositional logic, whereas the formula $(p \wedge \neg p) \hookrightarrow q$ is not valid in nonstandard propositional logic. (We note also that the analogue to the distressing propositional tautology $(p \Rightarrow q) \vee (q \Rightarrow p)$, namely $(p \hookrightarrow q) \vee (q \hookrightarrow p)$, is not valid in nonstandard propositional logic.)

As we promised in the previous section, we can now express logical implication in $\mathcal{L}^{\hookrightarrow}$, using $\hookrightarrow$, just as we can express logical implication in standard structures, using $\Rightarrow$.

Proposition 4.1: *Let φ_1 and φ_2 be formulas in $\mathcal{L}^{\hookrightarrow}$. Then φ_1 logically implies φ_2 in nonstandard structures iff $\varphi_1 \hookrightarrow \varphi_2$ is valid in nonstandard structures.*

The connective $\hookrightarrow$ is somewhat related to the connective $\rightarrow$ of relevance logic, which is meant to capture the notion of *relevant entailment.* In particular, it is not hard to show that if φ_1 and φ_2 are standard propositional formulas (and so have no occurrence of $\hookrightarrow$), then $\varphi_1 \rightarrow \varphi_2$ is a theorem of the relevance logic **R** [RR72, RM73][2] exactly if $\varphi_1 \hookrightarrow \varphi_2$ is valid in $\mathcal{NM}$ (or equivalently, φ_1 logically implies φ_2 in $\mathcal{NM}$). However, in formulas with nested occurrences of $\hookrightarrow$, the semantics of $\hookrightarrow$ is quite different from that of relevant entailment. In particular, while $p \hookrightarrow (q \hookrightarrow p)$ is valid in $\mathcal{NM}$, the analogous formula $p \rightarrow (q \rightarrow p)$ is not a theorem of relevance logic.

In $\mathcal{L}$, we cannot say that a formula φ is false. That is, there is no formula ψ such that $(M,s) \models \psi$ iff $(M,s) \not\models \varphi$. This is because no formula is true at the world t of Theorem 3.1, and so no $\psi \in \mathcal{L}$ can do the job, for any formula $\varphi \in \mathcal{L}$. What about the formula $\neg\varphi$? This formula says that $\neg\varphi$ is true, but does not say that φ is false. However, once we move to $\mathcal{L}^{\hookrightarrow}$, it is possible to say that a formula is false, as we shall see in the next proposition. In what follows, we add to $\mathcal{L}$ and $\mathcal{L}^{\hookrightarrow}$ the abbreviations *true* and *false*. In $\mathcal{L}$, we take *true* to be an abbreviation for some fixed standard tautology such as $p \Rightarrow p$, while in $\mathcal{L}^{\hookrightarrow}$, we take *true* to be an abbreviation for some fixed nonstandard tautology such as $p \hookrightarrow p$, In both cases, we abbreviate $\neg$*true* by *false.* In fact, it will be convenient to think of *true* and *false* as constants in the language (rather than as abbreviations) with the obvious semantics.

Proposition 4.2: *Let M be a nonstandard structure, and let s be a world of M. Then $(M,s) \not\models \varphi$ iff $(M,s) \models \varphi \hookrightarrow false$.*

A close examination of all the constructs in our logic shows that in fact the only nonstandard connective is $\neg$; all other connectives "behave" standardly. We now formalize this observation by considering certain transformations on formulas and structures.

Let M be a nonstandard structure. We define M^{st}, the *standardization* of M, to be the structure obtained by replacing the $*$ of M by the the identity function. Note that if M is

[2] A formula of the form $\varphi_1 \rightarrow \varphi_2$, where φ_1 and φ_2 are standard propositional formulas, is called a *first-degree entailment.* See [Dun77] for an axiomatization of first-degree entailments.

standard then $M^{st} = M$. Let φ be a standard formula. We define a nonstandard formula φ^{nst} by recursively replacing in φ all subformulas of the form $\neg\psi$ by $\psi \hookrightarrow \mathit{false}$ and all occurences of $\Rightarrow$ by $\hookrightarrow$. Note that φ^{nst} is negation free. We also define what is essentially the inverse transformation on negation-free nonstandard formulas. Let φ be a nonstandard negation-free formula. We define a standard formula φ^{st} by replacing in φ all occurences of $\hookrightarrow$ by $\Rightarrow$. Notice that the transformations ^{nst} and st are inverses when restricted to negation-free formulas.

Proposition 4.3: *Let M be a nonstandard structure, let s be a world of M, and let φ be a standard formula. Then $(M, s) \models \varphi^{nst}$ iff $(M^{st}, s) \models \varphi$.*

Corollary 4.4: *Let φ be a standard formula. Then φ is valid in standard structures iff φ^{nst} is valid in nonstandard structures.*

Another connection between standard propositional logic and NPL is due to the fact that negated propositions in NPL behave in some sense as "independent" propositions. We say that a formula φ is *pseudo-positive* if $\neg$ occurs in φ only immediately in front of a primitive proposition. For example, the formula $p \wedge \neg p$ is pseudo-positive, while $\neg(p \vee \neg p)$ is not. If φ is a pseudo-positive formula, then φ^+ is obtained from φ by replacing every occurrence $\neg p$ of a negated proposition by a new proposition $\bar{p}$. Note that φ^+ is a negation-free formula.

Proposition 4.5: *Let φ be a pseudo-positive formula. Then φ is valid in nonstandard structures iff φ^+ is valid in nonstandard structures.*

Corollary 4.6: *Let φ be a pseudo-positive formula. Then φ is valid in nonstandard structures iff $(\varphi^+)^{st}$ is valid in standard structures.*

We can use the above facts to obtain an axiomatization of NPL. To prove that a propositional formula ψ_1 in $\mathcal{L}^{\hookrightarrow}$ is valid, we first drive negations down until they apply only to primitive propositions, by applying the following equivalences: (a) $\neg\neg\varphi$ is equivalent to φ, (b) $\neg(\varphi \hookrightarrow \psi)$ is equivalent to $((\neg\psi \hookrightarrow \neg\varphi) \hookrightarrow \mathit{false})$, and (c) $\neg(\varphi \wedge \psi)$ is equivalent to $(\neg\varphi \hookrightarrow \mathit{false}) \hookrightarrow \neg\psi$. This gives us a pseudo-positive formula ψ_2 equivalent to ψ_1. By Corollary 4.6, it then suffices to prove that $(\psi_2^+)^{st}$ is valid in standard structures.

Consider the following axiom system N, where $\psi_1 \rightleftharpoons \psi_2$ is an abbreviation of $(\psi_1 \hookrightarrow \psi_2) \wedge (\psi_2 \hookrightarrow \psi_1)$:

PL. All formulas φ^{nst}, where φ is a valid formula of standard propositional logic

NPL1. $\neg\neg\varphi \rightleftharpoons \varphi$

NPL2. $\neg(\varphi \hookrightarrow \psi) \rightleftharpoons ((\neg\psi \hookrightarrow \neg\varphi) \hookrightarrow \mathit{false})$

NPL3. $\neg(\varphi \wedge \psi) \rightleftharpoons [(\neg\varphi \hookrightarrow \mathit{false}) \hookrightarrow \neg\psi]$

R0. From φ and $\varphi \hookrightarrow \psi$ infer ψ (modus ponens)

Again, one should view the axioms and inference rules above as *schemes*, i.e., N actually consists of all propositional $\mathcal{L}^{\hookrightarrow}$-instances of the above axioms and inference rules.

Theorem 4.7: *N is a sound and complete axiomatization for NPL.*

We note that PL can be replaced by the nonstandard version of any complete axiomatization of standard propositional logic (i.e, by applying the ^{nst} operator to a complete axiomatization of standard propositional logic).

What is a sound and complete axiomatization for the full nonstandard logic? Interestingly, it is obtained by modifying the axiom system K by (a) replacing propositional reasoning by nonstandard propositional reasoning, and (b) replacing standard implication ($\Rightarrow$) in the other axioms and rules by strong implication ($\hookrightarrow$). Thus, we obtain the axiom system, which we denote by $K^{\hookrightarrow}$, which consists of all instances (for the language $\mathcal{L}^{\hookrightarrow}$) of the axiom scheme and rules of inference given below:

A1$^{\hookrightarrow}$. $(K_i\varphi \wedge K_i(\varphi \hookrightarrow \psi)) \hookrightarrow K_i\psi$ (Distribution Axiom)
NPR. All sound inference rules of NPL
R1. From φ infer $K_i\varphi$ (Knowledge Generalization)

For both standard propositional logic and NPL, if Σ logically implies σ, then "from Σ infer σ" is a sound inference rule. As we noted earlier, the converse is true for standard propositional logic, but not for NPL in general. For example, consider the rule "from $\neg\varphi$ infer $\varphi \hookrightarrow \mathit{false}$", which we call *negation replacement.* It is not hard to verify that for any nonstandard formula φ, if $\neg\varphi$ is valid in nonstandard structures, then $\varphi \hookrightarrow \mathit{false}$ is also valid in nonstandard structures. Thus, negation replacement is a sound NPL inference rule. On the other hand, $\varphi \hookrightarrow \mathit{false}$ is clearly not a logical consequence of $\neg\varphi$ in nonstandard structures. Nevertheless, it can shown that testing soundness of nonstandard inference rules has the same computational complexity as testing logical implication in NPL; they are both co-*NP*-complete [FHV89].

Theorem 4.8: $K^{\hookrightarrow}$ *is a sound and complete axiomatization with respect to* $\mathcal{NM}$ *for formulas in the language* $\mathcal{L}^{\hookrightarrow}$.

When we presented the axiom system K we remarked that PR can be replaced by any complete axiomatization of standard propositional logic that includes modus ponens as an inference rule. Surprisingly, this is not the case here; if we replace NPR by all valid formulas of NPL with modus ponens as the sole propositional inference rule, then the resulting system would *not* be complete. It can shown, however, that NPR can be replaced by any complete axiomatization of NPL that includes modus ponens and negation replacement as inference rules. We discuss the details in the full paper.

The reader should note the similarity between the axiom system K for knowledge in standard Kripke structures and the nonstandard system $K^{\hookrightarrow}$. The latter is obtained from the former by replacing the inference rules for standard propositional logic by inference rules for nonstandard propositional logic and by replacing $\Rightarrow$ by $\hookrightarrow$ in the distribution axiom. Thus, one can say that in our approach agents are "nonstandardly" logically omniscient.

Since $\hookrightarrow$ can capture logical implication it is easy to see that our lower bound results for logical implication in the language $\mathcal{L}$ from Section 3 translate immediately to results on validity for the language $\mathcal{L}^{\hookrightarrow}$. We can show that these bounds are tight.

Theorem 4.9: *The validity problem for propositional* $\mathcal{L}^{\hookrightarrow}$*-formulas in* $\mathcal{NM}$ *is co-NP-complete and the validity problem for* $\mathcal{L}^{\hookrightarrow}$*-formulas in* $\mathcal{NM}$ *is PSPACE-complete.*

5 A Concrete Example

An interesting application of our approach is in the situation alluded to earlier, where there is a (finite) knowledge base of facts. Thus, the knowledge base can be viewed as a formula κ. A query to the knowledge base is another formula φ. There are two ways to interpret such a query. First, we can ask whether φ is a consequence of κ. Secondly, we can ask whether knowledge of φ follows from knowledge of κ. Fortunately, these are equivalent questions, as we now see.

Proposition 5.1: *Let φ_1 and φ_2 be $\mathcal{L}$-formulas. Then φ_1 logically implies φ_2 in $\mathcal{NM}$ iff $K_i\varphi_1$ logically implies $K_i\varphi_2$ in $\mathcal{NM}$.*

The problem of determining the consequences of a knowledge base (whether κ logically implies φ, or equivalently, by Proposition 5.1, whether $K_i\kappa$ logically implies $K_i\varphi$) is co-*NP*-complete, by Theorem 3.2, even when the database is propositional. However, there is an interesting special case where the problem is not hard.

Define a *clause* to be a disjunction of literals. For example, a typical clause is $p \vee \neg q \vee r$. Suppose that the knowledge base consists of a finite collection of clauses. Thus, κ is a conjunction of clauses. A formula (such as κ) that is a conjunction of clauses is said to be in *conjunctive normal form* (or *CNF*). Every standard propositional formula is equivalent to a formula in CNF (this is true even in our nonstandard semantics).

We now consider the question of whether κ logically implies another clause φ. In standard propositional logic, this problem is no easier than the general problem of logical implication in propositional logic, that is, co-*NP*-complete. By contrast, there is a polynomial-time decision procedure for deciding whether κ logically implies φ in nonstandard propositional logic. In fact, even when φ is a CNF formula (rather than just a clause), there is a polynomial-time decision procedure for deciding whether κ logically implies φ in nonstandard propositional logic. In particular, the task of computing whether a set of clauses logically implies another clause (and whether an agent's knowledge of a set of clauses logically implies his knowledge of another clause) is feasible.

Theorem 5.2: *There is a polynomial-time decision procedure for deciding whether κ logically implies φ in nonstandard propositional logic (or $K_i\kappa$ logically implies $K_i\varphi$ with respect to nonstandard structures), for CNF formulas κ and φ.*

Theorem 5.2 follows from results in [Lev84]. The precise relationship to Levesque's results will be clarified in the next section.

6 Standard-World Validity

Recall that a world s of a nonstandard structure $M = (S, \pi, \mathcal{K}_1, ..., \mathcal{K}_n, ^*)$ is *standard* if $s = s^*$. In a standard world, negation behaves classically, because at a standard world s, we have $(M, s) \models \neg\varphi$ iff $(M, s) \not\models \varphi$. As mentioned in the introduction, in the impossible worlds approach there is a distinction between standard and nonstandard worlds [Cre72, Cre73, Lev84, Ran82]. According to this approach, although an agent might consider a nonstandard world possible, the real world must be standard. Consequently, validity and logical implication are defined with respect to standard worlds. Formally, define a formula of $\mathcal{L}$ to be *standard-world valid* if it is true at every standard world of every nonstandard structure. The definition for *standard-world logical implication* is analogous.

At standard worlds, implication ($\Rightarrow$) behaves as it does in standard Kripke structures: that is, $\varphi_1 \Rightarrow \varphi_2$ holds at a standard world precisely if it is the case that if φ_1 holds, then φ_2 holds. We now have the following analogue to Proposition 4.1.

Proposition 6.1: *Let φ_1 and φ_2 be formulas in $\mathcal{L}$. Then φ_1 standard-world logically implies φ_2 iff $\varphi_1 \Rightarrow \varphi_2$ is standard-world valid.*

What about logical omniscience? Although the classical tautology $\varphi \vee \neg\varphi$ is standard-world valid, an agent may not *know* this formula at a standard world s, since the agent might consider an incomplete world possible. So agents do not necessarily know all standard-world valid formulas. The reason for this lack of knowledge is the inability of the agent to distinguish between complete and incomplete worlds.

Let φ be a propositional formula that contains precisely the primitive propositions $p_1, \ldots, p_k$. Define Complete(φ) to be the formula

$$(p_1 \vee \neg p_1) \wedge \ldots \wedge (p_k \vee \neg p_k).$$

Thus, Complete(φ) is true at a world s precisely if s is complete, at least as far as the primitive propositions in φ are concerned. If φ is a standard propositional tautology, then knowledge of Complete(φ) implies knowledge of φ. The next theorem follows from the results in [FH88].

Theorem 6.2: *Let φ be a tautology of standard propositional logic. Then K_i(Complete(φ)) logically implies $K_i\varphi$ in nonstandard structures.*

A similar phenomenon occurs with regard to closure of knowledge under material implication. The formula $K_i\varphi \wedge K_i(\varphi \Rightarrow \psi) \Rightarrow K_i\psi$ is not standard-world valid. This lack of closure results from the inability to distinguish between coherent and incoherent worlds; indeed, it is shown in [FH88] that $K_i\varphi \wedge K_i(\varphi \Rightarrow \psi) \Rightarrow K_i(\psi \vee (\varphi \wedge \neg\varphi))$ is standard-world valid. That is, if an agent knows that φ holds and also knows that $\varphi \Rightarrow \psi$ holds, then he or she knows that either ψ holds or the world is incoherent.

Let φ be a propositional formula that contains precisely the primitive propositions $p_1, \ldots, p_k$. Define Coherent(φ) to be the formula

$$((p_1 \wedge \neg p_1) \hookrightarrow \mathit{false}) \wedge \ldots \wedge ((p_k \wedge \neg p_k) \hookrightarrow \mathit{false}).$$

Thus, Coherent(φ) is true at a world s precisely if s is coherent, at least as far as the primitive propositions in φ are concerned. (Note that Coherent(φ) is not definable in $\mathcal{L}$ but only in $\mathcal{L}^{\hookrightarrow}$.) Knowledge of coherence implies closure of knowledge under implication.

Theorem 6.3: *Let φ and ψ be standard propositional formulas. Then $(K_i(\mathit{Coherent}(\varphi)) \wedge K_i\varphi \wedge K_i(\varphi \Rightarrow \psi)) \Rightarrow K_i\psi$ is standard-world valid.*

Propositions 6.2 and and 6.3 explain why the agents in Levesque's model [Lev84] are not logically omniscient: "logically" is defined there with respect to standard worlds, but the agents cannot distinguish standard from nonstandard worlds. If an agent's knowledge includes the distinction between standard and nonstandard worlds, i.e., we have the antecedents $K_i(Complete(\varphi))$ and $K_i(Coherent(\varphi))$ of Theorems 6.2 and 6.3, then this agent is logically omniscient.

Let us reconsider the knowledge base situation discussed earlier, where the knowledge base is described by a formula κ and the query is described by a formula φ. We saw earlier (Proposition 5.1) that in the nonstandard approach φ is a consequence of κ precisely when knowledge of φ is a consequence of knowledge of κ. Furthermore, implication of knowledge coincides in the standard and nonstandard approaches.

Proposition 6.4: *Let φ_1 and φ_2 be $\mathcal{L}$-formulas. Then $K_i\varphi_1$ standard-world logically implies $K_i\varphi_2$ iff $K_i\varphi_1$ logically implies $K_i\varphi_2$ in nonstandard structures.*

On the other hand, the two interpretations of query evaluation differ in the standard approach. In contrast to Proposition 5.1, it is possible to find φ_1 and φ_2 in $\mathcal{L}$ such that φ_1 standard-world logically implies φ_2, but $K_i\varphi_1$ does not standard-world logically imply $K_i\varphi_2$. The reason for this failure is that φ_1 standard-world logically implying φ_2 deals with logical implication in standard worlds, whereas $K_i\varphi_1$ standard-world logically implying $K_i\varphi_2$ deals with logical implication in worlds agents consider possible, which includes nonstandard worlds.

The difference between the two interpretations of query evaluation in the standard approach can have a significant computational impact. Consider the situation where both κ and φ are CNF propositional formulas. In this case, testing whether κ standard-world logically implies φ is co-NP-complete, while testing whether $K_i\kappa$ standard-world logically implies $K_i\varphi$ can be done in polynomial time by Theorem 5.2 and Proposition 6.4. (In fact, Levesque proved the latter result in [Lev84], from which we obtained Theorem 5.2 using Proposition 6.4.)

References

[AB75] A. Anderson and N. D. Belnap, *Entailment: the logic of relevance and necessity*, Princeton University Press, 1975.

[Bel77] N. D. Belnap, A useful four-valued logic, *Modern Uses of Multiple-Valued Logic* (G. Epstein and J. M. Dunn, eds.), Reidel, 1977, pp. 5–37.

[Che80] B. F. Chellas, *Modal Logic*, Cambridge University Press, 1980.

[Cre72] M. J. Cresswell, Intensional logics and logical truth, *Journal of Philosophical Logic* **1**, 1972, pp. 2–15.

[Cre73] M. J. Cresswell, *Logics and Languages*, Methuen and Co., 1973.

[Dun77] J. M. Dunn, Relevance logic and entailment, *Handbook of Philosophical Logic, Vol. III* (D. Gabbay and F. Guenthner, eds.), Reidel, 1977, pp. 117–224.

[FH88] R. Fagin and J. Y. Halpern, Belief, awareness, and limited reasoning, *Artificial Intelligence* **34**, 1988, pp. 39–76.

[FHV89] R. Fagin, J. Y. Halpern, and M. Y. Vardi, What is an inference rule?, 1989.

[Hal87] J. Y. Halpern, Using reasoning about knowledge to analyze distributed systems, *Annual Review of Computer Science, Vol. 2* (J. Traub et al., ed.), Annual Reviews Inc., 1987, pp. 37–68.

[Hin62] J. Hintikka, *Knowledge and Belief*, Cornell University Press, 1962.

[Hin75] J. Hintikka, Impossible worlds vindicated, *Journal of Philosophy* 4, 1975, pp. 475–484.

[Lad77] R. E. Ladner, The computational complexity of provability in systems of modal propositional logic, *SIAM Journal on Computing* **6**:3, 1977, pp. 467–480.

[Lak87] G. Lakemeyer, Tractable meta-reasoning in propositional logics of belief, *Tenth International Joint Conference on Artificial Intelligence (IJCAI-87)*, 1987, pp. 402–408.

[Lev84] H. Levesque, A logic of implicit and explicit belief, *Proc. of National Conference on Artificial Intelligence (AAAI-84)*, 1984, pp. 198–202.

[Ran82] V. Rantala, Impossible worlds semantics and logical omniscience, *Acta Philosophica Fennica* **35**, 1982, pp. 18–24.

[RK86] S. J. Rosenschein and L. P. Kaelbling, The synthesis of digital machines with provable epistemic properties, *Theoretical Aspects of Reasoning about Knowledge: Proceedings of the 1986 Conference* (J. Y. Halpern, ed.), Morgan Kaufmann, 1986, pp. 83–97.

[RM73] R. Routley and R. K. Meyer, The semantics of entailment, I, *Truth, Syntax, and Semantics* (H. Leblanc, ed.), North-Holland, 1973, pp. 194–243.

[RR72] R. Routley and V. Routley, Semantics of first degree entailment, *Noûs* **6**, 1972, pp. 335–359.

[Var86] M. Y. Vardi, On epistemic logic and logical omniscience, *Theoretical Aspects of Reasoning about Knowledge: Proceedings of the 1986 Conference* (J. Y. Halpern, ed.), Morgan Kaufmann, 1986, pp. 293–305.

[Wan89] H. Wansing, A general possible worlds framework for reasoning about knowledge and belief, 1989. Unpublished manuscript.

Preferential Logics: the Predicate Calculus case *

(extended abstract)

Daniel Lehmann[†] and Menachem Magidor[‡]

Abstract

Suppose a knowledge base contains information on how the world generally behaves and in particular contains the information that *birds, normally fly*. Suppose that we obtain the information that Tweety is a bird, why should we conclude that it is plausible that Tweety flies? The answer to this question is unexpectedly sophisticated since the *obvious* substitution rule has to be rejected. Our answer to this question is based on an extension to predicate calculus of the ideas presented in [7]. Preferential consequence relations over predicate calculi are defined. In addition to the rules satisfied by those relations in the propositional case, they satisfy two rules dealing with quantifiers. These rules are not enough to enable us to conclude that Tweety flies. The rational closure construction defined in [7] should be generalized to the predicate calculus case and, in the rational closure, Tweety should fly.

1 Introduction

Many systems that exhibit nonmonotonic behavior have been described and studied already in the literature. The general notion of nonmonotonic reasoning, though, has almost always been described only negatively, by the property it does not enjoy, i.e., monotony. We study here general patterns

*This work was partially supported by the Jean and Helene Alfassa fund for research in Artificial Intelligence and by a grant from the Basic Research Foundation, Israel Academy of Sciences and Humanities

[†]Department of Computer Science, Hebrew University, Jerusalem 91904 (Israel)

[‡]Department of Mathematics, Hebrew University, Jerusalem 91904 (Israel)

of nonmonotonic reasoning and try to isolate properties that could help us map the field of nonmonotonic reasoning by reference to positive properties. We concentrate on nonmonotonic consequence relations, defined in the style of Gentzen [3]. Both proof-theoretic and semantic points of view are developed in parallel.

Nonmonotonic logic is the study of those ways of inferring additional information from given information that do not satisfy the monotony property satisfied by all methods based on classical (mathematical) logic. In Mathematics, if a conclusion is warranted on the basis of certain premises, no additional premises will ever invalidate the conclusion. In everyday life, however, it seems clear that we, human beings, draw sensible conclusions from what we know and that, on the face of new information, we often have to take back previous conclusions, even when the new information we gathered in no way made us want to take back our previous assumptions. For example, we may hold the assumption that most birds fly, but that penguins are birds that do not fly and, learning that Tweety is a bird, infer that it flies. Learning that Tweety is a penguin, will in no way make us change our mind about the fact that most birds fly and that penguins are birds that do not fly, or about the fact that Tweety is a bird. It should make us abandon our conclusion about its flying capabilities, though. It is most probable that intelligent automated systems will have to do the same kind of (nonmonotonic) inferences.

Many researchers have proposed systems that perform such nonmonotonic inferences. The best known are probably: negation as failure [2], circumscription [9], the modal system of [10], default logic [12], autoepistemic logic [11] and inheritance systems [13]. In [6], [5], and [7] (see preliminary versions in [4] and [8]) the first steps towards a general framework in which those many examples could be compared and classified were taken.

In [5], a number of families of nonmonotonic consequence relations were defined. The underlying set of formulas was left quite unspecified, except for the fact that propositional connectives were supposed to be available. In fact the analysis found in [5] and later in [7] is really adequate only for propositional languages. We shall give here preliminary thoughts about the case of first order predicate calculi.

The rational closure of a conditional knowledge base will play a fundamental role in our treatment of predicate calculi. This construction has been proposed in [7] as a reasonable description of the set of conditional assertions entailed by another such set. There, the construction was defined only for finite knowledge bases and given a model-theoretic definition. Since then, this construction, for propositional languages, has been given both an abstract characterization and an algorithmic description. In the same time it has been generalized to arbitrary knowledge bases and appealing global properties of this construction have been shown to hold. This work is currently in progress.

2 Predicate Calculus: Why?

The purpose of this extended abstract is to examine the extension of the authors' previous work, that dealt with propositional languages, to predicate calculus. One may rightly ask whether this is a worthy enterprise. We shall first, therefore, discuss the status of the debate: predicate calculus vs. propositional calculus.

There is no doubt that, among mathematical logicians and especially those interested in the foundations of mathematics, predicate calculus is considered to be the language of choice, richer, more interesting. After all, predicate calculus is the universal language of mathematics and there is no way the full richness of mathematical reasoning may be captured by propositional logic. But, in this respect, the choices of mathematical logicians should not bear too heavily on us. Researchers in Artificial Intelligence have other concerns than studying mathematical reasoning, and all the evidence gathered during this last decade of fruitful research on nonmonotonic reasoning shows that the kinds of reasoning we have to analyze or realize are different in some essential ways from mathematical reasoning.

More to the point is the observation that, without exception, all systems proposed about ten years ago for nonmonotonic reasoning, used predicate calculus as their basic language. All traditional examples in the field are couched in predicate calculus terms, even when, as in the case of the Yale shooting problem for example, they may obviously be translated in propositional terms. One is therefore surprised to notice that almost none of the efforts in nonmonotonic reasoning have been devoted to analyze the role of quantifiers and free variables in nonmonotonic reasoning. One noticeable exception is Adams' [1], but his motivations are quite different. None of the systems proposed have rules to deal with quantifiers: one finds no introduction or elimination rules, the quantifiers simply disappear from the formalism by some magic, free variables appear syntactically but they are implicitely quantified universally. One of the most often used 'magic' is to consider a formula (or default) with free variables as a short-hand for the (possibly) infinite set of formulas obtained by replacing variables by ground terms. But this essentially means that a formula of predicate calculus stands for a set of propositional formulas. Looking at the examples traditional in the field, one is very hard put to find examples dealing with quantifier alternation, with functions, with formulas containing more than one free variable, with defaults whose antecedent and consequent do not contain the same variables. All the problems discussed in the literature on nonmonotonic reasoning may as well be discussed in the framework of propositional logic, and indeed some recent efforts, mainly in the autoepistemic stream, have decided, with good reason, to move to such a propositional framework. Our position is that we find no absolute necessity to move to the predicate framework, that extending our approach to predicate calculus is not at all easy, but that it is probably worthwhile trying, if only to learn more about the propositional case and to understand better what are exactly the problems raised by variables, functions and quantifiers. We shall present here a preliminary report on the state of our efforts.

The major question we are addressing may simply put in the following way: is $\mathrm{Bird}(x) \mathrel{|\!\sim} \mathrm{Fly}(x)$ a proper way of saying that *birds, normally, fly*?

3 Preferential Reasoning in Predicate calculus

Let L be a first order language, with equality. The greek letters α, β, and so on, will represent arbitrary formulas (not necessarily closed). The letters x, y and so on, variables. If α and β are formulas, then the pair $\alpha \mathrel{|\!\sim} \beta$ (read *if* α, *normally* β, or β *is a plausible consequence of* α) is called a conditional assertion (assertion in short). The formula α is the antecedent of the assertion, β is its consequent. The meaning we attach to such an assertion, and against which the reader should check the logical systems we shall discuss is the following: if α is true, I am willing to (defeasibly) jump to the conclusion that β is true. In particular, the intuitive meaning of the assertion $\mathrm{Bird}(x) \mathrel{|\!\sim} \mathrm{Fly}(x)$ is *If x is a bird, it may be sensibly concluded that it flies*, or, more precisely, *normal birds fly*. The reader should notice that we do *not* allow the application of propositional connectives or quantifiers to assertions. The object $\forall x(\mathrm{Bird}(x) \mathrel{|\!\sim} \mathrm{Fly}(x))$ is not a well-formed syntactic object for us. But, $(\forall x \text{Bird}(x)) \mid\!\sim (\forall x \text{Fly}(x))$ is an assertion. *Consequence relations* are sets of conditional assertions.

We shall now briefly describe the intended pragmatics. The queries one wants to ask an automated knowledge base are formulas (of L) and query β should be interpreted as: *is β expected to be true*? To answer such a query the knowledge base will apply some inference procedure to the information it has. This information may be divided into two different types. The first type of information consists of a set of conditional assertions describing the soft constraints (e.g. birds normally fly). This set describes what we know about the way the world generally behaves. This set of conditional assertions will be called the knowledge base, and denoted by **K**. The second type of information describes our information about the specific situation at hand (e.g. it is a bird). This information will be represented by a formula, α.

Our inference procedure will work in the following way, to answer query β. It will try to deduce (in a way that is to be discovered yet) the conditional assertion $\alpha \mid\!\sim \beta$ from the knowledge base **K**. This is a particularly elegant way of looking at the inference process: the inference process deduces conditional assertions from sets of conditional assertions. Clearly any system of nonmonotonic reasoning may be considered in this way.

The following properties of consequence relations have been introduced in [5]. They constitute *preferential reasoning* in the propositional case. In the framework of predicate calculus, the notation $\alpha \models \beta$ has to be understood in the restricted way: in all first order structures, all assignments that satisfy α also satisfy β.

(1) $\alpha \mid\!\sim \alpha$ **(Reflexivity)**

(2) $$\frac{\models \alpha \leftrightarrow \beta \;,\; \alpha \mid\!\sim \gamma}{\beta \mid\!\sim \gamma}$$ **(Left Logical Equivalence)**

(3) $$\frac{\models \alpha \rightarrow \beta \;,\; \gamma \mid\!\sim \alpha}{\gamma \mid\!\sim \beta}$$ **(Right Weakening)**

(4) $$\frac{\alpha \mid\!\sim \beta \;,\; \alpha \mid\!\sim \gamma}{\alpha \wedge \beta \mid\!\sim \gamma}$$ **(Cautious Monotony)**

(5) $$\frac{\alpha \mid\!\sim \beta \;,\; \alpha \mid\!\sim \gamma}{\alpha \mid\!\sim \beta \wedge \gamma}$$ **(And)**

$$(6)\quad \frac{\alpha \mid\!\sim \gamma \;,\; \beta \mid\!\sim \gamma}{\alpha \vee \beta \mid\!\sim \gamma} \qquad (\textbf{Or})$$

Now that we take L to be a first-order predicate calculus, we wish to add the following two rules. They will be discussed and justified below.

$$(7)\quad \frac{\alpha \mid\!\sim \beta}{\exists x \alpha \mid\!\sim \exists x \beta} \qquad (\exists - \textbf{intr})$$

$$(8)\quad \frac{\exists x \alpha \mid\!\sim \beta,\ x \text{ is not free in } \beta}{\alpha \mid\!\sim \beta} \qquad (\exists - \textbf{elim})$$

The eight rules above constitute the system **P** for predicate calculus. A consequence relation that satisfies them is said to be preferential. Let us discuss first the ($\exists$ – **elim**) rule, since this will be a short discussion. This rule is a special case of Monotony. Its justification is that if one is ready to jump to the conclusion that β, which does not involve x, is true on the knowledge that there is an element that satisfies α, one should jump to the same conclusion if one learns that x satisfies α since the new information about the value of the variable x does not change in any essential way our conclusions about the world (variables may take any value) as long as these conclusions do not involve x.

Our argument for accepting the rule ($\exists$ – **intr**) is the following. If normal birds fly and if I obtain information to the effect that there is at least one bird in the world, then it is sensible to conclude that there is at least one normal bird in the world and therefore there is at least one flying individual. More generally, we shall see that rule $\exists$ says that *if there is an individual that has property A then it is plausible that there is an individual that has property A and is normal for that property, i.e., there is a typical A*. Notice, indeed, that the following is a derived rule of **P**.

$$(9)\quad \frac{\alpha \mid\!\sim \beta}{\exists x \alpha \mid\!\sim \exists x\, (\alpha \wedge \beta)}$$

It implies that we shall not be able to consider situations where *normal birds fly, normal birds have feathers, normal birds have beaks, normal birds are not green* but in which we have information to the effect that there are birds but any bird that have beaks, feathers and flies is green. Such information is, for us, contradictory. In other words, we consider impossible situations in which there are birds but there is no typical bird. Such situations have been referred to in the literature as *the lottery paradox* or *the bird-shop paradox*. For us, such situations are indeed paradoxical. Whether this restriction to non-paradoxical situations is bearable is mainly a pragmatical question and only experience will tell. Notice, though, that *default* reasoning (in the largest possible meaning) is mainly useful when the number of individuals is very large, i.e., when we do not expect to have an exhaustive list of all those individuals available. Otherwise, it seems we could get full information and then classical monotonic reasoning is called for. At least, we are aiming at those situations in which there is no exhaustive list of individuals. In such situations, we may as well accept that there is a typical bird, perhaps at the cost of accepting that phantom birds *exist*, in the sense of the quantifier $\exists$. This quantifier would be badly chosen anyway to represent anything like *physical existence*. Should we accept other rules dealing with quantifiers? Two such candidates come to mind. They must be rejected. Let x be an individual variable and t a term, and α^x_t represents the result of replacing x by t in α and is defined only if no variable free in t clashes with a bound variable of α.

$$(10) \quad \frac{\alpha \mathrel{|\!\sim} \beta}{\forall x \alpha \mathrel{|\!\sim} \forall x \beta} \qquad (\forall)$$

$$(11) \quad \frac{\alpha \mathrel{|\!\sim} \beta}{\alpha^x_t \mathrel{|\!\sim} \beta^x_t} \qquad \textbf{(Substitution)}$$

The reasons to reject ($\forall$) are clear. Suppose we think that *birds, normally fly*, written as Bird$(x) \mathrel{|\!\sim}$ Fly(x), and we know that *we are talking only about birds*, written as $\forall x$Bird(x), we have no reason at all to conclude that *we are talking only about flying things*. The knowledge that everything is a bird has no bearing on our assumption that there may be birds that do not fly.

The reasons to reject **(Substitution)** are much more delicate and they seem to involve two-place predicates in an essential way. Suppose we hold the default that most pets are dogs or cats, or, equivalently, that normal pet owners have dogs or cats as pets. We would like to describe this default as: Pet$(x, y) \mathrel{|\!\sim}$ Dog$(y) \vee$ Cat(y). Suppose also that we know of an individual, John, who likes snakes. We would like to describe this in a default that says that most of John's pets are snakes. The natural way to do that is obviously: Pet(John, $y) \mathrel{|\!\sim}$ Snake(y). If we accepted the rule of **(Substitution)**, we would deduce from the first default: Pet(John, y) $\mid\!\sim$ Dog(y) $\vee$ Cat(y). With the second default, using **(And)** and the fact that the classes of dogs, cats and snakes have an empty intersection, we would deduce: Pet(John, y) $\mid\!\sim$ **false**, which means that it is completely unthinkable that John has a pet. This is obviously unwanted. What is revealed here is that the system **P**, in the propositional case, is such a powerful system that it is incompatible with the very powerful rule of **(Substitution)**. If one considers what happens in other nonmonotonic formalisms, one sees that the only reason **(Substitution)** is accepted by Reiter's Default Logic or McCarthy's Circumscription is that those formalisms are too weak by themselves (i.e., without some additional formalism) to choose between two different extensions: the one in which John's pet is a snake and the one in which it is a dog or a cat. The price Default Logic has to pay is very high: it cannot even conclude that John's pet is a snake, a dog or a cat. Circumscription fares a bit better, but cannot see, without external help, that the second default is more specific than the first one and should therefore preempt it. The fact that **(Substitution)** has to be rejected raises the question of how can we manage without it. How can we show that Tweety flies?

The system **P** is powerful, as was shown in [5], but it does not enable us to conclude that Tweety flies from the information that normal birds fly and that Tweety is a bird. This is the case because preferential reasoning is not capable of inferring the fact that Tweety is a normal bird from the fact that we have no reason to think that it is abnormal. This task must be delegated to the procedure of rational closure, a first limited version of which has been defined in [7]. But, before we discuss technical matters, let us describe on an informal level why Bird(Tweety) $\mid\!\sim$ Fly(Tweety) is derivable from, i.e., in the rational closure of, the knowledge base containing only Bird(x) $\mid\!\sim$ Fly(x). The property of **(Rational Monotony)** described in equation (13) guarantees that, if we have Bird(x) $\mid\!\sim$ Fly(x), we shall also have Bird(x) $\wedge\ x =$ Tweety $\mid\!\sim$ Fly(x), unless we have Bird(x) $\mid\!\sim x \neq$ Tweety. It will be the task of the rational closure operation to make sure that, in the absence of added information, the assertion Bird(x) $\mid\!\sim x \neq$ Tweety does not enter the rational closure. Now, from Bird(x) $\wedge\ x =$ Tweety $\mid\!\sim$ Fly(x), we shall infer, by propositional preferential reasoning that: Bird(x) $\wedge\ x =$ Tweety $\mid\!\sim$ Fly(x) $\wedge\ x =$ Tweety. The intuitive rationale behind this derivation is that completely obvious. Then $\exists x$ (Bird(x) $\wedge\ x =$ Tweety) $\mid\!\sim \exists x$ (Fly(x) $\wedge\ x =$ Tweety) follows by the rule ($\exists$ – **intr**). Replacing antecedent and consequent by logically equivalent formulas, we obtain: Bird(Tweety) $\mid\!\sim$ Fly(Tweety). This is indeed, we think, an exact description of why we are *right* to think that Tweety flies. In cases where there are some reasons to think that Tweety is not a normal bird (and preferential reasoning is quite good at discovering such situations) then Bird(x) $\mid\!\sim x \neq$ Tweety will be derivable (preferentially) and therefore in the rational closure. In such a case the assertion Bird(x) $\wedge\, x =$ Tweety $\mid\!\sim$ Fly(x) will typically not enter the rational closure.

4 Preferential models

We shall now briefly define preferential models (in the predicate calculus case), along the lines of [5], and show that the consequence relations that may be defined by those models are exactly the preferential relations. Similarly for ranked models and rational relations. The semantic restriction that corresponds to the rules ($\exists$ – **intr**) and ($\exists$ – **elim**) are quite natural, though not so easy to manipulate. We adapt the definition of a preferential model found in [5] to predicate calculus. The following definitions are also taken from [5] and justified there.

Preferential models give a model-theoretic account of the way one performs nonmonotonic inferences. The main idea is that the agent has, in his mind, a partial ordering on possible states of the world. State s is less than state t, if, in the agent's mind, s is *preferred* to or more *natural* than t. Now, the agent is willing to conclude β from α, if all *most natural* states that satisfy α also satisfy β.

Some technical definitions are needed. Let U be a set and $\prec$ a strict partial order on U, i.e., a binary relation that is antireflexive and transitive.

Definition 1 *Let $V \subseteq U$. We shall say that $t \in V$ is minimal in V iff there is no $s \in V$, such that $s \prec t$.*

Definition 2 *Let $V \subseteq U$. We shall say that V is smooth iff $\forall t \in V$, either $\exists s$ minimal in V, such that $s \prec t$ or t is itself minimal in V.*

We may now define the family of models we are interested in. The states will be labeled with worlds. A world should give a truth value to each formula, even formulas that are not closed, and therefore will be defined as a pair

$\langle M, f \rangle$ where M is a first order structure and f assigns an element of the domain of M to each variable.

Definition 3 *A* preferential *model* W *is a triple* $\langle S, l, \prec \rangle$ *where* S *is a set, the elements of which will be called states,* $l : S \mapsto \mathcal{U}$ *assigns a world to each state and* $\prec$ *is a strict partial order on* S *satisfying the following two conditions. The first one, the* smoothness condition *is:* $\forall \alpha \in L$, *the set of states* $\widehat{\alpha} \stackrel{\text{def}}{=} \{s \mid s \in S,\ s \models \alpha\}$ *is smooth, where* $\models$ *is defined as* $s \models \alpha$ *(read* s *satisfies* α*) iff* $l(s) \models \alpha$. *The second one* E *is:*

1. *if a state* s, *labeled with* $\langle M, f \rangle$, *is minimal in* $\widehat{\exists x \alpha}$, *then there exists a state* t *that is minimal in* $\widehat{\alpha}$ *and that is labeled with* $\langle M, f' \rangle$ *where* f' *differs from* f *at the most in the element it assigns to* x
2. *if a state* t *is minimal in* $\widehat{\alpha}$ *and labeled with* $\langle M, f \rangle$, *then there is a state* s, *labeled with* $\langle M, f' \rangle$, *where* f' *differs from* f *at the most in the element it assigns to* x, *that is minimal in* $\widehat{\exists x \alpha}$.

The model W *will be said to be finite if* S *is finite.*

The smoothness condition is only a technical condition needed to deal with infinite sets of formulas, it is always satisfied in any finite preferential model, and in any model in which $\prec$ is well-founded (i.e., no infinite descending chains).

We shall now describe the consequence relation defined by a model.

Definition 4 *Suppose a model* $W = \langle S, l, \prec \rangle$ *and* $\alpha, \beta \in L$ *are given. The consequence relation defined by* W *will be denoted by* $\mid\!\sim_W$ *and is defined by:* $\alpha \mid\!\sim_W \beta$ *iff for any* s *minimal in* $\widehat{\alpha}$, $s \models \beta$.

If $\alpha \mid\!\sim_W \beta$ we shall say that the model W satisfies the conditional assertion $\alpha \mid\!\sim \beta$, or that W is a model of $\alpha \mid\!\sim \beta$.

It is easy to see that any preferential model that satisfies our additional condition (E) defines a preferential consequence relation that satisfies the rules ($\exists$ – **intr**) and ($\exists$ – **elim**).

The representation theorem is the following.

Theorem 1 *Let* $\mid\!\sim$ *be a preferential relation. There is a preferential model that defines* $\mid\!\sim$.

Proof: The proof parallels the corresponding proof of [5], only the main steps will be sketched. The only difference is that we restrict our attention to a subset of the possible worlds. Let D be an infinite large enough set of constants not included in L. We shall consider first order structures on the extended language $L \cup D$.

Definition 5 *A first order structure M, on the extended language, is said to be satisfactory iff, given any formula α (in the original language) of the form $\exists x\beta$ and any assignment f of elements of the domain of M to the variables, for which the world $w = \langle M, f\rangle$ is normal for α, there is a constant $d \in D$ such that the world $\langle M, f^d_x\rangle$ (again we should have written d_M instead of d) is normal for β. A world $\langle M, f\rangle$ will be termed satisfactory iff M is satisfactory.*

The reader may check that, changing *world* to *satisfactory world* leaves the completeness proofs of [5] and [8] correct if only one can prove the following lemma 1. On the other hand, if a canonical model is built with satisfactory worlds only, then it satisfies (E), if we can prove lemma 2.

Lemma 1 *If $\alpha \not\mid\!\sim \beta$, then there exists a satisfactory world, that is normal for α and does not satisfy β.*

Proof: Let $\Delta \stackrel{\text{def}}{=} \{\neg\beta\} \bigcup \{\gamma \mid \alpha \mid\!\sim \gamma\}$. Clearly Δ is satisfiable (see [5]). Let T_0 be the logical closure of Δ (over the original language). We shall build an ascending sequence of consistent logically closed sets: T_i on larger and larger languages L_i. The languages L_i will contain the original language L and a finite subset of D. We are going to enumerate all pairs consisting of a formula α of the form $\exists x\beta$ (in the original language) and an assignment of elements of $D \cap L_i$ to some of the free variables of α. Suppose we have defined T_i and L_i and are now dealing with $\alpha = \exists x\beta$ and g that assigns an element of $D \cap L_i$ to some of the free variables of α. If γ is a formula (over L) we shall denote by γ_g the formula obtained by replacing those free variables of γ that have an image under g by their image. If there exists a formula γ (in the language L_i) such that $\alpha \mid\!\sim \gamma$ and $\gamma_g \notin T_i$ then choose any one of those γ's and take T_{i+1} to be the logical closure (over L_i) of $T_i \cup \{\neg\gamma_g\}$ and L_{i+1} to be L_i. The set T_{i+1} is clearly consistent. Otherwise, all such γ_g are in T_i. Let then d be an element of D not in L_i. We shall take L_{i+1} to be $L_i \cup \{d\}$ and T_{i+1} to be the logical closure of the set $\Delta_i = T_i \cup \{\left(\eta^d_x\right)_g \mid \beta \mid\!\sim \eta\}$. It is left to show that the set Δ_i is consistent. Suppose not. Then there is a finite subset of Δ_i that is inconsistent and, since $\mid\!\sim$ satisfies **And**, there is some η such that $\beta \mid\!\sim \eta$ and $T_i \models \neg\left(\eta^d_x\right)_g$. From $\beta \mid\!\sim \eta$, by ($\exists$ – **intr**) and **(Right Weakening)** (since x is not free in η^d_x), we have $\alpha \mid\!\sim \eta^d_x$. By hypothesis, then, $\left(\eta^d_x\right)_g$ must be in the set T_i. A contradiction to the fact that T_i is consistent. It is clear that, by dovetailing, one can arrange for the enumeration to contain all pairs of existential formulas and partial assignments into D. The set $T_\infty \stackrel{\text{def}}{=} \bigcup_{i=0}^{\infty} T_i$ is clearly consistent. Any world w that is a model for this set is clearly normal for α and does not satisfy β. Let us check it is satisfactory. Let M be the first order structure of w. Suppose $\alpha = \exists x \beta$ is a formula of L and f is an assignment of elements of D to the variables for which $\langle M, f\rangle$ is normal for α. The pair consisting of α and the assignment f restricted to the free variables of α has appeared somewhere in the enumeration. At this point we certainly did not take the first possibility, otherwise there would be a γ such that $\alpha \mid\!\sim \gamma$ and $\neg\gamma_f \in T_\infty$, which implies that $\langle M, f\rangle$ does not satisfy γ and is not normal for α. Therefore, at this point, we chose the second possibility and the new d introduced in the language at this point is such that for every γ such that $\beta \mid\!\sim \gamma$, w satisfies $\left(\gamma^d_x\right)_f$, i.e., $\langle M, f^d_x\rangle$ is normal for β. ∎

Lemma 2 *If a world w $\langle M, f\rangle$ is satisfactory then, given any formula of the form $\exists x\alpha$ for which w is normal, there is an element e in the domain of M such that the world $\langle M, f^e_x\rangle$ is satisfactory and satisfies all formulas β such that $\alpha \mid\!\sim \beta$.*

Proof: Take e to be d_M for the d whose existence is asserted by definition 5. ∎

5 Renaming

In the system presented so far the rule

$$(12) \quad \frac{\alpha(x) \mid\!\sim \beta(x)}{\alpha(y) \mid\!\sim \beta(y)} \qquad \textbf{(Renaming)}$$

when y is not a free variable of α or β, is not a derived rule. One may argue pro and con invariance under renaming of variables. The corresponding semantic restriction is not difficult to describe and the characterization theorem is not difficult either. The question of invariance under renaming seems to be completely orthogonal to the quest for rules dealing with quantifiers.

6 Rational closure

As we have argued above, the system of preferential reasoning in predicate calculus has one main weakness related to predicate calculus (it has other weaknesses that relate to propositional calculus too): *Tweety does not fly.* It is therefore necessary to build an additional layer of reasoning on top of preferential reasoning. The rational closure of a conditional knowledge base, has been proposed in [7] as a reasonable description of the set of conditional assertions entailed by another such set. There, this closure operation was defined in model-theoretic terms and for finite knowledge bases only. We have now a definition of rational closure that is both abstract and general. The idea, that we cannot develop here, is that the rational closure of a knowledge base, if it exists, is its preferred rational extension. *Rational* means that the consequence relation satisfies the following additional rule of **(Rational Monotony)**. A representation theorem for rational relations and ranked models (satisfying the condition (E)) is obtained without too much trouble, following the lines of the corresponding result in the propositional case.

(13) $$\frac{\alpha \wedge \beta \not\mid\!\sim \gamma \ , \ \alpha \not\mid\!\sim \neg\beta}{\alpha \not\mid\!\sim \gamma}$$ **(Rational Monotony)**

Preferred means least in the following ordering. In the next definition, and in the sequel, $\alpha < \beta$ for K means that $\alpha \vee \beta \mid\!\sim \neg\beta$ is in K.

Definition 6 *Let K_0 and K_1 be two rational consequence relations. We shall say that K_0 is preferable to K_1 and write $K_0 \prec K_1$ iff:*

1. *there exists an assertion $\alpha \mid\!\sim \beta$ in $K_1 - K_0$ such that for all γ such that $\gamma < \alpha$ for K_0, and for all δ such that $\gamma \mid\!\sim \delta$ is in K_0, we also have $\gamma \mid\!\sim \delta$ in K_1*

2. *For any γ, δ if $\gamma \mid\!\sim \delta$ is in $K_0 - K_1$ there is an assertion $\rho \mid\!\sim \eta$ in $K_1 - K_0$ such that $\rho < \gamma$ for K_1.*

The intuitive explanation behind definition 6 is the following. Suppose two agents, who agree on a common knowledge base, are discussing the respective merits of two rational relations K_0 and K_1. A typical attack would be: *your relation contains an assertion* $\alpha \mathrel{|\!\sim} \beta$ *that mine does not (and therefore contains unsupported assertions).* A possible defense against such an attack could be: *yes, but your relation contains an assertion* $\gamma \mathrel{|\!\sim} \delta$ *that mine does not, and you yourself think that* γ *describes a situation much more usual than the one described by* α. Such a defense much be accepted as valid. Definition 6 exactly says that the proponent of K_0 has an attack that the proponent of K_1 cannot defend against (this is part 1) but that he (i.e., the proponent of K_0) may find a defense against any attack from the proponent of K_1 (this is part 2 of the definition).

The relation $\prec$ among rational relations is, as expected, a strict partial order. We conjecture the following (for predicate calculus):

Conjecture 1 *If* **K** *is a finite knowledge base, it has a rational closure*

The corresponding result for propositional calculus has been proved. We also hope to provide an algorithmic characterization of the rational closure of a finite knowledge base over predicate calculus, similar to the one proposed for the propositional case. This characterization leads, again in the propositional case, to an efficient algorithm computing the rational closure of a finite knowledge base.

7 Discussion and conclusion

We have not shown yet that *Tweety flies* may be deduced from, i.e., is in the rational closure, $\overline{\mathbf{K}}$, of the knowledge base **K** that contains the single assertion $\text{Bird}(x) \mathrel{|\!\sim} \text{Fly}(x)$. From the discussion at the end of section 3, we know it is enough to show that the assertion $\text{Bird}(x) \mathrel{|\!\sim} x \neq \text{Tweety}$ is not the rational closure of **K** (by our conjecture such a closure exists). To show this, remark that the one-state model in which $x = \text{Tweety}$, Bird(Tweety) and Fly(Tweety) hold defines a rational relation R (since it is ranked) that extends **K**. But it does not contain $\text{Bird}(x) \mathrel{|\!\sim} x \neq \text{Tweety}$. By definition 6, then, there must be an assertion $\alpha \mathrel{|\!\sim} \beta$ in $R - \overline{\mathbf{K}}$, such that, in R, $\alpha < \text{Bird}(x)$. But this is impossible, since $\text{Bird}(x)$ is satisfied at the lowest level in the model.

References

[1] Ernest W. Adams. The logic of high probabilities. *Journal of Philosophical Logic*, 15:258, 1986.

[2] Keith L. Clark. Negation as failure. In H. Gallaire and J. Minker, editors, *Logics and Data Bases*, pages 293–322. Plenum Press, 1978.

[3] Gerhard Gentzen. *The Collected Papers of Gerhard Gentzen, edited by M. E. Szabo.* North Holland, Amsterdam, 1969.

[4] Sarit Kraus, Daniel Lehmann, and Menachem Magidor. Preferential models and cumulative logics. Technical Report TR 88-15, Leibniz Center for Computer Science, Dept. of Computer Science, Hebrew University, Jerusalem, November 1988.

[5] Sarit Kraus, Daniel Lehmann, and Menachem Magidor. Nonmonotonic reasoning, preferential models and cumulative logics. *Artificial Intelligence*, 1990. in press.

[6] Daniel Lehmann. Preferential models and cumulative logics. In Ehud Shapiro, editor, *Fifth Israeli Symposium on Artificial Intelligence, Vision and Pattern Recognition*, pages 365–381, Tel Aviv, Israel, December 1988. Information Processing Association of Israel.

[7] Daniel Lehmann. What does a conditional knowledge base entail? In Ron Brachman and Hector Levesque, editors, *Proceedings of the First International Conference on Principles of Knowledge Representation and Reasoning*, Toronto, Canada, May 1989. Morgan Kaufmann.

[8] Daniel Lehmann and Menachem Magidor. Rational logics and their models: a study in cumulative logic. Technical Report TR 88-16, Leibniz Center for Computer Science, Dept. of Computer Science, Hebrew University, Jerusalem, November 1988.

[9] John McCarthy. Circumscription, a form of non monotonic reasoning. *Artificial Intelligence*, 13:27–39, 1980.

[10] Drew McDermott and John Doyle. Non-monotonic logic I. *Artificial Intelligence*, 25:41–72, 1980.

[11] Robert C. Moore. Possible-world semantics for autoepistemic logic. In *Proceedings of AAAI workshop on nomonotonic reasoning*, pages 396–401, New Paltz, 1984.

[12] Raymond Reiter. A logic for default reasoning. *Artificial Intelligence*, 13:81–132, 1980.

[13] David S. Touretzky. *The Mathematics of Inheritance Systems.* Research Notes in Artificial Intelligece. Pitman, London — Morgan Kaufmann, Los Altos, 1986.

Nonmonotonic default modal logics

(Detailed abstract)

Michael Tiomkin

IBM Israel Scientific Center
Technion City
Haifa 32000, Israel

Michael Kaminski

Department of Computer Science
Technion – Israel Institute of Tecnology
Haifa 32000, Israel

ABSTRACT. Conclusions by failure to prove the opposite are frequently used in reasoning about an incompletely specified world. This naturally leads to logics for default reasoning which, in general, are nonmonotonic, i.e., introducing new facts can invalidate previously made conclusions. Accordingly, a nonmonotonic theory is called (nonmonotonically) *degenerate*, if adding new axioms does not invalidate already proved theorems. We study nonmonotonic logics based on various sets of defaults and present a necessary and sufficient condition for a nonmonotonic modal theory to be degenerate. In particular, this condition provides several alternative descriptions of degenerate theories. Also we establish some closure properties of sets of defaults defining a nonmonotonic modal logic.

1. Introduction

Nonmonotonic reasoning is very natural in Artificial Intelligence. For example, when an expert system derives a conclusion based on incomplete knowledge, this conclusion may be invalidated in the future by the new facts about the external world. In Prolog, with its *negation by failure* semantics, the proved goals can become invalid after the addition of new facts to the data base. Also while dealing with probabilistic reasoning, the derived probabilities of different events can change completely, when new facts are added to the knowledge base. Thus if one uses threshold probabilities for making conclusions, the accepted truths may change as well.

Logics which reflect nonmonotonic reasoning have been first introduced in [2], [7], [8], and [12]. More general approach to the question "What is a nonmonotonic system?" can be found in [1], [3], [5], and [6]. In particular, a detailed example of nonmonotonic reasoning can be found in [2]. Most of nonmonotonic logics are based on semantics and proof theory, both obtained via fixed points of some monotonic operators. The *default logic* of Reiter ([12]) is based on theories which are fixed points of such an operator. The logic of McDermott and Doyle ([8]) is based on the intersection of all fixed points of a similar operator. The *circumscription* of McCarthy ([7]) is based on a definition of a predicate as the minimal relation satisfying some property.

Later, McDermott in [9] introduced nonmonotonic modal logics which are based on the modal systems T, S4, and S5. These modal logics are more suitable for describing dynamic worlds. However, his logics are a little bit problematic in view of the following. First, it is unknown whether McDermott's logics based on the first order versions of T and S4 are consistent. In addition, the logic based on S5 degenerates to the monotonic one, cf. [9].

We shall study here nonmonotonic modal logics, which contain a *possibility operator M* and a *necessity operator L*. More precisely, logics which are extensions of the modal system T. Our definition of nonmonotonics logics is a relativization of that appearing in [9], namely, the nonmonotonic theory is the intersection of all extensions of the default theory presented in ([12]). The main difficulty of dealing with a nonmonotonic modal logic is that the underlying monotonic modal logic lacks a deduction theorem ($A, \varphi \vdash \psi$ implies $A \vdash \varphi \supset \psi$). For this reason we cannot prove that every (monotonically) consistent theory has a consistent nonmonotonic fixed point, etc., cf. [9] and Proposition 4 in Section 2. Despite of this, in modal logics which are extensions of T we have a "weak deduction theorem" stating that $A, \varphi \vdash \psi$ implies $A \vdash L^k\varphi \supset \psi$, for some k, where $L^0\varphi$ is φ, and $L^{k+1}\varphi$ is $LL^k\varphi$. Using this weak deduction theorem we can give a condition for a nonmonotonic default logic to be *degenerate*, i.e., to become monotonic. This condition is the main result of this paper, and states that a default modal logic degenerates if and only if the set of defaults is, in some sense, closed under negation. In particular, it provides an alternative proof of the degeneration of McDermott's S5.

Another version of nonmonotonic modal logics discussed in literature is *autoepistemic logic*, cf. [10], [11], and [4]. This logic is based on the modal logic K45 and restricted to the application of default reasoning to nonmodal formulas. Since T is not a sublogic of K45, the theory developed in this paper is not applicable to autoepistemic logics. However, it is possible to find some similarity between autoepistemic logic and the nonmonotonic *ground* logics introduced in Section 4.

The paper is organized as follows. In the next section we give the necessary definitions and derive some simple properties of nonmonotonic default logics. Section 3 contains the main result of this paper, i.e., a condition for the degeneration of nonmonotonic modal logics. Also in that section we prove that for any nonmonotonic default logic the set of defaults can be taken to be closed under the operators $\wedge$, $\vee$, and L. In Section 4, we present a slightly different version of McDermott's nonmonotonic logic that both is consistent and nondegenerate.

2. Monotonic and nonmonotonic modal logics

This section is organized as follows. First we give definitions of monotonic and nonmonotonic modal logics and derive some of their properties. Next, we discuss the nonmonotonic modal logics of McDermott ([9]), which constitute a particular case of nonmonotonic default modal logics.

The language **Lang** of modal logic is obtained from the language of the (first order) predicate calculus by extending it with a modal connective L (*necessarily*). As usual, the dual connective M (*possibly*) is defined by $\sim L \sim$. A formula without free variables is called a *sentence*, and the set of all sentences is denoted by **St**. We assume that **Lang** is countable.

In this paper we shall deal with modal logics which result from the classic predicate calculus by adding the rule of inference

Necessitation (NEC): $\varphi \vdash L\varphi$,

and all the instances of some subsets of the axiom schemata below.

M1. $L\varphi \supset \varphi$

M2. $L(\varphi \supset \psi) \supset (L\varphi \supset L\psi)$

M3. $\forall x\, L\varphi \supset L\forall x \varphi$

M4. $L\varphi \supset LL\varphi$

M5. $M\varphi \supset LM\varphi$

The system T contains axiom schemata M1 and M2 only. Adding M4 to T results in S4, and adding M5 to S4 results in S5. In this paper by modal logic we refer to any modal system that is an extension of T + M3 with additional axioms, e.g., T + M3 itself, S4 + M3, S5 + M3, etc.. Below these systems will be simply denoted by T, S4, and S5, respectively.

For a set of formulas $A \subseteq$ **Lang**, called *axioms*, we define the (monotonic) *theory of A*, denoted by Th(A), as

$$\mathrm{Th}(A) = \{\, \varphi \in \mathbf{Lang} : A \vdash \varphi \,\} \subseteq \mathbf{Lang}.$$

As usual, we write $A \vdash \varphi$, if there exists a sequence of formulas $\psi_1, \psi_2, \ldots, \psi_n = \varphi$ such that each ψ_i is an axiom or belongs to A or is obtained from some of the formulas $\psi_1, \psi_2, \ldots, \psi_{i-1}$ by one of the rules of inference: *modus ponens*, *generalization* or *necessitation*. Thus the relation $\vdash$ and the operator Th should be subscripted by T, S4 or S5, respectively. However, in this paper, if not specified otherwise, the results are true for every modal logic containing T, and the subscripts will be omitted.

Let $D \subseteq \mathbf{St}$ be a set of sentences called *defaults*. Following [8], [9], and [12] we define a *default logic* by adding to a modal logic, roughly speaking, the following "rule of inference".

$$\frac{\nvdash \sim\varphi}{\varphi}, \quad \varphi \in D. \tag{1}$$

This rule is read as

"for a default $\varphi \in D$, derive φ if $\sim\varphi$ is not provable".

However, the above rule is self-referring, and therefore it is ill-defined. A possible correct definition of nonmonotonic inference is given below. It is similar to that appearing in [9].

Definition 1. The nonmonotonic modal D-default theory of $A \subseteq \mathbf{Lang}$, denoted by $\mathbf{NTH}_D(A)$, is the intersection of $\mathbf{Lang}$ and all the *fixed points* of the operator $\mathbf{NM}_D^A$, defined below.

For a set of formulas F, $\mathbf{NM}_D^A(F)$ is defined by

$$\mathbf{NM}_D^A(F) = \mathrm{Th}(A \cup \mathbf{As}_D^A(F)),$$

where

$$\mathbf{As}_D^A(F) = \{\varphi \in D : \sim\varphi \notin F\} - \mathrm{Th}(A).$$

A set of formulas X is called a fixed point of $\mathbf{NM}_D^A$, if $\mathbf{NM}_D^A(X) = X$.

Thus

$$\mathbf{NTH}_D(A) = \mathbf{Lang} \cap \bigcap\{X : X = \mathbf{NM}_D^A(X)\}.$$

Remark 1. Since $\bigcap\varnothing = \mathbf{Lang}$, we can define $\mathbf{NTH}_D(A)$ as $\bigcap\{X : X = \mathbf{NM}_D^A(X)\}$. Also we trivially have

$$\mathbf{NM}_D^A(F) = \mathrm{Th}(A \cup \{\varphi \in D : \sim\varphi \notin F\}),$$

because

$$\mathrm{Th}(A \cup \{\varphi \in D : \sim\varphi \notin F\}) = \mathrm{Th}(A \cup (\{\varphi \in D : \sim\varphi \notin F\} - \mathrm{Th}(A))) = \mathrm{Th}(A \cup \mathbf{As}_D^A(F)).$$

Similarly to [12], a fixed point of $\mathbf{NM}_D^A$ can be considered as an acceptable set of beliefs that one may hold about incompletely specified changing world. I.e., a fixed point of $\mathbf{NM}_D^A$ realizes some defaults and rejects all the others. Alternatively, such a fixed point can be thought of as a "syntactic model" for A, or as a "minimal complete for D extension" of A with formulas from D. The nonmonotonic theory of A is the set of formulas which are believed in all the fixed points.

A set of axioms A is said to be *nonmonotonically inconsistent* (with respect to D), if $\mathbf{NTH}_D(A) = \mathbf{Lang}$, i.e., each formula can be derived in an inconsistent theory, exactly as in the case of monotonic logics. In particular, if for the set of axioms A, $\mathbf{NM}_D^A$ has no fixed points (models), then A is (nonmonotonically) inconsistent, because in this case we have $\mathbf{NTH}_D(A) = \mathbf{Lang}$. At the end of this section we present an example of a (monotonically) consistent set of axioms whose induced operator has no fixed points with respect to some set of defaults. This example is related to the nonmonotonic modal logics of McDermott, and to the nonmonotonic ground logics introduced in Section 4.

Another possibility for a set of axioms A to be (nonmonotonically) inconsistent is indicated by Proposition 1 below.

Proposition 1. ([12]) **Lang** *is a fixed point of* $\mathbf{NM}_D^A$ *if and only A is (monotonically) inconsistent. In this case* **Lang** *is the only fixed point of* $\mathbf{NM}_D^A$.

In this paper, if not specified otherwise, the words "consistent" and "inconsistent" refer to the monotonic case.

Fixed points of $\mathbf{NM}_D^A$ can be alternatively described by the following proposition.

Proposition 2. *Let F be a proper subset of* **Lang**. *Then F is a fixed point of* $\mathbf{NM}_D^A$ *if and only if it satisfies the following two conditions.*

(i) $F = \mathrm{Th}(A \cup (F \cap D))$, *and*

(ii) For any $\varphi \in D$ *either* $F \vdash \varphi$ *or* $F \vdash \sim\varphi$, *i.e., "F is complete for D".*

Condition (*i*) states that a fixed point is generated by the formulas added by the rule of nonmonotonic inference, i.e., that this rule is the only one used. Condition (*ii*) states that the rule of nonmonotonic inference is satisfied.

Corollary 1. ([8], [12]) *Let* F_1 *and* F_2 *be fixed points of* $\mathbf{NM}_D^A$. *If* $F_1 \subseteq F_2$, *then* $F_1 = F_2$.

Corollary 2. ([12]) *Let* $D' \subseteq D$ *be a set of defaults. Then any consistent fixed point of* $\mathbf{NM}_D^{A \cup D'}$ *is also a fixed point of* $\mathbf{NM}_D^A$.

Remark 2. Proposition 2 implies that if the set of defaults D is of finite cardinality n, then any set of axioms has at most 2^n fixed points. Therefore, in the propositional nonmonotonic modal logic based on a finite set of defaults, if the set of axioms A is finite, then the nonmonotonic theory $\mathbf{NTH}_D(A)$ is decidable. The decision procedure is as follows. Using condition (*ii*) of Proposition 2 and the decidability of propositional modal logics T, S4, and S5, it is possible to find all subsets D' of D such that $\mathrm{Th}(A \cup D')$ is a fixed point of $\mathbf{NM}_D^A$, i.e., satisfies condition (*ii*) of Proposition 2. Then for a formula φ one can decide whether for every D' as above we have $A \cup D' \vdash \varphi$, i.e., whether φ belongs to all fixed points of A.

Nonmonotonic default logics can be illustrated by the following example. In [9] McDermott introduced the nonmonotonic modal theory of A, denoted by TH(A), that is the intersection of **Lang** and all the fixed points of the operator NM_A.

NM_A is defined by

$$\mathrm{NM}_A(F) = \mathrm{Th}(A \cup \mathrm{As}_A(F)),$$

where

$$\mathrm{As}_A(F) = \{ M\varphi : \varphi \in \mathbf{St},\ \sim\varphi \notin F \} - \mathrm{Th}(A).$$

Thus

$$\mathrm{TH}(A) = \mathbf{Lang} \cap \bigcap \{ X : X = \mathrm{NM}_A(X) \}.$$

The above logic reflects the following "rule of inference" called *possibilitation.*

$$\frac{\nvdash \sim\varphi}{M\varphi}.$$

By the following proposition, this rule is equivalent to default rule (1) with the set of defaults $D_M = \{ M\varphi : \varphi \in \mathbf{St} \}$.

Proposition 3. *We have* $\mathrm{TH}(A) = \mathbf{NTH}_{D_M}(A)$, *where* $D_M = \{ M\varphi : \varphi \in \mathbf{St} \}$.

It was shown in [9] that McDermott's nonmonotonic based on S5 is equivalent to the (monotonic) S5 itself. Thus, trivially, it is consistent, i.e., the empty set of axioms is nonmonotonically consistent. Also, even though McDermott's nonmonotonic logics based on the propositional versions of T and S4 are consistent, cf. [9], nothing is known about the consistency of nonmonotonic logics based on the first order versions of T and S4. However it is not hard to show that the first order nonmonotonic T and S4 with *strong equality*, i.e., $M(x=y) \supset L(x=y)$, are consistent.

In Section 4 we present a slightly modified version of McDermott's logic, called nonmonotonic ground logic. This logic is (nonmonotonically) consistent and possesses many of the "nonmonotonic" properties of McDermott's logic. Moreover, it is nondegenerate even when the underlying modal logic is S5.

We close this section by an example of a consistent set of axioms that has no fixed points.

Proposition 4. *Let the underlying modal logic be first order T or S4, and let* ψ *be a sentence not containing modal connectives such that* $\nvdash \psi$*. If the set of defaults D is a subset of* $D_M = \{M\varphi : \varphi \in \mathbf{St}\}$ *and contains* $M{\sim}\psi$*, then the set of axioms* $\{ML\psi\}$ *is (nonmonotonically) inconsistent.*

3. Closure properties of sets of defaults and degeneration of nonmonotonic theories

First we establish a closure property of the set of defaults under the positive connectives $\wedge$, $\vee$, and L. This closure property can be considered as a motivation for Theorems 2 and 3 below.

Definition 2. Let $D \subseteq \mathbf{Lang}$. We say that D is *closed* under connectives $\wedge, \vee$, and L, if $\varphi, \psi \in D$ implies $\varphi \wedge \psi, \varphi \vee \psi, L\varphi \in D$. We define $\bar{D}$, the *closure* of D under the connectives $\wedge$, $\vee$, and L, to be the set of all formulas which can be obtained from formulas of D by means of the connectives $\wedge$, $\vee$, and L.

Theorem 1. *For every set of defaults D we have* $\mathbf{NTH}_D(A) = \mathbf{NTH}_{\bar{D}}(A)$*. Moreover,* $\mathbf{NM}_{\bar{D}}^A$ *and* $\mathbf{NM}_D^A$ *have the same fixed points.*

Theorem 1, naturally, suggests to ask what about the closure under negation. But as is shown in the sequel, if the set of defaults is closed under negation, then the corresponding nonmonotonic logic is monotonic.

Next we present the main result of the paper, namely, a condition for a nonmonotonic modal logic to degenerate to a monotonic one. In order to give a precise statement of this condition we observe that for any default $\varphi \in D$ and any fixed point F we have $L^i\varphi \vee L^j{\sim}\varphi \in F$, $i, j = 0, 1, \ldots$. Indeed, if $F = \mathbf{Lang}$, then the proposition is, trivially, true. Otherwise, by Proposition 2, either $F \vdash \varphi$, or $F \vdash {\sim}\varphi$. In the former case, by i applications of NEC, $F \vdash L^i\varphi$, which, in turn, implies $L^i\varphi \vee L^j{\sim}\varphi \in F$, because F is deductively closed. The case of $F \vdash {\sim}\varphi$ is treated similarly.

The set of formulas $\{L^i\varphi \vee L^j{\sim}\varphi : \varphi \in D,\ i, j = 0, 1, \dots\}$ will be referred to as the set of *axioms imposed by D* and will be denoted by Ax_D. In this notation the above observation can be restated as follows.

Proposition 5. *We have* $\mathrm{Th}(A \cup \mathrm{Ax}_D) \subseteq \mathbf{NTH}_D(A)$.

Now consider the properties of nonmonotonic default modal logics stated below.

1. For every default $\varphi \in D$ there exists a default $\psi \in D$ such that $A, \psi \vdash {\sim}\varphi$, and $A, \mathrm{Ax}_D, {\sim}\varphi \vdash \psi$. This property of D can be thought as "the closure under negation relatively to A".

2. $\mathbf{NTH}_D(A) = \mathrm{Th}(A \cup \mathrm{Ax}_D)$, i.e. the nonmonotonic theory on A is equal to the monotonic one augmented with the additional axioms imposed by D. Notice that by Proposition 6, Ax_D is the least set of additional axioms that could enjoy this property.

2′. For every $A' \supseteq A$, $\mathbf{NTH}_D(A') = \mathrm{Th}(A' \cup \mathrm{Ax}_D)$, i.e. the nonmonotonic theory on extensions of A is equal to the monotonic one augmented with the additional axioms imposed by D.

3. For every $A' \supseteq A$, $\mathbf{NTH}_D(A') \supseteq \mathbf{NTH}_D(A)$, i.e. the nonmonotonic theories of extensions of A do not invalidate the assumptions (nonmonotonically) deduced from A. In other words, the operator $\mathbf{NTH}_D$ is monotonic in A.

3′. For every $A'' \supseteq A' \supseteq A$, $\mathbf{NTH}_D(A'') \supseteq \mathbf{NTH}_D(A')$, i.e., the logic is monotonic in the extensions of A.

Theorems 2 and 3 below show that the above properties of nonmonotonic theories are tightly connected.

Theorem 2. *For any set of defaults D and for any set of axioms A we have*

$$\begin{array}{ccccc} 1 & \Rightarrow & 2' & \Rightarrow & 2 \\ & & \Updownarrow & & \Updownarrow \\ & & 3' & \Rightarrow & 3\,, \end{array}$$

where $\Leftrightarrow$ *denotes equivalence, and* $\Rightarrow$ *denotes implication.*

In order to close the diagram given by Theorem 2 we need additional assumptions on the set of defaults and the underlying modal logic.

Definition 3. We shall say that a set of formulas $\Phi \subseteq \mathbf{Lang}$ is *finitely based* if there exist formulas $\varphi_1, \varphi_2, \dots, \varphi_n$ such that every formula of Φ can be obtained from $\varphi_1, \varphi_2, \dots, \varphi_n$ by means of propositional and modal connectives. I.e., for every formula $\varphi \in \Phi$ there exits a formula φ' in the language of the propositional modal logic over the propositional variables $p_1, p_2, \dots, p_n$ such that φ results by the substitution of φ_i for p_i in φ', $i = 1, 2, \dots, n$. The set of formulas $\{\varphi_1, \varphi_2, \ldots, \varphi_n\}$ is called *a finite base for* Φ.

Theorem 3. *If the underlying modal logic contains* S4 *and the set of defaults is finitely based and closed under* $\wedge$, $\vee$, *and* L, *then property* **2** *implies property* **1**, *i.e., the five properties stated above are equivalent.*

In Theorem 3, the condition imposed on the set of defaults to be closed under $\wedge$, $\vee$, and L is required only for a technical reason. (Alternatively, in view of Theorem 1, we could talk about $\bar{D}$ in property 1.) However, it can be shown that the requirement of a finite base is essential.

Next we present some of almost immediate corollaries to Theorems 2 and 3. The first one gives a proof-theoretic version of the corresponding result in [9].

Corollary 1. *Let* TH(A) *be the nonmonotonic theory of McDermott defined in Section 2. Then* TH(A)=Th(A) *if and only if* Th(A) *contains the sentential part of* M5.

Corollary 2. *Let* **Lang** *be a language of propositional modal logic of finite signature (that is the set of propositional variables is finite), and let the underlying modal logic contain the propositional part of* S4. *If the set of defaults* D *is closed under* $\wedge$, $\vee$, *and* L, *then all the properties* **1**, **2**, **2′**, **3**, *and* **3′** *are equivalent.*

Corollary 3. *Let the set of defaults* D *be finitely based and let the underlying modal logic contain* S4. *If* $\mathrm{Th}(\varnothing)=\mathbf{NTH}_D(\varnothing)$, *then* $\mathrm{Th}(A)=\mathbf{NTH}_D(A)$ *for every set of axioms* A.

Remark 3. It can be easily shown that $L\varphi \vee L{\sim}\varphi \vdash_T L^i\varphi \vee L^j{\sim}\varphi$, $i, j = 0, 1, \ldots$. Thus Ax_D could be defined as $\{L\varphi \vee L{\sim}\varphi\}_{\varphi \in D}$.

4. Nonmonotonic ground logics

One of the undesirable properties of the nonmonotonic logics of McDermott is that a consistent set of axioms may have no fixed points, i.e., be nonmonotonically inconsistent. A possible reason for this may be the lack of clear separation between the defaults not containing modalities, which one can consider as the facts about the real world, and the defaults containing modalities, which are "metaformulas" supposed to interpret knowledge, necessity, contingency, etc.. In this section we propose a slightly modified version of the nonmonotonic logics of McDermott that seems to be more convenient to deal with. These logics, referred to as *nonmonotonic ground logics*, result from the set of defaults D_G that is defined as follows.

$$D_G = \{ M\varphi : \varphi \text{ is a sentence without modalities } \}.$$

In view of [4, Proposition 3.6], fixed points of nonmonotonic ground logics correspond to *minimal* autoepistemic extensions. However, the language of nonmonotonic ground logics is richer than that of the autoepistemic one, because the language of autoepistemic logic does not allow the occurrence of modal operators within the scope of quantifaers. In addition an S5-consistent set of axioms is also nonmonotonically consistent, cf. Proposition 8 below, whereas in autoepistemic logics there exist consistent sets of formulas which have no autoepistemic extension, cf. [4, Example 2.2].

As in the case of McDermott's logics based on T or S4, the consistent set of axioms $\{MLp\}$ is inconsistent in nonmonotonic ground logic based on T or S4, cf. Proposition 4. But, fortunately, for T, S4 and S5 every consistent set of axioms without modalities is also nonmonotonically consistent. Moreover, for S5 this is true for any set of axioms, even if it contains "metaformulas". The former, in particular, implies that the first order nonmonotonic theory resulting from the empty set of axioms is consistent in nonmonotonic ground logic, even if the underlying modal logic is T or S4. In addition, nonmonotonic ground logic is nondegenerate in S5. The precise statements of the above results are given below.

Proposition 6. *Let the underlying logic contain T and be contained in S5, and let A be a consistent set of axioms without modalities. Then* $\mathbf{NM}^A_{D_G}$ *has a unique consistent fixed point* $F_A = \mathrm{Th}(A \cup \{ M\varphi \in D_G : A \nvdash \sim\varphi \})$.

Proposition 7. *Let the underlying logic contain T and be contained in S5. If a set of axioms A does not contain modalities, and* Th(A) *is not complete in the predicate calculus, then there exists a consistent set of axioms* $A' \supset A$ *without modalities, such that* $\mathbf{NTH}_{D_G}(A') \not\supseteq \mathbf{NTH}_{D_G}(A)$.

Proposition 8. *Let the underlying modal logic be S5. If a set of axioms A is consistent, then* $\mathbf{NTH}_{D_G}(A)$ *is also consistent.*

Finally we would like to note that, in view of Remark 2 in Section 2, nonmonotonic propositional ground logics over a finite signature are decidable, because their set of defaults D_G is finite.

References

[1] M.R.B. Clarke and D.M. Gabbay, An Intuitionistic Basis for non-monotonic Reasoning, in: A. Mamdani et al. eds., *Non Standard Logics for Automated Reasoning*, Academic Press, 1987.

[2] D.M. Gabbay, Intuitionistic Basis for non-monotonic Logic I, in: D.W. Loveland ed., *Proceedings of the 6th conference of Automated Deduction*, Springer, Berlin, 1982, pp. 260-273 (Lecture Notes in Computer Science No. **138**).

[3] D.M. Gabbay, Theoretical foundations for non-monotonic reasoning expert systems, in: K.R. Apt ed., *Proceedings of the NATO Advanced Study Institute on Logics and Models of Concurrent Systems*, Springer, Berlin, 1985, pp. 439-457.

[4] K. Konolige, On the relation between default and autoepistemic logic, *Artificial Intelligence* **35** (1988), 343-382.

[5] D. Lehmann, Preferential models and cumulative logic, in: E. Shapiro ed., *Fifth Israeli Symposium on Artificial Intelligence Vision and Patter Recognition*, Information Processing Association of Israel, Tel Aviv, 1988, pp. 365-381.

[6] D. Makinson, General Theory of Cumulative Inference, in: M. Reinfrank et al. eds., *Proceedings of the 2nd international workshop on non-monotonic reasoning*, Springer, Berlin, 1989, pp. 1-18 (Lecture Notes in Computer Science No. **346**).

[7] J. McCarthy, Circumscription - A Form of Non-Monotonic Reasoning, *Artificial Intelligence* **13** (1980), 27-39.

[8] D. McDermott and J. Doyle, Non-Monotonic Logic I, *Artificial Intelligence* **13** (1980), 41-72.

[9] D. McDermott, NonMonotonic Logic II: Nonmonotonic Modal Theories, *Journal of ACM* **29** (1982), 33-57.

[10] R.C. Moore, Semantical Considerations on Nonmonotonic Logics, *Artificial Intelligence* **25** (1985), 75-94.

[11] R.C. Moore, Possible-world semantics for autoepistemic logic, in: M.L. Ginsberg ed., *Readings in Nonmonotonic Reasoning*, Morgan Kaufmann, Los Altos, California, 1987, pp. 137-142.

[12] R. Reiter, A Logic for Default Reasoning, *Artificial Intelligence* **13** (1980), 81-132.

EXPLANATORY BELIEF ASCRIPTION

NOTES AND PREMATURE FORMALIZATION

Kurt Konolige
Artificial Intelligence Center
Center for the Study of Language and Information
SRI International
333 Ravenswood Ave.
Menlo Park, California 94025/USA

1 Overview

In this paper we discuss the problem of ascribing beliefs to an agent, given partial knowledge of his beliefs. The particular kind of ascription we are interested in we call explanatory ascription, since it ascribes beliefs to an agent as a means of explaining the beliefs we already know he has.

We explore two approaches to explanatory ascription. In the first, we develop a model of belief called the derivational model, in which the derivation of one belief from another is made explicit. This model and its proof theory are formalized and used to solve a variation of the Wise Man Puzzle. For comparison, a second approach using an abductive framework and a standard modal logic of belief is developed. This approach leads to weaker conclusions than the derivational model, because closure conditions on derivations cannot be stated. On the other hand, the representational power of the two approaches differs, the abductive system being more expressive with respect to disjunctive information about belief, and the derivational model allowing nonmonotonic reasoning by the believer.

The next section of the paper gives some background in the area of belief ascription. The third section describes the problem of explanatory ascription, and some general properties that a successful approach should have. The fourth and fifth sections develop the derivational model and its proof theory, while the sixth describes an abductive framework and compares it to the derivational approach. Finally, we discuss some extensions to the language of the derivational model.

2 Belief ascription

Formalizations of belief are useful in AI for building systems that can represent and reason about the beliefs of other agents in cooperative situations. A typical example is an intelligent user interface to a database: an agent (the *user*) queries the system about a topic, and the system should respond in a helpful manner, making communication with the user efficient. It is well-known that extensive knowledge of the user's beliefs and intentions is required for this task [Pollack, 1986]. Since explicit communication of beliefs and intentions is limited, the system must implicitly ascribe them to the user. Here we concentrate on the process of belief ascription. Existing formalizations of belief can to some extent represent several types of ascription, which we call *deductive*, *closure*, and *analogical* ascription, but are inadequate for another type which we dub *explanatory* ascription. In this paper we develop and formalize a preliminary theory of explanatory belief ascription.

As an example of the various types of ascription, consider a simplified version of the Wise Man Puzzle with only two wise men. Each has a white hat, and it is common knowledge that there is one white hat. The first wise man says "I don't know the color of my hat," and the second wise man, on hearing this, says "My hat must be white."

As observers, we can ascribe to the second wise man the belief that his hat is white from our knowledge of his other beliefs: common knowledge of the existence of one white hat, knowledge of perceptual capabilities, and knowledge of the first wise man's ignorance of his own hat's color. This ascription is *deductive* in a suitable modal logic of belief[1]: given all of the facts above expressed in the logic, it follows that the second wise man believes his hat is white[McCarthy, 1978]. We use deduction within the belief logic to reason about the conclusions an agent must draw from an initial set of beliefs.

Deductive ascription can also be used to infer that an agent does *not* believe some fact. In the Wise Man Puzzle, the second wise man reasons that the first wise man does not believe his own hat is white, and thus can not believe that the second wise man's hat is black. More simply, if an agent believes a proposition, he does not believe its negation[2].

Another type of reasoning about ignorance is to be able to conclude that the first wise man does not know the color of his own hat, given his beliefs in the initial situation. This kind of reasoning requires a closure assumption about beliefs — the only beliefs the first wise man has that are relevant to his hat color are those presented in the puzzle. Belief ascription by closure is complicated to formalize, but recent approaches involving autoepistemic logic seem to be successful [Levesque, 1987].

A third type of ascription of belief is *analogical* in nature. The second wise man must reason that the perceptual capabilities of the first wise man are similar to his own, i.e., that he will recognize a white hat when he sees one, and form an appropriate belief. Analogical ascription is difficult to formalize, because it is only plausible: other information might cause the analogical ascription to be retracted. This type of ascription is widely used in plan recognition to make assumptions about another agent's knowledge of the effects of actions [Pollack, 1986, Konolige and Pollack, 1989].

These types of ascription all have a common core: they involve reasoning about the forward inferential connections of the beliefs of an agent. That is, they involve reasoning of the form: if an agent believes α, and β follows from α, then the agent must believe β. Even ascription by closure is a variation on this theme — there is no α believed by the agent such that β follows from α, therefore the agent does not believe β. By contrast, explanatory belief ascription is *abductive* in nature: one searches for a plausible explanation for the beliefs an agent is known to have. We discuss this process in the next section.

3 Explanatory belief ascription

Consider a variation of the Wise Man Puzzle for two wise men, that we will call the Easy Wise Man Puzzle. Suppose that the second wise man's hat is black, and thus the first wise man says "I know that my hat is white." The second wise man then says, "My hat must be black." How can we account for this conclusion? Intuitively, the second wise man must reason about what gave

[1] The simplest such logic, K, will do here.

[2] This is assuming an agent's beliefs to be consistent, which requires a belief logic with the modal axiom D.

rise to the first wise man's belief, that is, what other beliefs it must be based on. In this case, a plausible candidate is the belief that second wise man's hat is black. We call this kind of reasoning *explanatory* ascription, because it ascribes beliefs as a means of explaining the presence of other beliefs.

What are the general characteristics of explanatory ascription? Here we discuss some of its properties, as a guide to developing a formalization in the next section.

1. The ascription of belief obviously depends on what we take to be a model of belief. Without arguing for their appropriateness, we make two related assumptions. The first is that beliefs are related by derivation, that is, on the basis of certain beliefs, an agent will derive other beliefs. The aim is to keep this assumption as abstract as possible, so no particular symbol system or computational mechanism is assumed; but the model of belief must have some way of stating derivation relations. The second assumption is that a special set of beliefs, the primitive beliefs, acts as the foundation for all derived beliefs. This view is similar to that of the Truth Maintenance System [Doyle, 1979], in which all propositions are justified on the basis of some set of primitive propositions that need no justification.[3] The set of primitive beliefs will often include those that are based on observation.

2. Explanatory ascription is a kind of abductive inference, in that it involves reasoning from an observed belief of an agent back to the way the belief arose or was derived. In this respect it differs from the other types of ascription noted above. Several consequences should be noted.[4]

First, explanations should be minimal in some sense. For belief ascription, we want to ascribe just enough primitive beliefs to account for the observed facts, and no more. In this respect explanatory ascription differs from other types of forward reasoning ascription, which are generally additive. For instance, if beliefs β_1 and β_2 are both derivable from the belief α, and they are consistent with each other, then it is reasonable to ascribe belief in both of them. On the other hand, explanatory inference is not additive in this manner, but competitive. If α_1 and α_2 are both explanations for β, then even if they are mutually consistent, it would be unwise to ascribe both of them to an agent believing β.

The competitive nature of explanatory ascription is similar to that in the plan recognition process. In ascribing intentions to an agent whose actions are being observed, we seek to ascribe fragments of a plan that would connect the observed actions with the imputed goals of an agent [Konolige and Pollack, 1989]. Alternative plan fragments compete with one another as explanations of the observed actions. Local cues, such as preferences for one type of plan fragment over another, can be used to choose among the alternatives.

A similar story can be told in explanatory ascription of belief. Here the inferential connections between the beliefs, as well as beliefs themselves, are being ascribed. So, for example, in the case of the Easy Wise Man Puzzle, the second wise man ascribes to the first the belief in b_2, and also the inferential connection between this belief and the conclusion w_1.[5]

---

[3]The foundational theory of belief has an interesting history in the philosophy literature, and there are some compelling arguments against its full application (see, for example, [Harman, 1986]). Nevertheless it is a useful approximation.

[4]In other accounts of abduction, the properties we cite here are also recognized, e.g., [Levesque, 1989, Poole, 1988, Reiter, 1987]).

[5]b_i and w_i are convenient abbreviations for the propositions *wise man i's hat is black (or white)*.

A second characteristic of explanatory ascription is that there may be preferences among competing explanations. It may be much more likely, for example, that Ralph knows the combination of the lock because he saw someone else open it, rather than guessing it at random. Often this kind of preference information is based on knowing that certain derivations are more likely than others. Thus it is useful to have a language in which both beliefs and the derivational relations among them are represented.

3. Distinguishing between the derivational capabilities of an agent and his "factual" beliefs is important. For example, in the Easy Wise Man Puzzle, we have information about the possible derivations that the first wise man can make from his observation of the second wise man's hat. This includes *closure* information, that is, the knowledge that the only way in which he can conclude that his own hat is white is if he sees a black hat on the second wise man. On the other hand, we do not want to assume closure over factual information, since we do not have complete knowledge here.[6]

4. Belief derivation may be *nonmonotonic*. By this we mean that an agent may come to a conclusion on the basis of some proposition he does not believe, as well as those he does. This derivation is nonmonotonic in the sense that it may be retracted when the agent acquires new information. The presence of nonmonotonic derivation poses an additional challenge for explanatory ascription.

Most of the logics of belief used in AI work, including all those derivative of Hintikka's original possible-worlds formulation [Hintikka, 1962], do not seem adequate to account for these properties, even in an abductive framework. The main problem is that they do not explicitly represent relationships among beliefs, particularly that one belief is derived from or caused by other beliefs. Rather, the derivation of one belief from another (for an ideal reasoning agent) is implicitly given by the axioms of the belief logic. For example, an ideal agent would conclude q from p and $p \supset q$, and this is reflected in a normal modal logic by the fact that $B(q)$ follows from $B(p)$ and $B(p \supset q)$. There is never any need to reason explicitly about the derivation of belief: one simply starts with a set of known beliefs, and uses logical entailment in the belief logic to deduce all derived beliefs. In explanatory ascription, on the other hand, being able to reason explicitly about belief derivation is necessary, both for deciding among competing explanations, and in stating closure conditions. Hence the representation of derivation or causation among beliefs becomes important.

In the sequel, we develop a derivational model of belief in which the distinction between beliefs and their derivational relations is clearly drawn. From this we construct a competence theory of belief ascription, that is, we do not consider preferences among the explanations. The ascription theory is based on the simplifying assumption of a propositional belief language and monotonic derivation.

4 A derivational model of belief

As we have argued, an appropriate model of belief for explanatory ascription must take into account the derivational relationships among beliefs. Together with the hypothesis of a foundational theory,

[6] This distinction means that we cannot formalize the closure conditions by simply giving a set of sentences about an agent's beliefs, and then saying "the agent has no beliefs that do not follow from these sentences." In fact, this is the approach taken in [Levesque, 1987] and [Lifschitz, 1989]. In earlier work [Konolige, 1982], this author explored a different kind of closure condition relating the background knowledge of an agent to his factual beliefs.

we construct a simple derivational model of belief. First, we fix the possible model structures by defining a *frame.*

DEFINITION 4.1 *A* frame *consists of three elements: a set of propositions* $(p_1, p_2, \cdots)$, *a subset of these propositions called the* primitive *propositions, and a mapping* $\mathcal{D}$ *from sets of propositions to propositions. An element of* $\mathcal{D}$ *is called a* derivation, *and can be written as* $p_1, \cdots, p_n \mapsto q$. *The propositions* p_i *are called the antecedents, and* q *the conclusion. One proposition,* $\bot$, *is distinguished as the contradictory proposition, and is never primitive.*

A frame gives the possible beliefs and derivations among beliefs that an agent can have. A model, based on a frame, describes the beliefs of an agent in a particular situation.

DEFINITION 4.2 *A* derivational model *of belief over a frame* $\langle P, Prim, \mathcal{D}\rangle$ *is a tuple* $\langle B, D\rangle$. *The* belief set B *is a subset of* P, *and the* derivation set D *is a subset of* $\mathcal{D}$. *The following conditions must hold:*

1. *The contradictory proposition* $\bot$ *is not in* B.
2. *For every derivation* $p_1 \cdots p_n \mapsto q$ *of* D, *all propositions* p_i *and* q *are in* B.
3. *If* $d = p_1 \cdots p_n \mapsto q$ *is a derivation of* $\mathcal{D}$, *and all* p_i *are in* B, *then* $d \in D$.
4. *Every element of* B *is the root of a tree over* D *whose leaves are in Prim.*

Informally, a model gives the beliefs of an agent (component B), together with the derivational structure of those beliefs (component D). The conditions on B and D ensure that the set of beliefs is closed under well-founded derivation. The exclusion of $\bot$ means that the beliefs are noncontradictory. The definition of the derivational model is similar to admissible labelings of a TMS [Reinfrank *et al.*, 1989] with only monotonic rules.

It is straightforward to give models for the beliefs of the first Wise Man in the Easy Wise Man Puzzle. The propositions are w_1, b_1, w_2, and b_2. For the first Wise Man, w_2 and b_2 are primitive because they are observable. Since he knows that at least one hat is white, his derivational relation $\mathcal{D}$ is:

$$\begin{aligned} b_1 &\mapsto w_2 \\ b_2 &\mapsto w_1 \\ b_1, w_1 &\mapsto \bot \\ b_2, w_2 &\mapsto \bot \end{aligned} \tag{1}$$

There are three possible models using this frame:

model	B	D
m_1	$\emptyset$	$\emptyset$
m_2	b_1, w_2	$b_1 \mapsto w_2$
m_3	b_2, w_1	$b_2 \mapsto w_1$

The model in which both b_1 and b_2 are in the belief set leads to a contradiction.

The derivational model can be considered as a further development of the Deduction Model of belief [Konolige, 1986]. In contrast to possible-world model, the Deduction Model considers belief to be sentence-like data structures in the cognitive structure of an agent, who has a deductive apparatus for infering one belief from another. The most significant departure here is the inclusion of derivation as an explicit structural element of the model. Like the deduction model, the derivational model is free from the problem of logical omniscience. in which it is assumed that an agent knows all the logical consequences of his beliefs. However, an agents' beliefs are assumed to be closed under derivation — but the derivation mapping $\mathcal{D}$ of a frame may not be logically complete.

Another way in which the derivational model differs significantly is the inclusion of the derivation mapping of a frame. This mapping specifies all of the possible ways in which a belief can be derived from its fellows, and as such is a type of closure. The mapping may have an infinite number of members, but it can also be finite, or the number of derivations with a given proposition as the conclusion may be finite. With the appropriate language for describing models, it is very easy to express the closure conditions that prevail in many belief representation situations.

5 A language and proof system

Our formalization of the derivational model of belief will proceed in several parts. First we present a language for talking about belief, and give its semantics relative to the model. Then we define the notion of logical implication relative to a set of premises and a frame. Finally, we construct an axiomatic system and prove it sound and complete with respect to logical implication, when the frame is finite.

5.1 A belief language

A propositional language for belief, **B**, is defined relative to a derivational frame $\langle P, Prim, \mathcal{D}\rangle$. It contains:

- A set of modal atoms Bp, where $p \in P$. $p_1, \cdots, p_n \mapsto q \in \mathcal{D}$.
- A set of *ordinary* propositional atoms, and the boolean connectives.

The semantics is straightforward. An interpretation consists of a truth assignment v for all of the ordinary atoms, along with a derivational structure $m = \langle B, D\rangle$ over a frame $\mathcal{F}$. The normal rules for boolean connectives hold; the atoms are interpreted as follows:

1. $m, v \models_{\mathcal{F}} \phi$, for ϕ ordinary, iff $v(\phi) =$ true.
2. $m, v \models_{\mathcal{F}} \mathrm{B}p$ iff $p \in B$.

Note that interpretations are always defined relative to a frame. In the standard way, a set of sentences Γ of **B** defines the collection of models for which all of Γ are true, and a sentence ϕ true in all these models is a logical consequence of Γ; we write $\Gamma \models_{\mathcal{F}} \phi$.

5.2 Inference

Our knowledge about an agent is given by two collections of belief propositions and derivation relations. One collection is our knowledge of the possible belief derivations and primitive propositions an agent might have: the frame. For example, the frame for the Easy Wise Man Puzzle, from Equation 1 and the paragraph preceding it, gives the possible derivations of the first Wise Man from the primitive propositions b_2 and w_2. As noted above, an important part of the information given is the implicit closure condition: there are no other derivations the agent could make.

The other collection is our initial knowledge of the agent's beliefs, a finite set of sentences of B called the *base* or *premise set*. The base set $\{\mathrm{B}w_1, \neg\mathrm{B}b_1\}$ describes the first Wise Man as believing (at least) w_1 and not believing b_1. A base set may be incomplete, in that it may not contain all of the beliefs that are logical consequences of its members relative to the derivational semantics (the base set just given is incomplete with respect to b_2 and w_2).

Given a frame $\mathcal{F}$ and a base set O, what conclusions should we come to? At the least, we should conclude everything that is true in all models of $\mathcal{F}$ and O. That is, we conclude:

$$\{\phi \mid O \models_{\mathcal{F}} \phi\}. \tag{2}$$

This is the set of logical consequences of O, given a fixed frame $\mathcal{F}$.

As an example, consider the frame with primitive propositions $\{a_1, a_2\}$ and derivations

$$a_1 \mapsto p,\ a_2 \mapsto p,\ a_2 \mapsto q.$$

Suppose the base set is $\{\mathrm{B}a_1\}$. There are three models:

model	*B*	*D*
m_1	a_1, p	$a_1 \mapsto p$
m_2	a_2, p, q	$a_2 \mapsto p, a_2 \mapsto q$
m_3	a_1, a_2, p, q	$a_1 \mapsto p, a_2 \mapsto p, a_2 \mapsto q$

From these we can conclude $\mathrm{B}a_1 \vee \mathrm{B}a_2$, $\neg\mathrm{B}a_1 \supset \mathrm{B}q$, $\neg\mathrm{B}q \supset \neg\mathrm{B}a_2$, $\neg\mathrm{B}a_2 \supset \neg\mathrm{B}q$, etc. Note that, because of the implicit closure condition of the frame, we have greatly increased the ability to infer ignorance on the part of the agent.

As another example, consider the same frame with the base set $O = \{\mathrm{B}a_1, \mathrm{B}q\}$. There are two models, m_2 and m_3 of the previous example. We should conclude $\mathrm{B}a_2$, but not $\neg\mathrm{B}a_1$, since a_2 is a belief in m_3. Note that this is different from the conclusions we get by taking the models of O that are minimal in the primitive propositions believed: this would be m_2 alone, and $\neg\mathrm{B}a_1$ would be a conclusion.

Finally, consider the Easy Wise Man example of Equation 1. For the base set $\{\mathrm{B}w_1\}$, there is only one model, namely that for which $\mathrm{B}b_2$ holds.

Although it may not be obvious, the derivational semantics are sufficient for concluding the minimal abductive consequences of a base set. We prove this in the next section, where the derivational semantics is compared to the abductive framework.

5.3 Proof theory

The proof theory is a propositional system, with additional axioms for the modal atoms. Define the set $\mathrm{Ax}(\langle P, Prim, \mathcal{D}\rangle)$ as:

1. $\neg\mathrm{B}\,\bot$.

2. For every $p_1, \cdots, p_n \mapsto q \in \mathcal{D}$, $\mathrm{B}p_1 \wedge \cdots \wedge \mathrm{B}p_n \supset \mathrm{B}q \in \mathrm{Ax}(\langle P, Prim, \mathcal{D}\rangle)$.

3. Let $q \in P$, $q \notin Prim$, and $q \neq \perp$. If the number N of derivations of q in $\mathcal{F}$ is finite, then $\mathrm{B}q \supset \bigvee_{i=1}^{N}(\mathrm{B}p_1^i \wedge \cdots \wedge \mathrm{B}p_{k_i}^i) \in \mathrm{Ax}(\langle P, Prim, \mathcal{D}\rangle)$.

The first axiom states that beliefs are not contradictory. The second item contains axioms that state how beliefs are inferred by an agent via derivations. The third is basically Clark's completion of the first set of axioms, stopping at the primitive propositions. If a particular proposition has an infinite number of derivations, then we can't form the completion in the language **B**.

Define the theorems of a base set O on a frame $\mathcal{F}$ by:

$$O \vdash_{\mathcal{F}} \phi \quad \text{if and only if} \quad O \cup \mathrm{Ax}(\mathcal{F}) \vdash \phi. \tag{3}$$

We can prove the following soundness theorem:

THEOREM 5.1 *$O \models_{\mathcal{F}} \phi$ if $O \vdash_{\mathcal{F}} \phi$.*

There are conditions under which the converse is also true, so that the axiomatic system is complete.

THEOREM 5.2 *Suppose $\mathcal{F}$ is an acyclic frame such that every proposition is the conclusion of only a finite number of derivations. Then $O \vdash_{\mathcal{F}} \phi$ if $O \models_{\mathcal{F}} \phi$.*

For the Easy Wise Man frame, we get the following set of axioms:

$$\mathrm{Ax}(\mathcal{F}) = \{ \begin{array}{l} \mathrm{B}b_1 \equiv \mathrm{B}w_2 \\ \mathrm{B}b_2 \equiv \mathrm{B}w_1 \\ \neg(\mathrm{B}b_1 \wedge \mathrm{B}w_1) \\ \neg(\mathrm{B}b_2 \wedge \mathrm{B}w_2) \quad \} \end{array} \tag{4}$$

Besides knowledge of the derivational frame, the second wise man knows the following about the first wise man: he believes his own hat is white ($\mathrm{B}w_1$), and he can faithfully observe the color of the second wise man's hat ($b_2 \supset \mathrm{B}b_2$, $w_2 \supset \mathrm{B}w_2$). From these and the frame axioms it follows that:

$$\mathrm{Ax}(\mathcal{F}) \cup \{Bw_1, b_2 \supset \mathrm{B}b_2, w_2 \supset \mathrm{B}w_2\} \vdash b_2 \ .$$

This is the solution to the Easy Wise Man Puzzle using the model of derivational belief.

6 An abductive framework

In this section we compare the derivational model with a standard modal belief logic in an abductive framework. We show that, under suitable assumptions, the derivational model produces all the conclusions of the standard logic, but that the converse is not true.

We define a standard modal language **B′** based on the propositions P of a frame. The sentences of **B′** are all boolean combinations of P and the modal atoms $\mathrm{B}\phi$, where ϕ is an ordinary (nonmodal) sentence of **B′**. We are not interested in the complications of nested modal operators here. We have $\mathbf{B} \subset \mathbf{B}'$, since **B** excludes those modal atoms whose arguments are boolean combinations of the propositions P.

The set Pr is defined as $\{B\phi \mid \phi \in Prim\}$, that is, the set of primitive belief atoms. Take the logic to be propositional KD, that is, the simplest belief logic together with the axiom $D = \neg B \perp$ stating that beliefs are consistent. In the abductive framework, there is background information $\Sigma \subset B'$ about the world and the agent's beliefs. The background information might contain statements about the connections among the agent's beliefs, or between the agent's beliefs and the world. There is also a set of observations $O \subset B$ about the agent's beliefs, from which further beliefs are to be ascribed.

An *explanation* of the observations is a set $A \subset Pr$ such that

1. $\Sigma \cup A \models_{KD} O$.

2. A is consistent in KD.

3. A is minimal.

A *cautious explanation* is the disjunction of all the explanations, that is, $\bigvee_i A_i$. This is the minimum we can conclude in the abductive framework.

As an example consider the Easy Wise Man Puzzle. The background information, from the second wise man's point of view, consists of:

$B(w_1 \vee w_2)$	the first wise man believes at least one hat is white	
$w_1 \vee w_2$	and so it is	
$w_2 \supset B(w_2)$	he can observe the second wise man's hat	
$b_2 \supset B(b_2)$		
$B(b_1 \equiv \neg w_1)$	he believes black and white are mutually exclusive	(5)
$B(b_2 \equiv \neg w_2)$		
$b_1 \equiv \neg w_1$	as indeed they are	
$b_2 \equiv \neg w_2$		

From the observed fact Bw_1, there is only one possible explanation (which is also the cautious explanation), Bb_2. From this and the background information it follows that Bw_1, and also $\neg Bw_2$ (via the D axiom) and hence b_2. So by using a standard belief logic in an abductive framework, the second wise man can infer the color of his own hat.

The abductive framework actually produces only a subset of the conclusions of the derivational model: conclusions about the non-beliefs of the agent are lacking. Consider the same example, only with the observation set $O = \{\neg Bb_2\}$. The cautious explanation is the tautology $\neg \perp$, so we can conclude only what follows in KD from Σ and O; in particular, we cannot conclude $\neg Bw_1$, which is a consequence of the derivational model. The difference lies in the ability to state closure of the possible derivations in the derivational model. In this model, the only way in which w_1 could be derived by the agent is via the belief in b_2, and so not believing b_2 means he doesn't believe w_1.

It is possible to prove that, under the condition of complete derivation, the derivational model produces all of the conclusions of the standard model in the abductive framework. Define a complete set of derivations relative to a background theory as:

DEFINITION 6.1 $\text{Comp}(\Gamma, P, Q)$ *is the set of all derivations* $p_1, \cdots, p_n \mapsto q$ *such that*

1. $p_i \in P$ *and* $q \in Q$,

2. *$p_1, \cdots p_n$ is a minimal subset such that* $\Gamma \models_{KD} \mathrm{B}p_1 \wedge \cdots \wedge \mathrm{B}p_n \supset \mathrm{B}q$,

3. *either* $\mathrm{B}p_1 \wedge \cdots \wedge \mathrm{B}p_n$ *is consistent with* Γ, *or* $q = \perp$.

Divide the background theory Σ into two parts: a set Σ_d whose sentences contain modal atoms not in **B** (that is, with complex propositional arguments), and the rest Σ_b. We use Σ_d to generate derivations.

THEOREM 6.1 *Let* $\Sigma = \Sigma_d \cup \Sigma_b$ *be as defined above, and let* A *be the cautious explanation of some observation set* O *relative to* Σ. *Suppose* Σ_d *consists only of modal atoms and their negations. Let* $\mathcal{F}$ *be the frame* $\langle P, Prim, \mathrm{Comp}(\Sigma_d, Prim, P)\rangle$. *Then*

$$\Sigma_b \cup O \models_{\mathcal{F}} A .$$

7 Extensions

We briefly discuss several extensions to the formalization. These are preliminary ideas, and need further exploration.

7.1 Language

The belief language **B** is impoverished with respect to the model, since we assume a fixed frame, rather than allowing statements about the frame in the language. In part this is to distinguish knowledge of belief derivations from knowledge of factual belief, and in part to make it easy to state closure conditions on derivations. A reasonable extension would be to eliminate the assumption of a fixed frame, and expand the language to include statements about derivations, perhaps of the form $\mathrm{Der}(p_1, \cdots, p_n; q)$ to indicate that $p_1, \cdots, p_n \mapsto q$ is a derivation. To achieve closure over the derivations given by a set of premises, we could make inferences with respect to derivational models of the premises with *minimal frames*. This is equivalent to the present approach when the premises only contain the modal atoms Der as sentences.

7.2 Nonmonotonic belief derivation

A slight change in the definition of derivations allows us to add nonmonotonic derivations to the model. Instead of $p_1, \cdots p_n \mapsto q$, we take derivations to be $p_1 \cdots p_n; r_1 \cdots r_l \mapsto q$, where the r_i are the nonmonotonic antecedents of the derivation. The conditions on the model (Definition 4.2) must be modified:

2. For every derivation $p_1 \cdots p_n; r_1 \cdots r_l \mapsto q$ of D, all propositions p_i and q are in B, and r_j are not in B.

3. If $d = p_1 \cdots p_n; r_1 \cdots r_l \mapsto q$ is a derivation of $\mathcal{D}$, and all p_i are in B, and all r_j are not in B, then $d \in D$.

We make similar modifications in the proof theory, adding negative belief literals in the antecedent of the implications in $\mathrm{Ax}(\mathcal{F})$. Nothing else need be changed: the soundness and completeness theorem go through as before.

Surprisingly, we are able to formalize quite simply the behavior of an agent that does non-monotonic reasoning. However the belief language is still restrictive, limiting us to the case of a TMS-reasoner, a subset of a full default-logic type of reasoner [Reinfrank *et al.*, 1989].

8 Conclusion

The theory of belief ascription presented here accounts for some of the characteristic interaction of explanatory and deductive ascription. Previous formal work on belief ascription in AI has not addressed the problem of explanatory ascription.

We have developed an elaboration of the Deduction Model of belief, by making explicit the nature of derivation among beliefs. The advantages of this model are that it allows us to state closure conditions on the derivations in a straightforward manner, and keep them separate from closure conditions on "factual" beliefs, which are usually not desired. We have developed a proof theory for the model, and shown it to be sound, and complete under certain restrictions on finiteness in the derivational structure.

In comparison with a standard modal logic of belief in an abductive framework, the derivational model has good and bad points. On the one hand, for a restricted background theory, it gives all of the results of the abductive system, and in addition allows conclusions based on the closure of derivations that are not available in the abductive system. On the other hand, the expressivity of the language **B** is somewhat impoverished. Perhaps a good solution here is to expand the expressivity of **B** to talk about derivations; but then the problem of defining closure of these derivations appears.

Finally, we have indicated how the derivational model can deal with belief ascription when the agent is a nonmonotonic reasoner, something that cannot be done in the standard abductive framework.

9 Acknowledgements

I would like to thank David Israel and Martha Pollack for discussing these issues with me.

References

[Doyle, 1979] John Doyle. A truth maintenance system. *Artificial Intelligence*, 12(3), 1979.

[Harman, 1986] Gilbert Harman. *Change in View.* The MIT Press, Cambridge, Massachusetts, 1986.

[Hintikka, 1962] Jaako Hintikka. *Knowledge and Belief.* Cornell University Press, Ithaca, New York, 1962.

[Konolige and Pollack, 1989] Kurt Konolige and Martha Pollack. Ascribing plans to agents: Preliminary report. In *submitted to AAAI*, Detroit, Michigan, 1989.

[Konolige, 1982] Kurt Konolige. Circumscriptive ignorance. In *Proceedings of the American Association of Artificial Intelligence*, Pittsburgh, Pennsylvania, 1982. Carnegie-Mellon University.

[Konolige, 1986] Kurt Konolige. *A Deduction Model of Belief.* Pitman Research Notes in Artificial Intelligence, 1986.

[Levesque, 1987] Hector J. Levesque. All I know: an abridged report. In *Proceedings of the American Association of Artificial Intelligence.* Seattle, Washington, 1987.

[Levesque, 1989] Hector J. Levesque. A knowledge-level account of abduction. In *Proceedings of the International Joint Conference on Artificial Intelligence.* Detroit, Michigan, 1989.

[Lifschitz, 1989] Vladimir Lifschitz. Between circumscription and autoepistemic logic. In *Proceedings of the First International Conference on Knowledge Representation and Reasoning,* Toronto, Ontario, 1989.

[McCarthy, 1978] John McCarthy. Formalization of two puzzles involving knowledge. Unpublished note, 1978.

[Pollack, 1986] M. E. Pollack. *Inferring Domain Plans in Question-Answering.* PhD thesis, University of Pennsylvania, 1986.

[Poole, 1988] David Poole. A methodology for using a default and abductive reasoning system. Technical report, Department of Computer Science, University of Waterloo, Waterloo, Ontario, 1988.

[Reinfrank *et al.*, 1989] M. Reinfrank, O. Dressler, and G. Brewka. On the relation between truth maintenance and autoepistemic logic. In *Proceedings of the International Joint Conference on Artificial Intelligence.* Detroit, Michigan, 1989.

[Reiter, 1987] Raymond Reiter. A theory of diagnosis from first principles. *Artificial Intelligence,* 32, 1987.

AUTOEPISTEMIC MODAL LOGICS

Grigori Shvarts
Program Systems Institute
of the USSR Academy of Sciences
152140 Pereslavl-Zalessky, USSR

ABSTRACT

A modal approach to nonmonotonic reasoning was proposed by Drew McDermott and Jon Doyle in 1980–82. Almost immediately some disadvantages of that approach were pointed out. Robert Moore (1983) proposed his autoepistemic logic, which overcomes these difficulties. Later, some authors (Kurt Konolige, Paul Morris and others) found peculiarities of different kinds in Moore's logic and proposed rather complicated solutions to these problems. A careful mathematical analysis of Moore's and McDermott's approaches shows that Moore's logic is merely a special case of McDermott's logic, at least formally. The problems that arose in Moore's logic may find a simple and uniform solution by going back to McDermott's original concept.

INTRODUCTION

Moore [1] introduced autoepistemic logic for formalising reasoning of an agent which may contain references to the agent's own knowledge (or belief). This kind of reasoning, which Moore calls *autoepistemic*, has the nonmonotonicity property: The set of "theorems" does not increase with the set of "axioms." (Moore attributes this observation to Stalnaker's work [2] which is not available to the author.) The language of Moore's logic is the usual propositional language augmented by the modal operator L. The intended interpretation of $L\phi$ is: "the rational agent believes (or knows) ϕ". Because of nonmonotonicity, the set of autoepistemic consequences of a given premisses cannot be defined as the set of sentences obtained from the premisses by applying some axioms and inference rules. Instead, Moore [1] introduced the following fixed point construction.

Let A be any set of sentences in the modal propositional language. A set of sentences T is said to be a *stable expansion* of A iff

$$T = \{\psi : A \cup \{L\phi : \phi \in T\} \cup \{\neg L\phi : \phi \notin T\} \vdash \psi\}. \tag{1}$$

The sign $\vdash$ denotes here the usual tautological consequence relation. The stable expansion of A may be described informally as the set of beliefs of an ideal rational agent on the basis of the premisses A. Two sets of formulas added in (1) to A are produced by "positive introspection" ($\{L\phi : \phi \in T\}$) and "negative introspection" of the agent.

Moore's work was preceded by McDermott and Doyle's work [4], who attempted to formalise default reasoning, another important form of non-monotonic reasoning. The informal interpretation of $L\phi$ in [4] is "ϕ is provable." (As a primary modal operator, the dual operator $M = \neg L \neg$ is used in [4]; we use L for convenience.) The basic notion of [4] is the *fixed point* of a set A: T is a fixed point of A iff

$$T = \{\psi : A \cup \{\neg L\phi : \phi \notin T\} \vdash \psi\}. \tag{2}$$

Thus stable expansions differ from fixed points by the presence of the term $\{L\phi : \phi \in T\}$ in the right-hand side of the fixed point equation. Informally, fixed points are the possible sets of non-monotonic consequences of A. However, McDermott and Doyle's logic has some peculiarities. The most serious one is that a set of formulas may have a consistent fixed point containing both p and $\neg Lp$, which contradicts the intended interpretation of L.

McDermott [5] fixed this defect of the definition (2) by replacing the provability $\vdash$ in the classical propositional logic by the provability in some system of modal logic (with L identified with the necessity operator). He considered three well-known modal systems as possible bases for non-monotonic logic, namely the systems T, S4 and S5. But only the case of S5 was investigated in [5] in sufficient detail. It turned out that there are too many fixed points in this case; even the empty set (pure non-monotonic S5) has infinitely many fixed points. Moreover, the intersection of all fixed points of A is just the set of all monotonic S5-consequences of A, so that non-monotonic S5 collapses, in some sense, to the monotonic S5. But the non-monotonic T and S4 remained uninvestigated in [5], although, as we show in this paper, they have nice properties.

Moore [1] argued that McDermott and Doyle's logics are logics of autoepistemic reasoning, rather than of default reasoning, and considered his own logic a reconstruction of McDermott and Doyle's logic.

Later, some authors pointed out some defects of Moore's logic. Such defects are of two kinds: first, some sets of formulas have superfluous, or "ungrounded" stable expansions (Konolige [6]); second, some simple theories do not have stable expansions (Morris [7]). Solutions to these problems have been proposed. In order to get rid of superfluous expansions, Konolige [6] introduced the notions of moderately grounded and of strongly grounded extension, which are the strenghenings of the notion of stable expansion. On the other hand, Morris [7] introduced the notion of stable closure, which is a generalisation of the notion of stable expansion.

In this paper we argue that McDermott's non-monotonic modal logics may be viewed as autoepistemic logics, and Moore's logic is one of them, although the most important one. Many problems arising in Moore's logic may be solved within McDermott's logic by an appropriate choice of the underlying modal system. In particular, if we take S4 as the underlying system, then the ungrounded extensions found by Konolige disappear, and the additional extensions introduced by Morris take their place.

Accordingly, we shall call McDermott's non-monotonic modal logics the autoepistemic (modal) logics.

The paper is organized as follows. After some preliminaries in Section 1, we prove in Section 2 that Moore's logic is exactly McDermott's logic based on the modal logic known as "weak S5." In Section 3, the complete description of fixed points for McDermott's logics based on modal logics K, T, S4 and weak S5 is given. The proofs of propositions are collected in Appendix. The theorems are formulated in Appendix in more general (and more technical) form. This enables us to clarify the reasons for the differences between the nonmonotonic logics based on different modal logics; on the other hand, the reader interested only in applications to AI can avoid relatively complicated technical machinery. In Section 4 we apply the general results of Section 3 to concrete situations. In particular, we show, that using S4 as a basis for autoepistemic logic enables to avoid some difficulties appeared in Moore's logic.

1 PRELIMINARIES

We consider the usual propositional modal language with the logical connectives $\vee, \wedge, \supset, \neg$ and with the modal operator L (necessity). All modal logics in question have two inference rules: modus ponens $(\phi, \phi \supset \psi/\psi)$ and necessitation $(\phi/L\phi)$. Their axioms include all instances of propositional tautologies and some axiom schemata from the following list:

K $$L(\phi \supset \psi) \supset (L\phi \supset L\psi)$$

T $$L\phi \supset \phi$$

4 $$L\phi \supset LL\phi$$

5 $$\neg L\phi \supset L\neg L\phi.$$

K is the modal logic based on the single axiom schema K. T is K together with T, S4 is T together with 4, S5 is S4 together with 5, K45 (also called weak S5) is S5 without T.

If S is a logic and Γ is a set of sentences, then $\Gamma \vdash_S \phi$ means that ϕ is deducible from Γ by means of the axioms and inference rules of S. If S is classical propositional logic then we omit the subscript S.

By a *modal logic* we mean any logic in the modal propositional language which contains all instances of propositional tautologies, and whose inference rules are just modus ponens and necessitation.

NB. Some authors (e.g. Chellas [8], Konolige [6]) use $\Gamma \vdash_S \phi$ in a stronger sense: they mean that for some finite subset $\{A_1, \ldots, A_n\}$ of Γ, $\vdash_S (A_1 \wedge \ldots \wedge A_n) \supset \phi$. It is important to distinguish our understanding of $\vdash_S$ from the stronger one. For instance, we have $p \vdash Lp$, and in the stronger sense this this is not true. Our definition follows McDermott [5].

A *Kripke model* is a triple $\mathcal{M} = \langle M, R, V \rangle$, where M is a nonempty set (called the *set of worlds)*, R is a binary relation on M, and for each $\alpha \in M$, $V(\alpha)$ is a set of propositional variables, which are said to be *true* in the world α. The forcing relation $\langle \mathcal{M}, \alpha \rangle \models \phi$ (the formula ϕ is true in the world α of the model M) is defined inductively as follows: $\langle \mathcal{M}, \alpha \rangle \models p$ iff $p \in V(\alpha)$; $\langle \mathcal{M}, \alpha \rangle \models \phi \wedge \psi$ $(\phi \vee \psi)$ iff $\langle \mathcal{M}, \alpha \rangle \models \phi$ and (or) $\langle \mathcal{M}, \alpha \rangle \models \psi$; $\langle \mathcal{M}, \alpha \rangle \models \neg\phi$ iff not $\langle \mathcal{M}, \alpha \rangle \models \phi$; $\langle \mathcal{M}, \alpha \rangle \models L\phi$ iff for each β with $\alpha R \beta$, $\langle \mathcal{M}, \beta \rangle \models \phi$.

We write $\alpha \models \phi$ if it is clear from the context which $\mathcal{M}$ is meant.

We write $\mathcal{M} \models \phi$ iff for each $\alpha \in M$, $\langle \mathcal{M}, \alpha \rangle \models \phi$.

Any Kripke model is also called a K-*model.* If R is reflexive, then the K-model is called a T-*model*; if R is reflexive and transitive, then $\mathcal{M}$ is called an S4-*model*; if R is universal on M (i.e., $R = M \times M$), then $\mathcal{M}$ is called an S5-*model.* If R is transitive and Euclidean (i.e., $\alpha R \beta$ and $\alpha R \gamma$ implies $\beta R \gamma$), then $\mathcal{M}$ is called a K45-*model.* $\Gamma \models_S \phi$ means that for each S-model $\mathcal{M}$, if $\mathcal{M} \models \Gamma$ then $\mathcal{M} \models \phi$. It is well known that, if S is one of K, T, S4, S5 and K45, then, for each Γ and ϕ, $\Gamma \models_S \phi$ iff $\Gamma \vdash_S \phi$ (completeness theorems, see e.g. Chellas [8], McDermott [5]). (In monographs on modal logic, the completeness theorem is usually proved in a weaker form, for the empty Γ only. McDermott deduced the form we need from this weaker form. His method is applicable to any normal mod

A set T of formulas is called an *S-extension* of a set A iff

$$T = \{\psi : A \cup \{\neg L\phi : \phi \notin T\} \vdash_S \psi\}$$

Proposition 1.1. (McDermott [5]). *Let S, T be any normal modal logics contained in S5, and $S \subseteq T$. Then each S-extension of A is also a T-extension of A.*

T is called *stable* iff: (i) T is closed under tautological consequence, (ii) for each ϕ, if $\phi \in T$ then $L\phi \in T$, and (iii) for each ϕ, if $\phi \notin T$ then $\neg L\phi \in T$. Clearly, for each normal logic S, each S-extension is a stable set. T is called an S5-*set* iff for some S5-model $\mathcal{M}$, $T = \{\phi : \mathcal{M} \models \phi\}$. Moore [9] has proved that a consistent set is stable iff it is an S5-set.

An *objective formula* is a formula not containing occurrences of L.

2 MOORE'S LOGIC AND K45

Moore [1, p. 89] established the following connection between his logic and K45: T is a stable expansion of A iff

$$T = \{\psi : A \cup \{L\phi : \phi \in T\} \cup \{\neg L\phi : \phi \notin T\} \vdash_{K45} \psi\}.$$

Konolige [6] strengthened this result: T is a stable expansion of A iff

$$T = \{\psi : A \cup \{L\phi : \phi \in T_0\} \cup \{\neg L\phi : \phi \in \overline{T}_0\} \vdash_{K45} \psi\},$$

where T_0 is the set of all objective formulas in T, and $\overline{T}_0$ is the set of all objective formulas not in T.

Remark. Konolige writes $A \cup LA$ instead of A since he uses $\vdash$ in the stronger sense, see NB in Section 1. (3) is equivalent to Konolige's result since $\vdash_{K45} \phi \supset L\phi$ for each modalized ϕ.

Proposition 2.1. *If T is consistent, then T is a stable expansion of A iff T is a K45-extension of A.*

So Moore's logic may be considered a special case of McDermott's logic.

Remark. Proposition 2.1 fails for an inconsistent T. For instance, the theory $\{\neg Lp\}$ has two stable expansions: a consistent one, which does not contain p, and an inconsistent one (the set of all formulas). Only the consistent expansion is a K45-extension. In the rest of the paper we shall write "stable expansion" for "consistent stable expansion".

3 FORMAL PROPERTIES OF AUTOEPISTEMIC MODAL LOGICS

Konolige [6, p. 355] described a construction which enables us to construct a stable set W_A containing a given set A of objective formulas, such that W_A is a stable expansion of A, and the objective formulas in W_A are exactly the tautulogical consequences of A. W_A is described as an S5-set. We generalize this construction to arbitrary A and investigate in which cases the resulting stable set is an S-extension, and when all S-extensions can be constructed in this way.

By A^L we denote the set of all subformulas of (the elements of) A that begin with L. *A-formulas* are the formulas constructed from the elements of A^L and propositional variables by means of propositional connectives. If Φ is a set of formulas then $\neg\Phi$ denotes $\{\neg\phi : \phi \in \Phi\}$.

Let W be a consistent stable set containing A. Let $\Psi = A^L \cap W$, and $\Phi = A^L \setminus \Psi$. Obviously, if $L\psi \in W$ then $\psi \in W$, and if $L\phi \in \Phi$ then $\phi \notin \Phi$. Hence $A \cup \Phi \cup \Psi \cup \{\psi : L\psi \in \Psi\}$ is consistent,contained in W and does not imply ϕ for any $L\phi \in \Phi$ in the propositional calculus. This motivates the following definition.

Definition 3.1. Let $\Phi \subseteq A^L, \Psi = A^L \setminus \Phi$. Φ is said to be *admissible for A* iff $A \cup \neg\Phi \cup \Psi \cup \{\psi : L\psi \in \Psi\}$ is propositionally consistent and for each $L\phi \in \Phi$, ϕ is not a tautological consequence of $A \cup \neg\Phi \cup \Psi \cup \{\psi : L\psi \in \Psi\}$.

Let V be any valuation assigning the truth values 1 (true) and 0 (false) to propositional letters, and let Φ be any set of formulas beginning with L. Define $V_\Phi(p) = V(p)$ if p is a propositional variable, $V_\Phi(L\phi)$ =(0 if $L\phi \in \Phi$, 1 otherwise), and extend V_Φ to all formulas of modal language by means of the usual truth-tables.

Definition 3.2. Let Φ be admissible for A, $\Psi = A^L \setminus \Phi$. Define the *$\langle A, \Phi\rangle$-generated S5-model* $\mathcal{N}_{A,\Phi} = \langle N_{A,\Phi}, R, U_{A,\Phi}\rangle$ as follows. Set $N_{A,\Phi}$ to be the set of all valuations V such that $V_\Phi(A) = 1$ and for each $L\psi \in \Psi$, $V_\Phi(\psi) = 1$. Set R to be universal on $N_{A,\Phi}$, and for $V \in N_{A,\Phi}$ set $U_{A,\Phi}(V) = \{p : V(p) = 1\}$. Denote $W_{A,\Phi} = \{\phi : \mathcal{N}_{A,\Phi} \models \phi\}$.

$N_{A,\Phi}$ is nonempty, since $A \cup \{\neg L\phi : L\phi \in \Phi\} \cup \Psi \cup \{\psi : L\psi \in \Psi\}$ is propositionally consistent. Consequently, the model $\mathcal{N}_{A,\Phi}$ is well-defined.

Lemma 3.1. *If Φ is admissible for A and ϕ is an A-formula, then for each $V \in N_{A,\Phi}$, $\langle \mathcal{N}_{A,\Phi}, V\rangle \models \phi$ iff $V_\Phi(\phi) = 1$.*

Corollary 3.1. *$W_{A,\Phi}$ is a stable set containing $A \cup \neg\Phi \cup \Psi \cup \{\psi : L\psi \in \Psi\}$.*

Corollary 3.2. *$A \cup \neg\Phi \cup \Psi \cup \{\psi : L\psi \in \Psi\}$ is consistent with S5.*

Each Φ admissible for A defines a theory $W_{A,\Phi}$ which is stable and contains A. First we shall try to investigate in which cases $W_{A,\Phi}$ is an S-extension of A.

Definition 3.3. Let $\Phi \subseteq A^L$, $\Psi = A^L \setminus \Phi$. Φ is said to be *S-admissible for A* iff it is admissible for A and, in addition, for each $L\psi \in \Psi$, $A \cup \neg\Phi \vdash_S \psi$.

Theorem 3.1. *Let S be any modal logic contained in S5, and let Φ be S-admissible for A. Then $W_{A,\Phi}$ is an S-extension of A.*

Does a set Φ, S-admissible for A, uniquely determine the S-extension of A containing $\neg\Phi$? If S is S5 then this this not the case: Even the empty set (which is S5-admissible for itself) has infinitely many S5-extensions. But for many other logics this is the case.

Theorem 3.2. *Let S be any of K, T, S4, K45, and let Φ be S-admissible for A. Then $W_{A,\Phi}$ is the unique S-extension of A containing $A \cup \neg\Phi$.*

Note on the proof. The proof (see Appendix) is rather complicated and uses Kripke models for S. The key property of S which enables us to obtain the result is the following one. Let $\mathcal{M} = \langle M, R, V\rangle$ be an S-model, and let $\alpha \notin M$. Then for some R^* such that

$$R \cup (\{\alpha\} \times Rg(R)) \subseteq R^* \subseteq (\{\alpha\} \times (\{\alpha\} \cup M)) \cup R,$$

$< M \cup \{\alpha\}, R^*, V^* >$ is an S-model for each V^*, too. S5-models do not possess this property, K,T and S4 possess it trivially, and for K45 we can achieve it by a slight modification of the notion of K45-model (preserving, of course, the completeness theorem). The theorem holds for each modal logic possessing the above-mentioned property.□

Another question is whether every S-extension is $W_{A,\Phi}$ for some S-admissible for A set Φ.

Theorem 3.3. *Let S be K,T or S4. Then each S-extension of A equals $W_{A,\Phi}$ for some S-admissible Φ.*

Note on the proof. In addition to the property mentioned above, we need here the following closure property: If $< M, R, U >$ and $< N, Q, V >$ with $M \cap N = \emptyset$ are S-models, then

$$\langle M \cup N, R \cup (M \times N) \cup Q, U \cup V \rangle$$

is an S-model too. K, T and S4 possess this property trivially, but K45 does not. Again the theorem holds for each modal logic possessing these two properties.□

Theorem 3.3 is wrong for K45—for example, $A = \{Lp \supset p\}$ has a stable expansion $W_{A,\emptyset}$, but $\emptyset$ is not K45-admissible for A.

Definition 3.4. Let Φ be admissible for A, $\Psi = A^L \setminus \Phi$. Φ is said to be *propositionally admissible for A* iff for each $L\psi \in \Psi$, ψ is a tautological consequence of $A \cup \neg\Phi \cup \Psi$.

Theorem 3.4. *T is a stable expansion (or K45-extension) of A iff T is $W_{A,\Phi}$ for some Φ which is propositionally admissible for A.*

Theorem 3.4 can be obtained as a corollary to Theorems 1.1 and 1.2, see Appendix. In [10] we presented a simpler proof without any use of modal logic.

4 APPLICATIONS

Proposition 4.1. *Let S be any modal logic for which Theorem 3.2 is true, and let A be any set of objective sentences consistent with S. Then A has $W_{A,\emptyset}$ as its unique S-extension.*

Proposition 4.1 for the empty A was proved in [11] (directly, not as a corollary to the general theorems from the previous section).

For Moore's logic, this fact was established by Konolige [6]. Thus, for objective axioms there is no difference between autoepistemic K, T, S4, K45. But for arbitrary axioms all these logics are different.

The following two examples are taken from [11] too, but here we explain them more simply using the general results of Section 2.

Example 4.1. Let $A = \{L(Lp \supset LLp) \supset p\}$. In S4 this formula is equivalent to p. So, by Proposition 4.1, A has a unique S4-extension, namely $T = W_{p,\emptyset}$. Let A have a T-extension. Then, by Proposition 1.1, it must be T. Hence, by Proposition 3.2, $\emptyset$ is T-admissible for A, i.e., $A \vdash_T p$, which is wrong. So A has no T-extensions.

Example 4.2. $B = \{\neg Lp \supset p\}$ is known to have no stable expansions. But $B \vdash_T p$, hence $\emptyset$ is T-admissible for B, and B has a T-extension.

Example 4.3.. Consider the theory $C = \{Lp \wedge Lq \supset p \wedge q, \neg Lp \supset p\}$. Since $C \cup \{Lp, Lq\} \vdash p \wedge q$, $\emptyset$ is propositionally admissible for C, so $W_{C,\emptyset}$ is a stable expansion of C. It may be easily shown that there is no other set propositionally admissible for C. On the other hand, $\{Lq\}$ is the only set S4-admissible for C, so that $W_{C,Lq}$ is the only S4- extension of C. Thus, C has one S4-extension and one stable expansion, and the two are different.

$A = \{Lp \supset p\}$ has two K45-extensions, namely $T_1 = W_{A,\{Lp\}}$ and $T_2 = W_{A,\emptyset}$, but only the former is an S4-extension. These facts may be established using the results of Section 3.

Konolige [6] considered two examples:

$$A = \{Lp \supset p\},\ B = \{\neg Lp \supset q, Lp \supset p\}.$$

A has two stable expansions, T_1 and T_2, described above. Konolige considered T_2 an "anomalous" extension, since then "the agent's belief in P is grounded in her assumption that she believes P." In order to avoid this situation, Konolige introduced the notion of moderately grounded extension, and T_2 turned out to be not moderately grounded.

B has two extensions: $S_1 = W_{B,\{Lp\}}$ and $S_2 = W_{B,\emptyset}$. Konolige regards S_2 as anomalous too, but both S_1 and S_2 are moderately grounded. To eliminate S_2, he introduced the concept of strongly grounded extension—a rather complicated definition possessing some undesirable properties.

We suggest another possibility. If we consider, e.g., S4-extensions instead of K45-extensions, then T_2 and S_2 fail to be extensions, but T_1 and S_1 remain.

Let us consider, on the other hand, some examples of the lack of extensions. Morris [7] gives two such examples (we have simplified his notation).

The axiom set

$$C = \{\neg LB \supset A,\ \neg LA \supset \neg F,\ \neg LB \supset F, \neg F\}$$

is a "simplified taxonomy example". Here A should be understood as "Tweety is an abnormal animal", B should be understood as "Tweety is an abnormal bird", F should be understood as "Tweety can fly".

The second example is

$$D = \{\neg Lq \supset p, \neg Lr \supset \neg p\}$$

(the "Nixon paradox"; q stands for "Nixon is a Quaker", r stands for "Nixon is a Republican", p stands for "Nixon is a pacifist").

Morris considers it anomalous that C and D do not have stable expansions. He introduced the notion of stable closure. C has one stable closure, and D has two. Using the results of Section 3, we conclude that C has the unique S4-extension $W_{C,\{LA\}}$, and D has two S4-extensions, $W_{D,\{Lq\}}$ and $W_{D,\{Lr\}}$. All these extensions exactly coincide with Morris's stable closures.

Lifschitz [personal communication] considered it unsatisfactory that $\{Lp\}$ has no stable expansions. Again, $\{Lp\}$ has the unique S4-extension, which contains Lp and p.

Thus the use of S4-extensions instead of stable expansions allows us to avoid some "ungrounded" extensions and, on the other hand, to add some new extensions required in applications. But we do not assert that autoepistemic S4 is always "better" than Moore's logic. We only wanted to demostrate that the problems of different kind may get a uniform solution. We think that different aspects of autoepistemic reasoning should be reflected by different formalisations.

APPENDIX. PROOFS OF PROPOSITIONS

Proposition 2.1. *If T is consistent, then T is a stable expansion of A iff T is a K45-extension of A.*

Proof. Let T be a consistent stable expansion of A. Moore [1, p.89] proved that stable expansions contain all instances of all K45-axioms. Since T is closed under the necessitation rule, we have for each ψ,

$$\psi \in T \text{ iff } A \cup \{L\phi : \phi \in T\} \cup \{\neg L\phi : \phi \notin T\} \vdash_{K45} \psi.$$

If $\phi \in T$, then $L\phi \in T$, hence $\neg L\phi \notin T$. But $\neg L \neg L\phi \supset L\phi$ is a theorem of K45, hence for each $\phi \in T$, $\{\neg L\phi : \phi \notin T\} \vdash_{K45} L\phi$. Hence T is a K45-extension.

Let T be a K45-extension. Let $\mathcal{P}$ be propositional calculus augmented by the necessitation rule. Let Ax be the set of all instances of the modal axiom schemes of K45. Then for each ψ,

$$\psi \in T \text{ iff } A \cup \{\neg L\phi : \phi \notin T\} \cup Ax \vdash_{\mathcal{P}} \psi.$$

Hence

$$\psi \in T \text{ iff } A \cup \{\neg L\phi : \phi \notin T\} \cup \{L\phi : \phi \in T\} \cup Ax \vdash \psi$$

Moore [1, p. 89, the last paragraph of Section 4] proved, that this is equivalent to

$$\psi \in T \text{ iff } A \cup \{\neg L\phi : \phi \notin T\} \cup \{L\phi : \phi \in T\} \vdash \psi,$$

which proves the proposition.□

Lemma 3.1. *If Φ is admissible for A and ϕ is an A-formula, then for each $V \in N_{A,\Phi}$, $\langle \mathcal{N}_{A,\Phi}, V\rangle \models \phi$ iff $V_\Phi(\phi) = 1$.*

Proof. By induction on the complexity of ϕ. The only nontrivial case is when ϕ has the form $L\eta$ in the induction step. Since $L\eta \in A^L$, we have $L\eta \in \Phi$ or $L\eta \in \Psi$.

Let $V_\Phi(L\eta) = 0$. Then $L\eta \in \Phi$ and

$$A \cup \neg\Phi \cup \Psi \cup \{\psi : L\psi \in \Psi\} \nvdash \eta.$$

Since $\Phi \cup \Psi = A^L$, there exists a valuation W such that

$$W_\Phi(A) = W_\Phi(\{\psi : L\psi \in \Psi\}) = 1 \text{ and } W_\Phi(\eta) = 0.$$

This W is an element of $N_{A,\Phi}$; hence, by the induction hypothesis, $\langle \mathcal{N}, W\rangle \not\models \eta$, so that $\langle \mathcal{N}, V\rangle \models \neg L\eta$.

Let $V_\Phi(L\eta) = 1$. Then $L\eta \in \Psi$, hence for each $W \in N_{A,\Phi}$, $W_\Phi(\eta) = 1$. Hence, by the induction hypothesis, $W \models \eta$ for each $W \in N$, and $V \models L\eta$.□

Corollary 3.1. *$W_{A,\Phi}$ is a stable set containing $A \cup \neg\Phi \cup \Psi \cup \{\psi : L\psi \in \Psi\}$.*

Proof. Immediately follows from Lemma 3.1. (Recall that $W_{A,\Phi}$ is $\{\phi : \langle \mathcal{N}_{A,\Phi}, V\rangle \models \phi.\}$)□

Corollary 3.2. *$A \cup \neg\Phi \cup \Psi \cup \{\psi : L\psi \in \Psi\}$ is consistent with S5.*

Proof. All formulas in this set are true in the S5-model $\mathcal{N}_{A,\Phi}$. □

Untill the end of Appendix, we shall write $\mathcal{N}$ for $\mathcal{N}_{A,\Phi}$ and N for $N_{A,\Phi}$.

Theorem 3.1. *Let S be any modal logic contained in S5, and let Φ be S-admissible for A. Then $W_{A,\Phi}$ is an S-extension of A.*

Proof. It is sufficient to prove that for each ϕ and for $B = \{\neg L\eta : \text{for some } \alpha, \langle \mathcal{N}, \alpha \rangle \not\models \eta\}$,

$$\mathcal{N} \models \phi \text{ iff } A \cup B \vdash_S \phi \tag{A1}$$

The "if" part follows from Corollary 3.1, because S5 contains S.

Let us prove the "only if" part by induction on the maximal nesting depth of L in ϕ, $m(\phi)$. Assume that the "only if" part of (A1) is valid for each ϕ with $m(\phi) < n$, and assume $m(\phi) = n$ and $\mathcal{N} \models \phi$. We may assume that ϕ is in the conjunctive normal form, i.e., ϕ is $\phi_1 \wedge \ldots \wedge \phi_k$, and each ϕ_i has the form

$$\psi \vee \neg L\eta_1 \vee \ldots \vee \neg L\eta_l \wedge L\zeta_1 \vee \ldots \vee L\zeta_m \tag{A2}$$

with $m(\psi) = 0$, $l, m \geq 0$ and $\mathcal{N} \models \phi_i$.

If for some j and for some α, $\langle \mathcal{N}, \alpha \rangle \models \neg L\eta_j$, then for some β, $\langle \mathcal{N}, \beta \rangle \not\models \eta_j$. Hence $\neg L\eta_j \in B$ and $A \cup B \vdash_S \phi_i$.

If for some α and for some j, $\langle \mathcal{N}, \alpha \rangle \models L\zeta_j$, then $\mathcal{N} \models \zeta_j$. But $m(\zeta_j) < n$, hence, by the induction hypothesis, $A \cup B \vdash_S \zeta_j$. Applying the necessitation rule and the propositional logic, we obtain the derivability of ϕ_i.

The only remaining case is that of

$$\mathcal{N} \models L\eta_1 \wedge \ldots \wedge L\eta_l \wedge \neg L\zeta_1 \wedge \ldots \wedge \neg L\zeta_m.$$

Since $\mathcal{N} \models \phi_i$, we conclude $\mathcal{N} \models \psi$ from (A2). By Lemma 3.1, this means that ψ is a tautological consequence of $A \cup \neg\Phi \cup \Psi \cup \{\psi : L\psi \in \Psi\}$. Since Φ is S-admissible for A, and S contains the necessitation rule, we get $A \cup \neg\Phi \vdash_S \psi$. Hence $A \cup B \vdash_S \phi_i$. Thus, $A \cup B \vdash_S \phi_i$ in each case for each i, so that $A \cup B \vdash \phi$.□

A *frame* is a pair $\langle M, R \rangle$, where R is a binary relation on M.

Definition A1. Let S be a modal logic, and let $\mathcal{K}$ be a class of frames. We say that S *is characterized* by $\mathcal{K}$ if, for each set of formulas Γ and each formula ϕ, $\Gamma \vdash \phi$ if and only if the following condition is satisfied: For each Kripke model $\mathcal{M} = \langle M, R, V \rangle$ with $\langle M, R \rangle \in \mathcal{K}$, $\mathcal{M} \models \Gamma$ implies $\mathcal{M} \models \phi$.

We can say, for instance, that K is characterized by the class of all frames, T is characterized by the class of all reflexive frames, S4 is characterized by the class of all reflexive transitive frames, and S5 is characterized by the class of all universal frames (i.e., frames of the form $\langle M, M \times M \rangle$). K45 is characterized by the class of all transitive Euclidean frames.

Definition A2. Let $\mathcal{K}$ be a class of frames. We say that $\mathcal{K}$ *admits a quasi-amalgamation* if, for each $\langle M, R \rangle \in \mathcal{K}$ and for $\alpha_0 \notin M$, there exists a frame $\langle M \cup \{\alpha_0\}, R^* \rangle \in \mathcal{K}$ such that

$$(\{\alpha_0\} \times Rg(R)) \cup R \subseteq R^* \subseteq [\{\alpha_0\} \times (\{\alpha_0\} \cup M)] \cup R.$$

Such a frame is called *a quasi-amalgamation of $\langle M, R \rangle$ in $\mathcal{K}$.*

The notion of quasi-amalgamation is a generalisation of the well-known notion of amalgamation (see, for instance, Hughes and Cresswell [12]).

The classes of all frames, of all reflexive frames and of all reflexive and transitive frames admit a quasi-amalgamation. In each of these cases, a quasi-amalgamation of a frame $\langle M, R\rangle$ is given by the expression $\langle M \cup \{\alpha_0\}, R \cup \{\alpha_0\} \times (\{\alpha_0\} \cup M)\rangle$.

Theorem A1. *Let $\mathcal{K}$ be a class of frames admitting a quasi-amalgamation. Let S be characterized by $\mathcal{K}$, and let Φ be S-admissible for A. Then $W_{A,\Phi}$ is the only consistent S-extension of A containing $\neg\Phi$.*

Proof. $W_{A,\Phi}$ is an S-extension of A by Theorem 3.1, and contains $\neg\Phi$ by Corollary 3.1.

Let T be any consistent S-extension of A, and let $\neg\Phi \subseteq T$. T is stable; on the other hand, Moore [3] proved that stable sets coincide iff they contain the same objective formulas. Thus it is sufficient to prove that, for each ϕ with $m(\phi) = 0$,

$$\phi \in S \text{ if and only if } \mathcal{N} \models \phi.$$

Let us prove the "if" part first. If for each $\alpha \in N$, $\langle \mathcal{N}, \alpha\rangle \models \phi$, then, by Lemma 3.1, ϕ is a tautological consequence of $A \cup \neg\Phi \cup \Psi \cup \{\psi : L\psi \in \Psi\}$. Since Φ is S-admissible and S contains the necessitation rule, we have $A \cup \neg\Phi \vdash_S \phi$. But $A \cup \neg\Phi \subseteq T$ and T is deductively closed under S; hence $\phi \in S$.

"Only if": Assume that $\phi \in T$ but, for some $V \in N_{A,\Phi}$, $\langle \mathcal{N}, V\rangle \models \neg\phi$. Fix these V and ϕ. Since T is consistent with S, there is a Kripke model $\mathcal{M} = \langle M, R, W\rangle$ with $\langle M, R\rangle \in \mathcal{K}$ and $\mathcal{M} \models T$.

Consider the Kpipke model $\mathcal{M}^* = \langle M \cup \{\alpha_0\}, R^*, W^*\rangle$, where $\langle M \cup \{\alpha_0\}, R^*\rangle$ is a quasi-amalgamation of $\langle M, R\rangle$ in $\mathcal{K}$, $W^*(\alpha) = W(\alpha)$ for $\alpha \in M$, and $W^*(\alpha_0) = U_{A,\Phi}(V)$. Let us prove by induction on the complexity of ψ that, for each A-formula ψ,

$$\langle \mathcal{M}^*, \alpha_0\rangle \models \psi \text{ if and only if} \langle \mathcal{N}, V\rangle \models \psi. \tag{A3}$$

The only nontrivial step in the proof is the case when ψ has the form $L\eta$ in the induction step. Since $L\eta \in A^L$, we have $L\eta \in \Psi$ or $L\eta \in \Phi$.

If $\langle \mathcal{N}, V\rangle \not\models L\eta$, then $L\eta \in \Phi$ by Corollary 3.1. Hence $\neg L\eta \in T$, and, for some $\beta \in Rg(R), \langle \mathcal{M}, \beta\rangle \not\models \eta$. Hence $\langle \mathcal{M}^*, \beta\rangle \not\models \eta$. By Definition 2.3, $\alpha_0 R^* \beta$. Thus $\langle \mathcal{M}^*, \alpha_0\rangle \models \neg L\eta$.

If $\langle \mathcal{N}, V\rangle \models L\eta$, then $L\eta \in \Psi$. Hence, by Corollary 3.1, $\langle \mathcal{N}, V\rangle \models \eta$, and, by the induction hypothesis,

$$\langle \mathcal{M}^*, \alpha_0\rangle \models \eta. \tag{A4}$$

Since $A \cup \neg\Phi \subseteq T$, and Φ is admissible, we have $\eta \in T$. Hence, for all $\beta \in M$, $\langle \mathcal{M}^*, \beta\rangle \models \eta$. Then, from (A4), $\langle \mathcal{M}^*, \alpha_0\rangle \models L\eta$. (A3) is proven.

We have

$$T = Th_S(A \cup \{\neg L\psi : \psi \notin T\}). \tag{A5}$$

From (A3) and Corollary 3.1 we get:

$$\langle \mathcal{M}^*, \alpha_0\rangle \models A. \tag{A6}$$

For each $\psi \notin T$, for some $\beta \in Rg(R)$ we have $\langle \mathcal{M}^*, \beta\rangle \not\models \psi$; hence $\langle \mathcal{M}^*, \alpha_0\rangle \models \neg L\psi$. Since $\mathcal{M} \models T$, using (A5) and (A6) we get $\mathcal{M}^* \models T$. Hence $\langle \mathcal{M}^*, \alpha_0\rangle \models \phi$. But from (A3) and our assumption we get $\langle \mathcal{M}^*, \alpha_0\rangle \models \neg\phi$, contradiction.□

Theorem 3.2. *Let S be any of K, T, S4, K45, and let Φ be S-admissible for A. Then $W_{A,\Phi}$ is the unique S-extension of A containing $A \cup \neg\Phi$.*

Proof. The classes of all frames, of all reflexive frames, of all reflexive transitive frames characterize, respectively, the logics K, T and S4, so that we can apply Theorem A1. The class of all transitive Euclidean frames, which is known to characterize K45, does not admit a quasi-amalgamation. Let us call a frame $\langle M, R\rangle$ *strongly Euclidean* if it is transitive and, for each α and β from $Rg(R)$, $\alpha R\beta$. $\langle M \cup \{\alpha\}, \{\alpha\} \times Rg(R)\rangle$ is a quasi-amalgamation of this frame, and it is strongly Euclidean if the initial frame is strongly Euclidean. If $\langle M, R\rangle$ is transitive and Euclidean, then for $\alpha \in M$ the frame $\langle\{\beta \in M : \alpha = \beta \text{ or } \alpha R\beta\}, R|\{\beta \in M : \alpha = \beta \text{ or } \alpha R\beta\}\rangle$ is strongly Euclidean. From this fact we can easy deduce that K45 is characterized by class of all strongly Euclidean frames, and apply Theorem A1.□

Definition A3.. A class $\mathcal{K}$ of frames is said to be *closed* iff, for all $\langle M_1, R_1\rangle \in \mathcal{K}$ and $\langle M_2, R_2\rangle \in \mathcal{K}$ with $M_1 \cap M_2 = \emptyset$, the frame $\langle M_1 \cup M_2, R_1 \cup (M_1 \times M_2) \cup R_2\rangle$ belongs to $\mathcal{K}$, and $\mathcal{K}$ contains, along with each frame, all frames isomorphic to it.

Lemma A1. *Let $\Phi \subseteq A^L$, $\Psi = A^L \setminus \Phi$. Let $\mathcal{M}_1 = \langle M_1, R_1, V_1\rangle$ and $\mathcal{M}_2 = \langle M_2, R_2, V_2\rangle$ be Kripke models such that $M_1 \cap M_2 = \emptyset$, $\mathcal{M}_1 \models \neg\Phi$ and $\mathcal{M}_2 \models \psi$ for all $L\psi \in \Psi$. Let $\mathcal{M}$ be $\langle M_1 \cup M_2, R_1 \cup (M_1 \times M_2) \cup R_2\rangle$. Then, for each A-formula ϕ and for each $\alpha \in M_1$,*

$$\langle \mathcal{M}_1, \alpha\rangle \models \phi \text{ if and only if} \langle \mathcal{M}, \alpha\rangle \models \phi.$$

Proof. By induction on the complexity of ϕ. The only nontrivial step in the proof is the case when ϕ has the form $L\psi$.

Let $\langle \mathcal{M}, \alpha\rangle \models L\psi$. Then, for each $\beta \in M_1$ with $\alpha R_1 \beta$, $\langle \mathcal{M}, \beta\rangle \models \psi$. Hence, by the induction hypothesis, for all such β, $\langle \mathcal{M}_1, \beta\rangle \models \psi$, which means that $\langle \mathcal{M}_1, \alpha\rangle \models \phi$.

Let $\langle \mathcal{M}, \alpha\rangle \not\models L\psi$. Then, for some β with $\alpha R\beta$, $\langle \mathcal{M}, \beta\rangle \not\models \psi$. If $\beta \in M_1$, then, using the induction hypothesis, we get $\langle \mathcal{M}_1, \alpha\rangle \not\models L\psi$. Let $\beta \in M_2$. If $L\psi \in \Psi$, then $\mathcal{M}_2 \not\models \psi$, which contradicts the assumptions of the lemma. Thus, $L\psi \in \Phi$. Hence $\mathcal{M}_1 \models \neg L\psi$, and $\langle \mathcal{M}_1, \alpha\rangle \not\models L\psi$.
□

Theorem A2. *Let $\mathcal{K}$ be a closed class of frames, and let S be characterized by $\mathcal{K}$. Let T be any consistent S-extension of A. Let $\Psi = T \cap A^L$, and let $\Phi = A^L \setminus \Psi$. Then Φ is S-admissible for A.*

Proof. Since T is consistent with S, there is a model $\mathcal{M}_2 = \langle M_2, R_2, V_2\rangle$ with $\langle M_2, R_2\rangle \in \mathcal{K}$, $\mathcal{M}_2 \models T$. Since $A \cup \neg\Phi \subseteq T$, $A \cup \neg\Phi$ is consistent with S.

Let $L\psi \in \Psi$; since T is stable, $\psi \in T$.

Assume, on the contrary, that

$$A \cup \neg\Phi \not\vdash_S \psi. \tag{A7}$$

Then there is a model $\mathcal{M}_1 = \langle M_1, R_1, V_1\rangle$ with $\langle M_1, R_1\rangle \in \mathcal{K}$, $\mathcal{M}_1 \models A \cup \neg\Phi$, such that, for some $\alpha \in M_1$,

$$\langle M_1, \alpha\rangle \not\models \psi. \tag{A9}$$

We may assume $M_1 \cap M_2 = \emptyset$. Consider the model

$$\mathcal{M} = \langle M_1 \cup M_2, R_1 \cup (M_1 \times M_2) \cup R_2, V_1 \cup V_2\rangle.$$

By Lemma A1, $\mathcal{M} \models A$; clearly, for each $\neg L\psi \in T$, $\mathcal{M} \models \neg L\psi$. Since T is an S-extension of A, and $\mathcal{M}$ is a model of S, we have $\mathcal{M} \models T$. Hence $\mathcal{M} \models \psi$. But by (A8) and Lemma A1, $\langle \mathcal{M}, \alpha \rangle \not\models \psi$, contradiction. Thus (A7) is false, and Φ is S-admissible for A. □

Theorem 3.3. *Let S be K,T or S4. Then each S-extension of A equals $W_{A,\Phi}$ for some S-admissible Φ.*

Proof. The classes of all frames, of all reflexive frames and of all reflexive transitive frames all are closed and admit a quasi-amalgamation. The theorem follows from Theorems A2 and A1.□

Theorem 3.4. *T is a stable expansion (or K45-extension) of A iff T is $W_{A,\Phi}$ for some Φ which is propositionally admissible for A.*

Proof. Let $\Phi \subseteq A^L$, let Φ be propositionally admissible for A, and let $\Psi = A^L \setminus \Phi$. Let $B = A \cup \{\psi : L\psi \in \Psi\}$. We have $B \cup \neg\Phi \vdash \psi$ for each $\psi \in \Psi$. Hence Φ is S-admissible for B for each S contained in S5, and, in particular for K45. By Theorem 3.1 and Proposition 2.1, B has a stable expansion $T = W_{B,\Phi}$. Using the definition of $W_{B,\Phi}$, we conclude that $W_{B,\Phi} = W_{A,\Phi}$. Since, for each $L\psi \in \Psi$,

$$A \cup \{L\psi : \psi \in T\} \cup \{\neg L\psi : \psi \notin T\} \vdash \psi,$$

T is a stable expansion of A too.

Conversely, let T be a stable expansion of A. Let $\Psi = A^L \cup T$, $\Phi = A^L \setminus \Psi$. Let $L\psi \in \Psi$. Then ψ is a tautological consequence of $A \cup \{L\psi : \psi \in T\} \cup \{\neg L\psi : \psi \notin T\}$. Since $\psi \in A^L$, ψ is a tautological consequence of $A \cup \Psi \cup \neg\Phi$ also. Thus Φ is propositionally admissible for A.

Consider $B = A \cup \{\psi : L\psi \in \Psi\}$. $B \subseteq T$, so that T is a $K45$-extension of B, too. We have $B^L = A^L$ and, trivially, for $L\psi \in \Psi$, $B \cup \neg\Phi \vdash \psi$. Hence Φ is $K45$-admissible for B. Hence, by Theorem 3.2, T equals to $W_{B,\Phi}$. Let us recall the construction of the model $\mathcal{N}_{A,\Phi}$: We see that $W_{A,\Phi}$ coincides with $W_{B,\Phi}$.□

Proposition 4.1. *Let S be any modal logic for which Theorem 3.2 is true, and let A be any set of objective sentences consistent with S. Then A has $W_{A,\emptyset}$ as its unique S-extension.*

Proof. $A^L = \emptyset$, so that $\emptyset$ is trivially admissible for A. Apply Theorem 3.2.□

Acknowledgments

I am greatly indebted to Vladimir Lifschitz for the help in different ways. Discussions with Vladimir were very usefull and stimulating; he sent me newest papers on nonmonotonic logic, which are hardly available in the USSR, especially in such a little provincial town as Pereslavl-Zalessky. Vladimir polished my terrible English and helped to prepare camera-ready empy of the paper by using TEX.

The final version was prepared when I was in Stanford University as a visiting scholar. I am thankful to Professors Patrick Suppes and John McCarthy for the invitation to visit Stanford and for the help in arranging my visit.

References

[1] Moore, R.C., Semantical considerations on nonmonotonic logic. *Artificial Intelligence*, **25** (1985), 75–94.

[2] Stalnaker, R.A., *A Note on Non-Monotonic Modal Logic.* Department of Philosophy, Cornell University (1980).

[3] Lifschitz, V., The mathematics of nonmonotonic reasoning. *Proc. LICS-89.*

[4] McDermott, D. and Doyle, J., Nonmonotonic logic I. *Artificial Intelligence*, **13** (1980), 41–72.

[5] McDermott, D., Nonmonotonic logic II: Nonmonotonic modal theories. *Journal of the ACM*, **29**, 33–57.

[6] Konolige, K., On the relation between default and autoepistemic logic. *Artificial Intelligence*, **35** (1988), 342–382.

[7] Morris, P., Autoepistemic stable closures and contradiction resolution. In: Reinfrank e.a. (Eds.), *Non-Monotonic Reasoning (Lecture Notes in Artificial Intelligence, v.346)*, Springer, 1988, 60–73.

[8] Chellas, B.F., *Modal Logic: an Introduction.* Cambridge University Press, 1980.

[9] Moore, R.C., Possible world semantics for autoepistemic logic. In: M.Ginsberg (Ed.), *Readings on Non-Monotonic Reasoning.* Morgan Kaufmann, 1987, 137–142.

[10] Shvarts, G.F., Stable extensions of autoepistemic theories. In: *All-Union Conference on Artificial Intelligence (Proceedings)*, v. 1, 1988, 483–487 (in Russian).

[11] Shvarts, G.F., Nonmonotonic logics based on different modal logics. In:*COLOG-88. Papers Presented at the International Conference on Computer Logic. Part 2.* Tallinn, 1988.

[12] Hughes, G.E., Cresswell, M.J., *A Companion to Modal Logic.* Methuen, London, 1984.

References

EPISTEMIC SEMANTICS FOR FIXED-POINTS NON-MONOTONIC LOGICS

Fangzhen Lin
Yoav Shoham
Department of Computer Science
Stanford University

Abstract

Default Logic and Autoepistemic Logic are the two best-known fixed-points nonmonotonic logics. Despite the fact that they are known to be closely related and that the epistemic nature of Autoepistemic Logic is obvious, the only semantics that have been offered for Default Logic to date are complex and have little to do with epistemic notions [Etherington 1987]. In this paper we provide simple uniform epistemic semantics for the two logics. We do so by translating them both into a new logic, called GK, of Grounded Knowledge, which embodies a modification of preference semantics [Shoham 1987]. Beside their simplicity and uniformity, the semantics have two other advantages: They allow easy proofs of the connections between Default Logic and Autoepistemic Logic, and suggest a general class of logics of which the two logics are special cases.

1 INTRODUCTION

Existing nonmonotonic logics can be divided roughly into two kinds. One is based on fixed points, like default logic [Reiter 1980] or autoepistemic logic ([Moore 1983], [Konolige 1988], and [Levesque 1989]). The other is based on minimal models, like circumscription ([McCarthy 1980, 1984] and [Lifschitz 1987]) or minimal knowledge ([Halpern and Moses 1984], [Shoham 1987], and [Lin 1988]). While all those that are based on minimal models have a clear and intuitive semantics, some of those that are based on fixed-points do not have one yet. In spite of the fact that autoepistemic logic has a clear possible worlds semantics, and a close correspondence has been established between default and autoepistemic logics [Konolige 1988], similar semantics for default logic are still missing.[1]

[1]Etherington (1987) provides the first semantics for default logic. The semantics seem complicated and have little to do with autoepistemic logic, in spite of the close relationship between the two logics.

In this paper we provide a possible-world epistemic semantics for default logic as well as for autoepistemic logic. Among other things, the semantics clearly show the relationship, both similarities and differences, between the two logics. The semantics are largely in the spirit of Shoham's preference semantics [Shoham 1987]. In fact, they are largely motivated by the failure of Shoham's early attempt to provide preference semantics for default logic. Shoham's key idea is to translate a closed default

$$p : q/r$$

into something like

$$Kp \wedge \neg K \neg q \supset Kr$$

with knowledge (K) minimized. Although the translation works for normal defaults, i.e. when q and r are identical, it does not work for the general case. Intuitively speaking, the translation fails due to its wrong interpretation of the above default as "if p is known and $\neg q$ is not known (q is consistent) to be true, then r is also known to be true." This wrong interpretation does not meet the requirement that knowledge be not only minimal but also *grounded.* Our new semantics can be thought of accounting for groundedness of knowledge by the following informal reading of the same default rule: "if p is known to be true and $\neg q$ is not *assumed* to be true (q is *assumed* to be consistent), then r is known to be true – provided the assumption of the consistency of q can eventually be justified."

This suggests employing *two* epistemic modalities, K (for knowledge) and A (for assumption), which will be related to one another. Indeed, we will translate the above default rule into the sentence

$$Kp \wedge \neg A \neg q \supset Kr$$

and the process of justifying the assumption that q is consistent will correspond to first minimizing the knowledge K with A fixed, and then comparing the resulting knowledge and assumptions to see whether they agree.

Interestingly, the treatment of autoepistemic logic will be almost identical. It was shown in [Konolige 1988] that any autoepistemic theory can be transformed into an equivalent one in which every sentence has the form

$$Lp \wedge \neg L \neg q_1 \wedge \ldots \wedge \neg L \neg q_n \supset r$$

We will translate each such sentence into

$$Ap \wedge \neg A \neg q_1 \wedge \ldots \wedge \neg A \neg q_n \supset Kr$$

and keep the rest as in the default logic translation. Thus the only change required when moving from default logic to autoepistemic logic is the replacement of the first K by an A!

We now proceed to make this precise. We first define our basic logical language, which is simply a propositional one augmented by two epistemic modalities. Then in section 3 we define the logic GK of Grounded Knowledge, which is the result of imposing an augmented version of preference semantics on our basic language. In section 4 we offer translations of both default logic and autoepistemic logic into GK, translations that are similar but subtly different. We prove the correctness of the translations, and show how the common framework explicates the relationhsip between the two logics. Finally in section 5, we outline some of our ongoing further work.

2 THE BASIC LOGICAL LANGUAGE

Our language is a propositional one, augmented with two modalities K and A, which are at this point mutually unconstrained. Well-formed formulas are defined as usual. Intuitively $K\varphi$ means that φ is known or believed (the distinctions between the two are not important in this paper) to be true, while $A\varphi$ means that φ is assumed to be true.

A *Kripke structure* is a tuple (W, π, R_K, R_A), where W is a nonempty set, $\pi(w)$ a truth assignment to the primitive propositions for each $w \in W$, and R_K, R_A are binary relations over W (the accessibility relations for K and A, respectively). A *Kripke interpretation* M is a pair $(w, (W, \pi, R_K, R_A))$, where $w \in W$ and (W, π, R_K, R_A) is a Kripke structure.

We have not placed restrictions on the two accessibility relations so far. Indeed, our results are surprisingly insensitive to the properties of these relations. In particular, the reader may assume any of the major systems that have been used to capture epistemic notions – $S5$, $K45$, $KD45$ or $S4$.

The satisfaction relation "$\models$" between Kripke interpretations and formulas is defined as follows:

1. $(w, (W, \pi, R, T)) \models p$ iff $\pi(w)(p) = 1$, where p is a primitive proposition.
2. $M \models \varphi_1 \vee \varphi_2$ iff $M \models \varphi_1$ or $M \models \varphi_2$.
3. $M \models \neg\varphi$ iff it is not the case that $M \models \varphi$.
4. $(w, (W, \pi, R_K, R_A)) \models K\varphi$ iff $(w', (W, \pi, R_K, R_A)) \models \varphi$ for any $w' \in W$ such that $(w, w') \in R_K$.
5. $(w, (W, \pi, R_K, R_A)) \models A\varphi$ iff $(w', (W, \pi, R_K, R_A)) \models \varphi$ for any $w' \in W$ such that $(w, w') \in R_A$.

We say that a Kripke interpretation M is a *model* of a set of formulas S if M satisfies every member of S.

We conclude this section with two definitions that will be used throughout the remainder of the paper:

$$K(M) = \{\varphi \mid M \models K\varphi, \varphi \text{ is a base formula}\}$$

$$A(M) = \{\varphi \mid M \models A\varphi, \varphi \text{ is a base formula}\}$$

where a *base formula* is one that does not contain modal operators.

3 PREFERENCE SEMANTICS AND THE LOGIC GK

In this section we modify the semantics of our basic language, defining the logic GK. We will augment the semantical framework for nonmonotonic logics developed by Shoham (1987). Shoham's basic idea is that a nonmonotonic logic (called a *preference logic* by Shoham) can be viewed semantically as the result of imposing a partial order (called a *preference relation*) "$\sqsubset$" on interpretations of a monotonic logic. The syntax of the resulting logic is unchanged, but the definition of semantic entailment changes: Φ now entails φ if φ is true in all models of Φ that are minimal according to that partial order (but not necessarily in all models of Φ). This new notion of entailment is called *preferential entailment*, and is denoted by $\models_{\sqsubset}$. We start by endowing our basic language with such preference semantics.

To do so we define a preference relation on the Kripke interepretations defined in the previous section. The following relation "$\sqsubset$" has the effect of minimizing knowledge with assumptions fixed.

Definition 3.1 *Let M_i, $i = 1, 2$, be two Kripke interpretations. We say that M_1 is preferred over M_2, written $M_1 \sqsubset M_2$, if*

1. $A(M_1) = A(M_2)$
2. $K(M_1) \subset K(M_2)$.

M is a *minimal* model of S if M is a model of S and there is no other model M' of S such that $M' \sqsubset M$.

These semantics, however, are not sufficient for our purposes, as they do not capture the property of "groundedness" of knowledge. As was said in the introduction, the assumptions made by the agent should be justified. We capture this justification by an added requirement of the minimal models – that the assumptions coincide with the knowledge. This naturally leads to the following definition:

Definition 3.2 *Let S be a set of formulas, and M a Kripke interpretation. We say that M is a* preferred model *of S if*

1. *M is a minimal model of S, and*
2. $K(M) = A(M)$

Definition 3.3 *The logic GK is defined as follows:*

Syntax: The syntax of our basic language.

Semantic entailment: $\Phi \models_{GK} \varphi$ *iff* φ *holds in all preferred models of* Φ.

Example 3.1 In the following, p, q, r are primitive propositions.

$S_1 = \{Kp\}$ has a unique preferred model in the sense that M is a preferred model of $\{Kp\}$ iff $K(M)$ is the tautological closure of p, and $A(M) = K(M)$.

$S_2 = \{Kp \vee Kq, Kp \wedge \neg A\neg r \supset Kr, Kq \wedge \neg A\neg r \supset Kr\}$. We can distinguish two kinds of preferred models of S_2: One in which $Kp \wedge \neg Kq$ and Kr are true; and the other in which $Kq \wedge \neg Kp$ and Kr are true. Notice that Kr is true in all preferred models.

$S_3 = \{\neg Ap \supset Kp\}$ has no preferred models. For let M be a preferred model of S_3. If Ap is true in M, then Kp must be false because of the minimality of M. But then $K(M) \neq A(M)$ and M can not be a preferred model of S_3. Now if Ap is false in M, then Kp must be true in M because it is a model of S_3, this again will make $K(M) \neq A(M)$. ■

As we will see in the next section, S_1 corresponds to the default theory $(p, \emptyset)$, and S_3 to $(\emptyset, \{: \neg p/p\})$. There is no default theory that corresponds to S_2.

We conclude this section by proving a generalization of Reiter's Theorem 2.1 in [Reiter, 1980].

Theorem 1 *Let* $S = S_1 \cup S_2$ *be a set of formulas such that every member of* S_1 *has the form* Kp *and every member of* S_2 *the form*

$$Kp \wedge Aq \wedge \neg Ar_1 \wedge \ldots \wedge \neg Ar_n \supset Ks$$

where p, q, r_1, ..., r_n, s *are base formulas,* $n \geq 0$, *and both* Kp *and* Aq *may be absent (either* S_1 *or* S_2 *may be empty). Then a Kripke interpretation* M *is a preferred model of* S *iff*

1. $K(M) = A(M)$;
2. $K(M) = E_1 \cup E_2 \cup ...$, *where* E_i, $i = 1, 2, ...$, *are defined inductively as follows:*
   (a) $E_1 = \{p \mid Kp \in S_1\}$.
   (b) $E_{i+1} = Th(E_i) \cup \{s \mid Kp \wedge Aq \wedge \neg Ar_1 \wedge \ldots \wedge \neg Ar_n \supset Ks \in S_2$, *where* $p \in E_i, q \in A(M)$ *and* $r_1, r_2, ..., r_n \notin A(M)\}$, *where* $i > 0$ *and* $Th(E_i)$ *is the tautological closure of* E_i.

4 FIXED-POINTS NONMONOTONIC LOGICS

The two major fixed-points nonmonotonic logics in the AI literature are Reiter's default logic [Reiter, 1980] and Moore's autoepistemic logic [Moore, 1985]. By the above Theorem 1 and Theorem 2.1 in [Reiter, 1980], it is straightforward to translate default theories into sets of formulas in our logic GK. As we shall show in this section, a closely related but subtly different translation also exists for autoepistemic theories.

4.1 Default logic

Default logic was proposed by Reiter (1980) as a formalism for default reasoning. Default logic was originally defined with respect to a first-order language. For the sake of consistency with autoepistemic logic, the default logic adopted here is with respect to a propositional language. It is straightforward to extend the results to the first-order case (this is true because open defaults are defined as a shorthand for sets of closed defaults. See the concluding section for a discussion of quantifications over default rules). In this subsection, we define sentences as base formulas.

According to Reiter, a default theory, adopted to a propositional language, is a pair (W, D), where W is a set of sentences and D a set of defaults, which are expressions of the form

$$p : q_1, \ldots, q_n / r$$

where $p, q_1, \ldots, q_n, r$ are sentences. A set of sentences E is an extension of a default theory $\Delta = (W, D)$ if $\Gamma(E) = E$, where Γ is the operator defined as follows: for any set of sentences S, $\Gamma(S)$ is the smallest set of sentences satisfying the following conditins:

D1. $W \subseteq \Gamma(S)$

D2. $\Gamma(S)$ is closed under the tautological deduction.

D3. If $(p : q_1, \ldots, q_n / r) \in D$ and $p \in \Gamma(S)$, and $\neg q_1, \ldots, \neg q_n \notin S$ then $r \in \Gamma(S)$.

A default theory $\Delta = (W, D)$ is translated into the following set of formulas Δ_{GK} in GK:

1. If $p \in W$ then $Kp \in \Delta_{GK}$

2. If $(p : q_1, \ldots, q_n / r) \in D$ then

$$Kp \wedge \neg A \neg q_1 \wedge \ldots \wedge \neg A \neg q_n \supset Kr \in \Delta_{GK}$$

Theorem 2 *A consistent set of sentences E is a default extension of Δ iff there is a preferred model M of Δ_{GK} such that $E = K(M)$.*

4.2 Autoepistemic logic

Autoepistemic logic was proposed by Moore (1985) as a reformulation of McDermott and Doyle's nonmonotonic logic (1980). The language Moore used is a propositional one augmented by a modal operator L for belief. In the following, by a L-sentence we mean one that may contain the modal operator L but not K nor A.

Let S be a set of L-sentences. According to Moore, a set of L-sentences E is a *stable expansion (or AE extension)* of S if

$$E = Th(S \cup \{L\varphi \mid \varphi \in E\} \cup \{\neg L\varphi \mid \varphi \notin E\}) \tag{1}$$

where Th is the tautological closure operator. Konolige (1988) proves that for any set of L-sentences S, there is a set of L-sentences S' such that (a) a set E is a stable expansion of S iff it is a stable expansion of S'; (b) every member of S' is in *normal* form, that is, of the form:

$$Lp \wedge \neg Lq_1 \wedge \ldots \wedge \neg Lq_n \supset r$$

where $p, q_1, ..., q_n, r$ are base formulas, $n \geq 0$, and Lp may be absent. Thus without the lose of generality, in the following we assume that S is always a set of L-sentences of the normal form.[2]

For any such S, we define S_{GK} by the following equation:

$$S_{GK} = \{Ap \wedge \neg Aq_1 \wedge \ldots \wedge \neg Aq_n \supset Kr \mid Lp \wedge \neg Lq_1 \wedge \ldots \wedge \neg Lq_n \supset r \in S\}$$

Parallel to Theorem 2, we have the following result:

Theorem 3 *A consistent stable set of L-sentences E is a stable expansion of S iff there is a preferred model M of S_{GK} such that $K(M) = Base(E)$, where $Base(E)$ is the set of base formulas in E.*

By Theorem 1, the theorem is equivalent to the following propostion which is announced in [Lin and Shoham, 1989] and independently proved by Marek and Truszczynski (1989):

Proposition 4.1 *A stable set E is a stable expansion of S iff $Base(E) = E_2$ where*

1. $E_1 = \{p \mid p \in S$ *is a base formula*$\}$
2. $E_2 = Th(E_1 \cup \{r \mid Lp \wedge \neg Lq_1 \wedge \ldots \wedge \neg Lq_n \supset r \in S$, *where* $p \in Base(E)$ *and* $q_1, ..., q_n \notin Base(E)\})$.

[2] Theoretically, it is not necessary to use the normal form. Under the assumption that A satisfies S45 system, an arbitray L-sentence can be translated into a sentence in our language by inserting K in front of the L-sentence and replacing every L by A. The following Theorem 3 will also be true for this transformatioin.

Therefore by Theorem 2 and Theorem 3, under Konolige's transformation [Konolige 1988]:

$$p : q_1, \ldots, q_n / r \Rightarrow Lp \wedge \neg L \neg q_1 \wedge \ldots \wedge \neg L \neg q_n \supset r$$

the difference between default and autoepistemic logics lies in their different interpretations of the premise p. While default logic treats the premise p and the conclusion r in the same way (as knowledge in our terminology), autoepistemic logic treats the premise p and the consistency assumptions q's in the same way (as assumptions in our terminology). The effect of this difference is that the notion of default extensions is stronger than that of stable expansions, that is, under Konolige's transformation, if E is a default extension of a default theory and T is a stable set such that $Base(T) = E$, then T is also a stable expansions of the corresponding autoepistemic theory, but the converse is not true in general [Konolige 1988]. There is, however, a special case. If Δ is a default theory without premises, that is, if every default in Δ has the form:

$$: q_1, \ldots, q_n / r$$

then Konolige's transformation is exact, that is, a set of base sentence E is a default extension of Δ iff there is a stable set T such that $Base(T) = E$ and T is a stable expansion of the corresponding autoepistemic theory (this result is also proved in [Lin and Shoham 1989], and is now trivial according to our results).

5 CONCLUSIONS

We have defined the logic GK, of Grounded Knowledge, and provided two very similar transformations from default and autoepistemic logics into GK. The transformations provide for the first time a uniform epistemic semantics for both default and autoepistemic logics, and thus a common semantic background against which the two logics can be clearly compared.

As for our future work, the most important one is the extension of GK to the first-order case. As one might expect, there are several different ways of doing this. Ideally, we would like the extension to have the following properties:

1. It should provide a first-order extension of autoepistemic logic.

2. It should provide a truly first-order extension of default logic, i.e., we should have something like $\forall x(P(x) : Q(x)/R(x))$, instead of having only the open default $P(x) : Q(x)/R(x)$, which is considered a shorthand for a set of closed defaults.

3. It should be able to capture circumscription (since both GK and circumcription are minimal-model based). Particularly, like circumscription, it should have the ability to infer universal statements.

It turns out however that although it is easy to satisfy any single one of the above properties separately, it is quite difficult, if not impossible, to have a first-order GK to satisfy the three properties at the same time. We hope that we shall have a separate paper about first-order GK in the near future.

References

[1] Etherington, D.W. (1987), A semantics for default logic, *Proceedings of IJCAI–87*, Milan, Italy.

[2] Halpern, J. Y. and Y. O. Moses (1984), Towards a theory of knowledge and ignorance: preliminary report, IBM Technical Report RJ 4448 (48136), 1984.

[3] Konolige, K. (1988), On the relation between default logic and autoepistemic logic, *Artificial Intelligence*, 35 (1988) 343–382.

[4] Levesque, H. (1989), All I know: a study in autoepistemic logic, Technical Report KRR-TR-89-3, University of Toronto, 1989.

[5] Lifschitz, V. (1987a), Pointwise circumscription, in *Readings in Nonmonotonic Reasoning*, Morgan Kaufmann, 1987, ed. by M. Ginsberg.

[6] Lin, F. (1988), Circumscription in a modal logic, *Proceedings of the Second Conference on Theoretical Aspects of Reasoning about Knowledge*, Asilomar, California, 1988.

[7] Lin, F. and Y. Shoham (1988), Argument systems: a uniform basis for nonmonotonic reasoning, in the *Proceedings of the First International Conference on Principles of Knowledge Representation and Reasoning*, Toronto, 1989.

[8] McCarthy, J. (1980), Circumscription — A form of non-monotonic reasoning, *Artificial Intelligence* 13(1980) 27–39.

[9] McCarthy, J. (1986), Applications of circumscription to formalizing commonsense knowledge, *Artificial Intelligence* 28 (1986), 89–118.

[10] McDermott, D. and J. Doyle (1980), Nonmonotonic logic I, *Artificial Intelligence* 13(1980), 41–72.

[11] Marek, W. and M. Truszczynski (1989), Relating autoepistemic and default logics, in the *Proceedings of the First International Conference on Principles of Knowledge Representation and Reasoning*, Toronto, 1989.

[12] Moore, R. (1983), Semantical considerations on nonmonotonic logic, *Conference Proceedings of IJCAI-83*.

[13] Reiter, R. (1980), A logic for default reasoning, *Artificial Intelligence* 13(1980) 81–132.

[14] Shoham, Y. (1987), Nonmonotonic logics: meaning and utility, in *Proceedings of IJCAI–1987*, Milan, Italy.

SYSTEM Z: A NATURAL ORDERING OF DEFAULTS WITH TRACTABLE APPLICATIONS TO NONMONOTONIC REASONING(*)

Judea Pearl

Cognitive Systems Laboratory
Computer Science Department
University of California, Los Angeles

Abstract

Recent progress towards unifying the probabilistic and preferential models semantics for non-monotonic reasoning has led to a remarkable observation: Any consistent system of default rules imposes an unambiguous and natural ordering on these rules which, to emphasize its simple and basic character, we term "Z-ordering." This ordering can be used with various levels of refinement, to prioritize conflicting arguments, to rank the degree of abnormality of states of the world, and to define plausible consequence relationships. This paper defines the Z-ordering, briefly mentions its semantical origins, and illustrates two simple entailment relationships induced by the ordering. Two extensions are then described, maximum-entropy and conditional entailment, which trade in computational simplicity for semantic refinements.

1. Description

We begin with a set of rules $R = \{r : \alpha_r \rightarrow \beta_r\}$ where α_r and β_r are propositional formulas over a finite alphabet of literals, and $\rightarrow$ denotes a new connective to be given default interpretations later on. A truth valuation of the literals in the language will be called a *model*. A model M is said to *verify* a rule $\alpha \rightarrow \beta$ if $M \models \alpha \wedge \beta$ (i.e., α and β are both true in M), and to *falsify* $\alpha \rightarrow \beta$ if $M \models \alpha \wedge \neg \beta$.

Given a set R of such rules, we first define the relation of *toleration*.

(*) This work was supported in part by National Science Foundation grant #IRI-86-10155 and Naval Research Laboratory grant #N00014-89-J-2007.

Definition 1: A set of rules $R' \subseteq R$ is said to *tolerate* an individual rule r, denoted $T(r \mid R')$, if the set of formulas $(\alpha_r \wedge \beta_r) \bigcup_{r' \in R'} (\alpha_{r'} \supset \beta_{r'})$ is satisfiable, i.e., if there exists a model that verifies r and does not falsify any of the rules in R'.

To facilitate the construction of the desired ordering, we now define the notion of *consistency.*

Definition 2: A set R of rules is said to be *consistent* if for every non-empty subset $R' \subseteq R$ there is at least one rule that is tolerated by all the others, i.e.,

$$\forall R' \subseteq R, \exists\, r' \in R', \text{ such that } T(r' \mid R' - r') \tag{1}$$

This definition, named p-consistent in [Adams 1975] and ε-consistent in [Pearl 1988], assures the existence of an *admissible* probability assignment when rules are given a probabilistic interpretation. In other words, if each rule $\alpha \rightarrow \beta$ is interpreted as a statement of high conditional probability, $P(\beta \mid \alpha) \geq 1 - \varepsilon$, consistency assures that for every $\varepsilon > 0$ there will be a probability assignment P (to models of the language) that satisfies all these statements simultaneously. An identical criterion of consistency also assures the existence of an *admissible* preference ranking on models, when each rule $\alpha \rightarrow \beta$ is given a preferential model interpretation, namely, β is true in all the most preferred models of α [Lehmann and Magidor 1988].

A slightly more elaborate definition of consistency applies to databases containing mixtures of defeasible and nondefeasible rules [Goldszmidt and Pearl 1989a]. Note that the condition of consistency is stronger than that of mere satisfiability. For example, the two rules $a \rightarrow b$ and $a \rightarrow \neg b$ are satisfiable (if a is false) but not consistent. Intuitively, consistency requires that in addition to satisfying the constraint associated with the rule $a \rightarrow b$, the truth of a should not be ruled out as an impossibility. This reflects the common understanding that a conditional sentence "if a then b" is not fully satisfied by merely making a false; it requires that both a and b be true in at least one possible world, however unlikely.

The condition of consistency, Eq. (1), leads to a natural ordering of the rules in R. Given a consistent R, we first identify every rule that is tolerated by all the other rules of R, assign to each such rule the label 0, and remove it from R. Next, we attach a label 1 to every rule that is tolerated by all the remaining ones, and so on. Continuing in this way, we form an ordered partition of $R = (R_0, R_1, R_2, \cdots R_K)$, where

$$R_i = \{r : T(r \mid R - R_0 - R_1 - \cdots R_{i-1})\} \quad (2)$$

The label attached to each rule in the partition defines the **Z**-ranking or **Z**-ordering. The process of constructing this partition also amounts to testing the consistency of R, because it terminates with a full partition iff R is consistent [Goldszmidt and Pearl 1989a].

Theorem 1: The complexity of testing the consistency of a set of rules is $O[PS(n)N^2]$, where N is the number of rules, n the number of literals in R and $PS(n)$ the complexity of propositional satisfiability in the sublanguage characterizing the rules (e.g., $PS(n) = O(n)$ for Horn expressions).

Proof: Identifying R_0 takes $N \cdot PS(n)$ steps, identifying R_1 takes $(N - |R_0|)PS(n)$ steps, and so on. Thus, the total time it takes to complete the labeling is

$$PS(n)[N + (N - |R_0|) + (N - |R_0| - |R_1|) + \cdots] \leq PS(n)[N + (N-1) + \cdots]$$

$$= PS(n)\frac{N^2}{2} \quad (3)$$

In order to define the notions of entailment and consequence it is useful to translate the ranking among rules into preferences among models. The reason is that we wish to proclaim a formula g to be a plausible consequence of f, written $f \mid\!\sim g$, only if the constraints imposed by R would force the models of $f \wedge g$ to stand in some preference relation over those of $f \wedge \neg g$. For example, the traditional preferential criterion for g to be a rational consequence of f requires that all the most preferred models of f satisfy g, i.e., that all the most preferred models of f reside in $f \wedge g$ and none resides in $f \wedge \neg g$ [Shoham 1987]. We shall initially limit ourselves to such preference criteria that do not require substantial enumeration of models, i.e., that the preference between $f \wedge g$ and $f \wedge \neg g$ be readily tested using the partition defined in Eq. (2). To that purpose, we propose the following ranking on models. Using $\mathbf{Z}(r)$ to denote the label assigned to rule r,

$$\mathbf{Z}(r) = i \quad \textit{iff} \quad r \in R_i \ , \quad (4)$$

we define the rank associated with a particular model M as the lowest integer n such that all rules having $\mathbf{Z}(r) \geq n$ are satisfied by M,

$$\mathbf{Z}(M) = \min\{n : M \models (\alpha_r \supset \beta_r) \quad \mathbf{Z}(r) \geq n\} \quad (5)$$

In other words, the rank of a model is equal to 1 plus the rank of the highest-ranked rule falsified by the model. The rank associated with a given formula f is now defined as the lowest $\mathbf{Z}$ of all models satisfying f,

$$\mathbf{Z}(f) = \min \{\mathbf{Z}(M): M \models f\} \quad (6)$$

Note that, once we establish the ranking of the rules, the complexity of determining the $\mathbf{Z}$ value of any given M is $O(N)$; we simply identify the highest $\mathbf{Z}$ rule that is falsified by M and add 1 to its $\mathbf{Z}$. More significantly, determining the $\mathbf{Z}$ value of an arbitrary formula f requires at most N satisfiability tests; we search for the lowest i such that all rules having $\mathbf{Z}(r) \geq i$ tolerate $f \rightarrow true$, i.e.,

$$\mathbf{Z}(f) = \min\{i: T(f \rightarrow true \mid R_i, R_{i+1}, ...)\} \quad (7)$$

Eq. (5) defines a total order on models, with those receiving a lower $\mathbf{Z}$ interpreted as being more normal or more preferred. This ordering satisfies the constraints that for each rule $\alpha_r \rightarrow \beta_r$, β_r holds true in all the most-preferred models of α_r, namely, the usual preferential model interpretation of default rules. It can be shown (see Appendix I) that the rankings defined by Eqs. (4) and (5) correspond to a special kind of a preferential structure; out of all rankings satisfying the rule constraints, the assignment defined in Eq. (5) is the only one that is *minimal,* in the sense of assigning to each model the lowest possible ranking (or highest normality) permitted by the rules in R.

2. Consequence Relations

We are now ready to define two notions of nonmonotonic entailment. Given a knowledge base in the form of a consistent set R of rules, and some factual information f, we wish to define the conditions under which f can be said to entail a conclusion g, in the context of R.

Definition 3 (0-entailment): g is said to be *0-entailed* by f in the context R, written $f \vdash_0 g$, if the augmented set of rules $R \cup f \rightarrow \neg g$ is inconsistent.

Theorem 2: 0-entailment is semi-monotonic, i.e., if $R' \subseteq R$ then

$$f \vdash_0 g \text{ under } R \textbf{ whenever } f \vdash_0 g \text{ under } R'.$$

The proof is immediate, from the fact that if $R' \cup f \rightarrow \neg g$ is inconsistent, then $R \cup f \rightarrow \neg g$ must be inconsistent as well. Semi-monotonicity reflects a strategy of extreme caution; no consequence will ever be issued if it is possible to add rules to R (consistently) in such a way as to render the conclusion no longer valid. Thus, 0-entailment generates the maximal set of "safe" conclusions that can be drawn from R, and hence, was proposed in [Pearl 1989] as a *conservative core* that ought to be common to all nonmonotonic formalisms.

0-entailment was named p-entailment by Adams [1975], ε-entailment by Pearl [1988] and r-entailment by Lehmann and Magidor [1988]. Probabilistically, 0-entailment guarantees that conclusions will receive arbitrarily high probabilities (i.e., $P(g \mid f) \rightarrow 1$) whenever the premises receive arbitrarily high probabilities (i.e., $P(\beta_r \mid \alpha_r) \rightarrow 1 \; \forall r \in R$). In the preferential model interpretation, 0-entailment guarantees that $\kappa(f \wedge g) < \kappa(f \wedge \neg g)$ holds in *all* admissible ranking functions κ, namely, in all ranking functions $\kappa(M)$ that satisfy the rule constraints

$$\kappa(\alpha_r \wedge \beta_r) < \kappa(\alpha_r \wedge \neg \beta_r) \quad \forall r \in R \tag{8}$$

where, for every formula α,

$$\kappa(\alpha) = \min\{\kappa(M) : M \models \alpha\} . \tag{9}$$

Due to its extremely conservative nature, 0-entailment does not properly handle irrelevant features, e.g., from $a \rightarrow c$ we cannot conclude $a \wedge b \rightarrow c$ even in cases where R makes no mention of b. To sanction such inferences we now define a more adventurous type of entailment.

Definition 4: (1-entailment). A formula g is said to be 1-*entailed* by f, in the context R, (written $f \vdash_1 g$), if

$$\mathbf{Z}(f \wedge g) < \mathbf{Z}(f \wedge \neg g) . \tag{10}$$

Namely, there exists an integer k such that the set of rules ranked higher or equal to k tolerates $f \rightarrow g$ but does not tolerate $f \rightarrow \neg g$. Note that, once we have the **Z**-rank of all rules, deciding 1-entailment for a given query requires at most $2(1 + \log |R|)$ satisfiability tests (using a binary-search strategy). 1-entailment can be given a clear motivation in preferential model semantics. Instead of insisting that $\kappa(f \wedge g) < \kappa(f \wedge \neg g)$ hold in *all* admissible ranking functions κ, as was done in 0-entailment, we only require that it holds in the unique admissible ranking that is minimal, namely, the **Z**-ranking (see Appendix I).

Lehmann [1989] has extended 0-entailment in a slightly different way, introducing a consequence relation called *rational closure.* Rational closure is defined in terms of a relation called *more exceptional*, where a formula α is said to be more exceptional than β if

$$\alpha \vee \beta \vdash_0 \neg \alpha .$$

Based on this relation, Lehmann then used an inductive definition to assign a *degree* to each formula α in the language: $degree(\alpha) = i$ if $degree(\alpha)$ is not less than i and every β that is less exceptional than α has $degree(\beta) < i$. Finally, a sentence $\alpha \rightarrow \beta$ was defined to be in the rational closure of R iff $degree(\alpha) < degree(\alpha \wedge \neg \beta)$.

Goldszmidt and Pearl [1989b] have recently shown that $degree(\alpha)$ is identical to $\mathbf{Z}(\alpha)$ and, hence, rational closure is equivalent to 1-entailment. This endows the **Z**-ranking with an additional motivation in terms of exceptionality; $\mathbf{Z}(\alpha) > \mathbf{Z}(\beta)$ if α is more exceptional than β. Additionally, the computational procedure developed for 1-entailment renders membership in the rational closure decidable in at most $2(1 + \log |R|)$ satisfiability tests.

Lehmann [1989] has also shown that the rational closure can be obtained by syntactically closing the relation of 0-entailment under a rule suggested by Makinson called *rational monotony.* Rational monotony permits us to conclude $a \wedge b \vdash c$ from $a \vdash c$ as long as the consequence relation does not contain $a \vdash \neg b$. Rational monotony is induced by any admissible ranking function, not necessarily the minimal one defined by system-Z (see Appendix II). Thus, 1-entailment can be thought of as an extension of 0-entailment to acquire properties that are sound in any individual (admissible) ranking function.

1-entailment, though more adventurous than 0-entailment, still does not go far enough, as is illustrated in the next section.

3. Illustrations

Consider the following collection of rules R:

r_1 : "Penguins are birds"	$p \rightarrow b$
r_2 : "Birds fly"	$b \rightarrow f$
r_3 : "Penguins do not fly"	$p \rightarrow \neg f$
r_4 : "Penguins live in the arctic"	$p \rightarrow a$
r_5 : "Birds have wings"	$b \rightarrow w$
r_6 : "Animals that fly are mobile"	$f \rightarrow m$

It can be readily verified that r_6, r_5, and r_2 are each tolerated by all the other five rules in R. For example, the truth assignment $(p = 0, a = 0, f = 1, b = 1, w = 1, m = 1)$ satisfies both

$$b \wedge w \wedge (p \supset b) \wedge (b \supset f) \wedge (p \supset \neg f) \wedge (p \supset a) \wedge (f \supset m)$$

and

$$b \wedge f \wedge (p \supset b) \wedge (b \supset w) \wedge (b \supset \neg f) \wedge (p \supset a) \wedge (f \supset m).$$

Thus, r_6, r_5 and r_2 are each assigned a label 0 indicating that these rules pertain to the most normal state of affairs. No other rule can be labeled 0 because, once we assign p the truth value 1, we must assign 1 to b and 0 to f, which is inconsistent with $b \supset f$. The remaining three rules can now be labeled 1, because each of the three is tolerated by the other two. A network describing the six rules and their Z-labels is shown in Figure 1.

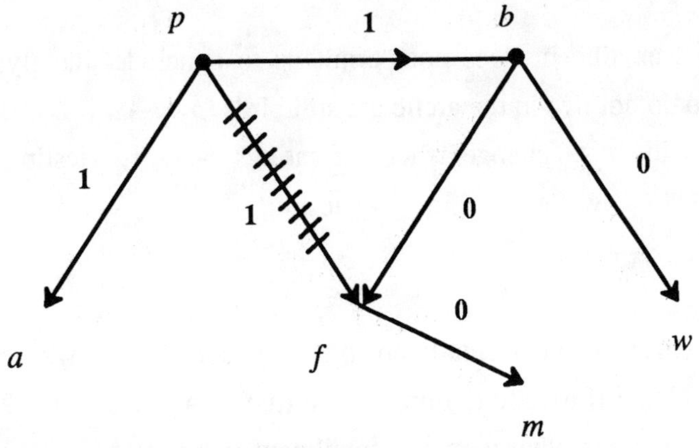

Figure 1.

The following are examples of plausible consequences one would expect to draw from R:

0-*entailed*	1-entailed	not-entailed
$b \wedge p \vdash \neg f$	$\neg b \vdash \neg p$	$p \vdash w$
$f \vdash \neg p$	$\neg f \vdash \neg b$	$p \wedge \neg a \vdash b$
$b \vdash \neg p$	$b \vdash m$	$p \wedge \neg a \vdash w$
$p \wedge a \vdash b$	$\neg m \vdash \neg b$	
	$p \wedge \neg w \vdash b$	

For example, to test the validity of $b \wedge p \vdash_0 \neg f$ we add the rule r_6: $b \wedge p \rightarrow f$ to R, and realize that the augmented set becomes inconsistent; no rule in the set $\{b \wedge p \rightarrow f, p \rightarrow b, p \rightarrow \neg f\}$ can be tolerated by the other two.

1-entailment sanctions plausible inference patterns that are not 0-entailed, among them rule chaining, contraposition and the discounting of irrelevant features. For example, we cannot conclude by 0-entailment that birds are mobile, $b \vdash m$, because neither $b \rightarrow m$ nor $b \rightarrow \neg m$ would render R inconsistent. However, m is 1-entailed by b, because the rule $b \rightarrow m$ is tolerated by all rules in R while $b \rightarrow \neg m$ is tolerated by only those labeled 1. Thus,

$$\mathbf{Z}(b \wedge m) < \mathbf{Z}(b \wedge \neg m),$$

confirming Eq. (10). Similarly, if c is an irrelevant feature (i.e., not appearing in R), we obtain $b \wedge c \vdash_1 f$ but not $b \wedge c \vdash_0 f$.

On the other hand, 1-entailment does not permit us to conclude that flying objects are birds ($f \vdash b$) or that penguins who do not live in the arctic are still birds ($p \wedge \neg a \vdash b$). This is because negating these consequences will not change their **Z**-ratings — in testing $f \vdash_1 b$ we have $\mathbf{Z}(f \wedge b) = \mathbf{Z}(f \wedge \neg b) = 0$, while in testing $p \wedge \neg a \vdash_1 b$ we have $\mathbf{Z}(p \wedge \neg a \wedge b) = \mathbf{Z}(p \wedge \neg a \wedge \neg b) = 2$.

There are cases, however, where 1-entailment produces conclusions whose plausibility may be subject to dispute. For example,(1) if we add to Figure 1 the rule $c \rightarrow f$ we obtain $\mathbf{Z}(c \rightarrow f) = 0$, which yields $c \vdash_1 \neg p$ and $c \wedge p \vdash_1 \neg f$. In other words, 1-entailment ranks the new class c to be as normal as birds, and penguins, by virtue of being exceptional kind of birds (relative to flying) are also treated as exceptional c's. Were the database to contain no information relative to birds, penguins and c's would be treated as equal status classes and the conclusion $p \wedge c \vdash \neg f$ would not be inferred. Thus, merely mentioning a property (f) by which a class (p) differs from its superclass (b) automatically brands that class (p) exceptional relative to any neutral class (c).

The main weakness of the system described so far is its inability to sanction property inheritance from classes to sub-classes. For example, neither of the two types of entailments can sanction the conclusion that penguins have wings ($p \rightarrow w$) by virtue of being birds (albeit exceptional birds). The reason is that the label 1 assigned to all rules emanating from p amounts to proclaiming penguins an exceptional type of birds in *all* respects, barred from inheriting *any* bird-like properties (e.g., laying eggs, having beaks, etc.). This is a drawback that cannot be remedied by methods based solely on the **Z**-ordering of defaults. The fact that $p \rightarrow w$ is tolerated by two extra rules ($p \rightarrow b$, and $b \rightarrow w$) on top of those tolerating $p \rightarrow \neg w$, remains undetected.

---

(1) This observation is due to Hector Geffner.

To sanction property inheritance, a more refined ordering is required which also takes into account the *number* of rules tolerating a formula, not merely their rank orders. One such refinement is provided by the maximum-entropy approach [Goldszmidt and Pearl 1989c] where each model is ranked by the sum of weights on the rules falsified by that model. Another refinement is provided by Geffner's conditional entailment [Geffner 1989], where the priority of rules induces a *partial* order on models. These two refinements will be summarized next.

4. The Maximum Entropy Approach

The maximum-entropy (ME) approach [Pearl 1988] is motivated by the convention that, unless mentioned explicitly, properties are presumed to be independent of one another; such presumptions are normally embedded in probability distributions that attain the maximum entropy subject to a set of constraints. Given a set R of rules and a family of probability distributions that are admissible relative the constraints conveyed by R (i.e., $P(\beta_r \rightarrow \alpha_r) \geq 1 - \varepsilon \;\; \forall\, r \in R$), we can single out a distinguished distribution $P^*_{\varepsilon, R}$ having the greatest entropy $-\sum_M P(M) \log(M)$, and define entailment relative to this distribution by

$$f \vdash_{ME} g \;\; \text{iff} \;\; P^*_{\varepsilon, R}(g \mid f) \underset{\varepsilon \to 0}{\rightarrow} 1 .$$

An infinitessimal analysis of the ME approach yields a ranking function κ on models, where $\kappa(M)$ corresponds to the lowest exponent of ε in the expansion of $P^*_{\varepsilon, R}(M)$ into a power series in ε. Moreover, this ranking function can be encoded parsimoniously by assigning an integer weight w_r to each rule $r \in R$ and letting $\kappa(M)$ be the sum of the weights associated with the rules falsified by M. The weight w_r, in turn, reflects the "cost" we must add to each model M that falsifies rule r, so that the resulting ranking function would satisfy the constraint conveyed by r, namely,

$$\min \{\kappa(M) : M \models \alpha_r \wedge \beta_r\} < \min \{\kappa(M) : M \models \alpha_r \wedge \neg \beta_r\} .$$

These considerations lead to a set of $|R|$ non-linear equations for the weights w_r which, under certain conditions, can be solved by iterative methods. Once the rule weights are established, ME-entailment is determined by the usual criterion

$$f \vdash_{ME} g \;\; \text{iff} \;\; \min \{\kappa(M) : M \models f \wedge g\} < \min \{\kappa(M) : M \models f \wedge \neg g\} .$$

where

$$\kappa(M) = \sum_{r: M \models \alpha_r \wedge \neg \beta_r} w_r$$

We see that ME-entailment requires minimization over models, a task that may take exponential time. In practice, however, this minimization is accomplished quite effectively in databases of Horn expressions, yielding a reasonable set of inference patterns. For example, in the database of Figure 1, ME-entailment will sanction the desired consequences $p \vdash w$, $p \wedge \neg a \vdash b$ and $p \wedge \neg a \vdash b$ and, moreover, it will avoid the undersirable pattern of concluding $c \wedge p \vdash \neg f$ from $R \cup \{c \rightarrow f\}$.

The weaknesses of the ME approach are two-fold. First, it does not properly handle causal relationships and, second, it is sensitive to the format in which the rules are expressed. This latter sensitivity is illustrated in the following example. From R = {Swedes are blond, Swedes are well-mannered}, ME will conclude that dark-haired Swedes are still well-mannered, while no such conclusion will be drawn from R = {Swedes are blond and well-mannered}. This sensitivity might sometimes be useful for distinguishing fine nuances in natural discourse, concluding, for example, that mannerisms and hair color are two independent qualities. However, it stands at variance with one of the basic conventions of formal logic, which treats $a \rightarrow b \wedge c$ as a shorthand notation of $a \rightarrow b$ and $a \rightarrow c$.

The failure to respond to causal information (see Pearl [1988, pp. 463, 519] and Hunter [1989]) prevents the ME approach from properly handling tasks such as the Yale shooting problem [Hanks and McDermott 1986], where rules of causal character are given priority over other rules. This weakness may perhaps be overcome by introducing causal operators into the ME formulation, similar to the way causal operators are incorporated within other formalisms of nonmonotonic reasoning (e.g., Shoham [1986], Geffner [1989]).

5. Conditional Entailment

Geffner [1989] has overcome the weaknesses of 1-entailment by introducing two new refinements. First, rather than letting rule priorities dictate a ranking function on models, a partial order on models is induced instead. To determine the preference between two models, M and M', we examine the highest priority rules that distinguish between the two, i.e., that are falsified by one and not by the other. If all such rules remain unfalsified in one of the two models, then this model is the preferred one. Formally, if $\Delta(M)$ and $\Delta(M')$ stand for the set of rules falsified by M and M', respectively, then M is preferred to M' (written $M < M'$) iff $\Delta[M'] \neq \Delta[M']$ and for every rule r in $\Delta[M] - \Delta[M']$ there exists a rule r' in $\Delta[M'] - \Delta[M]$ such that r' has a higher priority than r (written $r \prec r'$). Using this criterion, a model M will always be preferred to M' if it falsifies a proper subset of the rules falsified by M'. Lacking this feature in the **Z**-ordering has prevented 1-entailment from concluding $p \vdash w$ in the example of Section 3.

The second refinement introduced by Geffner is allowing the rule-priority relation, $\prec$, to become a partial order as well. This partial order is determined by the following interpretation of the rule $\alpha \rightarrow \beta$; if α is all that we know, then, regardless of other rules that R may contain, we are authorized to assert β. This means that $r: \alpha \rightarrow \beta$ should get a higher priority than any argument (a chain of rules) leading from α to $\neg \beta$ and, more generally, if a set of rules $R' \subset R$ does not tolerate r, then at least one rule in R' ought to have a lower priority than r. In Figure 1, for example, the rule $r_3: p \rightarrow \neg f$ is not tolerated by the set $\{r_1: p \rightarrow b, r_2: b \rightarrow f\}$, hence, we must have $r_1 \prec r_3$ or $r_2 \prec r_3$. Similarly, the rule $r_1: p \rightarrow b$ is not tolerated by $\{r_3, r_3\}$, hence, we also have $r_2 \prec r_1$ or $r_3 \prec r_1$. From the asymmetry and transitivity of $\prec$, these two conditions yield $r_2 \prec r_3$ and $r_2 \prec r_1$. It is clear, then, that this priority on rules will induce the preference $M < M'$, whenever M validates $p \wedge b \wedge \neg f$ and M' validates $p \wedge b \wedge f$; the former falsifies r_2, while the latter falsifies the higher priority rule r_3. In general, we say that a proposition g is conditionally entailed by f (in the context of R) if g holds in all the preferred models of f induced by every priority ordering admissible with R.

Conditional entailment rectifies many of the shortcomings of 1-entailment as well as some weaknesses of ME-entailment. However, having been based on model minimization as well as on enumeration of subsets of rules, its computational complexity might be overbearing. A proof theory for conditional entailment can be found in Geffner [1989].

Conclusions

The central theme in this paper has been the realization that underlying any consistent system of default rules there is a natural ranking of these defaults and that this ranking can be used to induce preferences on models and plausible consequence relationships. We have seen that the **Z**-ranking emerges from both the probabilistic interpretation of defaults and their preferential model interpretation, and that two of its immediate entailment relations are decidable in $O(N^2)$ satisfiability tests. The major weakness of these entailment relationships has been the blockage of property inheritance across exceptional subclasses. Two refinements were described, maximum-entropy and conditional entailment, which properly overcome this weakness at the cost of a higher complexity. An open problem remains whether there exists a tractable approximation to the maximum entropy or the conditional entailment schemes which permits inheritance across exceptional subclasses and, at the same time, retains a proper handling of specificity-based priority.

Acknowledgement

I am indebted to Daniel Lehmann for sharing his thoughts on the relations between *r*-entailment, ε-entailment, rational closure, and maximum-entropy. Hector Geffner and Moises Goldszmidt have contributed many ideas, and are responsible for the developments described in Sections 4 and 5.

References

[Adams 1975] Adams, E. 1975. *The logic of conditionals.* Dordrecht, The Netherlands: D. Reidel.

[Geffner 1989] Geffner, H. 1989. Default reasoning: causal and conditional theories. UCLA Cognitive Systems Laboratory *Technical Report (R-137),* December 1989. PhD. dissertation.

[Goldszmidt and Pearl 1989a] Goldszmidt, M. and Pearl, J. 1989. On the consistency of defeasible databases. *Proc. 5th Workshop on Uncertainty in AI,* Windsor, Ontario, Canada, pp. 134-141.

[Goldszmidt and Pearl 1989b] Goldszmidt, M. and Pearl, J. 1989. On the relation between rational closure and System-Z. UCLA Cognitive Systems Laboratory, *Technical Report (R-139),* December 1989. Submitted.

[Goldszmidt and Pearl 1989c] Goldszmidt, M. and Pearl, J. 1989. A maximum entropy approach to nonmonotonic reasoning. UCLA Cognitive Systems Laboratory, Technical Report R-132, in preparation.

[Hanks and McDermott 1986] Hanks, S. and McDermott, D. V. 1986. Default reasoning, nonmonotonic logics, and the frame problem. *Proc., 5th Natl. Conf. on AI (AAAI-86),* Philadelphia, pp. 328-33.

[Hunter 1989] Hunter, D. 1989. Causality and maximum entropy updating. *Intl. Journal of Approximate Reasoning.* 3 (no. 1) pp. 87-114.

[Lehmann 1989] Lehmann, D. 1989. What does a conditional knowledge base entail? *Proc. 1st Intl. Conf. on Principals of Knowledge Representation and Reasoning (KR'89),* Toronto, May 1989, pp. 212-222, San Mateo: Morgan Kaufmann Publishers.

[Lehmann and Magidor 1988] Lehmann, D. and Magidor, M. 1988. Rational logics and their models: a study in cumulative logics. Dept. of Computer Science, Hebrew University, Jerusalem, Israel, Technical Report #TR-88-16.

[Pearl 1988] Pearl, J. 1988. *Probabilistic Reasoning in Intelligent Systems: Networks of Plausible Inference,* San Mateo: Morgan Kaufmann Publishers.

[Pearl 1989] Pearl, J. 1989. Probabilistic semantics for nonmonotonic reasoning: a survey. *Proc. 1st Intl. Conf. on Principles of Knowledge Representation and Reasoning (KR'89),* Toronto, May 1989, pp. 505-516, San Mateo: Morgan Kaufmann Publishers.

[Shoham 1986] Shoham, Y. 1986. Chronological ignorance: Time, nonmonotonicity, necessity, and causal theories. *Proc., 5th Natl. Conf. on AI (AAAI-86),* Philadelphia, pp. 389-93.

[Shoham 1987] Shoham, Y. 1987. Nonmonotonic logics: meaning and utility. *Proc. Intl. Joint Conf. on AI (IJCAI-87),* Milan, pp. 388-393.

APPENDIX I: Uniqueness of The Minimal Ranking Function

Definition: A *ranking function* is an assignment of non-negative integers to the models of the language. A ranking function κ is said to be *admissible* relative to database R, if it satisfies

$$\min \{\kappa(M): M \models \alpha_r \wedge \beta_r\} < \min \{\kappa(M): M \models \alpha_r \wedge \neg \beta_r\} \qquad \text{(I-1)}$$

for every rule $r: \alpha_r \rightarrow \beta_r$ in R.

Let W stand for the set of models considered.

Definition: A ranking function κ is said to be *minimal* if every other admissible ranking κ' satisfies $\kappa'(M) > \kappa(M')$ for at least one model $M' \in W$.

Clearly, every minimal ranking has the property of "local compactness," namely, it is not possible to lower the rank of one model while keeping the ranks of all other models constant. Every such attempt will result in violating the constraint imposed by at least one rule in R. We will now show that local compactness is also a sufficient property for minimality, because there is in fact only one unique ranking that is locally compact.

Definition: An admissible ranking function κ is said to be *compact* if, for every $M' \in W$, any ranking κ' satisfying

$$\kappa'(M) = \kappa(M) \quad M \neq M'$$

$$\kappa'(M) < \kappa(M) \quad M = M'$$

is inadmissible.

Theorem (uniqueness): Every consistent R has a unique compact ranking $\mathbf{Z}(M)$ given by Eq. (5).

Corollary: Every consistent R has a unique minimal ranking given by the compact ranking $\mathbf{Z}(M)$ of Eq. (5).

Proof: We will prove that the ranking function $\mathbf{Z}$ given in Eq. (5) is the unique compact ranking. First we show, by contradiction, that $\mathbf{Z}$ is indeed compact. Suppose it is possible to lower the rank $\mathbf{Z}(M')$ of some model M'. Let $\mathbf{Z}(M')=I$. From Eq. (5) we know that M' falsifies some rule $r: \alpha \rightarrow \beta$ of rank $\mathbf{Z}(r)=I-1$, namely, $M' \models \alpha \wedge \neg \beta$, and there exists $\hat{M} \models \alpha \wedge \beta$ having $\mathbf{Z}(\hat{M})=I-1$. Lowering the rank of M' below I, while keeping $\mathbf{Z}(\hat{M})=I-1$ would clearly violate the constraint imposed by the rule $\alpha \rightarrow \beta$ (see Eq. (I-1)). Thus, $\mathbf{Z}$ is compact.

We now prove that $\mathbf{Z}$ is unique. Suppose there exists some other compact ranking function κ, that differs from $\mathbf{Z}$ on at least one model. We shall show that if there exists an M' such that $\kappa(M') < \mathbf{Z}(M')$ then κ could not be admissible, while if there exists an M' such that $\kappa(M') > \mathbf{Z}(M')$, then κ could not be compact. Assume $\kappa(M') < \mathbf{Z}(M')$, let I be the lowest κ value for which such inequality holds, and let $\mathbf{Z}(M')=J>I$. From Eq. (5), M' falsifies some rule $\alpha \rightarrow \beta$ of rank $J-1$, namely, $M' \models \alpha \wedge \neg \beta$ and every model M validating $\alpha \wedge \beta$ must obtain $\mathbf{Z}(M) \geq J-1$. By our assumption, $\kappa(M)$ must also assign to each such M a value not lower than $J-1 \geq I$. But this is incompatible with the constraint $\alpha \rightarrow \beta$ (see Eq. (I-1)). Thus, κ is inadmissible.

Now assume there is a non-empty set of models for which $\kappa(M) > \mathbf{Z}(M)$, and let I be the lowest $\mathbf{Z}$ value in which $\kappa(M') > \mathbf{Z}(M')$ holds for some model M'. We will show that κ could not be compact, because it should be possible to reduce $\kappa(M')$ to $\mathbf{Z}(M')$ while keeping constant the κ of all other models. From $\mathbf{Z}(M')=I$ we know that M' does not falsify any rule $\alpha' \rightarrow \beta'$ whose $\mathbf{Z}$ rank is higher than $I-1$. Hence, we only need to watch whether the reduction of κ can violate rules r for which $\mathbf{Z}(r)<I$. However, every such rule $r:\alpha \rightarrow \beta$ has a model $M \models \alpha \wedge \beta$ having $\mathbf{Z}(M)<I$, and every such model was assumed to obtain a κ rank equal to that assigned by $\mathbf{Z}$. Hence, none of these rules will be violated by lowering $\kappa(M')$ to $\mathbf{Z}(M)$. QED.

APPENDIX II: Rational Monotony of Admissible Rankings

Theorem: The consequence relation $\vdash$ defined by the criterion

$$f \vdash g \text{ iff } \kappa(f \wedge g) < \kappa(f \wedge \neg g)$$

is closed under rational monotony, for every admissible ranking function κ.

Proof: We need to show that for every three formulas a, b and c, if $a \vdash c$, then either $a \vdash \neg b$ or $a \wedge b \vdash c$. Assume $a \vdash c$ and $a \not\vdash \neg b$, namely,

$$\text{(i)} \qquad \kappa(a \wedge c) < \kappa(a \wedge \neg c)$$

$$\text{(ii)} \qquad \kappa(a \wedge \neg b) \geq \kappa(a \wedge b),$$

we must prove

$$\text{(iii)} \qquad \kappa(a \wedge b \wedge c) < \kappa(a \wedge b \wedge \neg c).$$

Rewriting (i) as

$$\kappa(a \wedge c) = \min\{\kappa(a \wedge c \wedge b, \kappa(a \wedge c \wedge \neg b)\} < \min\{\kappa(a \wedge b \wedge \neg c), \kappa(a \wedge \neg b \wedge \neg c)\} = \kappa(a \wedge \neg c)$$

we need to show only that the min on the left hand side is obtained at the second term, i.e., that

$$\min\{\kappa(a \wedge c \wedge b), \kappa(a \wedge c \wedge \neg b)\} = \kappa(a \wedge c \wedge \neg b).$$

But this is guaranteed by (ii), because the alternative possibility:

$$\kappa(a \wedge c \wedge b) < \kappa(a \wedge c \wedge \neg b)$$

together with (ii), would violate (i). QED

SEMANTICS FOR CONDITIONALS

Robert Stalnaker
Department of Linguistics and Philosophy
Massachusetts Institute of Technology
Cambridge, MA 02139

ABSTRACT

Model theoretic "possible worlds" analyses of conditionals were first developed in the late 1960's as a response to a philosophical problem - the problem of counterfactuals. Since then, they have been seen to be relevant to a range of problems that are of interest to the participants of this conference: knowledge representation, belief revision, probabilistic reasoning, nonmonotonic reasoning, deliberation and contingency planning. In this tutorial talk, I review the basic semantic apparatus, the logics of conditionals, and some of the applications are refinements of conditional semantics.

The basic idea of the analysis was very simple: a conditional statement, *if* Φ *then* Ψ, is true in a possible situation α if and only if the consequent Ψ is true in a possible situation (or a class of possible situations) that is a function of α and of the antecedent Φ. So to interpret conditional statements the semantical apparatus must contain a selection function taking a possible world and a proposition into a possible world or set of worlds representing the way the world would be if the antecedent were true. Alternative developments of this simple idea impose different constraints on such selection functions.

The logics of conditionals validated by this kind of semantic theory had some surprising properties, properties that distinguished them from logics of both the strict and material conditionals. Standard conditional inferences such as contraposition and hypothetical syllogism were invalidated by all versions of this semantics, and the logics all have a nonmonotonic character: the inference from *if* Φ *then* Ψ to *if* $(\Phi \wedge \Theta)$ *then* Ψ is invalid.

Philosophers have long distinguished two kinds of conditionals, usually called (with perhaps some grammatical impropriety) indicative and subjunctive conditionals. That there are semantic differences between the two kinds is demonstrated by contrasting pairs of examples, such as this famous one used by Ernest Adams to make the point:

If Oswald didn't shoot Kennedy, someone else did

If Oswald hadn't shot Kennedy, someone else would have.

Subjunctive conditionals are the main target of the semantic theories, but the same abstract analysis has been applied to indicative, epistemic, or "open" conditionals as well. I will review some of the issues concerning the relationship between the two kinds of conditionals.

There are some striking parallels between conditional propositions, as represented in the semantic theories, and conditional probabilities. A number of different strategies have been used to clarify and explain the relationship between conditionals and probability. The most straightforward hypothesis about this relation: that the absolute probability of a conditional proposition is always equal to the probability of the consequent on the condition of the antecedent - was shown to be untenable by David Lewis. I will review the Lewis triviality results and discuss what they show about the relation between probability and conditionals.

Conditionals interact with a range of concepts that have received analyses within the possible worlds framework. I will sketch very briefly some of the developments that show promise of helping to clarify, within this framework, the relationships between causal, temporal, epistemic and decision theoretic concepts.

COMMON KNOWLEDGE IN ECONOMICS

by

John Geanakoplos

Theories of rational decision-making recognize that agents often act on the basis of incomplete information. Before choosing, an agent must consider what he knows and what he does not know. A potential investor does not know that the price of a stock is going to go up, but he may have information which suggests it is likely to go up.

The most interesting economic environments involve more than one agent. In such situations agents must think not only about what they know, but also about what the others know. Nobody can buy stock unless somebody else is selling it. If the buyer has information suggesting the price will go up, perhaps he should consider that the seller might have information indicating that the price will go down. If the buyer further considers that the seller is willing to sell the stock having also taken into account that the buyer is willing to purchase the stock, should he still buy? Does the answer depend on how rational the agents are? For example, suppose one of them always ignores unpleasant news. Does that affect the chances for a sale?

Can rational agents agree to disagree? Is there a connection between this question and whether rational agents will speculate in the stock market? What relevance is the degree of rationality of the agents? Or the length of time they talk before agreeing to disagree?

A crucial role in the analysis of these questions is played by the notion of common knowledge. We say that an event E is common knowledge among a group of agents if each one knows it, and if each one knows that the others know it, and if each one knows that each one knows that the others know it, and so on. Common knowledge is thus the limit of a potentially infinite chain of reasoning about knowledge.

In different situations, different kinds of events are common knowledge, and with different consequences. Public events are the most obvious candidates for common knowledge, even when their occurrence is due to causes entirely independent of the agents in question. When the agents bring about the events themselves, as for example in collectively designing the rules of some game or agreeing to some contract, the plausibility of common knowledge is strengthened. Certain facts about human nature might also be taken to be common knowledge. We are especially interested, for example, in the consequences of the hypothesis that it is common knowledge that all agents are optimizers, i.e. maximize their utilities. Finally, it often comes about after lengthy periods of observing behavior that what people are going to do is common knowledge, though the reasons for their actions may be difficult to disentangle.

The purpose of this chapter is to survey some of the implications for economic behavior of the hypotheses that events are common knowledge, that actions are common knowledge, that optimization is common knowledge, and that rationality is common knowledge.

SELECTED REFERENCES

Aumann, R., "Agreeing to Disagree," The Annals of Statistics (1976), 4:1236-1239.

Cave, J., "Learning to Agree," Economic Letters (1983), 12:147-152.

Geanakoplos, J., "Game Theory without Partitions, and Applications to the Consensus," CFDP #914.

Geanakoplos, J., "Common Knowledge, Bayesian Learning, and Market Speculation with Bounded Rationality," mimeo, Yale University, 1988.

Milgrom, P. and N. Stokey, "Information, Trade, and Common Knowledge," Journal of Economic Theory (1982), 26:17-27.

Samet, D., "Ignoring Ignorance and Agreeing to Disagree," MEDS Discussion Paper, 1987, Northwestern University.

Sebenius J. and J. Geanakoplos, "Don't Bet On It: Contingent Agreements with Asymmetric Information," Journal of the American Statistical Association (1983), 78:424-426.

REACHING CONSENSUS ON DECISIONS

Paul J. Krasucki
Dept. of Mathematical Sciences
Rutgers University
Camden College of Arts and Sciences
Camden, NJ 08102
email: krasucki@cancer.rutgers.edu

ABSTRACT

We investigate how like-minded agents can reach consensus on their decisions even if they receive different information.

The model used here was introduced by Aumann, and subsequently refined by Geanakoplos and Polemarchakis, Bacharach, Cave, Parikh and Krasucki ([Aum76,GP82,Cav83,Bac85,PK]).

The main result is that when any number of like-minded agents communicate according to some *fair* protocol whether they want to trade or not, and their decision is based solely on whether the conditional probability of some fixed event exceeds some threshold value, they must reach consensus in a finite time.

We also investigate some necessary conditions which functions communicated have to satisfy in order to guarantee consensus in fair protocols.

1 INTRODUCTION

In order to investigate whether the difference in the kind of information received can justify the speculative trading between rational agents the following model was created ([Aum76,GP82, Cav83,Bac85,PK]).

Let W be a set of possible results of an experiment. There are two agents receiving some information about the result. Information is given by choosing one of the elements of the *ith* partition of W, P_i. It is assumed that P_i's are common knowledge among agents (so *type* of information available to agents is common knowledge). It is also assumed that agents always receive *true* information, if the actual state of the world is x, then for all i, $x \in P_i(x)$.

Both agents are interested in computing a probability of some fixed event, so they could make their decisions based on that. There is given some prior probability distribution on W, and it is shared by both agents. Without any additional information they would both have the same value: $p(E)$. But if an agent 1 learns that the result x is in $P_1(x)$, then he can compute a new probability as $p(E|P_1(x))$. This is his *posterior* probability of E. Similarly, an agent 2 can compute his posterior probability $p(E|P_2(x))$.

There is no a priori reason why $p(E|P_1(x)) = p(E|P_2(x))$, but surprisingly Robert Aumann [Aum76], has shown in 1976 that when the posteriors are common knowledge, then they must indeed be the same. Like-minded agents cannot "agree to disagree".

Aumann didn't address the question how the agents computed their posteriors and how could they become common knowledge. Geanakoplos and Polemarchakis [GP82] first investigated the procedure in which one agent computes his posterior, sends the value to the second agent, who in turn computes his new posterior excluding from his set of possible worlds all the worlds in which the first agent would have sent a different value. Subsequently he sends this new posterior back to the agent one, and process continues until (as they have proved), both agents' posteriors converge to the same value, which will happen after $k + l$ rounds where k, l are numbers of sets in information partitions of agents 1 and 2 respectively.

Cave [Cav83] and Bacharach [Bac85] noticed that the property of the conditional probability function that was crucial in both Aumann's and Geanakoplos-Polemarchakis' proofs is that if the conditional probability of some event is the same in two disjoint sets, then the conditional probability of this event in the union of the two sets will be the same as it was in both of them. This property was called *union consistency* by Cave and the *sure - thing principle* by Bacharach. Cave and subsequently Bacharach proved that if two agents communicate values of some function satisfying the sure-thing principle back and forth revising their sets of possible worlds and therefore recomputing values of the function, they will end up with the same values.

All these results generalise to the case when there are $n > 2$ agents and all the agents in turn communicate their values of a function so all of them hear all these values (and there is common knowledge among them of this fact). This was also investigated by Cave.

The situation where every announcement is public, corresponds in computer science to the case of a broadcast from a reliable source. In economics it corresponds to an auction.

However, prices are not always set up via auctions. Communication in the system is not always synchronous n-cast. There are also private communications between agents, inaccessible to others.

In fact, the situation when there are more than two agents involved, and agents communicate using person-to-person links inaccessible to other agents (binary channels) is much more difficult to analyse. This is because even if there are 3 agents, and their information partitions are common knowledge among them, if they communicate values of f in a ring (1 to 2, 2 to 3, 3 to 1 and so on) then, since 3 doesn't know what 2 has heard from 1 and he can usually imagine more then one scenario which made 2 send the value he has sent, so it is more difficult for him to exclude worlds.

This model was analysed first by Parikh and Krasucki in [PK]. They gave a general formula for updating agents knowledge in n-person case. They also defined a class of *fair* protocols, in which all the agents' information affect all other agents' knowledge. Of course if an agent doesn't communicate with anybody, we cannot expect consensus between this agent and the others.

Parikh and Krasucki showed that for $n > 2$ the sure-thing principle is not enough to guarantee consensus among agents communicating according to a fair protocol. They introduced stronger condition, *weak-convexity* which turned out to guarantee consensus in case of $n \leq 3$.

This condition was still not strong enough to guarantee consensus in case of $n > 3$ (an example was given in which four people communicate values of a weakly convex function according to a fair protocol without reaching consensus). They defined a property of *strong-convexity* which turned out to suffice to guarantee consensus for any number n of people communicating.

As a main result they proved that when any number of people communicate values of $f(X) = P(E|X)$ (expected value of some fixed event E) according to some fair protocol, they must reach consensus.

2 DECISIONS

In many cases agents base their decision whether to trade or not on the expected probability of a certain fixed event. If a probability of this event exceeds some value they will trade, otherwise not. Therefore the results asserting that in some cases agents always reach consensus on the value of conditional probability of an event are very important. They hint that the difference in available information might not be enough to justify trading between rational, like-minded agents.

All the consensus results obtained so far require that the agents send to each other their probabilities of the event E. In the market environment, where traders compete, it is unrealistic to assume that they will communicate to the others their assessment of probability. Instead they just communicate their *decision* (although the decision itself may be based on the assessment of probability). That's the case when a trader announces whether he is willing to trade without specifying what is his expected gain, or what kind of analysis lead him to his conclusions.

Our work shows that even if only decisions are communicated, in case where these decisions are based on a probability of a fixed event, consensus is guaranteed.

We talk about a model in which agents communicate values of "decision functions", functions with two-element range. We assume that the range is {0,1} (1 interpreted as "yes", 0 as "no").

The decision functions are the most difficult ones to analyse. They give least amount of information (except of constant functions, which give no information, but if everybody communicates value of the same constant function, consensus is trivially reached). The results of [PK] on strongly-convex functions are here of no help, since non-trivial two-valued functions cannot be strongly convex.

For two-valued functions weak-convexity is equivalent to union-consistency. By the result of [PK] consensus is guaranteed for $n \leq 3$ in such a case. We show that although in general union-consistency is not enough to guarantee consensus for $n > 3$, for the decision functions based on conditional probability consensus on their values in finitely many steps is guaranteed for any n and any fair protocol.

Formally, we prove consensus theorem for $f(X) = 1$ iff $P(E|X) > \alpha$ for some fixed event E and some constant α.

We also discuss some necessary conditions for guaranteeing consensus.

3 DEFINITIONS

All the notions defined here follow [PK].

W is the space of possible worlds. There is n participants with *finite* partitions P_i of W. P^+ is the common refinement (join) of the P_i (obviously P^+ is finite).

Let $cl(W, P^+)$ be the set of all subsets of W which are unions of elements of P^+ (we will call them *closed* sets).

We will consider functions $f : cl(W, P^+) \rightarrow \{0, 1\}$ (*decision functions*).

Let a *protocol* be a pair of functions $s(t), r(t)$ from the natural numbers (≥ 0) to the set {1,...,n} . t should be interpreted here as time and $s(t)$, $r(t)$ are, respectively, the sender and the recipient at time t. So $s(t) = i$, $r(t) = j$ means that at time t, i communicated with j (i sent a message which was received by j).

The protocol is *fair* iff every participant receives information from every other participant infinitely many times, possibly indirectly.

The simplest example of a fair protocol is a "round-robin" protocol, where the first person sends a value of f to the second person, second to third,...., and so on, until it reaches the last, nth person, who sends his value of f back to the first person. And this cycle is repeated forever. Formally, if participants are labeled from 0 to $n-1$, then this protocol can be expressed as $s(0) = r(0) = 0$ and for $t \geq 1$, $s(t) = r(t-1) = t \bmod n$.

Let $p = (s(t), r(t))$ be a protocol. We define by induction on t, the set of possible worlds for i at time t, given that the real world is x $C(x,i,t)$.

$$C(x,i,0) = P_i(x)$$

$$C(x,i,t+1) = \begin{cases} C(x,i,t) \cap f(C(x,s(t),t)) & \text{iff } i = r(t) \\ C(x,i,t) & \text{otherwise} \end{cases}$$

According to this definition, if i receives a message at t, then in order to obtain his set of possible worlds at $t+1$, he excludes from his set of possible worlds at t all the worlds incompatible with the received message.

We assume here for simplicity that communications are instantaneous and that always $s(t+1) = r(t)$. However both these assumptions are not necessary.

4 OVERVIEW OF THE USEFUL RESULTS

All the facts marked (P-K) are from [PK].

Fact 1 (P-K) : If all P_i are finite, then there is T s.t.

$$\forall x, i\, \forall t, t' \geq T\; C(x,i,t) = C(x,i,t')$$

so for every i we have some limiting partition of W (moreover this partition is finite). □

We use $C(x,i,\infty)$ to denote the limiting sets $C(x,i,T)$. Value $f(C(x,i,\infty))$ we call a *limiting value* of f for i at x. P^i, the set of limiting values for i is the set $\{f(C(x,i,\infty)) | x \in W\}$.

Let's define (following Bacharach) the *sure-thing principle* (Cave called the same condition *union consistency*):

Definition: Function $f : cl(W, P^+) \rightarrow D$ satisfies the *sure-thing principle* iff for every pair of disjoint sets $A, B \subseteq W$:

$$f(A) = f(B) \Rightarrow f(A \cup B) = f(A)$$

Fact 2 [Geanakoplos-Polemarchakis, Cave, Bacharach]: If two agents communicate values of a function satisfying the sure-thing principle, then they must reach consensus on the value of this function. □

Fact 3 (P-K) : If f is a decision function satisfying the sure-thing principle and the protocol P is fair then if 3 participants communicate values of f according to P then consensus on the value of f must be reached. □

Fact 4 (P-K) : If there is a space W, finite partitions P_1,...,P_n of W and a decision function f s.t. for some fair protocol Pr, the sets of possible limiting values are P^1,...,P^n, then there exist finite partitions $P'_1,\ldots, P'_n$ of W and protocol Pr' with the same graph as Pr such that executing Pr', we get the *same* set of limiting values, but no one gains any knowledge during the execution of Pr'. I.e. $C(x,i,1) = C(x,i,\infty)$ for all i,x. □

In particular, if no consensus was reached in the first case, then in the second case there will be no consensus, and moreover, no learning will take place.

Fact 5 (P-K) : There is a decision function f satisfying the sure-thing principle s.t. values of f are communicated among 4 agents according to some fair protocol and no consensus is reached. □

5 MAIN RESULT

We prove that in a case when a decision based on the conditional probability of a fixed event is communicated in a fair protocol between n agents, consensus is guaranteed. We state it as the following theorem:

Theorem 1 : If α is a rational number, then the decision function d_E

$$d_E(A) = \begin{cases} 1 & \text{iff } p(E|A) > \alpha \\ 0 & \text{otherwise} \end{cases}$$

based on conditional probability of E brings consensus when communicated according to a fair protocol.

Proof: First we prove that when W is finite and every point has some weight assigned to it, then if values of the decision function based on weighed average are communicated in a fair protocol, then consensus is reached. We state it as the following:

Main Lemma : If w is some weight distribution on finite W ($w : W \to R^+$) and if a decision function f defined by:

$$f(A) = \begin{cases} 1 & \text{iff } [\Sigma_{a_i \in A} w(a_i)]/|A| > \alpha \\ 0 & \text{otherwise} \end{cases}$$

is communicated in a fair protocol, then consensus is reached (for any fixed rational α).

Proof: Let's suppose that consensus is not reached. When we shift w, to get $w' : W \to R^+$, $w'(A) = w(A) - \alpha$, we can express f as:

$$f(A) = \begin{cases} 1 & \text{iff } \Sigma_{a \in A} w'(a) > 0 \\ 0 & \text{iff } \Sigma_{a \in A} w'(a) < 0 \end{cases}$$

If consensus is not reached in some fair protocol when values of f are communicated then there must be some *unstable* worlds, worlds x for which there are two agents i, j s.t. in a stabilised situation (when nothing more can be learned) i sends 0 and j sends 1.

Let's call the set of unstable worlds U. U is not empty. We can express U in two ways: $U = U_0 = U_1$ where

$$U_0 = \bigcup_{i,x} \{C(i,x,\infty) | f(C(i,x,\infty)) = 0,\ f(C(i \ominus 1, x, \infty)) = 1\}$$

and

$$U_1 = \bigcup_{j,x'} \{C(j,x',\infty) | f(C(j,x',\infty)) = 1,\ f(C(j \ominus 1, x', \infty)) = 0\}$$

($\ominus$ is a subtraction mod n).

For U_0 we have a sequence of inequalities of the form

$$\sum_{a \in C(i,x,\infty)} w'(a) < 0$$

Adding up this sequence we'll get inequality

$$\beta_1 = \sum_{a \in U_0} k_a \cdot w'(a) < 0$$

where k_a is the number of sets $C(i,x,\infty) \subseteq U_0$ s.t. $a \in C(i,x,\infty)$. Similarly by looking at U_1 we'll get

$$\beta_2 = \sum_{a \in U_1} l_a \cdot w'(a) > 0$$

where l_a is the number of sets $C(j,x',\infty) \subseteq U_1$ s.t. $a \in C(j,x',\infty)$.

If during the execution of one round of the protocol for a certain world x value communicated changed l_x times from 0 to 1, then value communicated must have changed the same number of times from 1 to 0. So $k_a = l_a$ for every a. Thus $\beta_1 = \beta_2$ and we get a contradiction. □

Now we return to the proof of the theorem:

Let $|P^+| = n$. Let's order elements of P^+: $X_1, \ldots, X_n$. Let $W' = \{x_1, \ldots, x_n\}$. There is a mapping $m : P^+ \to W'$, $m(X_i) = x_i$. We can extend m to all the closed subsets of W in a natural way: $m(X) = \bigcup\{m(X_i) | X_i \in P^+, X_i \subseteq X\}$.

If values of the function f are communicated according to the same protocol in W with partitions P_i as values of f' in W' with partitions P'_i (where $P'^k_i = \{x | X_l \subseteq P^k_i, m(X_l) = x\}$ and $f'(m(X)) = f(X)$), then consensus on f' is reached iff consensus on f is reached. So without loss of generality we can assume that our space W is finite.

If all the worlds are equally likely, then if we take $p(E \cap \{x\})$ to be the weight of x, then $p(E|A) > \alpha|W|$ iff an average weight of A is greater than α, so our theorem follows directly from the main lemma.

If weights of the points are different, we can create another set W'', and a mapping $\varphi : W'' \to W$, s.t. weights of all points are the same in W'', and for all sets in P''^+ (defined as $P''^k_i = \{x | \varphi(x) \in P^k_i\}$), $p(E|A) = p(\varphi(E)|\varphi(A))$ (we extend φ to a mapping $cl(W'', P''^+) \to cl(W, P^+)$ in the obvious way). So if there is no consensus in general case, there would be no consensus in a case where all the points are equally likely. This ends the proof of the theorem. □

Remark 1: The decision functions based on conditional probability satisfy the sure-thing principle. Unfortunately we cannot use it to get a contradiction by looking at the sets U_0 and U_1 since these sets represented as unions of sets of the form $C(i,x,\infty)$ are not necessarily disjoint unions. □

6 NECESSARY CONDITIONS FOR CONSENSUS

We proved that some decision functions always bring consensus among agents communicating their values according to fair protocols. We would like to find what conditions functions must satisfy so we could ever hope for consensus on their value.

Definition : Condition Φ is a *necessary condition* for guaranteeing consensus on the value of $f : cl(W, P^+) \rightarrow \{0, 1\}$ in a fair protocol iff for every f which doesn't satisfy Φ there are some partitions $P_i' \subseteq P^+$ s.t. for some $x \in W$ and for some fair protocol there is no consensus on the value of f in x in this protocol.

The idea here is that if our necessary condition is not satisfied, then without increasing the total amount of information in the system (join of new partitions is no finer than old P^+) we can change the *distribution* of information among agents so that in some world there will be no consensus.

Notice that the sure-thing principle is a necessary condition for guaranteeing consensus among any number of agents.

We will try to find some stronger necessary conditions for the case of more then two agents communicating.

Definition : Let's define a *domination relation* ($\succ_f$) generated by f on $cl(W, P^+)$ as $A \succ_f B$ iff A,B disjoint, f(A)$\neq$f(B) and $f(A \cup B) = f(A)$

Definition: The relation $\succ_f$ is *cyclic* iff there is a sequence of sets of worlds $A_1, ..., A_k$ s.t.

$$A_1 \succ_f A_2 \succ_f ... \succ_f A_k \succ_f A_1$$

This sequence we call a *cycle* of length k.

If $\succ_f$ is not cyclic we call it *acyclic.*

Note that the fact that $\succ_f$ is acyclic is equivalent to the fact that $< cl(W, P^+), \succ_f >$ is embeddable into $< R, > >$.

Fact 6 : All the cycles in $\succ_f$ are of even length. □

Definition : A set of sets of worlds $\mathcal{A} \subseteq cl(W, P^+)$ has *pairwise disjoint dominators with respect to f* iff

$$\forall A_1, A_2 \in \mathcal{A}\ f(A_1 - A_2) = f(A_1)$$

Intuitively, we don't want two sets in our collection to share some "strong" (dominating) subset of worlds. The other way of expressing this condition is to say that

$$\forall A_1, A_2 \in \mathcal{A}\ A_1 \cap A_2 \not\succ_f A_1 - A_2$$

Theorem 2: If $\succ_f$ is cyclic and there is a cycle $A_1 \succ_f A_2 \succ_f ... \succ_f A_n \succ_f A_1$ which has pairwise disjoint dominators with respect to f, then there exist partitions $P_1, ..., P_n$ of W s.t., when values of f are communicated in any world $x \in \bigcup A_i$ in an n-person round-robin protocol then no consensus is reached.

Proof: Suppose that we have a cycle in $\succ_f$ of length $n = 2m$ (see fact 6). $A_1 \succ_f A_2 \succ_f ... \succ_f A_n$, and $f(A_i - A_j) = f(A_i)$ for $i \neq j$. Let's assume that $f(A_{2k}) = 0$ and $f(A_{2k-1}) = 1$ for $k = 1, ..., n/2$. Now we construct partitions $P_1, ..., P_n$. In P_i we define A_j' in the following way: $A_j' = A_j - (A_i \cup A_{i+1})$:
$P_1 = \{A_1 \cup A_2, A_3', ..., A_n', W - \bigcup A_i\}$

$P_2 = \{A_2 \cup A_3, A'_1, A'_4, ..., A'_n, W - \bigcup A_i\}$
$P_3 = \{A_3 \cup A_4, A'_1, A'_2, A'_5, ..., A'_n, W - \bigcup A_i\}$
...
$P_n = \{A_n \cup A_1, A'_2, A'_3, ..., A'_{n-1}, W - \bigcup A_i\}$
In any world $x \in A_i$, all the people except the person $i-1$ send $f(A_i)$ while the person $i-1$ sends the opposite value. □

Corollary 1 : : If $\succ_f$ is cyclic, there is a cycle in $\succ_f$ built up of pairwise disjoint sets, then there exist partitions $P_1, ..., P_n$ of W s.t., when values of f are communicated in any world x in any of the sets forming the cycle in an n-person round-robin protocol then no consensus is reached. □

The question is whether cyclicity of $\succ_f$ is a sufficient condition for existence of partitions that might lead to a situation with no consensus reached. As we see on the following example, the answer to that is negative, therefore the additional condition (sets in a cycle have pairwise disjoint dominators), turns out to be essential.

Example 1 : This is a decision function with cyclic domination relation s.t. in every world, in every partition consensus on the value of f must be reached in every fair protocol.
$W = \{a, b, c, d, e\}$
$f(a) = f(b) = f(c) = f(d) = 1$
$f(e) = 0$ and $\forall i \in \{a, b, c, d\}$ $f(\{e, i\}) = 0$
$f(\{b, d, e\}) = f(\{a, c, e\}) = 0$
for all other sets A, $f(A) = 1$.

Clearly $\succ_f$ is cyclic, since

$$\{a\} \succ_f \{b, e\} \succ_f \{d\} \succ_f \{c, e\} \succ_f \{a\}$$

f has the following property: for any $B \subseteq A$, $\{e\} \succ_f A \rightarrow \{e\} \succ_f B$ (this is because e is the only element on which f gives value 0).

We prove that f guarantees consensus; suppose otherwise, then there are some agents i and $i+1$ s.t. i sends 0 and $i+1$ sends 1 in x. If i sends 0 in x, then $e \in C(i, x, \infty)$. Nothing is learned, so

$$C(i+1, x, \infty) \subseteq \bigcup\{C(i, x, \infty) | f(C(i, x, \infty) = 0\} = C(i, x, \infty)$$

But then $e \in C(i+1, x, \infty)$, and by the property of f mentioned earlier, $f(C(i+1, x, \infty)) = 0$, a contradiction. □

Remark 2: Not every decision function with an acyclic domination relation can be expressed as a decision based on weighed average. For example, if we have

$$\{a\} \succ_f \{b\} \text{ and } \{a\} \succ_f \{c\} \text{ but } \{b, c\} \succ_f \{a\}$$

then we cannot assign weights to a, b, c so that f would be based on averages of weights. □

7 SUMMARY

We proved that for any number of participants there is always consensus on the decision based on probabilities of some fixed event, provided that these decisions are communicated in some fair protocol.

We are not able at that point to establish complexity (how long it takes to reach consensus) as a function of partition sizes. Complexity here would have to be expressed in terms of *rounds* where one round is a sequence of communications s.t. everyone has a chance to contribute to everyone else's information (so protocols as: "exchange information between $n-1$ agents (in a circle) every time unit, and consult the remaining agent every 2^t time units (t is time used so far)" would not give us automatically high complexity).

Geanakoplos and Polemarchakis showed that in case of two agents communicating the complexity is linear. Their proof was based on the observation that if an agent removes a world from his set of possible worlds, he must remove the whole equivalence class (element of the other agents' partition), and this fact is common knowledge between the agents.

In the case of n agents it is no longer true. It seems that an agent may remove an arbitrary closed set. If all the partitions have n elements, there is 2^n closed sets, and we don't know if consensus is always guaranteed in polynomial number of rounds.

There are other natural examples of decision functions, which when communicated in a fair protocol must create consensus among participants. One such example is a decision based on maximum weight (in a case of finite W). We state it as the following fact:

Fact 7 : Every function $f : W \to \{0,1\}$ (where W - finite) of the form:

$$f(A) = \begin{cases} 1 & \text{iff } max(\{f(a) | a \in A\}) > \alpha \\ 0 & \text{otherwise} \end{cases}$$

for some fixed α, brings consensus in a fair protocol (the same is true for f defined as based on minimum). □

We introduced necessary condition decision functions must satisfy so that consensus is possible.

It remains open to find complete characterisation of functions which always create consensus in fair protocols.

Acknowledgements

I would like to thank prof. Rohit Parikh who introduced me to the consensus problems. Prof. Parikh who was my Ph.D. adviser gave me enormous help and encouragement while I was working on my Ph.D. thesis, which contains the results from this paper. Also, I would like to thank prof. Melvin Fitting for his valuable suggestions.

References

[Aum76] R. Aumann. Agreeing to disagree. *Annals of Statistics*, 4:1236–1239, 1976.

[Bac85] M. Bacharach. Some extensions of a claim of Aumann in an axiomatic model of knowledge. *Journal of Economic Theory*, 37:167–190, 1985.

[Cav83] J. Cave. Learning to agree. *Economics Letters*, 12:147–152, 1983.

[GP82] J. Geanakoplos and H. Polemarchakis. We can't disagree forever. *Journal of Economic Theory*, 28:192–200, 1982.

[PK] R. Parikh and P. Krasucki. Communication, consensus and knowledge. *to appear in Journal of Economic Theory.*

Agreeing to Disagree After All (Extended Abstract)

Yoram Moses

Department of Applied Math and CS
The Weizmann Institute of Science

Gal Nachum

Department of Computer Science
Tel Aviv University

Abstract

Bacharach and Cave independently generalized Aumann's celebrated agreement theorem to the case of *decision functions*. Roughly speaking, they showed that once two like-minded agents reach common knowledge of the actions each of them intends to perform, they will perform identical actions. This theorem is proved for decision functions that satisfy a condition that Bacharach calls the *sure thing condition*, which is closely related to Savage's *sure thing principle*. The assumption that any reasonable decision function should satisfy the sure thing condition seems to have been widely accepted as being natural and intuitive.

By taking a closer look at the meaning of the sure thing condition in this context, we argue that the technical definition of the sure thing condition does not capture the intuition behind Savage's sure thing principle very well. It seems to involve nontrivial hidden assumptions, whose appropriateness in the case of non-probabilistic decision functions is questionable. Similar trouble is found with the technical definition of the like-mindedness of two agents. Alternative definitions of the sure thing principle and like-mindedness are suggested, and it is shown that the agreement theorem does not hold with respect to these definitions. In particular, it is shown that the agreement theorem does not apply to a particularly appealing example attributed to Bacharach. Conditions that do guarantee the agreement theorem for decision functions are presented. Finally, we consider similar issues that arise in the case of communication among more than two agents, as studied by Parikh and Krasucki.

1 Introduction

In his seminal paper [Aum76], Aumann proved that agents that have the same prior probability distribution over the states of the world cannot agree to disagree. More precisely, once their posteriors for a certain event are common knowledge, these posteriors must coincide, despite the fact that they may be based on different information. In [Bac85,Cav83] Bacharach and Cave independently generalized Aumann's result from posterior probabilities to decision functions: Roughly speaking, they showed that once two like-minded agents reach common knowledge of the actions each of them intends to perform, they will perform identical actions. This theorem is proved for decision functions that satisfy a condition Bacharach calls the *sure thing condition*. The following story, due to Bacharach, is intended to vividly capture the essence of the generalized agreement theorem. We present here the version found in [Aum89].

> *A murder has been committed. To increase the chances of conviction, the chief of police puts two detectives on the case, with strict instructions to work independently, to exchange no information. The two, Alice and Bob, went to the same police school; so given the same clues, they would reach the same conclusions. But as they will work independently, they will, presumably, not get the same clues.*
>
> *At the end of thirty days, each is to decide whom to arrest (possibly nobody). On the night before the thirtieth day, they happen to meet in the locker room at headquarters, and get to talking about the case. True to their instructions, they exchange no substantive information, no clues; but both are self-confident individuals, and feel that there is no harm in telling each other whom they plan to arrest. Thus, when they leave the locker room, it is common knowledge between them whom Alice will arrest, and it is common knowledge between them whom Bob will arrest.*
>
> *Conclusion: They arrest the same people; and this, in spite of knowing nothing about each other's clues.*

In the case of this example, the theorem assumes that the rules by which each detective decides whom to arrest satisfy the sure thing condition. While the precise definition of this condition will be given in a later section, it is intuitively explained in [Aum89] as follows: "*Suppose that if you knew which of the mutually exclusive events J happened, you would do b (which is the same for all J). Then you will take the same action b if you only know that some J happened, without knowing which one. Thus, if Alice would arrest the butler if a certain blood stain is typed A, B, AB, or O, (perhaps for different reasons in each case), then she can arrest the butler without bothering to send the stain to the police laboratory.*" Throughout this paper, we will think of this explanation as corresponding to Savage's *sure thing principle* [Sav54].

By taking a close look at the proof of the agreement theorem, we will see that Bacharach's technical definition of the sure thing principle is considerably stronger than is implied by the intuitive explanation given above. Roughly speaking, it requires the decision function to be defined in a manner satisfying certain consistency properties at what amount to impossible situations. This is analogous to requiring a chess player's strategy to be defined, say, for a board with three kings. In addition, it turns out that the notion of like-mindedness implicitly used in [Bac85,Cav83,Aum89] doesn't quite correspond to the idea that given the same information the agents will reach the same decisions. The agreement theorem for decision functions is thus less applicable than initially thought. In particular, it does not directly capture the above murder story example.

It is, nevertheless, conceivable that once we make the appropriate definitions capturing the sure thing principle and like-mindedness, the agreement theorem will still hold. We show that this is not the case. In fact, we present a scenario consistent with the above murder story, in which the detectives are like-minded and satisfy the sure thing principle as described above, and yet Alice and Bob *agree to disagree after all.* Given these negative results, we turn to study whether there are other natural conditions one could make that do ensure the agreement theorem. It is shown that a strengthening of the sure thing principle, which we call the *inclusive sure thing principle*, does work.

Finally, we consider Parikh and Krasucki's extensions of Bacharach and Cave's agreement theorem to the case of communication among more than two agents [PK87]. In extending the previous work, Parikh and Krasucki's analysis suffers from similar shortcomings in terms of its applicability to deterministic decision functions. They present conditions that guarantee the agreement theorem for $n \geq 3$ agents. We show that their condition for $n = 3$ can be extended to an appropriate inclusive condition as above, while their condition for $n \geq 4$ cannot be extended in a nontrivial way.

This paper is organized as follows. In the next section we present the model of knowledge along the lines of [Aum89]. The agreement theorem is stated, proven, and discussed in Section 3. In Section 4 we reformulate the formal definitions of like-mindedness and the sure thing principle. Section 5 shows that the agreement theorem fails for the reformulated definitions, by presenting a "counterexample" scenario that is an instance of the murder story example. The agreement theorem is shown to hold with respect to an inclusive variant of the sure thing principle. Finally, the case of communication between more than two agents is discussed. Section 6 concludes with a discussion of the meaning of all this.

2 Knowledge and Common Knowledge

We begin by reviewing the model of knowledge used for the standard proof of the (generalized) agreement theorem. Our exposition will closely follow that of [Aum89]. We start with a set Ω whose members are called *states of the world.* An *event* e is defined as a subset of Ω. The family of all events is denoted by $\mathcal{E}$. An event in the ordinary sense of the word, such as "a crime has been committed", will be identified in the formalism with the set of all states of the world at which a crime has been committed. Inclusion of events corresponds to implication, union to disjunction, intersection to conjunction and complementation to negation. In addition, we have a set $\Pi = \{1 \ldots n\}$ of *agents*. For each agent $j \in \Pi$ we will assume that we are given a function $I_j : \Omega \to 2^\Omega$ satisfying:

1. $\omega \in I_j(\omega)$
2. $I_j(\omega)$ and $I_j(\omega')$ are either identical or disjoint.

I_j thus induces a partition of the states of Ω. I_j is called the *information function* of agent j. Intuitively $I_j(\omega)$ is the set of all those states of the world that are for agent j *indistinguishable* from ω. Thus, if ω is the true state of the world, j will usually not know this; he will know only that the true state is a member of $I_j(\omega)$. Put another way, $I_j(\omega)$ consists of all the states ω' that are considered by j to be possible when ω is the true state of the world. An event e is called a *possible state of knowledge* for agent j if $e = I_j(\omega)$ for some $\omega \in \Omega$.

A *knowledge operator* $K_j : \mathcal{E} \to \mathcal{E}$ is now defined as follows: for every event e,

$$K_j(e) = \{\omega \in \Omega \, : \, I_j(\omega) \subseteq e\}$$

In words, $K_j(e)$ is the event that j knows that e obtains. (Notice that when we interpret events as formulas, such a definition of knowledge has the properties of the modal system S5 [HM85].) The event that *everyone* in a set $N \subseteq \Pi$ of agents *knows* that e obtains is captured by an operator $E_N : \mathcal{E} \to \mathcal{E}$ defined as follows:

$$E_N(e) = \cap_{j \in N} K_j(e).$$

It is easy to verify that all members of N know e iff $E_N(e)$ holds. We can iterate the E_N operator, and define $E_N^1(e) = E_N(e)$, and $E_N^{m+1}(e) = E_N(E_N^m(e))$ for $m \geq 1$.

An event e is called *common knowledge* among a group N of agents, denoted $C_N(e)$, if they all know e, all know that all know it, all know that all know that all know it, and so on ad infinitum. Formally, we define

$$C_N(e) = \cap_{m=1}^{\infty} E_N^m(e).$$

We will generally omit the subscript N when either the set in question is the set Π of all agents or when its identity is clear from context.

An equivalent definition of common knowledge uses the notion of a greatest fixed point. An event e is a fixed point of a function $f : \mathcal{E} \to \mathcal{E}$ if $f(e) = e$; that is, if f maps the event e to itself. An event e is the *greatest fixed point* of f, if it is a fixed point of f and $e' \subseteq e$ for any other fixed point e' of f. An equivalent definition of $C_N(e)$ is as the greatest fixed point of the function

$$f(X) = E_N(e \cap X).$$

This definition seems to better reflect the way common knowledge actually arises. Common knowledge does not result from an infinite iterative process in which higher and higher levels of $E_N^m(e)$ are attained, but rather from a situation that is a fixed point of the E_N operator [HM89]. For other frequently used definitions of common knowledge, see [Aum76,HM89].

3 The Agreement Theorem

In order to prove the agreement theorem we need a few definitions. An *action function* d_j specifies agent j's actions at a given state, as a function of the agent's state of knowledge (the set of states of the world she considers possible). It follows that the value of $d_j(\omega)$ is completely determined by the set $I_j(\omega)$. We are therefore led to think of such functions as functions from nonempty subsets of Ω. Define a *decision function* to be a function D from nonempty subsets of Ω to a set $\mathcal{A}$ of actions. We say that the agent j using the action function d_j *follows the decision function* D if for all states ω it is the case that $d_j(\omega) = D(I_j(\omega))$. According to Bacharach, a decision function D is said to satisfy the *sure thing condition* (STC),[1] if whenever a nonempty event e is a disjoint union of a family of events $\{J\}$, on each of which $D(J) = b$, then also $D(e) = b$. (We will refer to this technical definition as the sure thing *condition*, as opposed to the sure thing *principle*, by which we refer to Savage's intuitive notion.) Finally, Bacharach defines two agents to be *like-minded* if they both follow the same decision function.

We are now in a position to state and prove the agreement theorem in the form found in [Bac85,Cav83,Aum89]. We will denote by "$d_1 = a$" the event consisting of all worlds $\omega \in \Omega$ for which $d_1(\omega) = a$. In words, the agreement theorem says that if two like-minded agents following a decision function that satisfies STC agree (attain common knowledge of the fact) that one of them intends to perform action a and the other intends to perform b, then $a = b$. This captures the fact that the agents cannot agree to disagree on what the appropriate course of action is.

Theorem 3.1: *[Agreement Theorem] Let* $\Pi = \{1,2\}$. *If the agents are like-minded, and follow a decision function D satisfying the sure thing condition, then*

$$[C(d_1 = a) \cap C(d_2 = b) \neq \emptyset] \quad \Rightarrow \quad a = b.$$

Proof: Set $e = C(d_1 = a) \cap C(d_2 = b)$. Because e is common knowledge, $K_1(e) = e$ and therefore e is a disjoint union of elements of the form $I = I_1(\omega)$. By definition of e, at every $\omega \in e$ we have $d_1(\omega) = a$, and hence $D(I_1(\omega)) = a$. Now, since e is a (nonempty) disjoint union of such sets I, the fact that D satisfies the sure thing condition implies that $D(e) = a$. Similar reasoning with respect to agent 2 shows that $D(e) = b$, and as a result we obtain $a = b$. ∎

3.1 Discussion

The agreement theorem is based on two assumptions: The like-mindedness of the agents, and the fact that their decision function satisfies the sure thing condition. The theorem immediately applies to the case in which the decision function yields the agent's posterior (conditional) probability of a particular event, based on a common prior probability distribution over the

[1] Cave uses the term *union consistent* to denote essentially the same property.

states of Ω, which is the case in Aumann's original agreement theorem [Aum76]. It has also been shown to apply in other situations originating from a common prior distribution, such as expectations or functions that maximize conditional expectations [Bac85,Cav83]. However, as exemplified in the murder story example, Bacharach intuitively argues that these assumptions apply to a very wide range of situations. He claims that the sure thing condition applies to "*just about any plausible theory of rational decision*", and interprets the agreement theorem as showing that, in general, "*differences in information alone cannot account for differences in behavior of rational persons ... any more than they can account for differences of opinion*" [Bac85]. We now attempt a critical assessment of this point of view.

3.1.1 Decision functions and STC

The proof of agreement theorem makes strong use of the fact that the decision function D is defined, and in a way that satisfies the sure thing condition, on the event e, which is a union of states of knowledge. But notice that an agent j's actions are completely determined once D is defined for all the events in $\mathcal{I} = \{I_j(\omega) : \omega \in \Omega\}$, which are all the possible states of knowledge of j. Extending D beyond $\mathcal{I}$ is intuitively analogous to extending a strategy for white in the game of chess to impossible board positions. For cardinality reasons it is obvious that $\mathcal{I}$ cannot include all the nonempty subsets of Ω. The following lemma characterizes a particularly interesting class of events that are definitely not possible states of knowledge for j:

Lemma 3.2: *If e' is a union of two or more different states of knowledge for j, then e' is not a possible state of knowledge for j.*

Proof: Let $e' = I_j(\omega)$ for some ω, and let ω' be a state such that $e' \supseteq I_j(\omega')$. Given that $\omega' \in I_j(\omega')$, we have $I_j(\omega) \cap I_j(\omega') \neq \emptyset$ and therefore $I_j(\omega') = I_j(\omega) = e'$. It follows that e' cannot be the union of two or more *different* states of knowledge for j. ∎

It follows that taking the union of states of knowledge in which an agent has differing knowledge does not result in a state of knowledge in which the agent is more ignorant. It simply does not result in a state of knowledge at all! If this is the case, however, then the technical definition of the sure thing condition does not quite capture the intuition given in the introduction for Savage's sure thing principle. It does not formalize the intuition that "if Alice would arrest the butler if a certain blood stain is typed A, B, AB, or O, (perhaps for different reasons in each case), then she can arrest the butler without bothering to send the stain to the police laboratory." (We will consider the question of how this intuition *can* be captured formally in a later section.) It is easy to check that for a decision function that is defined only on the agent's possible states of knowledge, the STC is never violated, since the decision function is not defined on nontrivial unions. Once we require a decision function to be extendible to such unions, however, the STC does appear to be a nontrivial consistency condition. Except that it no longer seems to capture our original intuition, and its actual meaning is quite unclear.

Returning to the proof of the agreement theorem, we see that it is based in a crucial way on the fact that the decision function D is defined on the event $e = C(d_1 = a) \cap C(d_2 = b)$. Since this event will generally be a nontrivial union of states of knowledge, Lemma 3.2 thus implies that e will in general *not* be a possible state of knowledge for either agent. As we have argued above, the assumption that the agents' decision functions are defined on e and that they satisfy the sure thing condition with respect to e and its subsets cannot be accepted without additional motivation. We conclude that it is no longer obvious that the agreement theorem, as stated, applies to cases such as Bacharach's murder story example.

3.1.2 Like-mindedness

In our story the two detectives are described as "like-minded". By this it is meant that given the same information they would behave in the same way. Technically, this property has been formalized by having both agents follow the same decision function. Indeed, this seems to capture the idea that given the same information, the agents should perform the same action. However, a closer inspection shows that here again there are some unexpected subtleties. Consider for example a situation where for some state ω we have $I_A(\omega) \subseteq K_A(e) \cap K_A \neg K_B(e)$. Let us denote $I_A(\omega)$ by I_a. In I_a, Alice knows that e obtains and at the same time knows that Bob does not know this. Clearly, I_a is not a possible state of knowledge for Bob, because this would require him to know that e obtains and at the same time to know that he (Bob) does not know this. So there is no sense in demanding that when Bob's state of knowledge is I_a he should take the same action that Alice does when she is in I_a. To be more precise, I_a is not a possible state of knowledge for Bob, and hence d_B — Bob's action function — need not be defined on I_a at all. Indeed, it is not hard to check that events that are possible states of knowledge for more than one agent are of a very special form:

Lemma 3.3: *If some event e' is a possible state of knowledge for both Alice and Bob, then $e' = C_{\{A,B\}}(e')$.*

It thus turns out that the vast majority of Alice's states of knowledge are not possible states of knowledge for Bob, and vice versa. As a result, the technical requirement that has been taken to capture the notion of like-mindedness does not capture the idea that Alice and Bob went to the same school and will act similarly given the same evidence.

Let us digress for a moment and consider an argument that has been brought up against our attack on the sure thing condition in the previous subsection. We claimed in Lemma 3.2 that a nontrivial union of an agent's state of knowledge does not result in a state of knowledge that is possible for that agent. One could, nevertheless, imagine a situation where a third agent is added, for whom the union is a possible state of knowledge. The point, however, is that there does not seem to be a good reason to relate what Alice and Bob do when their knowledge state is an element of the union, with what the third agent should do when in the union. In addition, of course, it is possible to prove an analogue of Lemma 3.3 that shows that a third agent's state of knowledge will coincide with the union only under rather particular circumstances.

4 Reformulating the conditions

The intuitive notions of like-mindedness and the sure thing principle are perfectly sensible. Even if, as we have argued, these notions are not formalized properly in [Bac85,Aum89], they definitely deserve to be given alternative formal definitions. This is what we will attempt to do in this section.

Let us start by reconsidering the notion of like-mindedness. When, for example, we say that the detectives in the murder story example are like-minded, we intuitively mean that given the same information they would act in the same way. The question is what we mean by "given the same information". Clearly, an agent's knowledge state determines the information it has. What Lemma 3.3 shows us is that the agents' having the same information is not the same as their having the same knowledge state. Indeed, decision functions usually depend only on certain aspects of the knowledge state. The toothpaste a detective regularly uses may be part of the description of a state ω, but the detective's decision will presumably not depend on this aspect of the world. We will thus want to consider agents as having the same information when their knowledge about the facts relevant to their decision is the same. What these facts are will in general depend on the model and the decision function. We remark that when a decision function truly depends on all aspects of the knowledge state, the lemma shows that the notion of different agents having the "same information" is not well defined in general. We will therefore consider reductions of the complete knowledge state to a state of knowledge about facts that are relevant to the decision; these will be called *states of relevant knowledge*. We will then be able to compare what different agents do when they are in the same state of relevant knowledge. However, to avoid the type of problems that arose in the previous section, a definition of like-mindedness seems to truly capture the notion only when every state of relevant knowledge that is possible for one agent is possible for the other agent as well. The concept of a state of relevant knowledge will also prove useful for reformulating the sure thing condition. In this case, however, we will be able to overcome the problem raised in Lemma 3.2 once we require that the union of states of relevant knowledge is always a possible state of relevant knowledge.

We now formalize the above discussion. A *projection* of Ω is a function $\rho : \Omega \to Q$, where Q is an arbitrary set. We extend such a projection ρ to events over Ω by defining $\rho(e) = \{\rho(\omega) : \omega \in e\}$. Given a model $(\Omega, I_1, I_2, \ldots)$, a decision function D is said to be ***admissible*** with respect to a set N of agents if there exists an associated projection ρ_D satisfying the following three conditions:

1. Whenever $\rho_D(e) = \rho_D(e')$, then $D(e) = D(e')$.
2. For all agents $j, j' \in N$ and states ω there exists a state ω' such that $\rho_D(I_j(\omega)) = \rho_D(I_{j'}(\omega'))$.
3. For every nonempty set $e \subseteq \Omega$ and agent $j \in N$ there exists a state ω' such that $\rho_D(I_j(\omega')) = \bigcup_{\omega \in e} \rho_D(I_j(\omega))$.

The first condition demands that the decisions taken according to D depend only on the knowledge about the relevant aspects of the world, as they are projected out by ρ_D. This guarantees that the projection ρ_D does not discard information that is relevant to the decision taken. The second condition says that every state of relevant knowledge that is possible for one agent of N is possible for any other. (N will often be a set of two agents; we do not intend for N to generally be the set of all agents.) Finally, the third condition guarantees that the union of states of relevant knowledge is itself a state of relevant knowledge.[2] A projection ρ_D satisfying the above conditions with respect to D and N we call a *relevance projection* for D and N. We remark that an admissible decision function D may have many different relevance projections (with respect to the same N; as usual, we will not mention the set N when it is clear from context). Notice that for any decision function, the identity projection mapping every state $\omega \in \Omega$ to itself and every event to itself will clearly satisfy the first condition. However, Lemmas 3.2 and 3.3 show that it does not satisfy the other two. The second and third conditions restrict the decision function so that the problems raised in the previous section do not apply.

We can now redefine the notion of like-mindedness as follows:

Definition 4.1: The agents in a set N are said to be *like-minded* if (i) they all follow the same decision function D, and (ii) D is admissible with respect to N.

Recall that, by the first condition, an agent's actions are a function of its state of relevant knowledge. As a consequence, our definition says precisely that like-minded agents act in the same way given the same (relevant) information.

The third condition requires that a union of states of relevant knowledge must itself be a state of relevant knowledge. Recall that our problem with Bacharach's definition of the sure thing condition was caused by the fact that the union of states of knowledge is in general not a state of knowledge (see Lemma 3.2). Thus, whereas unions of states of knowledge did not correspond to a state of knowledge of the disjunction of the states, unions of states of *relevant* knowledge do correspond to disjunctions of the relevant facts known in the states of knowledge being united. We can thus define the sure thing principle with respect to an admissible decision function as follows:

Definition 4.2: An admissible decision function D is said to satisfy the *projected sure thing condition* (PSTC) if there exists a relevance projection ρ_D corresponding to D such that whenever a set $\rho_D(e)$ is a disjoint union of the sets $\rho_D(J)$ for a family of events $\{J\}$ on each of which $D(J) = b$, then also $D(e) = b$.

Having introduced admissible decision functions, and redefined like-mindedness and the sure thing principle with respect to them, we are faced with a number of questions. First of all, we

[2] We make this requirement for ease of exposition. Technically, a slightly weaker condition would suffice. While our choice has the effect of making fewer decision functions admissible, this condition holds in many cases of interest.

should see whether such admissible decision functions arise in common scenarios. This will be done by providing a natural interpretation of the murder story example in which the detectives are like-minded, and follow an admissible decision function satisfying the projected sure thing condition. Once we do this, we will face the question of whether the agreement theorem holds with respect to the new definitions.

5 Agreement Theorem Revisited

We are now in a position to show the following:

Proposition 5.1: *[Disagreement Theorem] Like-minded agents following an admissible decision function that satisfies the projected sure thing condition (PSTC) may agree to disagree.*

In order to prove this proposition, we will construct an example in which the agreement theorem fails. Roughly speaking, the example will be an instance of the murder story; we will first give an informal presentation of the scenario, and later complete the formal details.

> There are initially three main suspects, called α, β, and γ. It is assumed that γ is the toughest of the three, followed by β, while α is the weakest. Therefore, α is more likely than β to cooperate in an interrogation, while β in turn is more likely than γ. The police school in Macho Macho maintains that at most one arrest should be performed in any investigation, in order to keep up the public's trust in the competence and integrity of its police. As a consequence, when it is known that a particular suspect is guilty of a crime, he is immediately brought to trial. When there is a doubt between two suspects, the weaker of the two is brought in and competently interrogated until the police discovers whether he is innocent. Finally, as long as there are more than two suspects, the investigation proceeds without any arrests being performed.
>
> In the particular instance being described, γ is the culprit. By the time Alice and Bob report to the chief of police, Alice has discovered that β is innocent, and is still in doubt whether it was α or γ that was at fault. Bob, on the other hand, was less successfull, and still considers each of the three a suspect. Alice therefore initially intends to suggest that α be arrested, while Bob would suggest that no arrests be made at this stage. Throughout their conversation, Alice insists on suggesting that α be arrested for interrogation, while Bob, not being able to use this information to rule out any of the suspects, insists on suggesting that no arrests be made. After a while it becomes common knowledge that Alice and Bob will stick to these conclusions, and they enter the chief's room having agreed to disagree.

It is obvious that Bob's declaration does not provide Alice with any useful information. Let us consider why Bob gains no relevant information from Alice's declaration. Alice's declaration implies that she has discovered about one of β and γ that he is innocent, and still considers the other one of them and α suspect. However, Bob cannot determine from Alice's declaration whom she has discovered as being innocent. As a consequence, he still considers each of α, β, and γ suspect after her declaration.[3] As a consequence, in their second round of declarations both Alice and Bob will stick to their original declarations. The exact same reasoning and the same declarations repeat themselves in each of the following rounds of Alice and Bob's conversation, until at some point they attain common knowledge of their respective suggestions. We now formalize this example.

5.1 Modeling the murder story scenario

Before we turn to the task of modeling the particular example described above, we wish to enrich Aumann's model of knowledge to one in which the internal structure of the states of the world is made more explicit. A state of the world consists of local states of a distinguished set of agents, and the state of the rest of the world, which we call the *environment.* (The environment will often contain additional agents; the agents that are singled out are typically the ones in whose states and knowledge we are most interested.) More formally, following work on reasoning about knowledge in distributed systems [HM89,Hal87], we will associate with every state of the world ω an *internal structure* $int(\omega)$ of the form $(\ell_1, \ldots, \ell_n, \ell_{env})$, where ℓ_j represents the local state of agent j, and ℓ_{env} represents the state of the environment. We will denote agent j's local state at $int(\omega)$ by ω_j, and the environment's state by ω_{env}. The actual states of the agent and of the environment will in general themselves have additional structure, depending on the particulars of the scenario being modeled.

Once we ascribe to each state of the world such internal structure, we can derive the information functions I_j directly from the internal structure, based on the agents' local states. Two worlds will be considered indistinguishable by agent j exactly if she has the same local state in both. Formally, we define

$$I_j(\omega) = \{\omega' : \omega_j = \omega'_j\}.$$

In effect, local states replace information functions as primitives of the model. We remark that adding such internal structure to states of the world and deriving the information functions in this manner can be done without loss of generality to any model of knowledge of the type described in Section 2. Specifically, assuming there are distinct names for all the states of the world, and for all the possible states of knowledge, we can simply take ω_j to be the name of $I_j(\omega)$, and take ω_{env} to be the name of ω. This construction yields a model isomorphic (with respect to knowledge) to the original one.

In the murder story application, the agents we wish to study carefully are Alice and Bob. We will thus associate with every state of the world an internal structure of the form $(\ell_A, \ell_B, \ell_{env})$. All relevant facts other than Alice and Bob's states will be modeled by the environment. Of

[3]The intuitive reason why Bob cannot suggest to interrogate α at this point is that if Bob would now interrogate α and discover that α is innocent, he could not say who should be indicted without a second arrest.

course, this environment may very well contain other agents related to the murder case, may involve their knowledge, etc. (The choice is up to us. We could just as well have chosen to model these additional agents as first rate citizens with their own local states. There are many ways to slice a cake.) Thinking in terms of agents' local states has the advantage that we can often define these states in a natural manner based on the scenario we are considering. This allows a careful study of what knowledge each agent obtains at any given point, and of how knowledge evolves over time.

The murder story scenario seems to involve three essential steps. The first stage involves the murder and all events up to the point at which the chief of police puts Alice and Bob on the case. The second stage is the detectives' inquiry stage, in which they each investigate various aspects of the murder case. Finally, the third case consists of their conversation in the locker room, resulting in their final report to the chief. Each of the detectives enters the second stage with a particular local state, which includes the wisdom gained in police school, and may also include personal tendencies as to how to perform the investigation. By the end of the second stage, the local state of each detective also contains the evidence s/he has obtained. In the third stage, Alice and Bob compare notes. They alternate turns in each announcing the action it would take given its current knowledge. Following each announcement, the contents of this announcement are appended to both agents' local states. We are thus assuming that Alice and Bob do not forget any of their discussion.[4] Notice that as a consequence of our defining an agent's knowledge based on its local state, the agents' relevant knowledge is updated automatically. Our model, taken from the distributed systems methodology, thus incorporates the evolution of agents' knowledge in a manner that is directly related to the change in the information they maintain. We remark that equivalent methods of updating agents' knowledge in the course of such a conversation are defined explicitly in [GP82,Mak83,Cav83,Bac85,PK87].

5.2 The counterexample

What remains to be done in order to complete the formal proof of Proposition 5.1 is to (i) describe the detectives' decision function, (ii) show that it is admissible and satisfies PSTC, and (iii) show that Alice and Bob agree to disagree in the particular scenario presented.

The detectives' decision function D can easily be described by specifying its relevance projection ρ_D, and by specifying the associated function D^r, whose domain consists of the sets $\rho_D(e)$. Formally, we will have $D(e) = D^r(\rho_D(e))$. Given a state ω of the world, we define $\rho_D(\omega)$ to be the actual murderer in the state ω, if the murder has already taken place in ω's

[4] This is purely an assumption we make for simplicity in this particular example. As is well-known, we could model forgetting in various ways too. For example, we could capture the idea that an agent only remembers the outcome of its test and the three latest announcements by having the local states contain exactly that information.

history. The definition of D^r is as follows:

$$\begin{array}{lll} D^r(\{\alpha\}) = indict(\alpha) & D^r(\{\beta,\gamma\}) = arrest(\beta) & \\ D^r(\{\beta\}) = indict(\beta) & D^r(\{\alpha,\gamma\}) = arrest(\alpha) & D^r(\{\alpha,\beta,\gamma\}) = \emptyset \\ D^r(\{\gamma\}) = indict(\gamma) & D^r(\{\alpha,\beta\}) = arrest(\alpha) & \end{array}$$

The set Q is thus $\{\alpha,\beta,\gamma\}$. An immediate corollary of a theorem of Geanakoplos and Polemarchakis in [GP82] states that if Q is finite, then Alice and Bob are guaranteed to reach common knowledge of the actions each one of them intends to perform, after a finite number of rounds.

Let us check that D is an admissible decision function. By defining D based on ρ_D, we have guaranteed that it satisfy the first admissibility condition. The second admissibility condition corresponds to the assumption, which we are implicitly making, that any subset of $\{\alpha,\beta,\gamma\}$ is a possible state of relevant knowledge for each of the detectives. Finally, the third condition is satisfied because D^r is defined on all nonempty subsets of Q and hence on all unions of states of relevant knowledge. It follows that D is admissible. The fact that D satisfies the projected sure thing condition is trivially satisfied, as there are no disjoint states of relevant knowledge on which the same decision is taken. (The only two state of relevant knowledge on which the same action is taken are $\{\alpha,\beta\}$ and $\{\alpha,\gamma\}$, but these are not disjoint.)

The actual scenario in the counterexample is one in which Alice finishes her inquiry (and enters the locker room) with $\{\alpha,\gamma\}$ as her state of relevant knowledge, while Bob has $\{\alpha,\beta,\gamma\}$. A simple proof by induction on the number of rounds now shows that in this particular example, Alice will forever have $\{\alpha,\gamma\}$ as her state of relevant knowledge, and hence will insist on deciding to arrest α, while Bob will have $\{\alpha,\beta,\gamma\}$ as his state, and will insist on continuing the investigation with no arrests. Now, since their decisions will become common knowledge after a finite number of steps, they will in fact end up *agreeing to disagree*!

5.3 Sufficient conditions for agreement

We now turn to study sufficient conditions for the agreement theorem. In order to do so, let us start by reconsidering why the theorem fails in the counterexample presented above. The point seems to be that whereas different states of knowledge of a given agent are guaranteed to be disjoint, different states of relevant knowledge are not guaranteed to be disjoint. However, in the spirit of STP and STC, union consistency is required by PSTC only for disjoint unions. Looking at the details of the example, Bob's state of relevant knowledge when they agree to disagree is $\{\alpha,\beta,\gamma\}$, and he remains uncertain whether Alice's state of knowledge is $\{\alpha,\beta\}$ or $\{\alpha,\gamma\}$. Observe that $D^r(\{\alpha,\beta\}) = D^r(\{\alpha,\gamma\}) = arrest(\alpha)$, while $D^r(\{\alpha,\beta\} \cup \{\alpha,\gamma\}) = D^r(\{\alpha,\beta,\gamma\}) = \emptyset$. We are thus led to the question of whether modifying PSTC to apply to arbitrary unions can salvage the agreement theorem for scenarios such as the murder story. Define an admissible decision function D to satisfy the *inclusive projected sure thing condition* (IPSTC) if whenever a set $X \subseteq Q$ is a union of a family of (not necessarily disjoint) subsets $\{Y\}$, on each of which $D^r(Y) = b$, then also $D^r(X) = b$. We can show:

Theorem 5.2: *Like-minded agents following an admissible decision function satisfying the inclusive projected sure thing condition (IPSTC) cannot agree to disagree.*

Proof: As in the proof of Theorem 3.1, set $e = C(d_1 = a) \cap C(d_2 = b)$. Again, because e is common knowledge, $K_1(e) = e$ and therefore e is a (disjoint) union of elements of the form $I = I_1(\omega)$. By definition of e, in every $\omega \in e$ we have $d_1(\omega) = a$, and hence $D^r(\rho_D(I_1(\omega))) = a$. Now, since e is a (nonempty) union of such sets I, we have by definition of ρ_D that $\rho_D(e)$ is the union of the corresponding sets $\rho_D(I)$. The fact that D satisfies the inclusive projected sure thing condition now implies that $D(e) = D^r(\rho_D(e)) = a$. Similar reasoning with respect to agent 2 shows that $D(e) = b$, and as a result we obtain $a = b$. ∎

The inclusive projected sure thing condition is clearly stronger than PSTC. However, for decision functions that do not originate from probabilistic reasoning, it does not seem to be much harder to accept the inclusive condition than it is to accept the original (exclusive) PSTC. Indeed, on second thought, it is not clear why disjointness appears in the blood stains motivation for STP quoted in the introduction. In non-probabilistic settings, restricting attention to disjoint unions is often quite unnatural. (In cases when a decision function is based on posterior probabilities or expectations, the disjointness requirement arises in a natural way.) Indeed, we consider the inclusive projected sure thing condition to be the more natural condition in the non-probabilistic case. We therefore conclude that, once the definitions are formulated appropriately and STP is replaced by inclusive STP, the agreement theorem does hold in the context of the murder story. In this case the statement that if the detectives use a reasonable decision function they cannot agree to disagree is justified. This also explains why our counterexample may seem somewhat contrived or unnatural: Any non-probabilistic decision function that satisfies PSTC but not IPSTC is likely to be somewhat unnatural.

It is interesting to note that PSTC does suffice when the projections of disjoint states of knowledge are guaranteed to be disjoint. We can thus state the following proposition:

Proposition 5.3: *Let $\Pi = \{1, 2\}$, and let $e = C(d_1 = a) \cap C(d_2 = b)$. Assume that (i) the agents are like-minded, (ii) they follow an admissible decision function D satisfying PSTC, and (iii) for $j \in \Pi$ and all $\omega, \omega' \in e$ it is the case that whenever $I_j(\omega) \cap I_j(\omega') = \emptyset$, then also $\rho_D(I_j(\omega)) \cap \rho_D(I_j(\omega')) = \emptyset$. Then*

$$[C(d_1 = a) \cap C(d_2 = b) \neq \emptyset] \quad \Rightarrow \quad a = b.$$

We can think of the requirement here as a combined condition, applying both to the decision function *and* to the protocol the agents are using for their interaction. It would be interesting to study other combined conditions that yield the agreement theorem.

5.4 More than two agents

Our final topic involves the question of how the analysis presented above applies to the case of more than two agents. It turns out that there are at least a couple of interesting types of scenarios that are worth considering in this case. One of them is the direct generalization of the agreement theorem to agreement among $n > 2$ agents. This corresponds to the case in which, say, three detectives, Alice, Bob, and Charlie are assigned to the case, and all three meet in the locker room and carry out a joint discussion of their intended actions. Everything any one of them says in this discussion immediately becomes common knowledge to all three. It is not hard to show that the results of [Aum76,Bac85,Cav83] and our above results all extend immediately to more than two agents in this case. However, in [PK87] Parikh and Krasucki considered a somewhat more practical situation in which the agents communicate in pairs, and the contents of a message are known only to the sender and the reciever of the message. They assume, however, that the communication protocol being used is *fair*,[5] and that the decision functions are real valued.

Definition 5.4: A decision function D is said to be *weakly convex* if for all $X, Y \subseteq \Omega$ we have

$$X \cap Y = \emptyset \Rightarrow \quad D(X \cup Y) = a \cdot D(X) + b \cdot D(Y),$$

for some $a, b \geq 0$ such that $a + b = 1$. D is *strongly convex* if it guarantees that $a, b > 0$.

Parikh and Krasucki show that the agreement holds for fair protocols with decision functions satisfying STC when there are $n = 2$ agents, and that this is not the case for $n > 2$. Weak convexity of D is a sufficient condition for the agreement theorem in the case of $n = 3$ agents, but not for $n > 3$. Finally, the agreement theorem holds in the context of fair protocols for $n \geq 4$ when D is strongly convex. We now review these results in light of our analysis.

The weak and strong convexity conditions, like the STC, are applied to disjoint unions of subsets of Ω. They therefore suffer from the same shortcomings as STC with respect to their intuitive meaning for deterministic or generally non-probabilistic decision functions. For the case of $n = 3$ we can obtain a positive result similar to Theorem 5.2. We define a decision function D to satisfy *inclusive weak convexity* if for all sets $X, Y \subseteq \Omega$ (not necessarily disjoint) it is the case that $D(X \cup Y) = a \cdot D(X) + b \cdot D(Y)$, for some $a, b \geq 0$ such that $a + b = 1$. An appropriate modification of the proof of [PK87] yields:

Proposition 5.5: *Three like-minded agents using a fair protocol and a continuous admissible decision function satisfying inclusive weak convexity cannot agree to disagree.*

It is possible to attempt to do the same for strong convexity and $n \geq 4$. Again, we would relax the disjointness requirement and obtain the notion of inclusive strong convexity. This, however, yields a rather meaningless result, as the following lemma shows:

[5] By a *protocol* they mean an a priori fixed list of sender-receiver pairs, specifying the order in which messages are sent. Given such a protocol, consider a graph whose vertices are the agents, where there is a directed edge from vertex i to vertex j exactly if i sends j an infinite number of messages according to the protocol. They call a protocol *fair* if its corresponding graph thus constructed is strongly connected.

Lemma 5.6: *A decision function D satisfying inclusive strong convexity is necessarily a constant function.*

Proof: For any $X \subseteq \Omega$ we have

$$D(\Omega) = D(X \cup \Omega) = a \cdot D(X) + b \cdot D(\Omega).$$

Since $a > 0$ and $a + b = 1$, we get $D(X) = D(\Omega)$. ∎

We are therefore unable to suggest any nontrivial positive result for fair protocols in the case $n \geq 4$.

6 Conclusions

We argued that formal definitions of the sure thing condition and the notion of like-mindedness used in [Aum89,Bac85,Cav83] do not capture their intended intuitive meaning. As a result, the agreement theorem of [Bac85,Cav83] is perhaps less widely applicable than was believed. It is important to note, however, that this theorem is both technically correct and of considerable practical significance. While not quite applying to arbitrary decision functions, it extends Aumann's original agreement theorem [Aum76] from agreeing on posteriors to many other interesting agreements, such as expectations, actions that maximize conditional expectations, etc. It seems not to directly apply in the presence of (non-probabilistic) nondeterminism in the agents' actions. In particular, it does not apply to the murder story example.

The reason that the technical definitions of like-mindedness and STC fail to capture their intended meaning seems to be that states of knowledge are a special subclass of the set of all events. This set is not closed under operations such as taking union, nor is it guaranteed to be symmetric with respect to the agents. Some of the structure of this set is more transparent once we model the internal structure of states of the world explicitly, as is done in the distributed systems literature, rather than implicitly, as in the game theoretic literature. The explicit modeling has the additional advantage that it provides useful machinery for the formalization of particular examples, and makes the evolution of knowledge over time more apparent.

Our definition of admissible decision functions and PSTC made it possible for us to consider the agreement theorem in the context of scenarios such as the murder story example. It is interesting to note, however, that it is not the case that posterior probability is a special case of an admissible decision function satisfying PSTC. (Recall that the STC is a proper generalization of posterior probability.) The reason for this is that our relevant knowledge states are constructed in a way that does not maintain information about the probabilities of the events known about. Indeed, the interaction of relevant knowledge and probability in this context is as yet somewhat unclear to us. We believe it deserves to be studied further. Perhaps the framework of Halpern and Tuttle in [HT89] could prove useful here.

We do not consider the results reported on in this abstract as showing that the claim made in the murder story is philosophically wrong. On the contrary, once the definitions are reformulated, and we consider an *inclusive* version of the sure thing principle, the agreement theorem is maintained. Our results mainly raise issues regarding how one should formalize concepts related to, and in the presence of, knowledge. They imply that Bacharach and Cave's original definitions and theorem do not apply to the murder story. It remains an interesting open problem whether there is a natural formulation of the agreement theorem that generalizes both our results and those of Bacharach and Cave. Such a theorem would at once apply both to probabilistic and to non-probabilistic situations, and would justify Bacharach's claim that "*differences in information alone cannot account for differences in behavior of rational persons ... any more than they can account for differences of opinion*" [Bac85].

Acknowledgments

We'd like to thank Robert Aumann for useful discussions and for comments on an earlier version of this abstract. His comments improved the presentation of the material in a substantial way. We also thank Yishai Feldman, Joe Halpern, and Moshe Vardi for useful discussions on the topic of this paper. Special thanks to Gadi Taubenfeld for drawing our attention to [Aum89], and thereby starting us off on this research project.

References

[Aum76] R. J. Aumann, Agreeing to Disagree, *The Annals of Statistics*, Vol 4 No 6, 1976, pp. 1236-1239.

[Aum89] R. J. Aumann, Notes on Interactive Epistemology, unpublished manuscript, version 89.04.06, 1989.

[Bac85] M. Bacharach, Some Extensions of a Claim of Aumann in an Axiomatic Model of Knowledge, *Journal of Economic Theory*, Vol 37, 1985 pp. 167-190.

[Cav83] J. A. K. Cave, Learning to Agree, *Economics Letters*, Vol 12, 1983, pp. 147-152.

[GP82] J. D. Geanakoplos and H. M. Polemarchakis, We Can't Disagree Forever, *Journal of Economic Theory*, Vol 28, 1982, pp. 192-200.

[Hal87] J. Y. Halpern, Using reasoning about knowledge to analyze distributed systems, *Annual Review of Computer Science*, Vol 2, J. Traub et al. eds., 1987, pp. 37-68.

[HM85] J. Y. Halpern and Y. Moses, A Guide to the Modal Logics of Knowledge and Belief, *Ninth International Joint Conference on Artificial Intelligence (IJCAI-85)*, 1985, pp. 480-490.

[HM89] J. Y. Halpern and Y. Moses, Knowledge and Common Knowledge in a Distributed Environment, *IBM RJ 4421*, 4th revision, September 1989. An early version appeared in *Proceedings of the 3rd ACM Symposium on Principles of Distributed Computing*, 1984, pp. 50-61.

[HT89] J. Y. Halpern and M. R. Tuttle, Knowledge, Probability, and Adversaries, *Proceedings of the 8th ACM Symposium on Principles of Distributed Computing*, 1989, pp. 119-128.

[Mak83] L. Makowski, Common Knowledge and Common Learning, unpublished manuscript, UC Davis, June 1983.

[PK87] R. Parikh and P. Krasucki, Communication, Consensus and Knowledge, unpublished manuscript, 1987.

[Sav54] L. J. Savage, *The Foundations of Statistics*, John Wiley and sons, 1954. 2nd revised edition by Dover Publications, 1972.

17

COSTLY ACQUISITION OF (DIFFERENTIATED) INFORMATION

Beth Allen
Department of Economics
University of Pennsylvania
3718 Locust Walk
Philadelphia, PA 19104-6297

ABSTRACT

Consumers' choices among many different types of information sub-σ-fields are examined in a large, perfectly competitive pure exchange economy in which information serves as a consumption good as well as a device to aid in the maximization of state-dependent utility. Analysis of derived preferences over information and wealth (and the resulting value of information function) implies that individual demands for information are well defined and upper hemicontinuous even though these correspondences fail to be convex valued. Sufficient conditions are given for the consistency of information acquisition decisions so that there exist equilibrium price vectors for physical goods and continuous equilibrium price functions for information in a general equilibrium model.

1 INTRODUCTION

This paper proposes a framework for studying individuals' economic decisions to purchase information for both its intrinsic consumption value and its function in the conditioning operation defining optimization problems under uncertainty. In contrast to the author's previous work (i.e., Allen (1986a, 1986b)) on the pure information case, this hybrid model permits information to confer direct utility in consumption so that literary merit and other aesthetic aspects of information can be included. Since I focus here on enriching the analysis to broaden consumers' uses of information, examination of a pure exchange economy is appropriate. [However, Allen (1990b) incorporates information production.]

A key feature of all this work is that information is viewed as a differentiated commodity, so that various types of information can be considered. Agents are hypothesized to costlessly combine information from limited numbers of diverse sources. The heterogeneity is analyzed by specifying a (metric) topological space of information sub-σ-fields, thereby defining similarity of information structures; see Allen (1983).

An early unpublished manuscript by Aumann (undated) shows that information production and sales can be admitted into a general equilibrium model quite easily under the usual assumptions, such as convexity. However, informational considerations inherently lead to the problems of indivisibilities (and hence nonconvexities), satiation, and price-dependent preferences, as well as (uncountably) infinite-dimensional commodity spaces for differentiated information.

2 THE MODEL

A large number of individually small consumers are able to trade not only ℓ ordinary commodities but also various pieces of information. They seek to maximize their ex ante (i.e., at the time when trading occurs) expected state-dependent utility of consuming physical goods and information. The model is similar to those studied in Allen (1986a, 1986b, 1990a, 1990b).

2.1 Uncertainty and Information

The underlying uncertainty is specified by an abstract probability triple $(\Omega, \mathbf{F}, \mu)$, where Ω is an arbitrary (possibly uncountable) set of states of the world, $\mathbf{F}$ is a σ-field of subsets of Ω which are interpreted as the measurable events eventually observable when consumption occurs, and μ is a (σ-additive) probability measure defined on $(\Omega, \mathbf{F})$. Consumers' unconditional prior probabilities may be subjective; they need not equal μ and different consumers may have different subjective probabilities. However, all must have the same null sets as μ. To simplify notation, I shall take μ to be the personal probability of each agent.

Pieces or types of information are modelled as sub-σ-fields of $\mathbf{F}$.

Sub-σ-fields having the same completion are identified because they invoke the same economic behavior almost surely. Then the set of these equivalence classes of sub-σ-fields of F is endowed with the topology induced by the metric (see Allen (1983, 1984), Allen and VanZandt (1989), and VanZandt (1989))

$$d(G,H) = \sup_{G\in G} \inf_{H\in H} \mu(G\Delta H) + \sup_{H\in H} \inf_{G\in G} \mu(G\Delta H).$$

[Some alternatives have been examined by Cotter (1986), Stinchcombe (1989), and VanZandt (1988).] Let $F^* = \{G \subset F | G$ is a complete sub-σ-field of $F\}$. The information available to agents is hypothesized to come from three compact subsets of F^*: (a) information which can be sold and which is not available (or "forgotten") after it is sold, (b) information which can be sold, but is retained (or "remembered") after the sale, and (c) information which cannot be sold or purchased, perhaps because of legal prohibitions, confidentially, adverse selection, or moral hazard. Call these disjoint sets K^a, K^b and K^c and let K be a compact subset of F^* such that $K \supset K^a \cup K^b \cup K^c$. Assume that all four sets are closed under the information combination operation $\sup : F \times F \to F$ defined by $\sup(G, H) = G \vee H = \sigma(G \cup H)$, the smallest (complete since G and H are) σ-field containing G and H. Information of class (a) or (b) can be purchased, and the purchaser can then use the information in calculating the conditional expected utility function to be maximized. On the other hand, an individual's endowment of class (c) information should be viewed as part of the intrinsic description of the agent. Class (c) information can be written, without loss of generality, as a single information sub-σ-field $I \in K^c$ while the information of types (a) and (b) possessed initially by a trader is assumed to consist of finitely many (not necessarily distinct) sub-σ-fields $\bar{G}^1, \bar{G}^2, \ldots, \bar{G}^A, \bar{H}^1, \ldots \bar{H}^B$ of K^a and K^b respectively. To summarize, class (c) information is unchangeable and should be treated like preferences, class (a) information is gone when it's sold (like commodity endowments) and class (b) information displays features of both other classes.

2.2 Agents' Characteristics

A trader is described by an initial endowment of physical goods, an initial endowment of information, and state dependent (cardinal) utility functions over consumption bundles of physical commodities. Initial endowments of the ℓ ordinary physical commodities are given by strictly positive vectors $e \in \bar{K}$, where $\bar{K}$ is a compact subset of $\mathbb{R}^{\ell}_{++}$. An initial endowment of information consists of a finite collection $[\bar{G}^1, \bar{G}^2, \ldots, \bar{G}^A, \bar{H}^1, \bar{H}^2, \ldots, \bar{H}^B, I]$ of (not necessarily distinct) information structures in K^a, K^b and K^c. Finally, state dependent utilities are specified by a measurable mapping $U : \Omega \to C^0(\mathbb{R}^{\ell}_{+} \times K, \mathbb{R})$ where $C^0(\mathbb{R}^{\ell}_{+} \times K, \mathbb{R})$ is given its Borel σ-field derived from the compact-open topology and F is the σ-field on Ω. For convenience, write $U(\omega) = u(\cdot;\cdot;\omega)$, where $u : \mathbb{R}^{\ell}_{+} \times K \times \Omega \to \mathbb{R}$ is jointly measurable (by Lemma 2.2 in Stinchcombe and White (1989)) from its continuity in the first two arguments and measurability in the third. Assume that for every $\omega \in \Omega$ and every $J \in K$, $u(\cdot;J;\omega)$ is strictly monotone (increasing) and strictly concave on $\mathbb{R}^{\ell}_{+}$. Assume also that there are compact convex subsets K^1 and K^2 of $C^0(\mathbb{R}^{\ell}_{+} \times K, \mathbb{R})$ and $C^0(\mathbb{R}^{\ell}_{+}, \mathbb{R})$ such that $u(\cdot;\cdot;\omega) \in K^1$ for every $\omega \in \Omega$ and $u(\cdot;J;\omega) \in K^2$ for all $J \in K$ and $\omega \in \Omega$.

For convenience, view the commodity space for differentiated information as a subset of a space of measures. Let M_K denote the set of integer-valued positive measures β on K with $\beta(K^a) \leq \bar{A}$, $\beta(K^b) \leq 2\bar{B}$ and $\beta(K^c) = 1$ for some fixed nonnegative integers $\bar{A}$ and $\bar{B}$ (at least one of which must be positive to permit agents to trade their information endowments). Give M_K the topology of weak convergence of measures, so that M_K is a compact set. Alternatively, measures in M_K can be written as the sum of a Dirac measure on

$K^c \supset \{\Omega, \emptyset\}$, at most $\bar{A}$ Dirac measures on K^a and at most $\bar{B}$ Dirac measures on K^b. Thus $\bar{A} + 2\bar{B} + 1$ gives an upper bound on the number of separate (but not necessarily distinct) information structures that an agent can consider, while the information endowment $[\bar{G}^1, \ldots, \bar{G}^A, \bar{H}^1, \ldots, \bar{H}^B, I]$ can be written as $\beta = \sum_{i=1}^{A} \delta(\bar{G}^i) + \sum_{i=1}^{B} \delta(\bar{H}^i) + \delta(I) \in \mathbf{M}_K$.

Throughout the paper, a price or price vector, denoted by $p \in \Delta = \{p \in \mathbb{R}^{\ell}_{++} \mid \sum_{j=1}^{\ell} p_j = 1\}$ states the relative price (normalized to lie in the unit simplex) for each of the ℓ ordinary physical goods. A price system (for information) refers solely to prices for information structures. A price system is a function in $C^+(K^a \cup K^b) = \{q : K^a \cup K^b \to \mathbb{R} \mid q$ is continuous, $q(G) \geq 0$ for all $G \in K^a$, and $q(H) \geq 0$ for all $H \in K^b\}$.

3 INDIVIDUAL BEHAVIOR

Agents can trade on both the markets for information and the markets for ordinary physical goods. They face a single budget constraint for these transactions. Consumers know all prices when they make their optimization decisions; they are also assumed to know their own endowments of physical goods and information and their own state-dependent utility functions defined over physical goods and information. Moreover, each trader knows the "rules" regarding the three types of information and is aware of the impossibility--due to the negligibility of each in the nonatomic continuum of agents--of affecting market prices.

Hence, the individual's utility maximization problem can be stated formally as follows:

Choose $x : \Omega \to \mathbb{R}^{\ell}_{+}$ and $G^1, \ldots, G^{A'} \in K^a$, $H^1, \ldots, H^{B'} \in K^b$ so as to maximize $E(u(x(\omega); \sigma(G^1 \cup \ldots \cup G^{A'} \cup H^1 \cup \ldots \cup H^{B'} \cup \bar{H}^1 \cup \ldots \cup \bar{H}^B \cup I);\omega) \,|\, \sigma(G^1 \cup \ldots G^A \cup H^1 \cup \ldots \cup H^{B'} \cup \bar{H}^1 \cup \ldots \cup \bar{H}^B \cup I))$ subject to

(i) $p \cdot x(\omega) + \sum_{i=1}^{A'} q(G^i) + \sum_{i=1}^{B'} q(H^i) \le p \cdot e + \sum_{i=1}^{A} q(\bar{G}^i) + \sum_{i=1}^{B} q(\bar{H}^i)$

(ii) $x : \Omega \to \mathbb{R}_+^\ell$ is $\sigma(G^1 \cup \ldots \cup G^{A'} \cup H^1 \cup \ldots \cup H^{B'} \cup \bar{H}^1 \cup \ldots \cup \bar{H}^B \cup I)$-measurable

(iii) $A' \le \bar{A}$ and $B' \le \bar{B}$.

[The conditional expectation is taken with respect to fixed versions of regular conditional probability. Of course the set of maximizers is an equivalence class of measurable functions from Ω to $\mathbb{R}_+^\ell$ which are equal μ-almost surely.]

Two strategies are available to analyze the solution. The direct approach focuses on the properties of conditional expected utility, which must be almost surely constant over states of the world that cannot be distinguished by the consumer's information. Hence the maximizers almost surely cannot differ over indistinguishable states either and the measurability constraint in (ii) becomes redundant. An alternative method due to VanZandt (1988) ignores the calculation of conditional expected utility and instead focuses on properties of the measurability constraint (ii). With either approach, continuity and compactness ensure the existence of maximizers while a generalized version of the Maximium Theorem gives upper hemicontinuity of the solution as prices change.

Theorem 1. The individual demand correspondence for ordinary physical goods and information is a nonempty, compact-valued and upper hemicontinuous correspondence from $\Delta \times C^+(K^a \cup K^b) \times \bar{K} \times C(K, L^1(\Omega, F, \mu; K^2)) \times M_K$ to $L^1(\Omega, F, \mu; \mathbb{R}_+^\ell) \times M_K$.

Proof. As in Allen (1986a), define the induced value of information $v(\gamma, w; e, u(\cdot;\bar{\gamma};\cdot), p, \beta) = \max\{Eu(x(\omega);\omega) \mid x : \Omega \to \mathbb{R}_+^\ell$ is γ-measurable and $p \cdot x(\omega) \le w$ for all $\omega \in \Omega\}$ where $u(\cdot;\bar{\gamma};\cdot) \in L^1(\Omega, F, \mu; K^2)$ is treated as a parameter. Thus, v is the maximum expected utility that the consumer can achieve given prices $p \in \Delta$ and wealth $w \in \mathbb{R}$ when the consumer "enjoys" information $\bar{\gamma} \in \mathbf{M}_K$ and is able to condition on the information $\gamma \in \mathbf{M}_K$. Continuity of $v : \mathbf{M}_K \times [0,\bar{C}] \times \bar{K} \times \mathbf{L}^1(\Omega,\mathbf{F},\mu;K^1) \times \Delta \times \mathbf{M}_K \to \mathbb{R}$ is proved in Proposition 3.8 of Allen (1986a), where $\bar{C}$ is the upper bound for wealth that is justified in the appendix.

Now restrict v to the "diagonal" $\gamma = \bar{\gamma}$ and define induced preferences--a complete symmetric transitive binary relation--on $\mathbf{M}_K \times [0, \bar{C}]$ by their graph $Gr(\leq) = \{(\gamma,w,\gamma',w') \in \mathbf{M}_K \times [0, \bar{C}] \times \mathbf{M}_K \times [0,\bar{C}] \mid v(\gamma,w) \leq v(w',\gamma')\}$. These preferences are well defined and continuous (by the continuity of v) and moreover, for the closed convergence topology, their graphs depend continuously on the parameters in $\bar{K} \times C(K, \mathbf{L}^1(\Omega,\mathbf{F},\mu;K^2)) \times \Delta \times \mathbf{M}_K$ by Theorem 4.1 of Allen (1986a).

Next, consider the following information demand problem: Given q and p,

$$\text{choose } \gamma \in \mathbf{M}_K \text{ and } w \in [0, \bar{C}] \text{ to maximize } v(\gamma,w;e,u(\cdot;\gamma;\cdot),p,\beta)$$

$$\text{subject to } w = p\cdot e + \sum_{i=1}^{A} q(\bar{G}^i) + \sum_{i=1}^{B} q(\bar{H}^i) - \sum_{i=1}^{A'} q(G^i) - \sum_{i=1}^{B'} q(H^i)$$

$$\text{and } \gamma = \delta(I) + \sum_{i=1}^{A'} \delta(G^i) + \sum_{i=1}^{B'} \delta(H^i) + \sum_{i=1}^{B} \delta(\bar{H}^i).$$

By compactness and continuity, maximizers exist and the Maximum Theorem guarantees that they form an upper hemicontinuous correspondence defined on $\bar{K} \times C(K, \mathbf{L}^1(\Omega,\mathbf{F},\mu;K^2)) \times \mathbf{M}_K \times \Delta \times C^+(K^a \cup K^b)$.

To finish, appeal to Corollary 10.12 in Allen (1983) to obtain $\mathbf{L}^1$ convergence of the individual demand functions $x : \Omega \to \mathbb{R}^\ell_+$. []

Observe that strict concavity of (state dependent and information parameterized) utilities implies that demands for physical commodities, given information trades, are necessarily single valued. On the other hand, one cannot eliminate the tendency for information demands to be set valued, at least for some price functions. The problem is that indivisibilities--the requirement that information sales and purchases involve only discrete integer-valued amounts of each information structure--generate nonconvexities in agents' feasible consumption sets for information (M_K is not convex even when K is trivial) and hence nonconvexities in information demand correspondences.

4 DISTRIBUTIONS AND EQUILIBRIUM

To complete the definition of an economy, I must specify the set of agents given by their endowments of information and physical commodities and (state dependent) utility functions. This is accomplished with a statistical description of agents' characteristics. Accordingly, equilibrium allocations are defined in terms of joint distributions on agents' characteristics and their resulting assignments of final information and state-dependent consumption of physical goods.

4.1 Distributions of Agents' Characteristics

To avoid measurability technicalities, I work with economies specified by a distribution on the (metric) space of agents' characteristics and with equilibrium distributions. Otherwise, the problem is that for a given representation, there need not exist equilibrium allocations. For my space of information bundles, the integral of a (uniformly bounded) correspondence with measurable graph is well defined, and nonempty, but it need not be convex valued or weak* closed. I can avoid this problem by considering sequences of "finite dimensional"--i.e., with finitely many types of information structures --approximations to M_K, since on Euclidean spaces the desired integrals are closed and convex-valued. Examination of the limit points (for the topology of weak convergence of probability measures) of equilibrium distributions for the approximations leads to existence of equilibrium.

Accordingly, an economy is defined as a distribution, or probability measure, ν on the measurable space $(\bar{K} \times L^1(\Omega, F, \mu; K^1) \times M_K, B(\bar{K} \times L^1(\Omega, F, \mu; K^1) \times M_K))$. Note that $\bar{K} \subset \mathbb{R}^{\ell}_{++}$ and M_K are compact metric spaces, while $L^1(\Omega, F, \mu; K^1)$ is a metric space. Recall that $K^1 \subset C^0(\mathbb{R}^{\ell}_{+}, \mathbb{R})$ is compact. The space of agents' characteristics is endowed with its product topology and the associated Borel σ-field. Denote the marginals on $\bar{K}$, $L^1(\Omega, F, \mu; K^1)$, and M_K by ν_1, ν_2, and ν_3 respectively. Note that ν_1 and ν_3 (which describe the distributions of agents' endowments of physical commodities and information structures) automatically have compact support.

A compact support hypothesis for distributions of agents' characteristics is a standard assumption meaning that agents are not too different; the set of preferences and endowments really present in the economy is "small" in a topological sense. For information demands and information allocations, the restriction to measures in M_K is a bit more problematic. Requiring these measures to concentrate on information structures in K simply says that agents can only demand information actually available. Boundedness (i.e., by $\bar{A} + 2\bar{B} + 1$) can be interpreted as a bounded rationality assumption concerning information processing, as it limits the number of distinct information structures that an agent can costlessly combine and utilize. Compactness of choice sets--the restriction to M_K--guarantees the existence of an optimal element when traders select information to be purchased; otherwise, information demands need not be well defined.

Assume further that information structures in $K^a \cup K^b$ are actually available in the economy in the following sense: Let $inc : M_K \to M_+$ be the inclusion map, where M_+ denotes the space of nonnegative finite measures on K, and let $\beta \in M_K$. Note that for every $S \in B(K)$--i.e., for every Borel subset of K--the mapping $\beta \to \beta(S)$, which takes M_K into $\mathbb{R}$, is measurable

(Mas-Colell (1975, Fact 1, p. 273)). Let $\int_{M_K} \text{inc}\, d\nu_3 \in M_+$ be defined by, for $S \in B(K)$, $(\int_{M_K} \text{inc}\, d\nu_3)(S) = \int_{M_K} \beta(S) d\nu_3(\beta)$. See Mas-Colell (1975, Fact 2, p. 274). Assume that $\text{supp}\,(\int_{M_K} \text{inc}\, d\nu_3) \supset K^a \cup K^b$. If this condition doesn't hold, one can replace $K^a \cup K^b$ by an appropriate smaller set, as it's meaningless to attempt to obtain prices for information structures which aren't available in the market.

As a device to guarantee that equilibrium prices for physical commodities are uniformly bounded away from zero, assume that there is a subset of agents of positive measure for whom $\beta(\mathbf{F}) \geq 1$; i.e., a nonnegligible fraction of agents are initially perfectly informed. Alternatively, assume that there is a subset of positive measure having utilities that are independent of the state of the world; this also serves to bound prices away from zero uniformly. These agents never purchase information unless their net information trades have the effect of increasing the amount that they have available to spend on physical goods. Thus, their budget sets always contain the set $\{x \in \mathbb{R}^\ell_+ \mid p \cdot x \leq p \cdot e\}$, regardless of information purchase decisions. Combined with the compactness of K^1 and $\bar{K}$, this implies that the boundary condition (that if $p_n \to p \in \partial\Delta$, then the sequence of excess demands is unbounded) is satisfied uniformly, for all $\omega \in \Omega$ and regardless of agents' information trades or the price system $q \in C^+(K^a \cup K^b)$ for information structures. An important implication is that there exists a compact subset $\Delta^K \subset \Delta$ (which does not depend on the prevailing price system in the markets for differentiated information) containing in its interior all possible market clearing prices for physical commodities; essentially Kakutani's fixed point theorem then guarantees that there are equilibrium prices for physical goods.

For technical reasons involving relative compactness of sets of equilibrium distributions, I must make an additional assumption to preclude the possibility that my space of agents' state-dependent utility functions is extremely large. Specifically, assume that either the space $L^1(\Omega, F, \mu; K^1)$ is separable (i.e., the σ-field F is separable) or that the marginal distribution ν_2, which is a probability measure on $L^1(\Omega, F, \mu; K^1)$, has separable support. To conserve notation, write $S^1 = L^1(\Omega, F, \mu; K^1)$ if this space is separable, and write $S^1 = \text{supp}\ \nu_2$ otherwise. In either case, S^1 is a complete separable metric space, and I can consider my original distribution economy to be defined by the (tight) probability measure ν on the complete separable metric space $\bar{K} \times S^1 \times M_K$. This guarantees that the economy ν has a standard representation--see Hildenbrand (1974).

4.2 The Definition of Equilibrium

General equilibrium requires, in addition to the conditions for equilibrium distributions of information, that each of the ℓ markets for a physical commodity clears on average, when agents' demands are defined by the maximization, subject to a budget constraint, of conditional expected utility given the equilibrium allocations of information. I use the condition that ordinary commodity markets clear only <u>on average</u> in order to obtain price vectors which do not depend on the state of the world. This simplifies the information choice problem and avoids the rational expectations existence problem that the informational content of price functions may be discontinuous. Moreover, my proof relies on the existence of convergent subsequences of prices, which would not necessarily hold for the case of state-dependent prices--unless there are only finitely many states of the world, in which case the individual's information choice problem trivially reduces to combinatorics. If prices were state dependent, the usual problems of obtaining existence of equilibrium with infinitely many agents and infinitely many commodities would arise.

Equilibrium involves <u>equilibrium distributions</u> with associated <u>equilibrium price systems</u> for information and <u>equilibrium price vectors</u> for ordinary goods. The use of distributions avoids measure theoretic obstacles of a purely technical nature.

Formally, a distribution (or probability measure) η on $\bar{K} \times L^1(\Omega,F,\mu;K^1) \times M_K \times M_K \times \mathbb{R}^\ell_+$ is an <u>equilibrium distribution</u> for the economy ν (defined as a distribution on $\bar{K} \times L^1(\Omega,F,\mu;K^1) \times M_K)$ if there is a price vector $p \in \Delta$ and a price system $q \in C^+(K)$ for information such that the following conditions are satisfied:

(i) $\eta_{123} = \nu$

(ii) $\int_{M_K} \text{inc}\, d\eta_4 \le \int_{M_K} \text{inc}\, d\eta_3$

(iii) $\int_{\mathbb{R}^\ell_+} \text{inc}\, d\eta_5 \le \int_{\bar{K}} \text{inc}\, d\eta_1$

(iv) $\eta\{(e,U,\beta,\gamma,x) \in \bar{K} \times L^1(\Omega,F,\mu;K^1) \times M_K \times M_K \times \mathbb{R}^\ell_+ \mid p\cdot x + \sum_{i=1}^{A'} q(G^i) + \sum_{i=1}^{B'} q(H^i) \le p\cdot e + \sum_{i=1}^{A} q(\bar{G}^i) + \sum_{i=1}^{B} q(\bar{H}^i)$ for $\beta = \delta(I) + \sum_{i=1}^{A} \delta(\bar{G}^i) + \sum_{i=1}^{B} \delta(\bar{H}^i)$ and $\gamma = \delta(I) + \sum_{i=1}^{A'} \delta(G^i) + \sum_{i=1}^{B'} \delta(H^i) + \sum_{i=1}^{B} \delta(\bar{H}^i)$ and if $(\gamma',x') \in M_K \times \mathbb{R}^\ell_+$ is such that $p\cdot x' + \sum_{i'=1}^{A''} q(G^{i'}) + \sum_{i'=1}^{B''} q(H^{i'}) \le p\cdot e + \sum_{i=1}^{A} q(\bar{G}^i) + \sum_{i=1}^{B} q(\bar{H}^i)$ for $\gamma' = \delta(I) + \sum_{i'=1}^{A''} \delta(G^{i'}) + \sum_{i'=1}^{B''} \delta(H^{i'}) + \sum_{i=1}^{B} \delta(\bar{H}^i)$, then for every γ'-measurable $x'(\cdot) : \Omega \to \mathbb{R}^\ell_+$ with $p\cdot x'(\omega) \le p\cdot x'$ for almost every $\omega \in \Omega$ and $\int_\Omega x'(\omega)d\mu(\omega) = x'$, there is a γ-measurable $x(\cdot) : \Omega \to \mathbb{R}^\ell_+$ with $p\cdot x(\omega) \le p\cdot x$ for almost every $\omega \in \Omega$ and $\int_\Omega x(\omega)d\mu(\omega) = x$ having the property that $\int_\Omega u(x'(\omega);\gamma';\omega)d\mu(\omega) \le \int_\Omega u(x(\omega);\gamma;\omega)d\mu(\omega)\} = 1$.

The definition associates (probabilistic) specifications of allocations (depending on agents' characteristics) with strictly positive price vectors for physical commodities and continuous nonnegative price systems for information. The consistency requirement (i) forces the distribution of agents' characteristics specified by the equilibrium distribution η to correspond to the economy ν. Condition (iii) says that the total assignment of each information structure under the equilibrium allocation does not exceed its total supply; recall that both expressions in the inequality (ii) are measures on K. Similarly, (iii) is a feasibility requirement for the allocation of physical goods--each expression is a vector in $\mathbb{R}_+^\ell$. Finally, condition (iv) requires that almost every agent's allocation maximize expected utility subject to the budget constraint given by p and q.

4.3 Existence of Equilibrium

This subsection contains the main result. It states that endogenous acquisition of differentiated information can be incorporated into a microeconomic pure exchange economy in which many negligible consumers take prices as given when choosing their trades of physical commodities and information, where information can be intrinsically preferred for its consumption properties as well as its use in the maximization of state dependent conditional expected utility. In other words, such a perfectly competitive general equilibrium model with purchases and sales of various types of "hybrid" information is consistent.

Theorem 2. For an economy ν satisfying all of the above assumptions, an equilibrium distribution exists; there is an equilibrium distribution η, an equilibrium price vector $p \in \Delta$ for physical goods, and an equilibrium price system $q \in C^+(K^a \cup K^b)$ for information.

Sketch of the proof. For brevity, details are omitted since they involve long and tedious but routine modifications of the proof for the pure information case; see Allen (1986b; Proof of Theorem 4.1 in Appendix II, pp. 20-30). Much of the strategy follows Mas-Colell's (1975) approach, but with the added complication that, in contrast to the standard differentiated commodity model analyzed there, information considerations necessitate price-dependent preferences. Hence all convergence arguments must be generalized to include their (continuous) dependence on varying prices. The basic idea is to approximate $K^a \cup K^b$ by finitely many sub-σ-fields and make a finite-dimensional fixed point argument to obtain equilibrium distributions and prices for the approximation. Finite-dimensionality also permits one to show that integration (over the nonatomic continuum of agents) preserves upper hemicontinuity of demand correspondences and gives, by Liapounov's Theorem, convex-valued aggregate excess demand even though individual demands fail to have this property due to indivisibilities (and hence nonconvexities) in information structures. Compactness is used to extract a subsequence converging weakly to an equilibrium distribution (by upper hemicontinuity of the equilibrium correspondence) for the original economy. Uniform equicontinuity yields--again, as the limit of a convergent subsequence--equilibrium prices with the desired properties. []

Remark. The device of obtaining equilibria for models with infinitely many commodities via limits of sequences with finite but large numbers of goods is due to Bewley (1972).

Acknowledgments

This research was supported by National Science Foundation Grant SES88-21442. Closely related work was also supported by NSF Grants IST79-18464, IST79-18464-A01, IST83-14096, and IRI85-20584.

References

Allen, Beth, 1983, Neighboring information and distributions of agents' characteristics under uncertainty, Journal of Mathematical Economics 12, 63-101.

Allen, Beth, 1984, Convergence of σ-fields and applications to mathematical economics, in G. Hammer and D. Pallaschke (eds.), Selected Topics in Operations Research and Mathematical Economics: Proceedings, Karlsruhe, West Germany. Heidelberg: Springer-Verlag Lecture Notes in Economics and Mathematical Systems Volume 226, 161-174.

Allen, Beth, 1986a, The demand for (differentiated) information, Review of Economic Studies 53, 311-323.

Allen, Beth, 1986b, General equilibrium with information sales, Theory and Decision 21, 1-33.

Allen, Beth, 1990a, Information as an economic commodity, American Economic Review, forthcoming.

Allen, Beth, 1990b, The supply of (differentiated) information, in preparation.

Allen, Beth and Timothy VanZandt, 1989, Uniform continuity of information combination: A corrigendum, mimeo, Department of Economics, University of Pennsylvania.

Aumann, Robert J., undated, A general equilibrium model with information, mimeo, Department of Mathematics, The Hebrew University of Jerusalem.

Bewley, Truman F., 1972, Existence of equilibria in economies with infinitely many commodities, Journal of Economic Theory 4, 514-540.

Cotter, Kevin D., 1986, Similarity of information and behavior with a pointwise convergence topology, Journal of Mathematical Economics 15, 25-38.

Hildenbrand, Werner, 1974, Core and Equilibria of a Large Economy. Princeton University Press.

Mas-Colell, Andreu, 1975, A model of equilibrium with differentiated commodities, Journal of Mathematical Economics 2, 263-295.

Stinchcombe, Maxwell B., 1989, Bayesian information topologies, Journal of Mathematical Economics, forthcoming.

Stinchcombe, Maxwell and Halbert White, 1989, Some measurability results for extrema of random functions over random sets, Economics Discussion Paper 89-18, University of California at San Diego.

VanZandt, Timothy, 1988, Information, measurability and continuous behavior, Center for Analytic Research in Economics and the Social Sciences Working Paper #88-18, University of Pennsylvania.

VanZandt, Timothy, 1989, The value of information and the Hausdorff metric on sub-σ-fields, mimeo, Department of Economics, Princeton University.

Appendix

Here I justify the claim that there is a uniform upper bound $\bar{C}$ on each agent's wealth w that is spent to purchase ordinary physical goods. Define

$\bar{V}(U,e,p,\beta) = \max\{\lambda \in \mathbb{R}_+ \mid$ for all constant functions $\bar{x} : \Omega \to \mathbb{R}^\ell_+$ which satisfy $p \cdot \bar{x} \le p \cdot e$, there is $x : \Omega \to \mathbb{R}^\ell_+$ which is F-measurable and satisfies $p \cdot x(\omega) \le p \cdot e - \lambda$ for almost every $\omega \in \Omega$ such that $\int_\Omega u(x(\omega);\beta;\omega)d\mu(\omega) \ge \int_\Omega u(\bar{x}(\omega);\beta;\omega)d\mu(\omega)\}$. The quantity $\bar{V}$ gives the maximum amount of "money" that a consumer would be willing to pay to condition demand (for physical commodities) on complete information. For all $(U,e,p,\beta) \in L^1(\Omega,F,\mu;K^1) \times \bar{K} \times \Delta^K \times M_K$, $\bar{V}$ is uniformly bounded. Recall from Section 4.1 that Δ^K denotes the compact subset of the open unit price simplex Δ which contains in its interior all possible market-clearing prices for physical commodities. Then an upper bound for wealth satisfying the budget constraint is given by $\bar{C} = (A+B) \max\{\bar{V}(U,e,p,\beta) \mid (U,e,p,\beta) \in L^1(\Omega,F,\mu;K^1) \times \bar{K} \times \Delta^K \times M_K\}$. This quantity bounds the amount that any agent would be willing to pay for information, while A+B bounds the number of (indivisible) information structures that can be sold from an initial endowment. Hence, I can restrict the choices of all agents to the compact metric space $M_K \times [0,\bar{C}]$.

DYNAMIC MODELS OF DELIBERATION AND THE THEORY OF GAMES

Brian Skyrms
Department of Philosophy
University of California, Irvine
Irvine, Ca. 92717
bskyrms@uci.bitnet

ABSTRACT

Deliberation can be modeled as a dynamic process. Where deliberation generates new information relevant to the decision under consideration, a rational decision maker will (processing costs permitting) feed back that information and reconsider. A firm decision is reached at a fixed point of this process - a deliberational equilibrium. Although there may be many situations in which informational feedback may be neglected and an essentially static theory of deliberation will suffice, there are others in which informational feedback plays a crucial role. From the point of view of procedural rationality, computation itself generates new information. Taking this point of view seriously leads to dynamic models of deliberation within which one can embed the theory of non-cooperative games.

In the sort of strategic situations considered by the theory of games, each player's optimal act depends on the acts selected by the other players. Thus each player must not only calculate expected utilities according to her current probabilities, but must also think about such calculations that other players are making and the effect on the probabilities of their acts, and of the import of other players thinking at this level as well, and so forth. In one idealized version of this problem, the players are endowed with enough initial common knowledge and computational resources so that each can emulate the reasoning of the others. A conjecture that all players have reached a firm decision as to the optimal act is consistent just in case it corresponds to a deliberational equilibrium on the part of each player. Under these idealized conditions, such a joint deliberational equilibrium on the part of the players is just a Nash equilibrium of the game. This embedding of classical game theory in the theory of dynamic deliberation suggests some non-classical extensions of the theory of strategic rationality. (I) Once one has a genuine dynamics one can ask a very rich set of questions instead of just asking which points are equilibria. As one illustration we can notice that notions of dynamical accessibility and stability of equilibria provide natural refinements of the Nash equilibrium concept. (II) In a more realistic theory, the highly idealized assumptions of common knowledge required for the coincidence of Nash equilibrium and joint deliberational equilibrium should be relaxed.

1 PHILOSOPHICAL ORIENTATION

The point of view adopted here depends on the cotenability of two principles. The first is that the principle of expected utility maximization is the touchstone of the theory of rationality in strategic as well as non-strategic contexts. The second is that a theory of deliberation should conceive of rationality as procedural. The first principle stands in direct opposition to a widely held view that rational decisions in the sort of situations treated by the theory of games demand an entirely different standard of rationality than those of agents dealing only with "nature". In a unified theory of rational decision, other decisionmakers should be regarded as part of nature, and rational decision will consist in maximizing one's expected payoff relative to one's uncertainty about the state of nature. The relevance of such a Bayesian viewpoint for the theory of games has become more widely appreciated as a result of fundamental papers by Harsanyi (1967), Aumann (1987), Pearce (1984), Bernheim (1984), and Kreps and Wilson (1982a), (1982b). The question which forms the basic theme of these investigations can already be found in von Neumann and Morgenstern (1944): when is a combination of strategies on the part of all the players of a game consistent with expected utility maximization on the part of all the players? The Nash equilibrium concept gives a sufficient but not a necessary condition for this to be true. The framework of this literature, although Bayesian, is still static. The focus is on a solution which satisfies a set of conditions rather than on the procedures by which the players attempt to arrive at an optimal decision.

The importance of the procedural aspect of rationality has long been emphasized by Simon (1957), (1972), (1986). In accordance with this point of view, common knowledge of rationality in strategic situations is to be thought of as common knowledge of a rational deliberational procedure. In such a situation, computations must be conceived of as generating new information. As a result, probabilities can change as a result of pure thought. There are provocative discussions of such a possibility under the name of "dynamic probability" in the writings of Good. [see Good (1983) Ch. 10 for a sample.] As probabilities evolve, so do expected utilities. There is some tension between the ideal of a full Bayesian analysis based on expected utility and a procedural approach which takes into account limitations of computational resources of the deliberators. But I do not think that the tension is so great that expected utility cannot play the central role in the analysis of deliberation. Nevertheless, the tension is responsible for some of the more interesting aspects of a deliberational approach to strategic rationality.

2 DYNAMIC DELIBERATION BASED ON ADAPTIVE RULES

Rational deliberators aim at maximizing expected utility. But in a situation where it is expected that new information may change your probabilities of the states of nature during deliberation, you may expect that your current expected utilities will be revised. Upon calculating expected utility the act which comes out on top may be more likely the act that looks best in the end than it was before that calculation, but it is by no means certain to be the optimal act at the end of deliberation. In such situation, then, calculations of expected utility should change the probabilities of the decisionmaker's acts in a way consistent with the decisiomaker's aiming at maximizing expected utility, but in a way which falls short of giving acts with non-maximal current expected utility probability zero. How should the decisionmaker's calculations of expected utility change the probabilities of her acts?

In principle, the decision maker might carry out an elaborate Bayesian preposterior analysis at each stage of deliberation but here we will be interested in modeling the case in which that is not feasible. Alternatively, the decisionmaker may modify probabilities of her acts according to some simple adaptive rule which reflects the fact that she is aiming for optimality. Let us say that a rule **seeks the good** just in case:

(1) it raises the probability of an act only if that act has utility greater than that of the status quo, and
(2) it raises the sum of the probabilities of all acts with utility greater than that of the status quo (if any).

[The expected utility of the status quo is just the average of the expected utilities of the pure acts, weighted by the decisionmaker's probabilities that she will do them.]
All dynamical rules which seek the good have the same fixed points. These are the states in which the utility of the status quo is maximal.

As a concrete example of such a rule we can take the function that Nash (1951) used to prove the existence of equilibria for finite non-zero sum games. Define the **Covetability** of an act in a state of indecision, p, as the difference in expected utility between the act and the state of indecision if the act is preferable to the state of indecision, and as zero if the state of indecision is preferable to the act COV(A) = MAX [U(A)-U(p), 0]. Then the Nash Map takes the decision maker from state of indecision p to state of indecision p' where each component p_i of p is changed to:

$$p'_i = [p_i + COV(A_i)] \;/\; [1 + \Sigma_i\, COV(A_i)]$$

Here a bold revision is hedged by averaging with the status quo. We can get a whole family of NASH MAPS by allowing different weights for the average:

$$p'_i = [\ k\ p_i + \text{COV}(A_i)]/[k + \Sigma_i\ \text{COV}(A_i)]$$

The constant k (k>0) is an index of caution. The higher k is,the more slowly the decision maker moves in the direction of acts which look more attractive than the status quo. In continuous time, one has the corresponding NASH FLOWS:

$$dp(A)/dt = [\text{Cov}(A) - p(A)\Sigma_j\ \text{Cov}(A_j)] \ / \ [k + \Sigma_j\ \text{Cov}(A_j)]$$

Let us model the deliberational situation in an abstract and fairly general way. A Bayesian has to choose between a finite number of acts: $A_1 ... A_n$. Calculation takes time for her; although its cost is negligible. We assume that she is certain that deliberation will end and she will choose some act (perhaps a mixed one) at that time. Her state of indecision will be a probability vector assigning probabilities to each of the n acts, which sum to one. These are to be interpreted as her probabilities now that she will do the act in question at the end of deliberation. A state of indecision, P, carries with it an expected utility; the expectation according to the probability vector $P = \langle p_1 ... p_n \rangle$ of the expected utilities of the acts $A_1 ... A_n$. The expected utility of a state of indecision is thus computed just as that of the corresponding mixed act. Indeed, the adoption of a mixed strategy can be thought of as a way to turn the state of indecision for its constituent pure acts to stone. We will call a mixed act corresponding to a state of indecision, its default mixed act. The decisionmaker's calculation of expected utility and subsequent application of the dynamical rule constitutes new information which may affect the expected utilities of the pure acts by affecting the probabilities of the states of nature which together with the act determine the payoff. In the typical game theoretical contexts they consist of the possible actions of the opposing players. For simplicity, we will assume here a finite number of states of nature.

The decision maker's personal state is then, for our purposes, determined by two things: her state of indecision and the probabilities that she assigns to states of nature. Her personal state space is the product space of her space of indecision and her space of states of nature. Deliberation defines a dynamics on this space. We could model the dynamics as either discrete or continuous, but for the moment, we will focus on discrete dynamics. We assume a dynamical function, ϕ, which maps a personal state $\langle x,y \rangle$ into a new personal state $\langle x',y' \rangle$ in one unit of time. The dynamical function, ϕ, has two associated rules: (I) the adaptive dynamical rule, D, which maps $\langle x,y \rangle$ onto x' and (II) the informational feedback process, I, which maps $\langle x,y \rangle$ onto y' (where $\langle x',y' \rangle = \phi\langle x,y \rangle$).]

A personal state <x,y> is a deliberational equilibrium of the dynamics, ϕ, if and only if ϕ<x,y> = <x,y>. If D and I are continuous, then ϕ is continuous and it follows from the Brower fixed point theorem that a deliberational equilibrium exists. Let N be the Nash dynamics for some k>0. Then if the informational feedback process, I, is continuous, the dynamical function <N,I> is continuous, and has a deliberational equilibrium. Then, since N seeks the good, for any continuous informational feedback process, I, <N,I> has a deliberational equilibrium <x,y> whose corresponding mixed act maximizes expected utility in state <x,y>. This is a point from which process I does not move y and process N does not move x. But if process N does not move x, then no other process which seeks the good will either. Therefore:

I: If D seeks the good and I is continuous, then there is a deliberational equilibrium, <x,y> for <D,I>. If D' also seeks the good then <x,y> is also a deliberational equilibrium for <D',I>. The default mixed act corresponding to x maximizes expected utility at <x,y>.

Now let us consider a situation in which two (or more) Bayesian deliberators are deliberating about what action to take in a finite non-cooperative non-zero sum matrix game. We assume here that each player has only one choice to make, and that the choices are causally independent in that there is no way for one player's decision to influence the decisions of the other players. Then, from the point of view of decision theory, for each player the decisions of the other players constitute the relevant state of the world which, together with her decision, determines the consequence in accordance with the payoff matrix. [If there are more than two players, we assume here that each player calculates the probability of combinations of acts of other players by taking the product of the individual probabilities.]

Suppose,in addition, that each player has an adaptive rule, D, which seeks the good (they need not have the same rule) and that what kind of Bayesian deliberator each player is, is common knowledge. Suppose also, that each player's initial state of indecision is common knowledge, and that other player's take a given player's state of indecision as their own best estimate of what that player will ultimately do. Then initially, there is a probability assignment to all the acts for all the players which is shared by all the players and is common knowledge.

Under these strong assumptions of common knowledge, an interesting informational feedback process becomes available. Starting from the initial position, player 1 calculates expected utility and moves by her adaptive rule to a new state of indecision. She knows that the other players are Bayesian deliberators who have just carried out a similar process. And she knows their initial states of indecision and their updating rules. So she can simply go through their calculations to see their new states of indecision and update her probabilities of their acts accordingly. We will call this sort of informational feedback process Updating by Emulation. Suppose that all the players update by emulation. Then, in this ideal case, the new state is common knowledge as well and the process can be repeated. Thus, the joint state of all players is common knowledge at all times.

A combination of strategies in a non-cooperative game is a **Nash equilibrium** just in case if all players know the others' strategies, each player's strategy maximizes her expected utility. It follows immediately from the foregoing that in our idealized model Nash equilibrium coincides with deliberational equilibrium:

II: **In a game played by dynamic deliberators with a common prior probability assignment, an adaptive rule which Seeks the Good, and Updating by Emulation, with common knowledge of all the foregoing, each player is at a deliberational equilibrium at a state of the system if and only if the assignment of the default mixed acts to each player constitutes a Nash equilibrium of the game.**

3 DYNAMIC DELIBERATION BASED ON INDUCTIVE RULES

In game theoretic situations there is an alternative way to conceptualize deliberational dynamics according to which the dynamics is driven by inductive rules. Given other players probabilities (for acts of players other than themselves), a player can calculate their expected utilities for their options just as they do. On some form of the hypothesis that the players are optimizers, each player makes an inductive inference about the eventual play of other players, and updates her probabilities accordingly. Given sufficient common knowledge, these calculations can be emulated. Then each player again knows the probabilities that other players have (for acts of players other than themselves) and thus can calculate their expected utilities, starting the cycle anew. On the inductive dynamics, no player needs to have subjective probabilities for her own acts. She only needs to have probabilities for other players' acts, and to think about other players' probabilities on her acts. An equilibrium in inductive dynamics is thus an equilibrium in degrees of belief. This is of special interest in connection with the theory of games because of a growing conviction among game theorists that the most viable interpretation of mixed equilibria is as equilibria in beliefs.

As a simple illustration let us consider 2 by 2 two person games, where the players rely on Laplace's rule of succession, treating each round of deliberation as a virtual trial. And suppose that it is common knowledge between them that they are such Laplacian deliberators. Then each can emulate the other's calculations and discover the other's current expected utilities and utilities at each stage of deliberation.

Laplace's rule is that given n instanciations of a given act, Ai in N trials, the probability of an instanciation on a new trial is:

Laplace: $pr(Ai) = (n + 1)/(N + 2)$

So initially our players each assign the other probability 1/2 for each act. Each player then calculates the other player's expected utilities, indentifies the act with highest expected utility and counts that act as exemplified on the first trial to get an updated probability over the other player's acts. Each player can now emulate the other player's calculation in this process to find the other player's updated probability. These process is then repeated, generating a trajectory in the joint belief space of the players. This space can be represented as the unit square with the y axis measuring Column's degree of belief that Row will play 2 and the x axis representing Row's degree of belief that Column will play 2.

If a player has more than two acts the natural generalization of LaPlace's rule is a rule used in Carnap's inductive logic. [Historical details are omitted here.] Suppose that column has m possible acts, A1 ...Am. After N trials in which act Ai has been chosen n times:

Carnap: $pr(Ai) = (n + 1)/(N + m)$

If two or more acts are tied for maximum expected utility on a round, then they are each is counted as having a "fractional success" with the fractions being proportion to the acts current probabilities and adding to one.

If the game has more than two players, we will assume as before that each player takes the product measure in computing the probabilities on combinations of acts by other players. [The assumption here is made for simplicity, not on principle. Ultimately it should be relaxed.] Under this assumption (and assuming again sufficient common knowledge to allow updating by emulation) the appropriate joint belief space is just the product of the belief simplices for each player, and deliberation generates an orbit in this space.

There is a clear sense in which deliberational equilibrium corresponds to Nash equilibrium for Carnap deliberators:

III. **If Carnap deliberators are at a point in the joint belief space, then they will stay at that point just in case that point is a Nash equilibrium in beliefs of the game.**

If the point is not a Nash equilibrium than some pure strategy used with positive probability by some player does not maximize expected utility. Then under the Carnap rule the probability of that strategy is diminished. Conversely, inspection of the Carnap rule show that if the point does not move then for every player every pure strategy used with positive probability must maximize expected utility for that player. Then the point is a Nash equilibrium. ||

But this result leaves open some questions. The Carnap rule specifies the initial beliefs of the players. They are built into the inductive rule. Carnap deliberation may not be able to reach some points in the joint belief space. In particular, in every game probabilities of one or zero are never reached by a finite number of stages of deliberation. This raises the question of **accessibility**. We will say that a point in the joint belief space is **accessible** under Carnap deliberation if Carnap deliberation converges to it as the number of stages of deliberation becomes arbitrarily great. Accessible points will be discussed in the next section.

Can inductive deliberational dynamics be consistent with adaptive deliberational dynamics? Well, it could be the case that each player could find no better adaptive rule than to look at virtual trials and apply Carnap to herself. If this were the case, then the adaptive and inductive deliberational dynamics would be two descriptions of the same process.

4 ACCESSIBLE POINTS

Since Carnap deliberation cannot start at a pure strategy and cannot reach one in a finite number of steps, the question is pressing whether there is a connection with the Nash equilibrium concept relevant to combinations of pure strategies. The following proposition gives an affirmative answer:

IV. Accessible points under Carnap deliberation (pure or mixed) are Nash equilibria.

Suppose not. Then at the point, p, some pure act, A, which does not maximize expected utility gets positive probability. By continuity of expected utility of the acts as a function of the probabilities, there is some neighborhood of p throughout which A does not maximize expected utility. Inspection of the Carnap rule shows that if deliberation converges to p, then the probability of A must - contrary to hypothesis - converge to zero. ||

Not every Nash equilibrium is accessible under the Carnap dynamics. What equilibria are accessible depends in part on the structure of the particular game in question, and on the a priori probabilities built into the Carnapian inductive logic. But there are some properties that accessible equilibria have in general under the Carnap dynamics, and which remain properties of accessible equilibria under various Bayesian generalizations of the Carnap dynamics.

Not all Nash equilibria are created equal. Consider the following game:

Example 1

	C1	C2
R1	1,1	-2,-2
R2	0,0	0,0

There is a Nash equilibrium in beliefs with Row believing with probability one that Column will do C2 and Column believing with probability one that Row will do R2. Doing R2 maximizes expected utility for row and doing either act has maximal expected utility for column.

Column's act C2 is weakly dominated by C1. That is, for some state of the world (i.e. R1), C1 gives column greater payoff than C2 and for all states of the world, C1 gives column at least as great a payoff as C2. Acts which are not weakly dominated are called admissible. Since C2 is inadmissible, if column is not absolutely certain about row choosing R2 - if column assigns each of Row's choices positive probability - then C2 would no longer maximize expected utility for column.

It is often assumed that a rational player will never choose an inadmissible act. However this conclusion is not a consequence of the postulate that players maximize expected utility. If Column's probability of R2 is 1, then his choice of the inadmissible act C2 does maximize expected utility. It is of some interest then, to see if there is a connection between accessibility and admissibility. For the Carnap dynamics one can show:

V. Accessible points under the Carnap dynamics only give positive probability to weakly admissible acts.

Suppose not. Then there is a weakly dominated act, A, which has positive probability at the accessible point, p. Since A is weakly dominated it does not maximize expected utility at any completely mixed point. Inspection of the rules shows that if deliberation converges to p, then probability of A must converge to zero.||

Readers familiar with Selten's (1975) notion of perfection can note that it is an immediate corollary that *in two person games, equilibria that are accessible under Carnap deliberation are perfect.* Due to limitations of space I cannot develop the concept of perfection here. Connections between accessibility, admissibility and perfection are discussed in more detail in Skyrms (forthcoming c).

Carnap's inductive rule may strike one as rather special. If so, it is of interest that that propositions III, IV and V continue to hold good when we generalize the Carnap dynamics to a wide class of Bayesian models. Suppose we model a process generating our evidence as being like sampling without replacement from an urn of unknown composition. The natural conjugate prior is the Dirichlet distribution. If there are m possible outcomes then the Dirichlet distribution is characterized by positive parameters $\alpha 1 \ldots \alpha m$. Take $\beta = \alpha 1 + \ldots + \alpha m$. The if n is the number of occurrences of Ai in N trials we get the general rule:

(Dirichlet) $Pr(Ai) = (n + \alpha i)/(N + \beta)$

If the αi are all 1 we get Carnap. [In his posthumously published systen, Carnap in fact moved to this parametric Bayesian rule.] Other choices of the parameters allow any starting point in the interior of the joint belief space of the players. It is easy to see that the reasoning used to establish propositions III-V holds good when (Dirichlet) is substituted for (Carnap). The results can be further generalized, using mixtures of Dirichlet priors to approximate arbitrary subjective priors. [See Diaconis and Ylvisaker (1984)]

One might, however, be tempted to overgeneralize. Consider the adaptive dynamics that underlies the game theory of Maynard Smith (1982):

(Darwin) NEWPr(Ai) = OldPr(Ai) [U(Ai)/U(Status Quo)]

In example 1, dynamic deliberation according to this rule can start at a completely mixed point and converge to an equilibrium where Pr(R2) = 1 and $2/3 < Pr(C2) < 1$. Such a equilibrium is imperfect and has Column using the inadmissible strategy, C2, with positive probability. The discussion of generalized evolutionary game theory in Samuelson (1988) is highly relevant to this point.

5 IMPRECISE PROBABILITIES

Our idealized model of games played by Bayesian deliberators makes the unrealistic assumption that at the onset of deliberation precise states of indecision of the players are common knowledge. Precise states of indecision are then maintained throughout deliberation. It is of interest to weaken this assumption as a move in the direction of greater realism and for the theoretical interest of the interaction of the dynamics and the imprecision of the beliefs. In this section, for simplicity, I will fix the dynamics as the Nash dynamics.

There are various ways in which imprecise states of indecision might be modeled. Here we will look at the computationally simplest alternative. Instead of taking a player's state of indecision to be a probability measure over his space of final actions, we will take it to be a convex set of probability measures. We focus here of the simplest case of 2 person games, where each player has only two possible actions, and a players state of indecision is given by a closed interval. If, for example, Row's probability of act 2 is to lie in the interval between Row's upper probability of act 2 = .7 and Row's lower probability of act 2 = .6 , then the extreme probability measure corresponding to Row's upper probability of act 2 is Pr(A2) = .7, Pr(A1) = .3 and the extreme measure corresponding to Row's lower probability of act 2 is Pr(A2) = .6, Pr(A1) = .4. The convex set in question is composed of all probability measures over the space [A1,A2] which can be gotten by a weighted average of the extreme measures.

How should Row calculate expected utilities given Column's probability interval? He should have a set of expected utilities, one corresponding to each possible point probability consistent with Column's probability interval. Because of the nature of the expectation however, Row need only compute the expected utilities relative to the endpoints of Column's interval with assurance that the other point utilities lie inbetween.

How should Row modify his probability sets in the light of new expected utility sets. He should have new probability sets corresponding to every point gotten by applying his dynamical law to a point chosen from the expected utility set and a point chosen from his old probability set. But for the Nash dynamics, and a large class of reasonable dynamical laws to which it belongs, it is a consequence of the form of the dynamical law that if old Pr2(A) is in the interval from oldPr1(A) to oldPr3(A) and oldU2(A) is between oldU1(A) and oldU3(A) then newPr2(A) is between newPr1(A) and newPr3(A). It is a consequence of these observations, that Row can achieve the results of point deliberation on every pair consisting of one point from his interval and one from column's interval, by performing four point computations on pairs consisting of one endpoint from his interval and one from columns interval. The new maximum and minimum probabilities of A among the four possibilities form the endpoints of his new probability for A. Here is the relevant subroutine:

```
SUB INTDYNAMICS
    CALL NASH(UPrR2,UPrC2) 'Call Nash dynamics applied to upper probabilities of R2 and C2
    Y1=OutPrR2' Set Y1 equal to the output for Pr(R2)
    X1=OutPrC2
    CALL NASH(UPrR2,LPrC2)
    Y2=OutPrR2
    X2=OutPrC2
    CALL NASH(LPrR2,UPrC2)
    Y3=OutPrR2
    X3=OutPrC2
    CALL NASH(LPrR2,LPrC2)
    Y4=OutPrR2
    X4=OutPrC2
    UPrR2=FNMAX(Y1,Y2,Y3,Y4)
    LPrR2=FNMIN(Y1,Y2,Y3,Y4)
    UPrC2=FNMAX(X1,X2,X3,X4)
    LPrC2=FNMIN(X1,X2,X3,X4)
END SUB
```

The general points made above continue to hold good mutatus mutandus for numbers of acts greater than two, with intervals being generalized to convex sets of probability measures and endpoints being generalized to extreme points. With regard to computational tractability, deliberational dynamics, as sofar developed, has a certain affinity for convex set representations of imprecise probabilities.

Returning to the case of two players each of which must choose between two acts, a state of indecision in the interval valued sense is now represented as a rectangle in the old space of indecision - the product of row and column's intervals. Points are considered degenerate intervals, and point states of indecision are special cases of rectangles of indecision. The area of a rectangle of indecision need not be preserved by deliberational dynamics. For example, players may start out with non-degenerate interval-valued probabilities, and be carried by deliberation to point probabilities. One might call such a process *elicitation of point probabilities through deliberation*. This process is illustrated in the case of a game with elements of both competition and coordination in figure 1. Here, in the game of Chicken, we have the orbit of [.4,.1],[.4,.1] converging to 0,0 and that of

[.6,.9],[.6,.9] converging to 1,1.

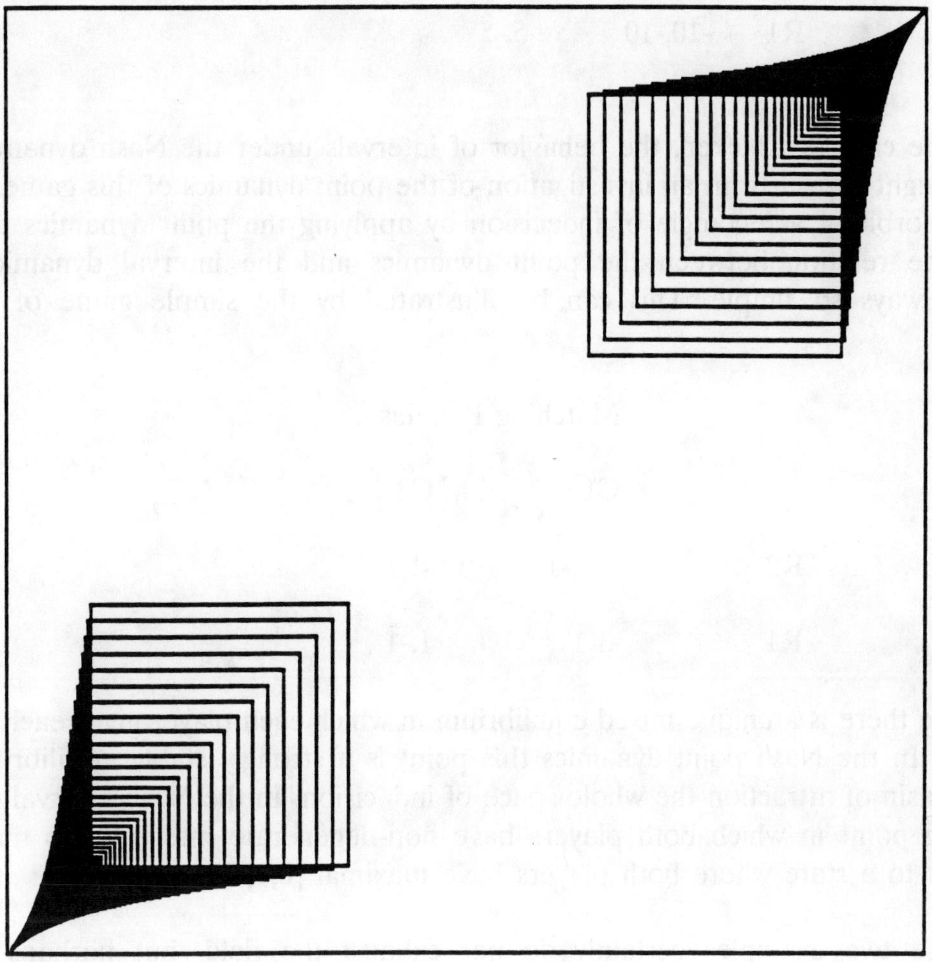

figure 1: Interval Deliberation in Chicken

Chicken

	C1	C2
R2	-5,5	0,0
R1	-10,-10	5,-5

In the case of Chicken, the behavior of intervals under the Nash dynamics is just what one might expect from an investigation of the point dynamics of this game. One can predict the orbit of a rectangle of indecision by applying the point dynamics to its four corners. The relation between the point dynamics and the interval dynamics is not, however, always so simple. This can be illustrated by the simple game of Matching Pennies:

Matching Pennies

	C1	C2
R2	1,-1	-1,1
R1	-1,1	1,-1

In this game there is a unique mixed equilibrium in which each player gives each act equal probability. In the Nash point dynamics this point is a strongly stable equilibrium which has as its basin of attraction the whole space of indecision. In the Nash interval dynamics, any starting point in which both players have non-degenerate intervals, no matter how small, leads to a state where both players have maximal [0,1] intervals.

These two examples certainly do not exhaust the field, but perhaps they are sufficient to allow a modest moral. The questions posed by imprecise beliefs cannot be adequately addressed in isolation from questions about the dynamics of deliberation.

Acknowledgement

This paper sketches parts of an area treated more fully in forthcoming publications [Skyrms (forthcoming a,b,c)]. The relevant research was partially supported by the National Science Foundation Grant SES-8721469 and by the John Simon Guggenheim Foundation.

References

Aumann, R. J. 1987. "Correlated Equilibrium as an Expression of Bayesian Rationality" *Econometrica* 55:1-18.

Bernheim, B. D. 1984. "Rationalizable Strategic Behavior" *Econometrica* 52:1007-1028.

Binmore, K. 1987. "Modeling Rational Players I and II" *Economics and Philosophy* 3, 179-214; 4, 9-55.

Brown, G. W. 1951. "Iterative Solutions of Games by Fictitious Play" in *Activity Analysis of Production and Allocation* (Cowles Commission Monograph) New York: Wiley. 374-376.

Carnap, R. 1950. *Logical Foundations of Probability* Chicago: University of Chicago Press.

Carnap, R. 1952. *The Continuum of Inductive Methods* Chicago: University of Chicago Press.

Carnap, R. 1971. "A Basic System of Inductive Logic, Part 1" in *Studies in Inductive Logic and Probability* vol. I ed. R. Carnap and R. C. Jeffrey. Berkeley: University of California Press.

Carnap, R. 1980. "A Basic System of Inductive Logic ,Part 2" in *Studies in Inductive Logic and Probability* vol. II ed. R. C. Jeffrey. Berkeley: University of California Press.

Diaconis, P. and Ylvisaker, D. 1984. "Quantifying Prior Opinion" in *Bayesian Statistics 2* ed. J. M. Bernardo et al. Amsterdam: North Holland.

Eells, E. 1984. "Metatickles and the Dynamics of Deliberation" *Theory and Decision* 17: 71-95.

Good, I. J. 1965. *The Estimation of Probabilities:An Essay on Modern Bayesian Methods* Cambridge, Mass.: MIT Press.

Good, I. J. 1983. *Good Thinking: The Foundations of Probability and Its Applications* Minneapolis: University of Minnesota Press.

Harper, W. 1988. "Causal Decision Theory and Game Theory: A Classic Argument for Equilibrium Solutions, a Defense of Weak Equilibria, and a New Problem for the Normal Form Representation" in *Causation in Decision, Belief Change, and Statistics* ed. Harper and Skyrms. Dordrecht:Kluwer. 25-48.

Harsanyi, J. C. 1967. "Games with Incomplete Information Played by Bayesian Players" parts I,II,III *Management Science* 14:159-183, 320-334, 486-502.

Harsanyi, J. C. 1973. "Games with Randomly Disturbed Payoffs: A New Rationale for Mixed Strategy Equilibrium Points" *International Journal of Game Theory* 2:1-23.

Harsanyi, J. C. and Selten, R. 1988. *A General Theory of Equilibrium Selection in Games* Cambridge,Mass.: MIT Press.

Kreps, D. and Wilson, R. 1982a. "Sequential Equilibria" *Econometrica* 50:863-894.

Kreps, D. and Wilson, R. 1982b. "Reputation and Incomplete Information" *Journal of Economic Theory* 27:253-279.

Maynard Smith, J. 1982. *Evolution and the Theory of Games* Cambridge: Cambridge University Press.

Nash, J. 1951. "Non-Cooperative Games" *Annals of Mathematics* 54:286-295.

Pearce, D. G. 1984. "Rationalizable Strategic Behavior and the Problem of Perfection" *Econometrica* 52:1029-1050.

Samuleson, L. 1988. "Evolutionary Foundations for Solution Concepts for Finite, Two-Player, Normal-Form Games" in *Proceedings of the Second Conference on Theoretical Aspects of Reasoning about Knowledge* ed. M. Vardi. Los Altos, California: Morgan Kaufmann. 211-226.

Selten, R. 1975. "Reexamination of the Perfectness Concept of Equilibrium in Extensive Games" *International Journal of Game Theory* 4:25-55.

Simon, H. 1957. *Models of Man* New York: Wiley.

Simon, H. 1972. "Theories of Bounded Rationality" In *Decision and Organization* ed. C.B.McGuire and R. Radner. Amsterdam: North Holland.

Simon, H. 1986. "Rationality in Psychology and Economics" In *Rational Choice* ed. Hogarth and Rader. Chicago: University of Chicago Press.

Skyrms, B. 1984. *Pragmatics and Empiricism* New Haven: Yale University Press.

Skyrms, B. 1986. "Deliberational Equilibria" *Topoi* 5:59-67.

Skyrms, B. 1988. "Deliberational Dynamics and the Foundations of Bayesian Game Theory" In *Epistemology* [Philosophical Perspectives v.2] ed. J.E.Tomberlin. Northridge: Ridgeview.

Skyrms, B. 1989. "Correlated Equilibria and the Dynamics of Rational Deliberation" *Erkenntnis* 31: 347-364.

Skyrms, B. forthcoming a. *The Dynamics of Rational Deliberation* Cambridge, Mass: Harvard University Press.

Skyrms, B. forthcoming b. "Ratifiability and the Logic of Decision" in *Philosophy of the Human Sciences* (Midwest Studies in Philosophy vol. 15) University of Minnesota Press: Minneapolis, Minnesota.

Skyrms, B. forthcoming c. "Inductive Deliberation, Admissible Acts and Perfect Equilibrium" in *Essays in the Foundations of Rational Decision* ed. M. Bacharach and S. Hurley. Oxford: Blackwells.

Smith, C. A. B. 1966. "Consistency in Statistical Inference and Decision" *Journal of the Royal Statistical Society, Series B* 23: 1-37.

Spohn, W. 1982. "How to Make Sense of Game Theory" in *Studies in Contemporary Economics vol2:Philosophy of Economics* ed. W. Stegmuller et. al. Heidelberg and New York: Springer Verlag.

von Neumann, J. and Morgenstern, O. 1947. *Theory of Games and Economic Behavior* Princeton: Princeton University Press.

A Note on the Consistency of Game Theory*

by

Itzhak Gilboa**

Abstract

It has been claimed in the literature that classical game theory is inconsistent, since it (implicitly) assumes that all players are rational and that this is common knowledge among them, while these two assumptions seem to be contradictory. The purpose of this note is to suggest a framework which allows the formalization of these implicit axioms in a consistent way.

The main idea is to distinguish between conceivable and possible states of the world, while both exist as formal objects in the theory. Thus we may require that the players would make rational choices only at possible states of the world, and that this fact be common knowledge at all (conceivable) states, where the impossible ones are present in the model for the sole purpose of formally presenting the players' reasoning.

It seems that the new concept of possible states of the world is an analytical tool which may have further (theoretical) applications.

---

*I wish to thank Philip Reny and Cristina Bicchieri for the discussions which motivated this note, and the encouragement to write it down. I am also grateful to Robert Aumann, Ehud Kalai, Dov Samet, Moshe Vardi and Lenore Zuck for helpful discussions.

**KGSM/MEDS, Northwestern University, 2001 Sheridan Road, Leverone Hall, Evanston, Illinois 60208.

1. **Motivation**

Let us consider the two-person game given in figure 1. Reny (1988), following Kreps, Milgrom, Roberts and Wilson (1982) claimed that one cannot assume that rationality is common belief, let alone common knowledge, at every node of the game, since should player II arrive at node 2 his/her belief that player I is rational would be inconsistent with player I's actual behavior at node I, if rationality of both were indeed common belief at this node.

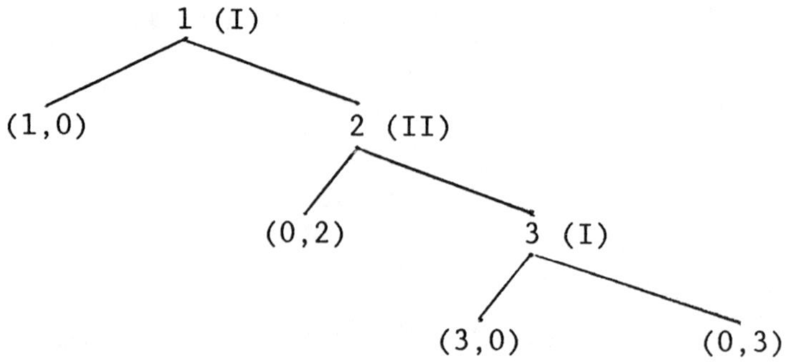

Figure 1
(Arabic numbers denote decision nodes, Latin ones - players)

Bicchieri (1988a,b,c and 1989) has carried this argument one step further to claim that traditional game theory, implicitly assuming common knowledge of rationality, is inconsistent. (See also Bonanno (1988).)

While game theorists seem to be willing to admit that common knowledge of rationality is not a very likely assumption in certain contexts (see Selten (1978), Rosenthal (1981), Kreps et al. (1982), Aumann (1988), Aumann-Sorin (1989) and the literature on bounded rationality), most of them would probably find the claim of inconsistency rather disturbing, partly because there are situations in which these assumptions are quite reasonable, and partly because being unrealistic is hardly as strong a flaw of a mathematical model as being inconsistent (in fact, the former sometimes seems to be a merit.) We are therefore challenged to come up with a viable mathematical model that would solve the problem explained above.

We introduce here two possible answers; the first, which we find somewhat unsatisfactory, is along the lines of traditional game theory, while the second uses the new concept of "possible" states of the world.

2. **The Traditional Reply**

We can simply write down the axioms of rationality being common knowledge at any state of the world--following Aumann (1974,1976,1987) in some formalized form as suggested, say, in Gilboa (1988) or Kaneko (1987). The meaning of "rationality" here may be somewhat unclear, but let us assume, for simplicity, that it consists of a set of axioms specifying what would each player do given any possible knowledge, and that this specification is, indeed, what we expect it to be (Later on we will present a slightly more sophisticated version of this axiom.) Then we can translate the well-known backward-induction argument to a theorem stating that in the game above there is a single state of the world at which player I plays left at node 1, thus terminating not only the game but also the discussion. The questions of why did player I play that way, what he/she thought player II would think should I play right and so forth are meaningless in this model; they may be very interesting as questions **about** the model, suggesting the unreasonability of its assumptions, but they cannot imply that the model is inconsistent.

The difficulty with this answer is that the model one ends up with does not seem to capture the players' reasoning, even if the scenario dictated by it is actually followed by them. It is somewhat disturbing that there are no states of the world corresponding to the other nodes of the game tree; after all, it seems **conceivable** that they would materialize, even if we ended up convincing ourselves that this cannot be the case. Indeed, one has to think about those possibilities in order to exclude them. Without having a state of the world as a "name" for each such possibility we cannot claim to have formalized the implicit assumption of game theory; in the model presented above it was only the outside observer who reasoned and understood the backward induction; the players themselves did not.

3. A Digression: Counterfactuals and Proofs by Negation

Noting that the (standard) model described above, flawed as it is, was rich enough to allow for a proof of the "rational" outcome, we may ask what distinguishes this perfectly valid proof-by-negation from the counterfactual argument we would like our players to conduct. The answer suggested by the discussion above is quite simple: both a counterfactual argument and a proof by negation may be described as considering a statement (not p) in the presence of the statements (not p implies q) and (not q), from which p is deduced. However, we may distinguish between them as follows: if the latter two statements are tautologies, that is, if they are true at each and every conceivable state of the world--then this is a mathematical proof by negation; if, on the other hand, there are conceivable states of the world at which this argument does not hold--this is a counterfactual reasoning.

4. An Alternative Reply

The obvious reply which the above discussion seems to suggest is the following: we have to begin with a set of conceivable states of the world S, which is large enough to describe any outcome of the game. Thus, if we analyze a game in an extensive form, there will be at least as many states of the world as there are terminal nodes ("leaves"), and in a normal-form analysis--as many as entries in the (super-)matrix of the game. (In fact, one would have to have more states of the world, since for each player a state of the world has to specify what would occur as a result of every possible action of this player, and not only of the one actually chosen at it. However, for simplicity we may ignore the counterfactual elements in the states of the world.) Events, surprisingly enough, will be subsets of states of the world, and in particular, every node in the game tree will correspond to an event containing all the leaves that may be reached from it.

The main novelty is the following: we will use a non-empty subset P of S, interpreted as the set of **possible** states, as a formal object in our model, which may be an object of players' knowledge. Thus, in a model such as Gilboa (1988), it will be meaningful to ask, say, whether at a certain state of the world a certain player considers another state (or the same one) to be possible or not, and so forth. Adhering to Savage's (1954) principle of a state-of-the-world "resolving all uncertainty," the answers to all such questions will be a part of the description of a state, including states which are conceivable but not possible according to some states (possibly - not even in the possible set according to themselves.)

We will also find it useful to extend the definition of possibility to events. Again, in a very general model each state may define each event to be possible or not, without any relationship to the possible states of the world. However, we will extend the consistency assumptions in Gilboa (1988), which say, for instance, that every pair of states of the world define any third one in the same way, to include the following:

1. According to every state of the world, an event is possible if and only if it has a non-empty intersection with the set of possible states.

2. The definition of the set P is identical across states. (Note that this assumption also implies that the definition of P is common knowledge.)

3. The event P is common knowledge at every state in it. (One may require that P be common knowledge over all S, thereby making the states of the world outside it inconsistent since what players know at those states need no longer be true at them; this inconsistency should not pose a problem: one simply has to modify the axiom saying that what a player knows is true to apply only to possible states of the world.)

A set P with the above properties still does not enjoy the special status we would like it to have: so far, "possible" is just a word that we --the game theorists--and the players can use in the same way. The meaning of this word will be given to it by the actual behavior of both the players and ourselves. (Although, to a certain extent, assumption (3) already says something about the set P beyond its mere definition.) As we will shortly see, the set P will be incorporated into game-theoretic axioms to make it meaningful to the players; however, we, as outside observers, will have to be interested in this set P as well. Namely, a fact that is proven to hold at each state of the world in P would have to be construed as "true," i.e., as an implication of the theory.

Assuming that the players are endowed with a reasonable reasoning ability, which is also common knowledge, we deduce that whatever we can prove to be impossible (namely, whatever state of the world we can prove is not in P) can also be proven by the players, and has to coincide with their knowledge of the definition of P. However, the definition of P--as known to the players--may be more restrictive. There may be sets satisfying our axioms, the occurrence of which cannot be proved from game-theoretic axioms. To avoid unwarranted exclusion of states we have to explicitly assume that all players consider as possible every state that cannot be proved impossible by game-theoretic assumptions. (Which are also assumed to be common knowledge, as in Gilboa-Schmeidler (1988).) We will assume that these assumptions are parameterized by an event A: for every A (to be thought of as a candidate for the set of possible states P) each axiom may have a different meaning. (This will hopefully become clearer in the example of the "common sense" axiom below.)

We are therefore led to the following axiom on the set P: there is a finite sequence $S = A_0 \supset A_1 \supset \ldots \supset A_k = P$ such that A_i can be proven from A_{i-1} and the game-theoretic assumptions for A_{i-1} $(1 \le i \le k)$, and this chain is maximal with respect to this property. (I.e., no proper subset of P can be proved from P and the game-theoretic assumptions corresponding to P.)

We can now describe a notion of rationality which may be common knowledge without leading to a contradiction: this assumption is close to the "common sense" assumption in Gilboa-Schmeidler (1988), and it basically says that players do not choose dominated strategies. We have to be more specific here and understand domination in the following way: an action x (of player i) is dominated by an action y (of the same player) at a decision node n with respect to a set A if at n player i knows that at every state of the world compatible with n (i.e., contained in the event associated with n), which is also in A, the action y guarantees him/her a strictly higher payoff than x. With this definition in mind, let us now define the axiom of **common sense with respect to A** to be the following: for every player i, and every node n, **if** (the event associated with) **n is A-possible** (namely, intersects A) and if an action x is strictly dominated by an action y at n with respect to A, then if i reaches n, i will not choose x.

Let us assume that the only game-theoretic assumptions are common sense and common knowledge (of all the model's assumptions, hence also of itself.) Then it is quite straightforward to translate the well-known backward induction arguments to show that the undominated solutions dictated by them constitute a valid P. Moreover, in the game given above, as in every finite game, P is unique. (In perfect-information extensive-form games without "ties," the unique P is a singleton.)

Thus, we are able to reconstruct the backward induction argument by proving (outside the model, but if you will--also inside it) that the only consistent set P is the singleton at which player I plays left at node 1. The main point is that the contradiction disappears since nodes 2 and 3 are impossible, (and this is common knowledge,) so that the rationality assumption is vacuously satisfied at these nodes. Finally, the advantage this admittedly more cumbersome model has over the previous one is that it is rich enough to describe every relevant and conceivable aspect of each player's decision problem, and thus to formally describe the players' reasoning.

5. Possible Applications of the Possible Set

5.1 Weak Domination

Let us consider weak domination, instead of strict one, in the definition of "common sense." This will serve as another example of the possibility set, showing that it may not be unique, and suggesting a certain refinement of it. The following discussion can also be viewed as another theoretical application of the notion of the possibility set, in which it provides some further insight on the elimination of weakly dominated strategies.

Consider the following normal-form game:

		player II	
		L	R
player I	T	(1,1)	(1,1)
	B	(1,1)	(0,0)

Figure 2

Obviously, player I's B is weakly dominated by T, and similarly player II's R is weakly dominated by L. There are three valid possibility sets: $P_1 = \{(T,L),(T,R)\}$, $P_2 = \{(T,L),(B,L)\}$ and $P_3 = \{(T,L)\}$. (In all three cases the chain of reasoning is of length 1. However, one may decide at the first stage whether to use the common sense assumption to eliminate both B and R, or only one of them. At any rate, after the first elimination the resulting strategies define a possibility set.)

At first glance, P_3 seems to be the most appealing one, as it is the only symmetric set (which is a natural choice for a symmetric game,) and the outcome it predicts seems plausible. However, upon a more careful scrutiny its validity as exhausting all that may possibly occur appears somewhat dubious: precisely if the players know (as opposed to "believe with a high probability") that (T,L) should be the outcome of the game, this knowledge cannot be justified: if player I, for instance, actually knows that player II is about to play L, there is no reason for him not to play B. In a way, the very knowledge of the "theory" represented by P_3 casts a shadow of doubt on this theory. (Note that this is a considerably less fundamental flaw than being a "self-refuting theory" in the sense of Bicchieri (1989): here the theory is logically consistent; it only seems somewhat arbitrary.)

If we wish to avoid this type of problem we can, in general, propose the following definition: a possibility set is **maximal** if it is maximal with respect to set inclusion. Obviously, P_3 is not maximal, while P_1 and P_2 are.

The fact that common knowledge of common sense--with weak domination rather than strict one--does not yield a unique maximal possibility set, nor a symmetric one for symmetric games, may be considered a theoretical disadvantage of weak domination. Naturally, this is closely related to the fact that weak domination is not inherited by subgames, which also implies that reduced games (with respect to it) are not unique. See Gilboa-Kalai-Zemel (1989) for further discussion.

5.2 Imperfectly Rational Players

The framework described above may be used to describe other models, and, in particular, ones which make less stringent rationality assumptions. For instance, by relaxing the assumption that the possibility set is common knowledge, one may assume that all players are actually rational, and even that this fact is known by all to a certain degree, but that it fails to be common knowledge. Introducing probability into the model may also allow us to quantify the extent of irrationality by the subjective probabilities of those states of the world (which are, in fact, impossible) and the level of knowledge at which they occur. (For instance, one may argue that a system of beliefs in which every player is actually rational, but suspects the others of being irrational, is, on the whole, "more rational" than one in which the players actually are irrational.)

These ideas have, of course, been suggested before (see, for instance, Aumann (1988)), but it seems it would be difficult to formally capture the distinction between violations of rationality occurring at different levels of knowledge without having the distinction between "possible" and "conceivable" states of the world as a basis.

References

Aumann, R. J. (1974), "Subjectivity and Correlation in Randomized Strategies," **Journal of Mathematical Economics 1**, 67-95.

Aumann, R. J. (1976), "Agreeing to Disagree," **Annals of Statistics 4**, 1236-1239.

Aumann, R. J. (1987), "Correlated Equilibrium as an Expression of Bayesian Rationality," **Econometrica 55**, 1-18.

Aumann, R. J. (1988), "Irrationality in Game Theory," a paper presented at the OSU conference on game theory, July 1988.

Aumann, R. J., and S. Sorin (1989), "Cooperation and Bounded Recall," **Games and Economic Behavior 1**, 5-39.

Bicchieri, C. (1988a), "Strategic Behavior and Counterfactuals," **Synthese** 76, 135-169.

Bicchieri, C. (1988b), "Common Knowledge and Backward Induction: A Solution to the Paradox," in the **Proceedings of the Second Conference on Theoretical Aspects of Reasoning about Knowledge**, edited by M. Vardi, Morgan-Kaufmann, 381-393.

Bicchieri, C. (1988c), "Backward Induction without Common Knowledge", in the **Proceedings of the Philosophy of Science Association Meeting**, Oct. 1988.

Bicchieri, C. (1989), "Self-Refuting Theories of Strategic Interaction: A Paradox of Common Knowledge," **Erkenntnis 30**, 69-85.

Bonanno, G. (1988), "The Logic of Rational Play in Games of Perfect Information," mimeo.

Gilboa, I. (1988), "Information and Meta-Information," in the **Proceedings of the Second Conference on Theoretical Aspects of Reasoning about Knowledge**, edited by M. Vardi, Morgan-Kaufmann, 227-243.

Gilboa, I., E. Kalai and E. Zemel (1989), "On the Order of Eliminating Dominated Strategies," Northwestern University discussion paper.

Gilboa, I. and D. Schmeidler (1988), "Information-Dependent Games: Can Common Sense be Common Knowledge?" **Economics Letters 27**, 215-221.

Kaneko, M. (1987), "Structural Common Knowledge and Factual Common Knowledge," RUEE Working Paper No. 87-27, Hitotsubashi University.

Kreps, D., P. Milgrom, J. Roberts and R. Wilson (1982), "Rational Cooperation in the Finitely Repeated Prisoner's Dilemma," **Journal of Economic Theory 27**, 245-252.

Reny, P. (1988), "Rationality, Common Knowledge and the Theory of Games," mimeo.

Rosenthal, R. W. (1981), "Games of Perfect Information, Predatory Pricing and the Chain-Store Paradox," **Journal of Economic Theory 25**, 92-100.

Savage, L. J. (1954), **The Foundations of Statistics**, Wiley, NY.

Selten, R. (1978), "The Chain-Store Paradox," **Theory and Decision 9**, 127-1589.

On the Strategic Advantages of a Lack of Common Knowledge

Barton L. Lipman
GSIA
Carnegie Mellon University
Pittsburgh, PA 15213

ABSTRACT

I illustrate the surprising strategic effects a lack of common knowledge can have in a simple example. I analyze a two–person bargaining game in which the seller makes a single take–it–or–leave–it offer. The seller knows everything except possibly what information the buyer has. If it is common knowledge that the buyer knows the value of the object or if it is common knowledge that the buyer does not know the value, then the buyer's expected payoff is zero. However, if the seller does not know what the buyer knows, then the buyer may be able to obtain some of the gains from trade. In the exogenous information case, where there is a fixed probability q that the buyer is informed, if q is far enough from zero and one, the buyer's expected payoff is strictly positive. However, if the seller is almost sure of what the buyer knows, the buyer's expected payoff is zero. Surprisingly, the endogenous information case, where, after seeing the seller's offer, the buyer decides whether or not to become informed, is quite different. If the cost of obtaining information is zero, we get the same outcome as it is common knowledge that the buyer is informed. However, if the cost of obtaining the information is small but strictly positive, the buyer's payoff is strictly positive. As the cost goes to zero, the limit of the buyer's payoff is strictly positive and may even be virtually all of the gains from trade.

2. INTRODUCTION

Much research in economics over the past decade has demonstrated the fact that the distribution of knowledge is of crucial importance for predicting outcomes. Changing the specification of "who knows what and when they learn it" can greatly affect the equilibrium outcome.[1] What is less well understood is how knowledge about the knowledge of others affects equilibrium outcomes. (The small amount of literature on this subject is discussed below.) Typically, we assume that "who knows what and when they learn it" is common knowledge. Informally, a statement p is said to be common knowledge among the players if all statements of the form "everyone knows that everyone knows that ... knows that p" are true. In this paper, I show by example that relaxing the assumption that "who knows what" is common knowledge can have very surprising implications.

---

1 For classic examples, see Kreps and Wilson [1982a] and Milgrom and Roberts [1982].

I consider a simple two–player bargaining game. Throughout, the seller is taken to be informed about everything except possibly the information of the buyer. The seller makes a single take–it–or–leave–it offer, which the buyer can accept or reject. It is easy to see that when it is common knowledge that the buyer is perfectly informed, the seller's bargaining power enables him to extract all the gains from trade. It is also straightforward to show that when it is common knowledge that the buyer is imperfectly informed, the buyer, again, receives none of the gains from trade. I relax the assumption that the seller knows what the buyer knows in two ways.

First, I consider the case of exogenous information, Here the information of the buyer is exogenously determined—the buyer is either informed or not and the seller does not know which. I show that the buyer obtains some of the gains from trade if the seller is sufficiently unsure about what the buyer knows. However, near certainty, the outcome is continuous in the probability that the buyer is informed. If the seller is almost sure that the buyer is informed or almost sure that the buyer is uninformed, the buyer's share of the surplus is small or zero.

The second case is endogenous information. Here the buyer has the option of becoming informed at a cost. Surprisingly, the outcome is *not* continuous in the cost at zero. The outcome when the cost of becoming informed is zero is the same as the outcome when it is common knowledge that the buyer is informed. For any strictly positive cost, however, the buyer's expected payoff is bounded away from zero. In fact, in some cases, the buyer receives virtually all of the surplus when the cost of becoming informed is close to zero! As discussed in Lipman [1989], one can view a game with endogenous information acquisition as a model of bounded rationality. Under this interpretation, the example indicates that complete rationality and "almost complete rationality" can be very different in extensive form games.

In Section 3, I set out the model, briefly discuss the equilibrium when the buyer's information is common knowledge, and analyze the exogenous information case. Section 4 considers the endogenous information case and offers concluding remarks. Proofs are in Section 5.

A Comment on Interpretation. A number of authors have argued that common knowledge of the information structure is without loss of generality. Let S_0 be the set of all possible states of the world. Suppose we represent the information of player i about S_0 by a partition of S_0. Aumann [1987] gives the following argument that the assumption that the partitions are common knowledge is without loss of generality. Suppose that player j thinks that player i's partition could be either Π_1 or Π_2. Then it must be true that there is a state of the world in which i's partition is Π_1 and another in which it is Π_2 and player j cannot tell these states apart. That is, the collection of states in S_0 is not a complete specification of the set of states of the world. In particular, we require a bigger state space in which we can represent the uncertainty about the knowledge of others regarding S_0. In the bigger space, say S_1, the information structure regarding S_1 will be common knowledge if S_1 is appropriately chosen.[2] In this sense, a lack of common knowledge at one level is equivalent to common knowledge in a higher-level state set.

My assumptions are consistent with this view. I assume that the information structure is common knowledge. However, I assume common knowledge at a higher level than is usually analyzed. In most bargaining models, it is assumed that a party is either informed or uninformed about the payoffs to various possible agreements and that which parties are informed is common knowledge.[3] By contrast, I assume in Section 3.1, for example, that the seller is informed, that there is a probability that the buyer is informed, and that these facts are common knowledge.

Related Literature. While there is a large literature on common knowledge (see, *e.g.*, Aumann [1976], Geanakoplos and Polemarchakis [1982], and Mertens and Zamir [1985]), only a few authors have explored the implications of a lack of common knowledge. Milgrom and Roberts [1982, Appendix B] discuss the possibility that lack of common knowledge could generate predation in Selten's [1978] Chain-Store game. Aumann [1988] gives an example in which the paradox of Rosenthal's [1981] centipede game is resolved by allowing for the possibility that rationality is not common knowledge. Rubinstein [1989] uses the coordinated attack problem to show that "almost common knowledge" is quite different from common knowledge. Neyman [1989] analyzes the effect of relaxing common knowledge assumptions in finitely repeated games.

3. EXOGENOUS INFORMATION

The basic game I consider has one seller, one buyer, and a single indivisible unit of a good. The seller proposes a price to the buyer. The buyer can then accept or reject. If he accepts, they trade at the proposed price. The payoff to the seller is the price minus his cost; the payoff to the buyer is the value of the good to him minus the price. If the buyer rejects the offer, the game ends and each player gets a payoff of zero. I assume throughout that the buyer's valuation is always larger than the seller's costs, so that trade is efficient. I also assume that the seller knows his costs and the buyer's valuation.

Formally, there is a finite set of possible states of the world, $S \subset [0,1]$, with $0, 1 \in S$. The buyer's valuation is given by a function $v : [0,1] \to \mathbf{R}_+$ and the seller's costs by $c : [0,1] \to \mathbf{R}_+$. Of course, these functions are only relevant at points in S, but, for reasons that will be clear shortly,

[2] See Brandenburger and Dekel [1985], Tan and Werlang [1985], and Gilboa [1988] for various formalizations of this argument. See also Mertens and Zamir [1985].

[3] See, for example, the papers in the recent *Journal of Economic Theory* symposium [1989].

it is convenient to define them on a broader domain. Without loss of generality, I assume that $v(s)$ is weakly increasing in s with $v(1) > v(0)$. Trade is always efficient in the sense that there is a $k > 0$ such that $v(s) - c(s) \geq k$ for all $s \in [0,1]$. Throughout, I assume that the seller knows the true state of the world. The buyer has a prior probability distribution f over S such that $f(s) > 0$ for all $s \in S$.[4]

While assuming S is finite simplifies much of the mathematics, it is inconvenient in that some results depend on how far apart the values of v and c are across states. For this reason, I sometimes assume that the largest distance between consecutive values of $v(s)$ or $c(s)$ for $s \in S$ is $\psi(n)$, where n, the number of states, is "large" and $\psi(n) \to 0$ as $n \to \infty$. When this assumption is used, I state it more succinctly by simply saying that n is large. It is only when I assume that n is large that the properties of $v(\cdot)$ and $c(\cdot)$ over all of $[0,1]$ are relevant.

I analyze the pure strategy sequential equilibria of variations on this game. Intuitively, a sequential equilibrium specifies strategies and beliefs for each player. Each player's strategy is required to be a best reply to the other player's strategy given his beliefs. Each player's beliefs are required to be consistent with the other player's strategy and Bayes' rule where applicable. A well known problem is the fact that the sequential equilibrium concept does not provide useful restrictions on beliefs off the equilibrium path. This allows players to "threaten with beliefs"—that is, they can adopt intuitively implausible beliefs off the equilibrium path which justify punitive actions in response to the deviation. The ability to punish deviations arbitrarily greatly enlarges the set of equilibria. In this context, this problem is especially troubling since my intent is to compare equilibria under various information structures. Naturally, I do not want the comparisons to hinge on what kinds of uncertainty allow the buyer more flexibility to threaten with his beliefs.

Consequently, I use refinements of sequential equilibria which eliminate some forms of threatening with beliefs. In Section 4, I focus on sequential equilibria in which no player ever uses a dominated strategy. This eliminates the buyer's ability to threaten to use a dominated strategy which punishes the seller. In Section 3.2, I use much stronger notion, namely perfect sequential equilibrium (see Grossman and Perry [1986]). Intuitively, this equilibrium concept eliminates sequential equilibria in which off the equilibrium path beliefs do not always use "sensible explanations" for the deviation when such explanations exist.

3.1 Common Knowledge

The simplest case is where whether or not the buyer is informed is common knowledge. When

---

[4] My assumptions on V and C are consistent with any degree of correlation between V and C as well as independence. Vincent [1989] shows that correlation between V and C can have strong consequences in bargaining models.

the buyer is informed, the game is as follows. First, Nature chooses s according to the probability distribution f. The seller observes Nature's choice and chooses an offer of a price $p(s)$. The buyer observes s and $p(s)$ and then can either accept or reject. The payoffs to the buyer and seller are $(p(s) - c(s), v(s) - p(s))$ if the buyer accepts; the payoffs if he rejects are $(0,0)$. When the buyer is uninformed, the game is the same except the buyer only observes $p(s)$. I refer to these games as G_i and G_u respectively.

If the buyer is informed, the fact that the seller has all the bargaining power implies that he gets all the gains from trade. More specifically, it is well-known that the unique sequential equilibrium of G_i has the seller choosing $p(s) = v(s)$ and the buyer accepting any $p \leq v(s)$. Not surprisingly, if the buyer does not know the value of the good and this fact is common knowledge, this informational disadvantage does not help him. It is true that there is no longer an equilibrium in which the seller offers $p(s) = v(s)$ and the buyer accepts. If the buyer would accept any such offer, the seller only offers the largest value of $v(s)$. However, if we rule out sequential equilibria which rely on "threatening with beliefs," the buyer's expected payoff is necessarily zero. More specifically, we have the following result.[5]

Theorem 1. *The buyer's expected payoff is zero in every perfect sequential equilibrium of G_u.*

In a perfect sequential equilibrium of G_u, the seller offers a price satisfying

$$p = \mathrm{E}[v(s) \mid p \geq c(s)]$$

if this at least covers his costs. Clearly, this makes the buyer's expected payoff zero. Intuitively, the seller wishes to set the price as high as possible and so sets it at the point where the buyer is just indifferent between accepting and rejecting the price, taking account of the information revealed by the fact that the seller is willing to trade at that price. Since the buyer is indifferent, it must be true that his expected payoff is zero—that is, he gets none of the gains from trade.

In short, if what the buyer knows is common knowledge, the seller's bargaining power makes the buyer's expected payoff is zero whether he knows his valuation or not. However, if the seller does not know whether the buyer knows his valuation, this reduces his bargaining power, potentially enabling the buyer to get a strictly positive payoff.

3.2 Equilibrium without Common Knowledge

Suppose the seller does not know the buyer's prior beliefs regarding the state. More specifically, Nature chooses s according to a nondegenerate probability distribution f. The seller observes

---

[5] The proof, messy but not difficult, is omitted. It is available from the author by request.

Nature's choice and offers a price $p(s)$. With probability $q \in (0,1)$, the buyer observes s and $p(s)$. Otherwise, the buyer observes only $p(s)$. Finally, the buyer can accept or reject with payoffs as above. Let G_q denote this game. The structure of G_q—including the value of q—is assumed to be common knowlege.

Clearly, if the buyer is informed, he accepts iff $p \leq v(s)$. Because of this, if q is close to 1, the strategies from the complete information case (appropriately modified) are still an equilibrium. To see this, suppose the seller offers $p(s) = v(s)$. The best reply for the buyer, if not informed, is to always accept. Is the seller's strategy a best reply? It is easy to see that his strategy is optimal iff for all s

$$v(s) - c(s) \geq (1-q)[v(1) - c(s)].$$

(Recall that $v(s)$ is increasing and that 1 is the largest value of s.) Rearranging:

$$q \geq q^*(s) = \frac{v(1) - v(s)}{v(1) - c(s)}.$$

Let q^* denote the largest value of $q^*(s)$ for $s \in S$. It is easy to use the assumptions on v and c to show that $q^* \in (0,1)$. Hence if q is close enough to 1, there is a sequential equilibrium in which the buyer receives no surplus. In fact, every perfect sequential equilibrium for $q \geq q^*$ has this property.

If $q \in (0, q^*)$, though, it simply is not credible for the seller to price at the buyer's valuation. If the buyer expects the seller to do so, the seller deviates to charging $v(1)$. Because of this, the informed buyer necessarily receives a strictly positive payoff. This also may enable the uninformed buyer to gain part of the surplus. However, consider what happens as q becomes small. Intuitively, we would expect the analysis to parallel the case where q is large—that is, for small enough q, the seller is essentially unconcerned with the behavior of the informed buyer. If q is sufficiently small, then, the seller always offers the highest price the uninformed buyer will accept. As in Theorem 1, this leaves the uninformed buyer indifferent between accepting and rejecting, giving him an expected payoff of zero. Unfortunately, the analysis is not quite so simple, since some types of sellers would earn negative profits at this price. In G_u, these types make no offer. In this game, though, these types offer higher prices in the hope that the buyer is informed. In part because of this, the analysis of the case where q is close to zero is more complex than the case where q is close to one. However, the result is the same: if the seller is almost sure of what the buyer knows, the buyer's payoff is close to zero. These observations are summarized in the following theorem, proved in the Appendix.[6]

---

[6] Perfect sequential equilibria often do not exist. While general existence results for this game are difficult, it is easy to show existence for a variety of special cases.

Theorem 2. *The buyer's expected payoff is zero for all $q \geq q^*$ in every perfect sequential equilibrium of G_q. For $q \in (0, q^*)$, the informed buyer's expected payoff is strictly positive if n is "large," though the uninformed buyer's payoff can be zero or strictly positive. However, as $q \downarrow 0$, the buyer's expected payoff in any sequence of perfect sequential equilibria of G_q goes to zero.*

In short, if q is far from zero and one, the buyer, at least if he is informed, earns a positive payoff. However, for q close to zero or one, the buyer's expected payoff is close to zero. In this sense, the outcome is continuous as a function of the seller's knowledge about the buyer's knowledge.

4. ENDOGENOUS INFORMATION

When the buyer can choose whether or not he knows his valuation, this continuity disappears. To be specific, suppose that after the seller makes his offer, the buyer can learn his valuation at a cost of $\delta \geq 0$.[7] If $\delta = 0$, the outcome is the same as the complete information world: the seller offers a price equal to the buyer's valuation, the buyer costlessly learns his valuation, and accepts. However, the outcome changes radically for $\delta > 0$ but small. We will see that the buyer's payoff is bounded away from 0 for all sufficiently small $\delta > 0$. In particular, the limit as $\delta \downarrow 0$ of the infimum of the buyer's payoff is strictly positive and can be quite large.

Formally, the game considered in this section is as follows. First, Nature chooses s according to the probability distribution $f(s)$. The seller observes s and offers a price $p(s)$. The buyer observes only $p(s)$ and then can choose to observe s. Then the buyer decides whether or not to accept. If the buyer does not observe s, the payoffs are exactly as in the previous section. If the buyer does observe s, the seller's payoff is as above, while the buyer's payoff is reduced by δ. I refer to this game as G_δ.

The case where $\delta = 0$ is quite simple. It is easy to see that not learning s given any $p \in (v(0), v(1))$ is a dominated strategy when $\delta = 0$. Hence in every sequential equilibrium where neither player uses a dominated strategy, the buyer learns s. Knowing this, the seller always sets $p(s) = v(s)$ and the buyer accepts. Hence we have the following theorem.

Theorem 3. *If $\delta = 0$, G_δ has a unique sequential equilibrium without use of dominated strategies in which the seller offers $p(s) = v(s)$, the buyer learns s whenever $p \in (v(0), v(1))$, and the buyer accepts any $p \leq v(s)$. Hence the buyer's expected payoff is zero.*

Suppose instead that δ is strictly positive but small. In this case, the strategies of Theorem 3

[7] The results are entirely unaffected by allowing the buyer the option of learning his valuation either before or after the seller's offer.

cannot possibly be an equilibrium. Since the seller's offer reveals $v(s)$ perfectly, the buyer will not pay any strictly positive amount to learn s. More generally, we see that it is no longer a dominated strategy to not learn s. Whenever the seller's strategy is such that there is a zero probability that the price is above $v(s)$, then the buyer's strict best response is to accept the offer without learning s. Hence it becomes credible for the buyer to not learn s, preventing the seller from extracting all the gains from trade.

To state the implications of this, for any $\delta > 0$, let $p(\delta)$ be the p which solves

$$\delta = \sum_{s \in \{s' \mid p \geq v(s')\}} f(s)[p - v(s)].$$

For any p, let $s^*(p)$ be the largest s such that $p > c(s')$ for all $s' \leq s$.

Theorem 4. *For any $\delta > 0$, every sequential equilibrium of G_δ gives the buyer an expected payoff of at least*

$$\inf_{p \in [v(0), p(\delta)]} \sum_{s \leq s^*(p)} f(s)[v(s) - p].$$

The proof of this result, contained in the Appendix, is not difficult. I will say that a price is automatically rejected (accepted) in an equilibrium if the buyer responds to that offer by rejecting (accepting) it without learning s. Let p be the lowest price the seller offers in some equilibrium which is not automatically rejected. Clearly, no offer above p is automatically accepted—if it were, the seller would never offer p. Also, p must be automatically accepted. If it is not, then it must be true that the buyer responds by learning the state. Since this is costly, the buyer would only do this if there exists an s such that $p(s) = p$ and $v(s) < p$. Hence it must be true that $v(0) < p$. But then, since every offer is either automatically rejected or leads the buyer to learn s, we see that when $s = 0$, the seller does not trade. But this cannot be an equilibrium since the seller could do better in this case by offering $v(0) - \epsilon$ when $s = 0$. (Recall that $v(0) > c(0)$.) It is not hard to show that if p is automatically accepted, it must be smaller than $p(\delta)$. If it were larger, the buyer would be better off learning s and rejecting the offer when $p > v(s)$. Finally, as shown in the Appendix, the seller offers p at least when $s \leq s^*(p)$. Since the buyer's expected payoff conditional on any price must be nonnegative, the lower bound given in Theorem 4 follows.[8]

The contrast between Theorems 2 and 4 is striking. When information is exogenous, the seller's uncertainty about the buyer's knowledge helps the informed buyer if q is small enough, but

---

8 It is not difficult to construct examples of pure strategy sequential equilibria with undominated strategies for this game, so a comparison of Theorems 3 and 4 is not vacuous. One can often achieve the lower bound on the buyer's expected payoff.

may never help the uninformed buyer. When information is endogenous, the situation is reversed: the lower bound on the buyer's expected payoff is based on his payoff when he chooses to remain ignorant. It is easy to construct examples in which the buyer's expected payoff is strictly positive if and only if the seller's offer leads him to remain uninformed.

The contrast between Theorems 3 and 4 is also surprising. First, notice that the lower bound on the buyer's expected payoff immediately implies the discontinuity referred to above. As $\delta \downarrow 0$, $p(\delta) \downarrow v(0)$, so the lower bound converges to

$$\sum_{s \leq s^*(v(0))} f(s)[v(s) - v(0)].$$

If there is at least one $s' > 0$ such that $c(s') < v(0)$, then $s^*(v(0)) \geq v'$. (Note that this must be true if n is sufficiently large.) Hence the limit as $\delta \downarrow 0$ of the buyer's payoff is at least $f(s')[v(s') - v(0)] > 0$. Thus the buyer's payoff as a function of δ is discontinous at $\delta = 0$.

Notice also that this lower bound can be quite strong. For example, suppose that $c(s) < v(0)$ for all s. (This must hold if the buyer's valuation is independent of the seller's costs by the assumption that trade is always efficient.) In this case, $s^*(p) = 1$ for any $p \geq v(0)$. Thus the lower bound is just $E(v) - p(\delta)$. Hence as $\delta \downarrow 0$, the buyer's payoff converges to at least $E(v) - v(0)$. Of course, the buyer can never get a larger payoff than this since the seller never offers a lower price than $v(0)$. Hence the limit of the buyer's payoff is exactly $E(v) - v(0)$. This holds even if $c(s) = v(0) - \epsilon$ for all s. In this case, the seller's payoff is ϵ, so that the buyer receives almost all the surplus!

Why is the equilibrium outcome discontinuous in δ at $\delta = 0$?[9] Intuitively, when the buyer has the ability to learn his valuation, this prevents the seller from setting the price much above the buyer's valuation. As $\delta \downarrow 0$, the probability that the price strictly exceeds the buyer's valuation must go to zero. At the same time, as long as $\delta > 0$, it is not an equilibrium for the seller to set the price equal to the buyer's valuation. If he does so, the buyer will never pay any strictly positive amount to learn his valuation since the seller's price reveals it to him. But then the seller has an incentive to deviate to the highest possible price. Even as $\delta \downarrow 0$, this effect prevents the seller from increasing the price up to the buyer's valuation.

---

[9] This discontinuity does not occur when the equilibrium notion is sequential equilibria since the sequential equilibrium correspondence is upper semicontinuous in payoffs (Kreps and Wilson [1982b]). However, the sequential equilibrium which is the limit as $\delta \downarrow 0$ requires the buyer to not learn s in response to some price offers above $v(0)$. This strategy is dominated when $\delta = 0$, even though it is not when $\delta > 0$. As this illustrates, the correspondence giving sequential equilibria in which no player uses a dominated strategy is not upper semicontinuous.

In short, when the buyer's valuation is common knowledge or if the buyer's ignorance about his valuation is common knowledge, the buyer gets none of the gains from trade. If, however, the buyer's information or ignorance is not common knowledge, the buyer does better. Even when the cost of learning his valuation is infinitesimal, the fact that the seller cannot be certain of what the buyer knows prevents the seller from getting all the surplus. Intuitively, the lack of common knowledge gives the buyer enough of an informational advantage to guarantee himself some of the surplus. This is analogous to the way the buyer gets some of the gains from trade in bargaining games where he knows his valuation and the seller does not.

It is worth noting the importance of the timing assumed in these results. The key to the result is the way the information conveyed by the seller's offer interacts with the buyer's decision to learn the state. If, for example, the buyer could learn the state before the seller's offer but not after the offer, the discontinuity would not occur. (If he has the option of learning the state either before or after, my results are unaffected.) Similarly, this discontinuity would not be present if we replace the bargaining model used here with a k–double auction (see, for example, Satterthwaite and Williams [1989]). In a k–double auction, the buyer and seller *simultaneously* make price offers, say p_b and p_s. If $p_s > p_b$, no trade occurs. If $p_s \leq p_b$, trade takes place at a price of $kp_b + (1-k)p_s$ where $k \in [0,1]$. The simultaneity of the procedure means that the buyer would have to make his decision about learning s before getting to see the seller's offer. Hence the discontinuity in δ at $\delta = 0$ would not arise.

5. APPENDIX

5.1 Proof of Theorem 2

Lemma 1. *Let $\bar{p}$ be the largest price the uninformed buyer accepts in some perfect sequential equilibrium. Then the seller always offers either $v(s)$ or $\bar{p}$. If $v(s) < \bar{p}$, the seller offers $v(s)$ if*

$$v(s) - c(s) > (1-q)[\bar{p} - c(s)]$$

and offers $\bar{p}$ if the reverse strict inequality holds. If $v(s) > \bar{p}$, he offers $v(s)$ if

$$q[v(s) - c(s)] > \bar{p} - c(s)$$

and $\bar{p}$ if the reverse strict inequality holds. If the buyer is informed, he accepts any $p \leq v(s)$. If he is uninformed, he accepts any value of $v(s) \leq \bar{p}$ and accepts $\bar{p}$.

Proof: Consider any s with $v(s) < \bar{p}$. Suppose that in equilibrium this type of seller only sells to the informed buyer. Then it must be true that $p(s) \leq v(s)$. Clearly, though, we cannot have $p(s) < v(s)$ since the seller could strictly increase the price and be better off as the informed buyer would continue to purchase. Hence if he sells only to the informed buyer, $p(s) = v(s)$. If he sells only to the uninformed buyer, we must have $p(s) = \bar{p}$, since this is the largest price the uninformed buyer accepts. Finally, if he sells to both types of buyer, we must have $p(s) \leq v(s)$. Suppose $p(s) < v(s)$. Consider the deviation to $v(s) - \epsilon$ where $\epsilon > 0$ but is small enough that $v(s) - \epsilon > p(s)$ and $v(s) - \epsilon > v(s')$ for all s' such that $v(s') < v(s)$. Clearly, the informed buyer accepts this offer. Suppose the uninformed buyer accepts. Then the seller certainly deviates in state s. Notice, however, that there is no state s' with $v(s') < v(s)$ in which the seller would deviate. Since $v(s) - \epsilon > v(s')$, if the seller in state s' deviated, he would only sell to the uninformed buyer. By assumption, though, $v(s) < \bar{p}$, so the seller in state s' could do better by selling to the uninformed buyer at $\bar{p}$. Hence for any s' such that the seller deviates, we must have $v(s') \geq v(s)$. Hence it is optimal for the uninformed buyer to accept the offer, breaking the proposed equilibrium. Therefore, if the seller does sell to both types in a state with $v(s) < \bar{p}$, we must have $p(s) = v(s)$. The same argument can be used to show that if $v(s) < \bar{p}$, then the seller in state s will not sell only to the informed buyer at $p(s) = v(s)$. If he were only able to sell to the informed buyer at $p = v(s)$, he could deviate down ϵ and attract the uninformed buyer, leading to a higher payoff.

Hence for states such that $v(s) < \bar{p}$, the seller either sells to both types of buyers at $v(s)$ or only to the uninformed buyer at $\bar{p}$. Essentially the same argument establishes that if the payoff to the seller from selling to both types at $v(s)$ is larger than the payoff to selling only to the uninformed at $\bar{p}$, then in equilibrium, the seller offers $v(s)$ and both types do accept. In other words, the seller has both options in equilibrium and chooses the one which yields the higher profits. Thus for states such that $v(s) < \bar{p}$, $p(s) = v(s)$ if

$$v(s) - c(s) > (1 - q)[\bar{p} - c(s)]$$

and $p(s) = \bar{p}$ if the opposite strict inequality holds, as stated in the lemma.

Suppose, then, that $v(s) > \bar{p}$. Clearly, then, the seller either sells to both types of buyer at $\bar{p}$ or sells only to the informed buyer. If he does the latter, we must have $p(s) = v(s)$. Hence, again, the statement of the lemma is verified. Finally, suppose that $v(s) = \bar{p}$. The seller can sell to both types at $\bar{p}$ or at a lower price. At any higher price, he cannot sell to either type. Clearly, $p(s) = \bar{p}$ is optimal. ▌

Lemma 2. *If $q \geq q^*$, then the buyer's expected payoff is zero in every perfect sequential equilibrium.*

Proof: Suppose, contrary to the lemma, that there is a perfect sequential equilibrium in which the buyer's payoff is strictly positive. Let $\bar{p}$ be the highest price the uninformed buyer accepts. By Lemma 1, the seller always offers either $v(s)$ or $\bar{p}$. Hence if the buyer has a strictly positive expected payoff, it must be true that there is some state s such that $p(s) = \bar{p} < v(s)$. Clearly, this means that we must have $\bar{p} < v(1)$. But, by the definition of q^*, the fact that $q \geq q^*$ implies that every seller prefers to offer $v(s)$, a contradiction. ▌

Lemma 3. *If $q \in (0, q^*)$, then the buyer's expected payoff if he is informed is strictly positive if n is sufficiently large.*

Proof: Suppose not. Since the informed buyer's expected payoff cannot be strictly negative, it must be zero. Again, let $\bar{p}$ be the largest price the uninformed buyer accepts. By Lemma 1, either $p(s) = v(s)$ or $p(s) = \bar{p}$. If the informed buyer's payoff is zero, either $p(s) = v(s)$ for all s or $\bar{p} \geq v(s)$ for all s such that $p(s) = \bar{p}$. Clearly, if $\bar{p} > v(s)$ for some s such that $p(s) = \bar{p}$, the uninformed buyer rejects $\bar{p}$, a contradiction. Hence for every s such that $p(s) = \bar{p}$, we have $v(s) = \bar{p}$. But then $p(s) = v(s)$ for all s. Since $q < q^*$, this implies $\bar{p} < v(1)$.

It is easy to see that $\bar{p} \geq v(0)$. Otherwise, the seller in state 0 could deviate to $v(0) - \epsilon$ and be strictly better off (as this must be accepted by both the informed and uninformed buyer). Let $\bar{s}$ denote the largest s such that $v(s) \leq \bar{p}$ and let $\bar{s}_+$ denote the smallest state with $v(s) > v(\bar{s})$. Since, by definition, $v(\bar{s}_+) > \bar{p}$, the uninformed buyer does not accept a price of $v(\bar{s}_+)$. Hence the seller in state $\bar{s}_+$ sells only to the informed buyer. He prefers this to deviating down to a price of $\bar{p}$ iff

$$q[v(\bar{s}_+) - c(\bar{s}_+)] \geq \bar{p} - c(\bar{s}_+) \geq v(\bar{s}) - c(\bar{s}_+). \tag{1}$$

Recall that the maximum distance between consecutive values of $v(s)$ or of $c(s)$ is $\psi(n)$. Together with (1), this implies

$$\psi(n) \geq (1 - q)[v(\bar{s}) - c(\bar{s})] \geq (1 - q^*)k$$

for all $q \leq q^*$. (Recall that $v(s) - c(s) \geq k$ for all $s \in [0, 1]$, where $k > 0$.) Hence, since $\psi(n) \to 0$ as $n \to \infty$, we can choose n large enough that (1) cannot hold for any $q \in (0, q^*)$. ▌

Lemma 3 shows that when $q \in (0, q^*)$ and n is large, we cannot have an equilibrium in which $p(s) = v(s)$ for all s. Since we cannot have $p(s) \geq v(s)$ for all s with a strict inequality for some s, this implies that the informed buyer earns a strictly positive expected payoff. This does not, however, guarantee that the uninformed buyer earns a strictly positive payoff. I now show that the uninformed buyer's payoff converges to 0 as $q \downarrow 0$ for every sequence of perfect sequential equilibria. Suppose not. Let $p_q(s)$ denote the seller's strategy as a function of q along this sequence of equilibria. Let $\bar{p}_q$ denote the largest price the uninformed buyer will accept as a function of q. Then

$$\lim_{q \downarrow 0} \sum_{s \in \hat{S}_q} [v(s) - \bar{p}_q] f(s) > 0 \tag{2}$$

where $\hat{S}_q = \{s \mid p_q(s) = \bar{p}_q\}$. A necessary condition for (2) is

$$\bar{p}_q < \mathrm{E}[v(s) \mid s \in \hat{S}_q]$$

for all q sufficiently small. Suppose there is no $s' \notin \hat{S}_q$ with $v(s') \leq \bar{p}_q$ such that the seller is indifferent between charging $v(s')$ and $\bar{p}_q$. Then there is an $\epsilon > 0$ such that no seller with $s' \notin \hat{S}_q$ and $v(s') \leq \bar{p}_q$ would deviate to $\bar{p}_q + \epsilon$ if the uninformed buyer would accept this price, but for every $s \in \hat{S}_q$, the seller would deviate. Let $\hat{S}_q^+$ denote the set of s such that the seller deviates. Clearly, $\hat{S}_q \subseteq \hat{S}_q^+$ and $v(s) > \bar{p}_q + \epsilon$ for all $s \in \hat{S}_q^+ \setminus \hat{S}_q$. Hence we can then make ϵ small enough that

$$\mathrm{E}[v(s) \mid s \in \hat{S}_q^+] > \bar{p}_q + \epsilon,$$

so the uninformed buyer's best response is to accept, breaking the proposed equilibrium.

Hence there must be some $s' \notin \hat{S}_q$ with $v(s') \leq \bar{p}_q$ such that the seller is indifferent between $v(s')$ and $\bar{p}_q$. Let S_q^I denote the set of such s. The argument above can easily be extended to show that we must have

$$\mathrm{E}[v(s) \mid s \in \hat{S}_q \cup S_q^I] \leq \bar{p}_q. \tag{3}$$

By definition, $s \in S_q^I$ iff

$$v(s) - c(s) = (1 - q)[\bar{p}_q - c(s)].$$

Clearly, then, for any $\epsilon > 0$, we can choose q small enough that we will have $\bar{p}_q - v(s) < \epsilon$ for all $s \in S_q^I$. This implies that there is a $\bar{q} > 0$ and a unique value of $v(s)$, say v^*, such that all $s \in S_q^I$ for $q \leq \bar{q}$ have $v(s) = v^*$.

For $q < \bar{q}$, then, (3) implies

$$\bar{p}_q \geq \frac{\Pr[s \in \hat{S}_q]}{\Pr[s \in \hat{S}_q \cup S_q^I]} \mathrm{E}[v(s) \mid s \in \hat{S}_q] + \frac{\Pr[s \in S_q^I \setminus \hat{S}_q]}{\Pr[s \in \hat{S}_q \cup S_q^I]} v^*$$

which can be rewritten as

$$\Pr[s \in \hat{S}_q \cup S_q^I](\bar{p}_q - v^*) > \Pr[s \in \hat{S}_q](\mathrm{E}[v(s) \mid s \in \hat{S}_q] - v^*) \geq 0.$$

But since $\lim_{q \downarrow 0} \bar{p}_q = v^*$, the left-hand side goes to zero, so the middle term must as well. By (2),

$$v^* = \lim_{q \downarrow 0} \bar{p}_q < \lim_{q \downarrow 0} \mathrm{E}[v(s) \mid s \in \hat{S}_q],$$

so we must have

$$\lim_{q \downarrow 0} \Pr[s \in \hat{S}_q] = 0.$$

However, this contradicts (2). ▌

5.2 Proof of Theorem 4.

Fix a sequential equilibrium and let $p_1 < \ldots < p_k$ be the set of prices offered by the seller in equilibrium which are not automatically rejected. As shown in the text, p_1 must be automatically accepted and for every $i > 1$, the buyer must respond to p_i by learning s.

Let $s^*(p_1)$ be the largest s such that $p_1 > c(s')$ for all $s' \leq s$. (Let $s^*(p_1) = 1$ if $p_1 > c(s)$ for all s.) Suppose that $p(s) \neq p_1$ for some $s \leq s^*(p_1)$. Let $\tilde{s}$ denote the smallest such s. Since the seller would receive a strictly positive payoff in state $\tilde{s}$ if he offered p_1, it must be true that he receives a larger payoff by offering p_i for some $i > 1$. Let $p(\tilde{s}) = \tilde{p}$. Since the buyer learns s in response to p_i for all $i > 1$, it must be true that $\tilde{p} \leq v(\tilde{s})$ as the seller would receive zero in state $\tilde{s}$ otherwise. By assumption, the seller offers p_1 for every $s < \tilde{s}$, so that $\tilde{s}$ must be the smallest s such that $p(s) = \tilde{p}$. But recall that $v(s)$ is weakly increasing in s. Hence the fact that $v(\tilde{s}) \geq \tilde{p}$ implies that $v(s) \geq \tilde{p}$ for every s such that $p(s) = \tilde{p}$. But then the fact that $\delta > 0$ implies that the buyer will not learn s in response to $\tilde{p}$, a contradiction. Hence the seller offers p_1 for every $s \leq s^*(p_1)$.

Let $S(p_1)$ denote the set of s such that $p(s) = p_1$. Since the buyer does not learn s in response to p_1, it must be true that

$$\sum_{s \in S(p_1)} [v(s) - p_1] f(s) \geq \sum_{s \in S(p_1)} \max[v(s) - p_1, 0] f(s) - \delta$$

or, letting $S^-(p_1)$ denote the set of $s \in S(p_1)$ with $v(s) \leq p_1$,

$$\delta \geq \sum_{s \in S^-(p_1)} [p_1 - v(s)] f(s). \tag{4}$$

By definition, $c(s^*(p_1)) > p_1$. Since $v(s) > c(s)$ for all s, $v(s^*(p_1)) > p_1$. Since $v(s)$ is weakly increasing, then, every s with $v(s) \leq p_1$ is smaller than $s^*(p_1)$. Since every such s is in $S(p_1)$, $S^-(p_1)$ is just the set of s such that $v(s) \leq p_1$. So we can rewrite (4) as

$$\delta \geq \sum_{s \in \{s' | p_1 \geq v(s')\}} f(s)[p_1 - v(s)]. \tag{5}$$

Let $p(\delta)$ be the value of p_1 such that this holds with equality. It is easy to show that a unique $p(\delta)$ exists for every $\delta > 0$. Since the right–hand side of (5) is increasing in p_1, (5) implies $p_1 \leq p(\delta)$.

Summarizing, there is a $p_1 \in [v(0), p(\delta)]$ such that p_1 is offered at least when $s \leq s^*(p_1)$. If the seller offers p_1 in some state $s > s^*(p_1)$, it will necessarily be true that $v(s) > p_1$ since $v(s)$ is increasing and $v(s^*(p_1)) > p_1$. Hence a lower bound on the buyer's expected payoff can be constructed by supposing that the buyer receives a payoff of zero in every state $s \in S(p_1)$ such that $s > s^*(p_1)$. Furthermore, conditional on any price, the buyer's expected payoff is nonnegative. Thus we can construct a lower bound by assuming that the buyer's payoff is zero when any price other than p_1 is offered. Hence a lower bound on the buyer's expected payoff is

$$\inf_{p_1 \in [v(0), p(\delta)]} \sum_{s \leq s^*(p_1)} [v(s) - p_1] f(s). \blacksquare$$

Acknowledgements

I thank Debra Holt and Sugato Bhattacharyya for helpful comments.

References

Aumann, R., "Agreeing to Disagree," *Annals of Statistics*, 4, 1976, 136–1239.

Aumann, R., "Correlated Equilibrium as an Expression of Bayesian Rationality," *Econometrica*, 55, January 1987, pp. 1–18.

Aumann, R., "Preliminary Notes on Irrationality in Game Theory," working paper, 1988.

Brandenburger, A., and E. Dekel, "Hierarchies of Beliefs and Common Knowledge," Graduate School of Business, Stanford University working paper, 1985.

Geanakoplos, J., and H. Polemarchakis, "We Can't Disagree Forever," *Journal of Economic Theory*, 28, 1982, 192–200.

Gilboa, I., "Information and Meta Information," in M. Y. Vardi, ed., *Proceedings of the Second Conference on Theoretical Aspects of Reasoning about Knowledge*, Los Altos: Morgan Kaufmann Publishers, 1988, pp. 227–244.

Grossman, S., and M. Perry, "Perfect Sequential Equilibria," *Journal of Economic Theory*, June 1986, pp. 97–119.

Kreps, D., and R. Wilson, "Reputation and Imperfect Information," *Journal of Economic Theory*, 27, August 1982a, 253–279.

Kreps, D., and R. Wilson, "Sequential Equilibria," *Econometrica*, 50, July 1982b, 863–894.

Lipman, B., "How to Decide How to Decide How to . . . : Limited Rationality in Decisions and Games," Carnegie Mellon University working paper, 1989.

Mertens, J.-F., and S. Zamir, "Formalization of Bayesian Analysis for Games with Incomplete Information," *International Journal of Game Theory*, 14, 1985, pp. 1–29.

Milgrom, P., and J. Roberts, "Predation, Reputation, and Entry Deterrence," *Journal of Economic Theory*, 27, August 1982, 280–312.

Neyman, A., "Games without Common Knowledge," working paper, 1989.

Rosenthal, R., "Games of Perfect Information, Predatory Pricing, and the Chain Store Paradox," *Journal of Economic Theory*, 25, 1981, pp. 92–100.

Rubinstein, A., "The Electronic Mail Game: Strategic Behavior Under 'Almost Common Knowledge,' " *American Economic Review*, 79, June 1989, 385–391.

Satterthwaite, M., and S. Williams, "Bilateral Trade with the Sealed Bid k–Double Auction: Existence and Efficiency," *Journal of Economic Theory*, 48, June 1989, pp. 107–133.

Selten, R., "The Chain–Store Paradox," *Theory and Decision*, 9, 1978, 127–159.

Symposium on Noncooperative Bargaining, *Journal of Economic Theory*, June 1989.

Tan, T. C. C., and S. R. C. Werlang, "On Aumann's Notion of Common Knowledge—An Alternative Approach," University of Chicago working paper, 1985.

Vincent, D., "Bargaining with Common Values," *Journal of Economic Theory*, June 1989, pp. 47–62.

Hypothesis Formation and Language Acquisition with an Infinitely-Often Correct Teacher

Sanjay Jain *
Dept. of Computer Science
University of Rochester
Rochester, New York 14627

Arun Sharma †
Dept. of Comp. and Inf. Sciences
University of Delaware
Newark, DE 19716

ABSTRACT

The presence of an "infinitely-often correct teacher" in scientific inference and language acquisition is motivated and studied. The treatment is abstract.

In the practice of science, a scientist performs experiments to gather experimental data about some phenomenon, and then tries to construct an explanation (or theory) for the phenomenon. A model for the practice of science is an inductive inference machine (a scientist) learning a program (an explanation) from the graph (set of experiments) of a recursive function (phenomenon). It is argued that this model of science is not an adequate one as scientists, in addition to performing experiments, make use of some approximate explanation (based on the "state of the art") about the phenomenon under investigation. An attempt has been made to model this approximate explanation as an additional information in the scientific process. It is shown that inference power of machines is improved in the presence of an approximate explanation. The quality of this approximate information is modeled using certain "density" notions. It is shown that additional information about a "better" quality approximate explanation enhances the inference power of learning machines as scientists more than a "not so good" approximate explanation.

*Supported by NSF grant CCR 832-0136.
†Supported by NSF grant CCR 871-3846.

Inadequacies in Gold's paradigm of language learning are investigated. It is argued that Gold's model fails to incorporate any additional information that children get from their environment. Children are sometimes told about some grammatical rule that enumerates elements of the language. These rules are some sort of additional information. Also, children are being given some information about what is not in the language. Sometimes, they are rebuked for making incorrect utterances or are told of a rule that enumerates certain non-elements of the language. An attempt has been made to extend Gold's model to incorporate both these kinds of additional information. It is shown that either type of additional information enhances the learning power of formal language learning devices.

INTRODUCTION

A model of scientific inference which involves learning of *predictive* explanations for phenomena [Gol67, BB75, CS83] may be described thus. Picture a scientist performing all the possible experiments (in any order) on a phenomenon, noting the result of each experiment while simultaneously, but algorithmically, conjecturing a succession of candidate explanations (programs) for predicting the results of all possible experiments. In this model, the set of all pairs of the form (*experiment, corresponding result*) associated with each phenomenon is taken to be coded by a function from $\mathcal{N}$ to $\mathcal{N}$, where $\mathcal{N}$ is the set of natural numbers. A criterion of success is for the scientist eventually to conjecture a program which he/she never gives up and which correctly predicts the results of all the possible experiments on the phenomenon, i.e., which correctly computes the function which codes the set of pairs associated with the phenomenon.

L. Blum and M. Blum [BB75] and Case and Smith [CS83] consider variations on the above criterion of success in which the final program is allowed to make up to a mistakes, where a is a natural number. The motivation for considering anomalies in [CS83] comes from the fact that physicists sometimes do employ explanations with anomalies.

This is a naive model of science. A scientist has more information available than just the result of experiments. C.S. Peirce [Pei58], [Rei70] argues that science is a non-terminating process of successive approximations. A scientist has some approximate explanation of the phenomenon based on the "state of the art" knowledge about that phenomenon. The model described above does not take in to account the presence of this additional information. In this paper, we make an attempt to model this additional information.

An *inductive inference machine* (IIM) is an algorithmic device which takes as its input a set of data given one element at a time, and which from time to time, as it is receiving its input, outputs programs. [KW80], [AS83], [Cas86], and [OSW86] contain surveys of work on inductive inference machines. Henceforth, we will concern ourselves with the problem in which an inductive inference machine is required to infer a program for a recursive function from its graph. This problem, as illustrated above, is analogous to the "naive" model of science. We describe below our approach to modeling additional information to a scientist.

An inductive inference machine is presented, as additional information, with a program which computes a partial function that (1) agrees infinitely often with the function being learned; and (2) does not contradict the function being learned. In other words, this additional information is an infinitely often correct teacher. However, the second restriction that this teacher not contradict the function being learned, we feel, makes our approach a simplistic one. We model the quality of this infinitely often correct teacher by using certain "density" notions from [Roy86].

A notion related to "scientific" inference of functions is the inductive inference of a type 0 grammar for a recursively enumerable language. To model language learning in children, Gold introduced the seminal notion of *identification* [Gol67]. We will use this paradigm as our model of language learning and refer to it as **TxtEx**-*identification* following [CL82]. According to this paradigm, a child (modeled as a machine) receives (in arbitrary order) all the well-defined strings of a language (a *text* for the language), and simultaneously, conjectures a succession of candidate grammars for the language being received. A criterion of success is for the child to eventually conjecture a correct grammar and to never change its conjecture thereafter. If, in this scenario, we replace the child machine by an arbitrary machine **M**, then we say that the machine **M** **TxtEx**-identifies the language. **TxtEx** is defined to be the class of sets $\mathcal{L}$ of r.e. languages such that some machine **TxtEx**-identifies each language in $\mathcal{L}$.

We study the effect of additional information in language learning. In this case, the language learning machine is provided with a grammar for a subset of the language being learned. It is also required that the "density" of difference between the two languages is no more than a certain, prespecified amount. The section on language learning contains an extensive discussion of the issues involved.

Fulk [Ful85, Ful80] and Jain and Sharma [JS89a] consider other approaches to modeling the presence of additional information in inductive learning. We now proceed formally.

NOTATIONS

$\mathcal{N}$ is the set of natural numbers. $\mathcal{I}^+$ is the set of positive integers. $*$ denotes any finite natural number. Unless otherwise specified, i, j, k, l, m, n denote integers. d, d_1, d_2 etc. denote real numbers between 0 and 1 (inclusive). a, b and c range over $(\mathcal{N} \cup \{*\})$. $\emptyset$ denotes the null set. $\text{card}(S)$ denotes the cardinality of the set S. max, min denote the maximum and minimum of a set respectively. $\subseteq$ denotes subset. $\subset$ denotes proper subset. For any two functions f_1 and f_2, $f_1 =^n f_2$ means that $\text{card}(\{x \mid f_1(x) \neq$

$f_2(x)\}) \leq n$. $f_1 =^* f_2$ means that card$(\{x \mid f_1(x) \neq f_2(x)\})$ is finite. For any two sets S_1 and S_2, $S_1 =^n S_2$ means card$((S_1 - S_2) \cup (S_2 - S_1)) \leq n$. $S_1 =^* S_2$ means card$((S_1 - S_2) \cup (S_2 - S_1))$ is finite. δf and ρf denote the domain and range of the function f respectively.

L denotes a *recursively enumerable* subset of $\mathcal{N}$. $\mathcal{L}$ denotes a set of *recursively enumerable* (r.e.) languages. $\mathcal{E}$ denotes the class of all *recursively enumerable* languages. φ denotes a standard *acceptable* programming system [Rog58], [Rog67], [MY78]. φ_i denotes the function computed by program i in the φ-system. $W_i = \delta\varphi_i$. The set of all total recursive functions of one variable is denoted by $\mathcal{R}$. $\mathcal{S}, \mathcal{S}_1...$ denote subsets of $\mathcal{R}$. $2^{\mathcal{S}}$ denotes the power set of $\mathcal{S}$. $\langle i, j\rangle$ stands for an arbitrary computable one to one encoding of all pairs of natural numbers onto $\mathcal{N}$ [Rog67].

PRELIMINARIES

In this section, we briefly describe the fundamental paradigms that model language learning and scientific inference.

Definition 1 [Gol67] An *Inductive Inference Machine* (IIM) is an algorithmic machine which takes as its input a set of data given one element at a time, and which from time to time, as it is receiving its input, outputs programs.

IIMs have been used in the study of identification of programs for recursive functions as well as learning of grammars for languages [BB75] [CS83] [Che81] [Ful85] [Gol67] [OSW86] [Wie78]. For a survey of this work see [AS83], [OSW86], [KW80], and [Cas86].

Definition 2 If L is a language, i is a *grammar* for L iff $W_i = L$.

Definition 3 A *text* for a language L is a mapping t from $\mathcal{N}$ into $(\mathcal{N} \cup \{\#\})$ such that L is the set of natural numbers in the range of t.

Intuitively, a text for a language is an enumeration of the objects in the language with #'s representing pauses in the listing of such objects. Variables σ and τ, with or without subscripts, range over finite initial segment of texts. content$(\sigma) = \rho\sigma - \{\#\}$. $|\sigma|$ denotes the length of the finite initial segment σ. t, t' range over texts for languages. $\overline{t_n}$ denotes the initial segment of t with length n. $\sigma \subset t$ means σ is an initial segment of t. content$(t) = \rho t - \{\#\}$; intuitively it is a set of meaningful things presented in text t.

$\mathbf{M}(\sigma)$ is the last output of $\mathbf{M}$ after receiving input σ (note that σ can be encoded as a natural number). We will assume that $\mathbf{M}(\sigma)$ is always defined. $\mathbf{M}(t)\downarrow = i$ iff $(\overset{\infty}{\forall} n)[\mathbf{M}(\overline{t_n}) = i]$. We write $\mathbf{M}(t)\downarrow$ iff $(\exists i)[\mathbf{M}(t)\downarrow = i]$.

Definition 4 [Gol67] [CL82] **M** $\mathbf{TxtEx}^a$*-identifies* L (written: $L \in \mathbf{TxtEx}^a(\mathbf{M})$) iff for any text t for L, $\mathbf{M}(t)\downarrow$ and $W_{\mathbf{M}(t)} =^a L$.

Definition 5 $\mathbf{TxtEx}^a = \{\mathcal{L} \subseteq \mathcal{E} \mid (\exists \mathbf{M})[\mathcal{L} \subseteq \mathbf{TxtEx}^a(\mathbf{M})]\}$.

Essentially the concepts from Definitions 4 and 5 ($a = 0$ case) constitute Gold's influential language learning paradigm. The generalization of Gold's paradigm to the $a > 0$ case above was motivated by the fact that humans rarely learn a language perfectly. The $a > 0$ case in Definitions 4 and 5 is due to Case and Lynes [CL82]. Osherson and Weinstein [OW82b, OW82a] had independently introduced the $a = *$ case.

In inference of programs for recursive functions by IIMs, the input sequence $\langle 0, f(0)\rangle, \langle 1, f(1)\rangle, \ldots$ is presented to the IIM. For all recursive functions f, $f|^n$ denotes the finite initial segment $((\langle 0, f(0)\rangle), (\langle 1, f(1)\rangle), \ldots, (\langle n, f(n)\rangle))$.

Definition 6 [Gol67] [BB75] [CS83] **M** $\mathbf{Ex}^a$*-identifies* f (written $f \in \mathbf{Ex}^a(\mathbf{M})$) iff both $\mathbf{M}(f)\downarrow$ and $\varphi_{\mathbf{M}(f)} =^a f$.

Definition 7 $\mathbf{Ex}^a = \{\mathcal{S} \subseteq \mathcal{R} \mid (\exists \mathbf{M})[\mathcal{S} \subseteq \mathbf{Ex}^a(\mathbf{M})]\}$.

The motivation for considering anomalies in the final program in Definitions 6 and 7 comes from the fact that physicists sometimes do employ explanations with anomalies [CS83]. The $a = *$ case was introduced by L. Blum and M. Blum [BB75] and the other $a > 0$ cases were introduced by Case and Smith [CS83].

Case and Smith [CS83] introduced another infinite hierarchy of identification criterion which we describe below. "**Bc**" stands for *behaviorally correct.* Barzdin [Bar74] independently introduced a similar notion. We now define these new criteria, both in the context of scientific inference and language learning.

Definition 8 [CS83] **M** $\mathbf{Bc}^a$*-identifies* f (written: $f \in \mathbf{Bc}^a(\mathbf{M})$) iff, **M** fed f outputs over time an infinite sequence of programs $p_0, p_1, p_2, \ldots$ such that $(\overset{\infty}{\forall} n)[\varphi_{p_n} =^a f]$.

Definition 9 [CS83] $\mathbf{Bc}^a = \{\mathcal{S} \subseteq \mathcal{R} \mid (\exists \mathbf{M})[\mathcal{S} \subseteq \mathbf{Bc}^a(\mathbf{M})]\}$.

Definition 10 [CL82] **M** $\mathbf{TxtBc}^a$*-identifies* L (written: $L \in \mathbf{TxtBc}^a(\mathbf{M})$) iff, for all texts t for L, **M** outputs over time an infinite sequence of grammars $g_0, g_1, g_2, \ldots$ such that $(\overset{\infty}{\forall} n)[W_{g_n} =^a L]$.

Definition 11 [CL82] $\mathbf{TxtBc}^a = \{\mathcal{L} \subseteq \mathcal{E} \mid (\exists \mathbf{M})[\mathcal{L} \subseteq \mathbf{TxtBc}^a(\mathbf{M})]\}$.

We usually write **Ex** for $\mathbf{Ex}^0$, **TxtEx** for $\mathbf{TxtEx}^0$, **Bc** for $\mathbf{Bc}^0$, and **TxtBc** for $\mathbf{TxtBc}^0$.

Theorem 1 just below states some of the basic hierarchy results about the $\mathbf{Ex}^a$ and $\mathbf{Bc}^a$ classes.

Theorem 1 *For all* $n \in \mathcal{N}$,
(a) $\mathbf{Ex}^n \subset \mathbf{Ex}^{n+1}$.
(b) $\bigcup_{n\in\mathcal{N}} \mathbf{Ex}^n \subset \mathbf{Ex}^*$.
(c) $\mathbf{Ex}^* \subset \mathbf{Bc}$.
(d) $\mathbf{Bc}^n \subset \mathbf{Bc}^{n+1}$.
(e) $\bigcup_{n\in\mathcal{N}} \mathbf{Bc}^n \subset \mathbf{Bc}^*$.
(f) $\mathcal{R} \in \mathbf{Bc}^*$.

Parts (a), (b), (d), and (e) are due to Case and Smith [CS83]. Part (f) is due to Harrington [CS83]. Blum and Blum [BB75] first showed that $\mathbf{Ex} \subset \mathbf{Ex}^*$. Barzdin [Bar74] independently showed $\mathbf{Ex} \subset \mathbf{Bc}$.

Theorem 2 just below states some of the basic results in language learning.

Theorem 2 [CL82] *For all* $i, n \in \mathcal{N}$,
(a) $\mathbf{TxtEx}^{n+1} - \mathbf{TxtEx}^n \neq \emptyset$.
(b) $\mathbf{TxtEx}^{2n+1} - \mathbf{TxtBc}^n \neq \emptyset$.
(c) $\mathbf{TxtEx}^{2n} \subset \mathbf{TxtBc}^n$.
(f) $\bigcup_n \mathbf{TxtBc}^n \subset \mathbf{TxtBc}^*$.

ADDITIONAL INFORMATION FOR FUNCTION INFERENCE

We define the following notions of "density" from [Roy86].

Definition 12 [Roy86] *Density* of a set $A \subseteq \mathcal{N}$ in a finite and nonempty set B (denoted: $\mathbf{d}(A; B)$) is $\mathrm{card}(A \bigcap B)/\mathrm{card}(B)$.

Intuitively, $\mathbf{d}(A; B)$ can be thought of as the probability of selecting an element of A when choosing an arbitrary element from B.

Definition 13 [Roy86] *Density* of a set $A \subseteq \mathcal{N}$ (denoted: $\mathbf{d}(A)$) is $\lim_{n\to\infty} \inf\{\mathbf{d}(A; \{z \mid z \leq x\}) \mid x \geq n\}$.

Definition 14 [Roy86] The *asymptotic agreement* between two partial functions f and g (denoted: $\mathbf{aa}(f, g)$) is $\mathbf{d}(\{x \mid f(x) = g(x)\})$.

Definition 15 [Roy86] The *asymptotic disagreement* between two partial functions f and g (denoted: $\mathbf{ad}(f, g)$) is $1 - \mathbf{aa}(f, g)$.

We now describe our notion of additional information to an inductive inference machine learning a program from the graph of a recursive function. An IIM, trying to infer a program for a function f, is given as additional information, a program for a partial recursive function g which agrees with f to some extent. In Definition 16 just below, we precisely define what we mean by "a partial function g agrees with f to some extent".

Definition 16 Suppose d is a real number in the interval $[0, 1]$. A partial function p is said to be *d-conforming* with a recursive function f iff, p satisfies the following two conditions:
(1) $p(x)\downarrow \Rightarrow p(x) = f(x)$, i.e., p does not contradict f.
(2) $\mathbf{d}(\{x \mid p(x) = f(x)\}) \geq d$.

Using Definition 16, we define below our new learning criterion for identification of a program from graph of a recursive function in the presence of an infinitely-often correct teacher.

Definition 17 Suppose d is a real number in the interval $[0, 1]$. Suppose $a \in \mathcal{N} \cup \{*\}$. A machine $\mathbf{M}$ $\mathbf{Ap}^d\mathbf{Ex}^a$-*identifies* a function f (written: $f \in \mathbf{Ap}^d\mathbf{Ex}^a(\mathbf{M})$) iff when provided with a program for a partial function p which is d-conforming with f, $\mathbf{M}$ on f converges to a program i such that $\varphi_i =^a f$.

Definition 18 Suppose d is a real number in the interval $[0, 1]$. Suppose $a \in \mathcal{N} \cup \{*\}$. $\mathbf{Ap}^d\mathbf{Ex}^a = \{\mathcal{S} \subseteq \mathcal{R} \mid (\exists \mathbf{M})[\mathcal{S} \subseteq \mathbf{Ap}^d\mathbf{Ex}^a(\mathbf{M})]\}$.

We similarly define the corresponding identification criterion for **Bc** inference.

Definition 19 Suppose d is a real number in the interval $[0, 1]$. Suppose $a \in \mathcal{N} \cup \{*\}$. A machine $\mathbf{M}$ $\mathbf{Ap}^d\mathbf{Bc}^a$-*identifies* a function f (written: $f \in \mathbf{Ap}^d\mathbf{Bc}^a(\mathbf{M})$) iff when provided with a program for a partial function p which is d-conforming with f, $\mathbf{M}$ on f, outputs an infinite sequence of programs $p_1, p_2, \ldots$ such that $(\overset{\infty}{\forall} n)[\varphi_{p_n} =^a f]$.

Definition 20 Suppose d is a real number in the interval $[0, 1]$. Suppose $a \in \mathcal{N} \cup \{*\}$. $\mathbf{Ap}^d\mathbf{Bc}^a = \{\mathcal{S} \subseteq \mathcal{R} \mid (\exists \mathbf{M})[\mathcal{S} \subseteq \mathbf{Ap}^d\mathbf{Bc}^a(\mathbf{M})]\}$.

In the above identification criteria, p — an approximation to f, is a good plausible additional information to a machine trying to learn a program for f from its graph. However, p may be a very bad approximator locally for large intervals which may be of importance. To overcome this situation, we use the notion of "uniform density" from [Roy86] to define a new identification criterion.

Definition 21 [Roy86] The *uniform density* of a set A in intervals of length $\geq n$ (denoted: $\mathbf{ud}_n(A)$) is $\inf(\{d(A; \{z \mid x \leq z \leq y\}) \mid x, y \in \mathcal{N}$ *and* $y - x \geq n\})$. *Uniform density* of A (denoted: $\mathbf{ud}(A)$) is $\lim_{n\to\infty} \mathbf{ud}_n(A)$.

Definition 22 [Roy86] The *asymptotic uniform agreement* between two partial functions f and g (denoted: $\mathbf{aua}(f,g)$) is $\mathbf{ud}(\{x \mid f(x) = g(x)\})$.

Definition 23 [Roy86] The *Asymptotic uniform disagreement* between two partial functions f and g (denoted: $\mathbf{aud}(f,g)$) is $1 - \mathbf{aua}(f,g)$.

Using the notion of *uniform density* we define an improved learning criterion. Definition 24 just below is an analogous notion to Definition 16 for this new density notion.

Definition 24 Suppose d is a real number in the interval $[0,1]$. A partial function p is said to be *d-uniform conforming* with a recursive function f iff, p satisfies the following two conditions:
(1) $p(x)\downarrow \Rightarrow p(x) = f(x)$, i.e., p does not contradict f.
(2) $\mathbf{ud}(\{x \mid p(x) = f(x)\}) \geq d$.

Definition 25 Suppose d is a real number in the interval $[0,1]$. Suppose $a \in \mathcal{N} \cup \{*\}$. A machine $\mathbf{M}$ $\mathbf{UAp}^d\mathbf{Ex}^a$*-identifies* a function f (written: $f \in \mathbf{UAp}^d\mathbf{Ex}^a(\mathbf{M})$) iff when provided with a program for a partial function p, which is d-uniform conforming with f, $\mathbf{M}$ on f converges to a program i such that $\varphi_i =^a f$.

Definition 26 $\mathbf{UAp}^d\mathbf{Ex}^a = \{\mathcal{S} \subseteq \mathcal{R} \mid (\exists \mathbf{M})[\mathcal{S} \subseteq \mathbf{UAp}^d\mathbf{Ex}^a(\mathbf{M})]\}$.

We similarly define the corresponding identification criterion for **Bc** inference.

Definition 27 Suppose d is a real number in the interval $[0,1]$. Suppose $a \in \mathcal{N} \cup \{*\}$. A machine $\mathbf{M}$ $\mathbf{UAp}^d\mathbf{Bc}^a$*-identifies* a function f (written: $f \in \mathbf{UAp}^d\mathbf{Bc}^a(\mathbf{M})$) iff when provided with a program for a partial function p, which is d-uniform conforming with f, $\mathbf{M}$ on f, outputs an infinite sequence of programs $p_1, p_2, \ldots$ such that $(\overset{\infty}{\forall} n)[\varphi_{p_n} =^a f]$.

Definition 28 $\mathbf{UAp}^d\mathbf{Bc}^a = \{\mathcal{S} \subseteq \mathcal{R} \mid (\exists \mathbf{M})[\mathcal{S} \subseteq \mathbf{UAp}^d\mathbf{Bc}^a(\mathbf{M})]\}$.

In what follows, we will refer to the two types of additional information as **Ap** and **UAp** type. Intuitively, **UAp** type additional information is a stronger type additional information, and hence we would expect the corresponding criteria of identification to be stronger. Since any $\mathbf{UAp}^d$ type additional information is also an $\mathbf{Ap}^d$ additional information we have the following two propositions.

Proposition 1 $(\forall a \in \mathcal{N} \cup \{*\})(\forall d \in [0,1])$ $[\mathbf{Ap}^d\mathbf{Ex}^a \subseteq \mathbf{UAp}^d\mathbf{Ex}^a]$.

Proposition 2 $(\forall a \in \mathcal{N} \cup \{*\})(\forall d \in [0,1])$ $[\mathbf{Ap}^d\mathbf{Bc}^a \subseteq \mathbf{UAp}^d\mathbf{Bc}^a]$.

Following theorems deal with the trade-offs between anomalies in the conjectured program, additional information, and types of identification criteria.

Theorem 3 $(\forall d \in (0,1])(\forall m \in \mathcal{N})$ $[\mathbf{UAp}^d\mathbf{Ex} - \mathbf{Ap}^1\mathbf{Bc}^m \neq \emptyset]$.

Theorem 3 says that there are classes of recursive functions that can be identified with some positive **UAp** type additional information but *cannot* be **Bc** identified with any predetermined number of anomalies allowed per program, and even the best possible **Ap** type additional information. In other words the best possible **Ap** type additional information and a more general criterion of inference cannot, in general, compensate for any **UAp** type additional information.

As a contrast, Theorem 4 below says that there are classes of recursive functions that can be **Ex**-identified with **Ap** type additional information but cannot be **Bc**-identified with any predetermined number of anomalies and **UAp** type additional information if the density associated with **Ap** type additional information is better than the one associated with **UAp** type additional information.

Theorem 4 $(\forall d_2 > d_1 \mid d_1, d_2 \in [0,1])(\forall k \in \mathcal{N})$ $[\mathbf{Ap}^{d_2}\mathbf{Ex} - \mathbf{UAp}^{d_1}\mathbf{Bc}^k \neq \emptyset]$.

Theorems 3 and 4 above together with Theorem 5 below give a complete picture about the relationship between different **Ex** and **Bc** identification criteria with **Ap** and **UAp** type additional information.

Theorem 5 $(\forall i \in \mathcal{N})$

1) $\mathbf{Ex}^{i+1} - \mathbf{UAp}^1\mathbf{Ex}^i \neq \emptyset$.
2) $\mathbf{Bc}^{i+1} - \mathbf{UAp}^1\mathbf{Bc}^i \neq \emptyset$.
3) $\mathbf{Ex}^* - \bigcup_i \mathbf{UAp}^1\mathbf{Ex}^i \neq \emptyset$.
4) $\mathbf{Bc} - \mathbf{UAp}^1\mathbf{Ex}^* \neq \emptyset$.

In summary: the results in this section give us corollaries that imply that both **Ap** and **UAp** type of additional information enhance scientific inference power of machines with respect to both **Ex** and **Bc** identification criteria. Also, in general **UAp** type of additional information results in a bigger enhancement as compared to a similar **Ap** type of additional information.

ADDITIONAL INFORMATION FOR LANGUAGE LEARNING

Formal language learning theory was originally motivated by the study of language learning in children. It relied on early claims of psycholinguists that children are rarely if ever informed of grammatical errors, instead they are only presented with strings in the language. Based on this, Gold [Gol67] developed the notion of **TxtEx**-identification. However, it turns out that the class **TxtEx**, which contains sets of *r.e.* languages that can be **TxtEx**-identified by some language learning machine, contains "small" classes of languages. For instance, none of the classes of languages in the

Chomsky hierarchy (regular, context free, context sensitive, and r.e.) are contained in **TxtEx**. This led Gold to two possible conclusions. One was that the class of natural languages is much "smaller" than previously thought, and the other was that children are being given additional information in some subtle way. Angluin [Ang80a] [Ang80b] and Wiehagen [Wie77] [KW80] address the first conclusion of Gold. We will concern ourselves, in this section, with the second conclusion of Gold.

It is not uncommon for an elder person (a parent or teacher) to tell a child some small grammatical rule that enables the child to enumerate a list of elements of the language. Basically, this additional information (the grammatical rule) enables the child to know certain elements of the language before it knows it by *text* presentation. This kind of additional information can be modeled in the Gold paradigm by requiring that in addition to a *text* for the language, the language learning device be provided with a grammar for a subset of the language. It turns out that this kind of additional information indeed increases the language learning power of learning machines. We further model the quality of this additional information by measuring the "density of agreement" of the language, whose grammar is provided as additional information, with the one being learned. Not surprisingly, a "better quality" additional information enhances the learning power more than a "not so good" additional information. We now define this "density" notion and the new language learning criteria.

Definition 29 The density of a language L_1 in an infinite language L_2 (denoted by $\mathbf{d}(L_1; L_2)$) is defined as follows: Let $x_1 < x_2 < x_3, \ldots$ be the elements of L_2. $\mathbf{d}(L_1; L_2) = \mathbf{d}(\{i \mid x_i \in L_1\})$.
Similarly, uniform density of L_1 in L_2 (denoted: $\mathbf{ud}(L_1; L_2)$) is $\mathbf{ud}(\{i \mid x_i \in L_1\})$.

Definition 30 Suppose d is a real number in the interval $[0, 1]$. A Language L' is said to be *d-language conforming* with a recursively enumerable language L iff, L' satisfies the following two conditions:

(1) $L' \subseteq L$,
(2) $\mathbf{d}(L'; L) \geq d$.

Definition 31 Suppose d is a real number in the interval $[0, 1]$. A Language L' is said to be *d-language uniform conforming* with a recursively enumerable language L iff, L' satisfies the following two conditions:

(1) $L' \subseteq L$,
(2) $\mathbf{ud}(L'; L) \geq d$.

Definition 32 Let $d \in [0, 1]$ and $a \in (\mathcal{N} \cup \{*\})$. A machine $\mathbf{M}$ $\mathbf{Ap}^d\mathbf{TxtEx}^a$*-identifies* a language L (written: $L \in \mathbf{Ap}^d\mathbf{TxtEx}^a(\mathbf{M})$) iff when provided with a grammar for a language L', which is *d-language conforming* with L, as an additional information, $\mathbf{M}$ on any text for L converges to a grammar i such that $W_i =^a L$.

Definition 33 $\mathbf{Ap}^d\mathbf{TxtEx}^a = \{\mathcal{L} \subseteq \mathcal{E} \mid (\exists \mathbf{M})[\mathcal{L} \subseteq \mathbf{Ap}^d\mathbf{TxtEx}^a(\mathbf{M})]\}$.

We can similarly define $\mathbf{UAp}^d\mathbf{TxtEx}^a$, $\mathbf{Ap}^d\mathbf{TxtBc}^a$, and $\mathbf{UAp}^d\mathbf{TxtBc}^a$ criteria of language learning. Clearly, these criteria are analogs of the similar criteria for function inference. All the theorems in function inference carry over to language learning.

Above, we were concerned with additional information that *supplements* the information a child is already receiving in the form of a *text* for the language. In other words, the additional information that we just modeled, is about what is in the language and not about what is not in the language. However, literature of speech language pathology and linguistics contains extensive refutations of the claim that children receive no negative data [BB64][Dal76]. Intuitively, it is clear that children are receiving information about the complement of the language they are trying to learn. If a child's utterances do not have the desired effect, it somehow works as a clue that the utterance is not in the language. An elder person (a parent or a teacher) either rebukes the child or tells it specifically that something is not in the language. Better still, an elder person can provide the child with a rule that enumerates a list of strings which are not members of the language. This kind of additional information can be modeled in the Gold's paradigm by requiring that the language learning device be provided with a grammar for a subset of the complement of the language being learned. It turns out that even this kind of additional information enhances the language learning power of learning devices.

Fulk [Ful85, Ful80] investigated a different approach to additional information about the complement of a language. He showed that being given *text* for a language and a grammar for the complement is equivalent to being given *text* for it and enumeration of a non-empty, finite sequence of grammars, the last of which is a grammar for the complement. However, we feel, a grammar for the complement of the language is too much additional information, and children certainly are not being given a rule that lists everything that is ungrammatical. We further employ the above density notions to differentiate a "good quality" additional information about the complement from a "not so good quality" additional information. As in the previous case, better the additional information, more is the enhancement achieved in learning power of language learning devices. We now define this notion.

Definition 34 Let $d \in [0,1]$. Let $a \in (\mathcal{N} \cup \{*\})$. A machine $\mathbf{M}$ $\mathbf{ACp}^d\mathbf{TxtEx}^a$-*identifies* a language L (written: $L \in \mathbf{ACp}^d\mathbf{TxtEx}^a(\mathbf{M})$) iff when provided with a grammar for a language L', which is *d-language conforming* with the complement of L (i.e. $\mathcal{N} - L$), as an additional information, $\mathbf{M}$ on any text for L converges to a grammar i such that $W_i =^a L$.

Definition 35 $\mathbf{ACp}^d\mathbf{TxtEx}^a = \{\mathcal{L} \subseteq \mathcal{E} \mid (\exists \mathbf{M})[\mathcal{L} \subseteq \mathbf{ACp}^d\mathbf{TxtEx}^a(\mathbf{M})]\}$.

We can similarly define $\mathbf{UACp}^d\mathbf{TxtEx}^a$, $\mathbf{ACp}^d\mathbf{TxtBc}^a$, and $\mathbf{UACp}^d\mathbf{TxtBc}^a$ criteria of language learning.

Finally, we define a language learning criteria that incorporates additional information both about elements of the language (positive information) and about elements of the complement of the language (negative information). This kind of additional information is better than just providing positive additional information or just providing negative additional information.

Definition 36 Let $d_1, d_2 \in [0,1], a \in (\mathcal{N} \cup \{*\})$. A machine $\mathbf{M}$ $\mathbf{Ap}^{d_1}\mathbf{ACp}^{d_2}\mathbf{TxtEx}^a$-*identifies* a language L (written: $L \in \mathbf{Ap}^{d_1}\mathbf{ACp}^{d_2}\mathbf{TxtEx}^a(\mathbf{M})$) iff when provided with grammars for languages L_1, which is d_1-*language conforming* with L, and L_2, which is d_2-*language conforming* with the complement of L (i.e. $\mathcal{N} - L$), as additional information, $\mathbf{M}$ on any text for L converges to a grammar i such that $W_i =^a L$.

Definition 37 $\mathbf{Ap}^{d_1}\mathbf{ACp}^{d_2}\mathbf{TxtEx}^a = \{\mathcal{L} \subseteq \mathcal{E} \mid (\exists \mathbf{M})[\mathcal{L} \subseteq \mathbf{Ap}^{d_1}\mathbf{ACp}^{d_2}\mathbf{TxtEx}^a(\mathbf{M})]\}$.

We can similarly define the following criteria of language learning.

1) $\mathbf{Ap}^{d_1}\mathbf{UACp}^{d_2}\mathbf{TxtEx}^a$,
2) $\mathbf{UAp}^{d_1}\mathbf{ACp}^{d_2}\mathbf{TxtEx}^a$,
3) $\mathbf{UAp}^{d_1}\mathbf{UACp}^{d_2}\mathbf{TxtEx}^a$,
4) $\mathbf{Ap}^{d_1}\mathbf{ACp}^{d_2}\mathbf{TxtBc}^a$,
5) $\mathbf{Ap}^{d_1}\mathbf{UACp}^{d_2}\mathbf{TxtBc}^a$,
6) $\mathbf{UAp}^{d_1}\mathbf{ACp}^{d_2}\mathbf{TxtBc}^a$,
7) $\mathbf{UAp}^{d_1}\mathbf{UACp}^{d_2}\mathbf{TxtBc}^a$.

All the results in function inference have a counterpart in language learning. These results along with the following theorems give us corollaries that imply that providing either positive or negative additional information enhances language acquisition power of formal devices with respect to both **TxtEx** and **TxtBc** identification criteria. Also, providing both positive and negative additional information to a language learning device is better than just providing one of them.

Theorem 6 *For all* $k \in \mathcal{N}$,

1) $\mathbf{TxtEx}^{k+1} - \mathbf{UAp}^1\mathbf{UACp}^1\mathbf{TxtEx}^k \neq \emptyset$,
2) $\mathbf{TxtBc}^{k+1} - \mathbf{UAp}^1\mathbf{UACp}^1\mathbf{TxtBc}^k \neq \emptyset$,
3) $\mathbf{TxtEx}^* - \bigcup_k \mathbf{UAp}^1\mathbf{UACp}^1\mathbf{TxtEx}^k \neq \emptyset$,
4) $\mathbf{TxtBc} - \mathbf{UAp}^1\mathbf{UACp}^1\mathbf{TxtEx}^* \neq \emptyset$,
5) $\mathbf{TxtEx}^{2k+1} - \mathbf{UAp}^1\mathbf{UACp}^1\mathbf{TxtBc}^k \neq \emptyset$,
6) $(\mathbf{U})\mathbf{Ap}^{d_1}(\mathbf{U})\mathbf{ACp}^{d_2}\mathbf{TxtEx}^{2k} \subseteq (\mathbf{U})\mathbf{Ap}^{d_1}(\mathbf{U})\mathbf{ACp}^{d_2}\mathbf{TxtBc}^k$,
7) $\mathcal{E} \notin \mathbf{UAp}^1\mathbf{UACp}^1\mathbf{TxtBc}^*$.

Theorem 7 $(\forall d > 0)[\mathbf{UAp}^d\mathbf{TxtEx} - \mathbf{Ap}^1\mathbf{UACp}^1\mathbf{TxtBc}^* \neq \emptyset]$.

Theorem 8 $(\forall d > 0)[\mathbf{UACp}^d\mathbf{TxtEx} - \mathbf{UAp}^1\mathbf{ACp}^1\mathbf{TxtBc}^* \neq \emptyset]$.

Theorem 9 $(\forall d_1, d_2 \mid d_2 > d_1)[\mathbf{Ap}^{d_2}\mathbf{TxtEx} - \mathbf{UAp}^{d_1}\mathbf{UACp}^1\mathbf{TxtBc}^* \neq \emptyset]$.

Theorem 10 $(\forall d_1, d_2 \mid d_2 > d_1)[\mathbf{ACp}^{d_2}\mathbf{TxtEx} - \mathbf{UAp}^1\mathbf{UACp}^{d_1}\mathbf{TxtBc}^* \neq \emptyset]$.

University of Rochester Technical Report No. 282 [JS89b] contains a detailed account of this paper.

ACKNOWLEDGEMENTS

We would like to thank John Case and Mark Fulk for advice and encouragement. Zuzana Dobes, Lata Narayanan, and Rajeev Raman provided helpful discussions. Department of CS at SUNY Buffalo and the Xerox University Grants Program to University of Rochester provided the equipment support. Sanjay Jain was supported by NSF grant CCR 832-0136 and Arun Sharma was supported by NSF grant CCR 871-3846.

References

[Ang80a] D. Angluin. Finding patterns common to a set of strings. *Journal of Computer and System Science*, 21:46–62, 1980.

[Ang80b] D. Angluin. Inductive inference of formal languages from positive data. *Information and Control*, 45:117–135, 1980.

[AS83] D. Angluin and C. Smith. A survey of inductive inference: theory and methods. *Computing Surveys*, 15:237–289, 1983.

[Bar74] J. A. Barzdin. Two theorems on the limiting synthesis of functions. *Latv. Gos. Univ. Uce. Zap.*, 210:82–88, 1974.

[BB64] R. Brown and U. Bellugi. Three processes in the child's acquisition of syntax. *Harvard Educational Review*, 34:133–151, 1964.

[BB75] L. Blum and M. Blum. Toward a mathematical theory of inductive inference. *Information and Control*, 28:125–155, 1975.

[Cas86] J. Case. Learning machines. In W. Demopoulos and A. Marras, editors, *Language Learning and Concept Acquisition*, Ablex Publ. Co., 1986.

[Che81] K. Chen. *Tradeoffs in Machine Inductive Inference.* PhD thesis, SUNY/Buffalo, 1981.

[CL82] J. Case and C. Lynes. Machine inductive inference and language identification. *Lecture Notes in Computer Science, Springer-Verlag, Berlin*, 140, 1982.

[CS83] J. Case and C. Smith. Comparision of identification criteria for machine inductive inference. *Theoretical Computer Science*, 25:193–220, 1983.

[Dal76] P. Dale. *Language Development, Structure and Function.* Holt, Reinhart, and Winston, New York, 1976.

[Ful80] M. Fulk. Inductive inference with additional information. *Journal of Computer and System Science*, to appear, 1980.

[Ful85] M. Fulk. *A Study of Inductive Inference machines.* PhD thesis, SUNY/ Buffalo, 1985.

[Gol67] E.M. Gold. Language identification in the limit. *Information and Control*, 10:447–474, 1967.

[JS89a] S. Jain and A. Sharma. *Knowledge of an Upper Bound on Grammar Size Helps Language Learning.* Technical Report 283, University of Rochester, 1989.

[JS89b] S. Jain and A. Sharma. *Learning with an Infinitely Often Correct Teacher.* Technical Report 282, University of Rochester, 1989.

[KW80] R. Klette and R. Wiehagen. Research in the theory of inductive inference by gdr mathematicians–a survey. *Information Sciences*, 22:149–169, 1980.

[MY78] M. Machtey and J. Young. *An Introduction to the General Theory of Algorithms.* North Holland, New York, 1978.

[OSW86] D. Osherson, M. Stob, and S. Weinstein. *Systems that Learn, An Introduction to Learning Theory for Cognitive and Computer Scientists.* MIT Press, Cambridge, Mass., 1986.

[OW82a] D. Osherson and S. Weinstein. Criteria of language learning. *Information and Control*, 52:123–138, 1982.

[OW82b] D. Osherson and S. Weinstein. A note on formal learning theory. *Cognition*, 11:77–88, 1982.

[Pei58] C.S. Peirce. In A.W.Burks, editor, *Collected Papers*, Harvard University Press,Cambridge Mass., 1958.

[Rei70] F. E. Reilly. In *Charles Pierce's Theory of Scientific Method*, Fordham University Press,New York, 1970.

[Rog58] H. Rogers. Godel numberings of partial recursive functions. *Journal of Symbolic Logic*, 23:331–341, 1958.

[Rog67] H. Rogers. *Theory of Recursive Functions and Effective Computability.* McGraw Hill, New York, 1967.

[Roy86] J. Royer. Inductive inference of approximations. *Information and Control*, 70:156–178, 1986.

[Wie77] R. Wiehagen. Identification of formal languages. *Lecture Notes in Computer Science, Springer-Verlag, Berlin*, 53:571–579, 1977.

[Wie78] R. Wiehagen. Characterization problems in the theory of inductive inference. *Automata, Languages and Programming 1978, Lectures Notes in Computer Science*, 62:494–508, 1978.

Nexttime is Not Necessary
(Extended Abstract)

Edith Spaan
Department of Mathematics and Computer Science
University of Amsterdam
Plantage Muidergracht 24, 1018 TV Amsterdam

Abstract

We investigate the propositional modal logic of knowledge and time for distributed systems. Previous results by Halpern and Vardi [HV89] and Ladner and Reif [LR] illustrate that the validity problems for a number of these logics are highly intractable; in particular they prove a number of Π_1^1-completeness results. The logics considered by the above authors contain at least two out of the three temporal logic operators: "sometimes", "nexttime", and "until". Although their proofs rely heavily on either the "nexttime" or the "until" operator, we show that the completeness results remain valid if we restrict the temporal operators to "sometimes".

1 Introduction

Recently, there has been a lot of interest in the logics of knowledge and time as a tool for analyzing the behavior of distributed systems. In [HV89], Halpern and Vardi categorize these logics in terms of two parameters: the language used and the class of distributed systems considered. The languages they consider depend on the number of processors, the absence or presence of an operator for common knowledge and the use of linear versus branching time. As in [HV89], we denote these languages by $CKL_{(m)}$, $KL_{(m)}$, $CKB_{(m)}$ and $KB_{(m)}$, where m is the number of processors, C denotes the presence of an operator for common knowledge, and L and B stand for linear and branching time. All of these languages include temporal operators for nexttime, until and sometimes.

We will now briefly describe the classes of systems considered in [HV89]. We view a distributed system as a set of possible runs of the system. We assume that runs proceed in discrete steps, and if r is a run then (r, i) (for $i \in \mathbb{N}$) describes the state of the system at the i-th step of run r. We say that a processor knows a fact φ at a given point, if φ is true at all points (r', i') that the processor considers possible at that point.

A processor does not forget if the set of runs it considers possible stays the same or decreases over time. The dual notion is no learning: we say that a processor does not learn if the set of runs it considers possible stays the same or increases over time. A system is synchronous if all processors have access to a global clock. Finally, a system has a unique initial state if no processor can distinguish $(r, 0)$ from $(r', 0)$ for all runs r and r'.

We use $\mathcal{C}$ to represent the class of all models and use subscripts nf, nl, $sync$ and uis to indicate classes of models where, respectively, all processors do not forget, all processors do not learn, where time is synchronous, and where there exists a unique initial state.

In [HV89], Halpern and Vardi completely characterize the computational complexity for all combinations of their languages and classes of models, including some results from [LR]. We will now state all combinations that are undecidable and their respective complexity class.

Theorem 1.1 (HV89)

1. *The validity problem for $CKL_{(\geq 2)}$ and $CKB_{(\geq 2)}$ is Π_1^1-complete with respect to $\mathcal{C}_{(nf)}$, $\mathcal{C}_{(nf,uis)}$, $\mathcal{C}_{(nf,sync)}$, $\mathcal{C}_{(nf,nl)}$, $\mathcal{C}_{(nf,sync,uis)}$, $\mathcal{C}_{(nf,nl,sync)}$, $\mathcal{C}_{(nl,sync)}$ and $\mathcal{C}_{(nl)}$.*
2. *The validity problem for $CKL_{(\geq 2)}$, $KL_{(\geq 2)}$, $CKB_{(\geq 2)}$ and $KB_{(\geq 2)}$ is Π_1^1-complete with respect to $\mathcal{C}_{(nf,nl,uis)}$.*
3. *The validity problem for $CKL_{(\geq 2)}$, $KL_{(\geq 2)}$, $CKB_{(\geq 2)}$ and $KB_{(\geq 2)}$ is co-r.e.-complete with respect to $\mathcal{C}_{(nl,uis)}$.*

Since the validity problem for linear temporal logic with the three operators mentioned earlier is PSPACE-complete, while the validity problem for linear temporal logic with just $\Diamond$ (sometimes) as temporal operator is only co-NP-complete [SC], it will be interesting to examine the impact on the complexity if we restrict the temporal operators in our languages to $\Diamond$ for linear time (resp. $\forall\Diamond$ and $\exists\Diamond$ for branching time). Let $CK\overline{L}_{(m)}$, $K\overline{L}_{(m)}$, $CK\overline{B}_{(m)}$ and $K\overline{B}_{(m)}$ denote the languages where $\Diamond$ (resp. $\forall\Diamond$ and $\exists\Diamond$) are the only temporal operators. Although the proofs in [LR, HV89] rely heavily on the use of either the nexttime or the until operator, it turns out that, by using new techniques, we get the same complexity results if we restrict the temporal operators to $\Diamond$ (resp. $\forall\Diamond$ and $\exists\Diamond$). Using approximately the same techniques, we can prove that the well-known Π_1^1-hardness result for two-dimensional temporal logic [Ha] goes through if we restrict the temporal operators to the sometimes operators in both directions $\Diamond_u$ and $\Diamond_r$.

The rest of the paper is organized as follows. In the next section we describe the formal model according to [HV86, HV89]; in section 3 we describe the specific problems encountered if we have only $\Diamond$ as a temporal operator; in section 4 we prove the analogue of 1 for the linear time language $CK\overline{L}_{(\geq 2)}$, by forcing models to be gridlike; in section 5 we prove the analogue of 2 and 3 for the linear time cases and a Π_1^1 lower bound for two-dimensional linear logic, by appropriately modifying the proof of Ladner and Reif [LR]. Finally, in section 6, we prove that for all classes of models considered, the validity problems for the branching time languages $CK\overline{B}_{(m)}$ (resp. $K\overline{B}_{(m)}$) are at least as hard as the corresponding validity problems for $CK\overline{L}_{(m)}$ (resp. $K\overline{L}_{(m)}$).

2 Syntax and Semantics

We start by giving the syntax of languages $CKL_{(m)}$ and $CKB_{(m)}$. We assume we have a set of propositional variables Φ and define the set of $CKL_{(m)}$ and $CKB_{(m)}$ formulas as follows:

- if $p \in \Phi$ then p is a $CKL_{(m)}$ ($CKB_{(m)}$) formula.
- if φ, ψ are $CKL_{(m)}$ ($CKB_{(m)}$) formulas, then so are $\neg\varphi$ and $\varphi \wedge \psi$.
- if φ is a $CKL_{(m)}$ ($CKB_{(m)}$) formulas, then so are $K_k\varphi$ (k knows φ), $E\varphi$ (everyone knows φ) and $C\varphi$ (φ is common knowledge).
- if φ, ψ are $CKL_{(m)}$ formulas, then so are $\bigcirc\varphi$ (nexttime φ), $\Diamond\varphi$ (sometimes φ) and $\varphi U \psi$ (φ until ψ).
- if φ, ψ are $CKB_{(m)}$ formulas, then so are $\forall\bigcirc\varphi$, $\exists\bigcirc\varphi$, $\forall\Diamond\varphi$, $\exists\Diamond\varphi$, $\forall\varphi U\psi$, $\exists\varphi U\psi$.

We define T, $\vee$ and $\rightarrow$ in the usual way from $\neg$ and $\wedge$. In addition, we define for linear time $\Box\varphi$ (always φ) as an abbreviation of $\neg\Diamond\neg\varphi$, and for branching time we view $\forall\Box\varphi$ (resp. $\exists\Box\varphi$) as an abbreviation of $\neg\exists\Diamond\neg\varphi$ (resp. $\neg\forall\Diamond\neg\varphi$).

We define the sublanguages $KL_{(m)}$ (resp. $KB_{(m)}$) as the set of $CKL_{(m)}$ (resp. $CKB_{(m)}$) formulas without the C operator. By restricting the temporal operators in each language to $\Diamond$ (resp. $\forall\Diamond$ and $\exists\Diamond$), we get the corresponding languages $C\overline{KL}_{(m)}$, $\overline{KL}_{(m)}$, $C\overline{KB}_{(m)}$ and $\overline{KB}_{(m)}$.

We will now give the semantics for $CKL_{(m)}$. A linear time model M for m processors is a tuple $(R, \pi, \sim_1, \ldots \sim_m)$, where R is a set of runs, $\pi : R \times \mathbb{N} \rightarrow \mathcal{P}(\Phi)$ assigns to each point the set of propositional variables that are true at that point, and $\sim_k$ is an equivalence relation on $R \times \mathbb{N}$. Note that we use the definition from [HV86]. We define $(M, r, i) \models \varphi$ (φ is satisfied by point (r, i) of M) with induction on φ:

- $(M, r, i) \models p \iff p \in \pi(r, i)$
- $(M, r, i) \models \neg\varphi \iff (M, r, i) \not\models \varphi$
- $(M, r, i) \models \varphi \wedge \psi \iff (M, r, i) \models \varphi \wedge (M, r, i) \models \psi$
- $(M, r, i) \models K_k\varphi \iff \forall (r', i') \sim_k (r, i) : (M, r', i') \models \varphi$
- $(M, r, i) \models E\varphi \iff \forall k \leq m : (M, r, i) \models K_k\varphi$
- $(M, r, i) \models C\varphi \iff \forall n : (M, r, i) \models E^n\varphi$
- $(M, r, i) \models \bigcirc\varphi \iff (M, r, i+1) \models \varphi$
- $(M, r, i) \models \Diamond\varphi \iff \exists j \geq i : (M, r, j) \models \varphi$
- $(M, r, i) \models \varphi U \psi \iff \exists i' \geq i : (M, r, i') \models \psi \wedge \forall i'' (i \leq i'' < i' \Rightarrow (M, r, i'') \models \varphi)$

Given a model M for m processors, we define $\sim_c$ as the transitive closure of $\bigcup_{k=1}^{m} \sim_k$. Then $(M, r, i) \models C\varphi$ if and only if $\forall (r', i') \sim_c (r, i) : (M, r', i') \models \varphi$.

We will now give the semantics for $CKB_{(m)}$. A branching time model M for m processors is a tuple $(F, \pi, \sim_1, \ldots \sim_m)$ where F is a forest, π assigns to each point of F the set of propositional variables that are true at that point, and $\sim_k$ is an equivalence relation on points of F. We assume that each node in F has some successor. We will view F as a tuple $< R_F, =_F >$ where R_F is the set of the infinite branches of F that start at the root of some tree in F. (r, i) denotes the i-th node of r and $(r, i) =_F (r', i)$ if and only if (r, i) and (r', i) denote the same node of F. We will define $(M, r, i) \models \varphi$ with induction on φ. We only give the clauses for $\exists\Diamond$ and $\forall\Diamond$, the other temporal operators are defined analogously.

- $(M, r, i) \models \forall\Diamond\varphi \iff \forall (r', i) =_F (r, i)\ \exists j \geq i : (M, r', j) \models \varphi$
- $(M, r, i) \models \exists\Diamond\varphi \iff \exists (r', i) =_F (r, i)\ \exists j \geq i : (M, r', j) \models \varphi$

As usual, we say that a formula φ is valid with respect to a class of models $\mathcal{D}$, if and only if for all models $M \in \mathcal{D}$ and for all points (r, i) of M : $(M, r, i) \models \varphi$. A formula φ is satisfiable with respect to $\mathcal{D}$ if and only if there is some model $M \in \mathcal{D}$ and some point (r, i) of M such that $(M, r, i) \models \varphi$.

We will now define the classes of models of [HV89]:

- Processor k does not forget in M if for all $r, r' \in R$ and $i, i' \in \mathbb{N}$: if $(r,i) \sim_k (r',i')$ then $\forall j \leq i \; \exists j' \leq i'$ such that $(r,j) \sim_k (r',j')$.
- Processor k does not learn in M if for all $r, r' \in R$ and $i, i' \in \mathbb{N}$: if $(r,i) \sim_k (r',i')$ then $\forall j \geq i \; \exists j' \geq i'$ such that $(r,j) \sim_k (r',j')$.
- Time is synchronous in M if for all $r, r' \in R$ and $i, i' \in \mathbb{N}$ and all processors k: $(r,i) \sim_k (r',i')$ implies that $i = i'$.
- M has a unique initial state if for all $r, r' \in R$ and all processors k: $(r,0) \sim_k (r',0)$.

We use $\mathcal{C}$ to represent the class of all models and use subscripts $nf, nl, sync, uis$ to indicate classes of models where, respectively, all processors do not forget, all processors do not learn, where time is synchronous, and where there is a unique initial state.

3 From Points to Intervals

Since all upper bounds follow directly from the corresponding upper bounds from [HV89], it will be enough to prove the corresponding lower bounds. As in [HV89], all Π_1^1 lower bounds for linear time will be proved by a reduction from the recurrence problem for nondeterministic Turing machines. A Turing machine is recurrent if and only if it has an infinite computation that starts on the empty tape and reenters its start state infinitely often. If $A_1, A_2, A_3, \ldots$ is a recursive enumeration of the 1-tape, right-infinite nondeterministic Turing machines, then $\{n \mid A_n \text{ is recurrent}\}$ is Σ_1^1-complete [HPS]. To prove a Π_1^1 lower bound for the validity problem with respect to a certain class of models $\mathcal{D}$, it will be sufficient to construct for an arbitrary 1-tape, right-infinite NTM A a formula φ_A such that A is recurrent if and only if φ_A is satisfiable with respect to $\mathcal{D}$.

In all our proofs, it is essential that the constructed formulas force runs to encode certain strings. The obvious way to encode some string on run r starting at i is by letting $(r, i+j)$ encode the j-th symbol of the string. However, if we restrict the temporal operators to just $\diamond$, we can't distinguish adjacent points satisfying the same set of formulas. To solve this problem, we introduce a propositional variable *tick*, alternating on runs. *tick* partitions each run into an infinite number of intervals. For all n, let $[r,i]_n$ be the set of points in the n-th interval of r starting at i (Note that we start counting the intervals from 0).

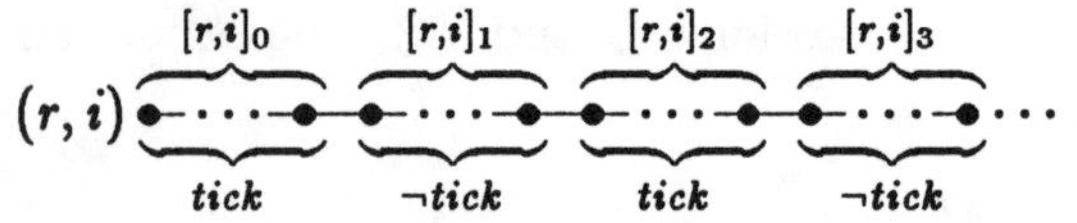

We will encode strings at consecutive intervals of a run. We say that (r,i) encodes some string if and only if each point in the j-th interval of (r,i) ($[r,i]_j$) encodes the j-th element of the string. It is possible to mark a fixed number of consecutive intervals on a run by propositional constants. Let *1-int*(p, up_p) be the conjunction of the following formulas:

$\Diamond p \wedge \Box(p \wedge tick \rightarrow \Box(\neg tick \rightarrow \Box\neg p)) \wedge \Box(p \wedge \neg tick \rightarrow \Box(tick \rightarrow \Box\neg p))$

p holds somewhere at some interval, and p holds nowhere outside that interval.

$\Box(tick \wedge \Diamond(p \wedge tick) \rightarrow \Diamond(\neg tick \wedge \Diamond p) \vee p)$

$\Box(\neg tick \wedge \Diamond(p \wedge \neg tick) \rightarrow \Diamond(tick \wedge \Diamond p) \vee p)$

p holds exactly at some prefix of an interval

$\Box(p \wedge tick \rightarrow \Diamond(up_p \wedge \neg tick)) \wedge \Box(p \wedge \neg tick \rightarrow \Diamond(up_p \wedge tick))$

up_p holds at somewhere after the p interval.

$\Box(up_p \wedge \neg tick \rightarrow \Box(tick \rightarrow \Box\neg up_p)) \wedge \Box(up_p \wedge tick \rightarrow \Box(\neg tick \rightarrow \Box\neg up_p))$

if up_p holds somewhere at some interval,
then up_p holds nowhere outside that interval.

$\Box(p \rightarrow \Box((\neg up_p \wedge \Diamond up_p) \rightarrow p))$

Thus, $(r, i) \models$ *1-int*(p, up_p) if and only if there is exactly 1 interval at which p holds, p holds nowhere else and up_p holds exactly at some prefix of the next interval.
Therefore if $(r, i) \models$ *1-int*$(p_0, p_1) \wedge$ *1-int*$(p_1, p_2) \wedge \ldots \wedge$ *1-int*(p_{n-1}, up_p) then there are n consecutive intervals on r after i such that p_j holds at exactly the j-th interval.

Now we can define $\models$ and $\sim_k$ on intervals:

$[r, i]_n \models \varphi \iff \forall (r, j) \in [r, i]_n : (r, j) \models \varphi$

(Note that $[r, i]_n \not\models \varphi$ does not imply that $[r, i]_n \models \neg\varphi$)

$$[r, i]_n \sim_k [r', i']_{n'} \iff \forall (r, j) \in [r, i]_n \exists (r', j') \in [r', i']_{n'} : (r, j) \sim_k (r', j') \wedge$$
$$\forall (r', j') \in [r', i']_{n'} \exists (r, j) \in [r, i]_n : (r, j) \sim_k (r', j')$$

Though the specific classes considered do imply specific behavior for the epistemic relations with respect to points, not much of this behavior carries over to intervals. For example, it is perfectly possible for a model in $C_{(sync)}$ not to be synchronous with respect to intervals. However, the following formula ψ_k will force that some of the structural properties of points hold for intervals as well.

$$K_k \Box((tick \rightarrow K_k tick) \wedge (\neg tick \rightarrow K_k \neg tick))$$

Lemma 3.1 *If $M \in C_{(nf)}$, $(M, r, i) \models \psi_k$ and $(r, j) \sim_k (r', j')$ for some $(r, j) \in [r, i]_n (n > 0)$, then*

- *there exists some i' such that $(r, i) \sim_k (r', i')$*
- *for all i', if $(r, i) \sim_k (r', i')$ then $(r', j') \in [r', i']_n$ and $\forall n' < n : [r, i]_{n'} \sim_k [r', i']_{n'}$.*

Lemma 3.2 *If $M \in C_{(nl,sync)}$ and $(r, i) \sim_k (r', i)$, then $\forall n : [r, i]_n \sim_k [r', i]_n$*

We leave the proofs of these two lemmas to the reader. They are similar to the proofs in [HV89] that force not necessarily synchronous models to be essentially synchronous.

4 Forcing Models to be Gridlike

Theorem 4.1 *The validity problem for $CK\overline{L}_{(\geq 2)}$ is Π^1_1-complete with respect to $C_{(nf)}$, $C_{(nf,uis)}$, $C_{(nf,sync)}$, $C_{(nf,nl)}$, $C_{(nf,sync,uis)}$ and $C_{(nf,nl,sync)}$.*

Since the Π_1^1 upper bounds for these classes follow directly from [HV89], it will be enough to prove the lower bounds for two processors. Given an arbitrary 1-tape, right infinite NTM A, we will construct a formula φ_A such that:

- A recurrent $\Rightarrow$ φ_A satisfiable with respect to $\mathcal{C}_{(nf,nl,sync)}$ and $\mathcal{C}_{(nf,sync,uis)}$.
- φ_A satisfiable with respect to $\mathcal{C}_{(nf)}$ $\Rightarrow$ A recurrent.

This implies a Π_1^1 lower bound for all six classes. Fix a 1-tape right-infinite NTM A. Suppose A has state space S, start state $s_0 \in S$; tape alphabet Γ; $b \in \Gamma$: the blank; and transition function δ. We use a special symbol # to mark the left side of the tape. Let CD (set of cell descriptors) be the set $\Gamma \cup \{\#\} \cup (S \times \Gamma)$. We view the IDs of A as infinite strings over CD, where $<s, a>$ denotes a cell with contents a, which is currently read by the head while A is in state s. A starts on the empty tape in state s_0, so the start ID of A (id_0) is equal to $\#<s_0, b>b^\omega$. Now suppose $id_0 \vdash id_1 \vdash id_2 \vdash \cdots$ is an infinite computation of A. Then for all n: $id_n = \#x_{n,1}x_{n,2}\ldots x_{n,n}x_{n,n+1}b^\omega$ ($x_{n,i} \in$ CD). The idea is to encode this computation in a model, by letting the runs represent the IDs (using the interval techniques of the previous section), and using the epistemic relations to simulate the transition function.

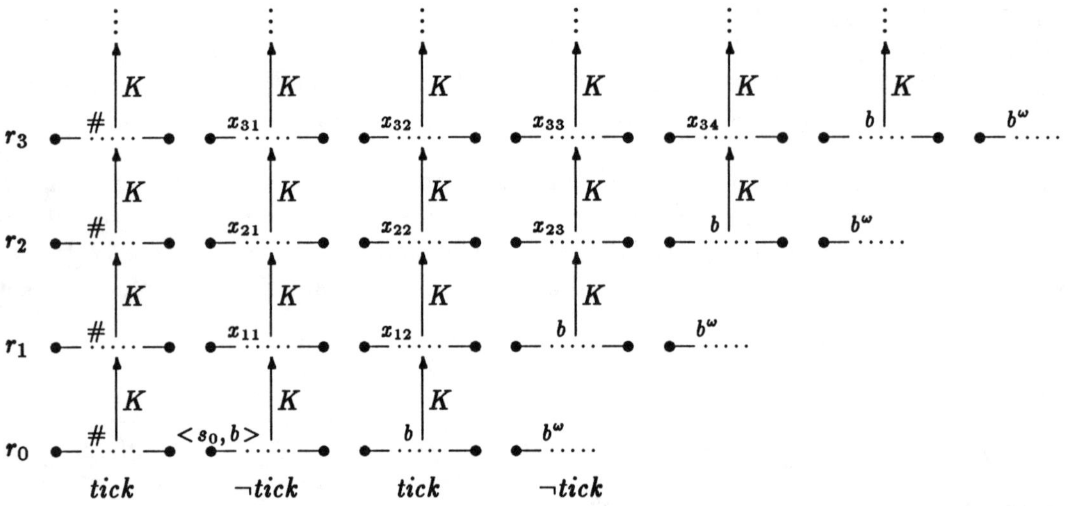

Since the encoding of IDs will be done at the intervals of runs, we start by partitioning each run into an infinite number of intervals, using the propositional variable *tick*. The following formula φ_1 will take care of this:

$$C\Box((tick \rightarrow \Diamond\neg tick) \wedge (\neg tick \rightarrow \Diamond tick))$$

The epistemic relation $\xrightarrow{K}$ is used to determine the contents of a cell at the next step of a computation. Therefore, it should not be reflexive, transitive or symmetric. As in [HV89], we use both epistemic relations $\sim_1$ and $\sim_2$ and introduce a propositional variable p_Δ to avoid reflexivity. Now we define the relation $\xrightarrow{K}$ and its associated modal operator K as follows:

$$(r,i) \xrightarrow{K} (r',i') \Longleftrightarrow \exists r'', i'' : (r,i) \sim_1 (r'',i'') \sim_2 (r',i') \wedge (r'',i'') \models \neg p_\Delta \wedge (r',i') \models p_\Delta$$
$$K\psi := K_1(\neg p_\Delta \rightarrow K_2(p_\Delta \rightarrow \psi))$$

Let φ_2 be the conjunction of the following formulas:

$$C((p_\Delta \rightarrow \Box p_\Delta) \wedge (\neg p_\Delta \rightarrow \Box \neg p_\Delta))$$

$$C\Box C(\neg K_1 p_\Delta \wedge \neg K_2 \neg p_\Delta)$$

If $(r_0, i_0) \models \varphi_2$ and $(r, i) \sim_c (r_0, i_0)$ then the value of p_Δ on r from i upwards is constant, and by the second conjunct we can take an infinite number of $\xrightarrow{K}$ steps from each point on r after i. This will ensure that we encode an infinite computation.

Since we are interested in the behavior of $\xrightarrow{K}$ with respect to intervals, we define:

$$[r,i]_n \xrightarrow{K} [r',i']_{n'} \iff \forall (r,j) \in [r,i]_n \exists (r',j') \in [r',i']_{n'} : (r,j) \xrightarrow{K} (r',j') \wedge$$
$$\forall (r',j') \in [r',i']_{n'} \exists (r,j) \in [r,i]_n : (r,j) \xrightarrow{K} (r',j')$$

For the IDs to match up right, we need synchrony and no forgetting of $\xrightarrow{K}$ with respect to intervals. Let φ_3 be the following formula:

$$C\Box((tick \rightarrow Ctick) \wedge (\neg tick \rightarrow C\neg tick))$$

By lemma 3.1 and the fact that p_Δ is constant on runs we obtain the following lemma:

Lemma 4.2 *If $(r_0, i_0) \models \varphi_3$, $(r, i) \sim_c (r_0, i_0)$, $(r, j) \xrightarrow{K} (r', j')$, and $(r, j) \in [r, i]_n (n > 0)$, then*

- *there exists some i' such that $(r, i) \xrightarrow{K} (r', i')$*
- *for all i', if $(r, i) \xrightarrow{K} (r', i')$ then $(r', j') \in [r', i']_n$ and $\forall n' < n : [r, i]_{n'} \xrightarrow{K} [r', i']_{n'}$.*

Now we turn to the encoding of IDs. We will encode IDs on runs where p_Δ holds. To encode the cell descriptors, we introduce for each $x \in \mathrm{CD}$ a propositional variable p_x. Let φ_4 be the formula

$$C\Box(p_\Delta \rightarrow \bigvee_{x \in \mathrm{CD}} (p_x \wedge \neg \bigvee_{y \in \mathrm{CD}, y \neq x} p_y))$$

If $(r_0, i_0) \models \varphi_1, \ldots, \varphi_4$ and $(r, i) \sim_c (r_0, i_0)$ and p_Δ holds at (r, i) then each point on r after i encodes exactly one cell descriptor.

We say that the n-th interval of $(r, i)([r, i]_n)$ encodes $x \in \mathrm{CD}$, if each point in $[r, i]_n$ encodes x. To encode the start ID (id_0) at the first run, we introduce the following formula φ_{start} (up_s is a dummy variable):

$$p_\Delta \wedge \textit{1-int}(p_\#, p_{<s_0,b>}) \wedge \textit{1-int}(p_{<s_0,b>}, up_s) \wedge \Box(p_\# \vee p_{<s_0,b>} \vee p_b)$$

To simulate the transition function we just have to make sure that $\xrightarrow{K}$ points to the corresponding cell of a next ID. Suppose $id \vdash id'$. The only cells that can be affected by the transition are the cell holding the state and its neighbors. On each run we mark the 3 consecutive intervals corresponding to these cells with propositional variables *left*, *state*, *right*. Let $\varphi_{5,1}$ be the conjunction of the following formulas (up_{state} is a dummy variable):

$$C(p_\Delta \rightarrow \textit{1-int}(left, state) \wedge \textit{1-int}(state, right) \wedge \textit{1-int}(right, up_{state}))$$

$$C\Box(p_\Delta \wedge \bigvee_{<s,a>\in S\times\Gamma} p_{<s,a>} \rightarrow \mathit{state})$$

Now we can force the transition on all non-marked cells. Let $\varphi_{5,2}$ be the conjunction of the following formulas:

$$\bigvee_{x\in \mathrm{CD}} C\Box(p_\Delta \wedge (\neg \mathit{left} \wedge \neg \mathit{state} \wedge \neg \mathit{right}) \wedge p_x \rightarrow Kp_x)$$

$$C\Box(p_\Delta \wedge (\neg \mathit{left} \wedge \neg \mathit{state} \wedge \neg \mathit{right}) \wedge \Box p_b \rightarrow K\Box p_b)$$

Now the transition on the three marked intervals. Let $N(x,y,z)$ be the set of successor triples of $< x,y,z >$ as given by the transition function δ. Let $\varphi_{5,3}$ be the following formula:

$$C(p_\Delta \wedge \Diamond(\mathit{left} \wedge p_x) \wedge \Diamond(\mathit{state} \wedge p_y) \wedge \Diamond(\mathit{right} \wedge p_z) \longrightarrow \bigvee_{(x',y',z')\in N(x,y,z)} (\Box(\mathit{left} \rightarrow Kp_{x'}) \wedge \Box(\mathit{state} \rightarrow Kp_{y'}) \wedge \Box(\mathit{right} \rightarrow Kp_{z'})))$$

Let φ_5 be the conjunction of $\varphi_{5,1}, \varphi_{5,2}$ and $\varphi_{5,3}$. By lemma 4.2, if $(r,i) \models \varphi_1, \ldots, \varphi_5$ and (r,i) encodes some ID $id = x_0 \ldots x_{n-1} b^\omega$ of A, and for some $j \in [r,i]_m (m > n+1)$, $(r,j) \xrightarrow{K} (r',j')$ then there exists some i' such that $(r,i) \xrightarrow{K} (r',i')$ and (r',i') encodes a successor ID $y_0 \ldots y_n b^\omega$ of id.

Since by φ_2, we can take an infinite number of $\xrightarrow{K}$ steps from any point in the model, we know that we encode an infinite computation of A.

The only thing left to be done now, is to force the encoded computation to be recurrent. That is, at each time in the computation, there must be some later time where the computation is in the start state. To be able to express this requirement in a formula, we must be able to discriminate at each time those IDs which occur at some later step in the computation. Therefore, we time stamp each run that encodes an ID with the time of the computation. Say (r,i) is at time t if and only if exactly the $(t+2)$-nd and $(t+3)$-rd interval of (r,i) are marked with $\mathit{time}_1, \mathit{time}_2$. The first run is at time 0; we will mark the second and third intervals on this run with time_1 and time_2. Let φ_6 be the conjunction of the following two formulas (with up_{time} a new dummy variable):

$$C(p_\Delta \rightarrow \mathit{1\text{-}int}(\mathit{time}_1, \mathit{time}_2) \wedge \mathit{1\text{-}int}(\mathit{time}_2, up_{time})) \wedge C\Box(p_\Delta \wedge \mathit{time}_2 \rightarrow K\,\mathit{time}_1)$$

$$\mathit{1\text{-}int}(p_{<s_0,b>}, \mathit{time}_1)$$

That is, each p_Δ run is time stamped, and by lemma 4.2, if $(r,i) \sim_c (r_0,i_0)$ and (r,i) is at time t, and $(r,j) \xrightarrow{K} (r',j')$ for some $j \in [r,i]_m (m > t+2)$, then for each i' such that $(r,i) \xrightarrow{K} (r',i')$: (r',i') is at time $t+1$. By the second conjunct, (r_0,i_0) is at time 0.

To check whether an infinite computation is recurrent or not, we need to discriminate between runs that encode IDs in the start state and those that are in a different state. To this end we introduce the following formula φ_7:

$$C(\Diamond \bigvee_{x\in\Gamma} p_{<s_0,x>} \rightarrow \Box\, \mathit{startstate}) \wedge C(\Box \bigwedge_{x\in\Gamma} \neg p_{<s_0,x>} \rightarrow \Box\neg \mathit{startstate})$$

If $(r_0, i_0) \models \varphi_1, \ldots, \varphi_7$ and $(r, i) \sim_c (r_0, i_0)$ and (r, i) encodes an ID, then *startstate* is constant on the run, *startstate* is true if the state of the encoded ID is the start state, false otherwise.

Finally, we state the formula to force recurrence φ_{rec}

$$C\Box(\Diamond C(p_\Delta \wedge time_2 \rightarrow startstate))$$

Let φ_A be the conjunction of φ_1 to φ_7, φ_{start} and φ_{rec}. Suppose $(M, r_0, i_0) \models \varphi_A$ for some $M \in \mathcal{C}_{(nf)}$. Then (r_0, i_0) encodes id_0. Suppose $(r, i) \sim_c (r_0, i_0)$ and (r, i) encodes some ID id at time t. By φ_{rec}, for each i' there must exist some $i'' \geq i'$ such that $(r, i'') \models C(p_\Delta \wedge time_2 \rightarrow startstate)$. In particular, there must exist some $m > 0$ and some j such that $(r, j) \in [r, i]_{t+3+m}$ and $(r, j) \models C(p_\Delta \wedge time_2 \rightarrow startstate)$. By φ_2, we can take $m \xrightarrow{K}$ steps from (r, j), say $(r, j)(\xrightarrow{K})^m(r', j')$. By φ_5, there must exist some i' such that $(r, i)(\xrightarrow{K})^m(r', i')$, (r', i') encodes some ID id' such that $id(\vdash)^m id'$ and $(r', j') \in [r', i']_{t+3+m}$. By φ_6, (r', i') is at time $t + m$, but then $(r', j') \models time_2 \wedge p_\Delta$ and therefore *startstate* is true at run r'. Thus, id' is in the start state. Since (r, i) was chosen arbitrarily, we have showed that M encodes a recurrent computation of A.

To conclude the proof of theorem 4.1, we still have to show that φ_A is satisfiable with respect to $\mathcal{C}_{(nf,nl,sync)}$ and $\mathcal{C}_{(nf,sync,uis)}$ if A is recurrent. As the proof is straightforward, we leave this to the reader.

Theorem 4.3 *The validity problem for $CK\overline{L}_{(\geq 2)}$ is Π^1_1-complete with respect to $\mathcal{C}_{(nl,sync)}$.*

We will show that formula φ_A works for $\mathcal{C}_{(nl,sync)}$ as well, i.e. A recurrent $\Leftrightarrow$ φ_A is satisfiable with respect to $\mathcal{C}_{(nl,sync)}$. By lemma 3.2, we can prove the following analogue of lemma 4.2.

Lemma 4.4 *If $M \in \mathcal{C}_{(nl,sync)}$, $(r, i) \models \varphi_3$ and $(r, i) \xrightarrow{K} (r', i)$, then $\forall n : [r, i]_n \xrightarrow{K} [r', i]_n$*

Analogous to the the proof of theorem 4.1, if $(M, r_0, i) \models \varphi_1, \ldots, \varphi_6$, $(r_0, i) \sim_c (r, i) \xrightarrow{K} (r', i)$ and (r, i) encodes some ID id at time t then, using lemma 4.4, (r', i) encodes a successor ID of id at time $t + 1$.

Suppose $(M, r_0, i) \models \varphi_A$ for some $M \in \mathcal{C}_{(nl,sync)}$. Then (r_0, i) encodes id_0. Suppose $(r, i) \sim_c (r_0, i)$ and (r, i) encodes some ID id at time t. As in the previous proof, there must exist some $m > 0$ and some j such that $(r, j) \in [r, i]_{t+3+m}$ and $(r, j) \models C(p_\Delta \wedge time_2 \rightarrow startstate)$. By φ_2, we can take $m \xrightarrow{K}$ steps from (r, i), say $(r, i)(\xrightarrow{K})^m(r', i)$. By φ_5 and φ_6, we know that (r', i) encodes some ID id' such that $id(\vdash)^m id'$ and (r', i) is at time $t + m$. By $(nl, sync)$, $(r, j) \sim_c (r', j)$ and by lemma 4.4, $(r', j) \in [r', i]_{t+m+3}$. Therefore, *startstate* is true at run r'. Thus, id' is in the start state. Since (r, i) was chosen arbitrarily, we have showed that M encodes a recurrent computation of A. Again, we leave the other direction of the equivalence to the reader.

Theorem 4.5 *The validity problem for $CK\overline{L}_{(\geq 2)}$ is Π^1_1-complete with respect to $\mathcal{C}_{(nl)}$.*

In our proof of the Π^1_1 lower bound of Theorem 4.3, it was essential that formula φ_3 forced synchrony with respect to intervals. This is not the case for models in $\mathcal{C}_{(nl)}$, since lemmas 3.2 and 4.4 do not hold for non-synchronous models. However, in [HV89] it is shown that we can force synchrony on finite prefixes of runs. This will enable us to force synchrony with respect to intervals on finite prefixes of runs. This will suffice to prove a Π^1_1 lower bound with respect to $\mathcal{C}_{(nl)}$ with minor changes to φ_A. Details are left to the full paper.

5 Variations on a Theme by Ladner and Reif

Theorem 5.1 *The validity problem for $K\overline{L}_{(\geq 2)}$ and $CK\overline{L}_{(\geq 2)}$ is Π_1^1-complete with respect to $\mathcal{C}_{(nf,nl,uis)}$.*

Since the Π_1^1 upper bounds for these classes follow directly from [HV89], it will be enough to prove the Π_1^1 lower bound for $K\overline{L}_{(2)}$. In [LR], Ladner and Reif prove that the validity problem for $KB_{(2)}$ is undecidable with respect to $\mathcal{C}_{(nf,nl,uis)}$. In particular, they construct for each deterministic Turing machine T a formula that forces a run to encode an infinite computation of T. As pointed out in [HV89], their proof can be trivially modified to obtain a Π_1^1 lower bound for $KL_{(2)}$. We will use the main idea of Ladner and Reif's proof to obtain for each nondeterministic Turing machine A a $K\overline{L}_{(2)}$ formula that encodes the recurrence problem for A.

Let A be a 1-tape right-infinite NTM. Suppose A has state space S, start state $s_0 \in S$; tape alphabet Γ; $b \in \Gamma$: the blank; and transition function δ. Let Δ be the set $\Gamma \cup \{\#, \$\} \cup (S \times \Gamma)$. We start by giving [LR]'s definitions extended to nondeterministic Turing Machines.

We view the IDs of A as finite strings of the form: $\$a_0\$a_1\$\ldots\$a_n\$$ with $a_0 \ldots a_n \in \Gamma^*(S\times\Gamma)\Gamma^*$. A starts on the empty tape in state s_0 and we define the start ID of A id_0 as the string $\$<s_0, b>\$$. Define an infinite computation as an infinite string over Δ of the form: $\#^{m_0} id_0 \#^{m_1} id_1 \#^{m_2} \ldots$ with for each i : $m_i > 0$, $id_i \vdash id_{i+1}$, $|id_i| = 2i + 3$.

Define a function *collapse* : $\Delta^\omega \cup \Delta^* \rightarrow \Delta^\omega \cup \Delta^*$, that replaces multiple contiguous occurrences of the same symbol by one occurrence, that is:

$$collapse(a_0^{m_0} a_1^{m_1} a_2^{m_2} \ldots) = a_0 a_1 a_2 \ldots \in \Delta^\omega \text{ (if for all } i\text{: } m_i > 0, a_i \neq a_{i+1})$$
$$collapse(a_0^{m_0} a_1^{m_1} a_2^{m_2} \ldots a_r^{m_r}) = collapse(a_0^{m_0} a_1^{m_1} a_2^{m_2} \ldots a_r^{\omega}) = a_0 a_1 a_2 \ldots a_r \text{ (if for all } i\text{: } m_i > 0, a_i \neq a_{i+1})$$

Suppose σ and τ are infinite computations of the form:

$$\sigma = \#\#\#\#\#\# id_0 \#\#\# id_1 \#\#\# id_2 \#\#\# \cdots$$
$$\tau = \# \;\; id_0 \;\# \;\; id_1 \;\; \# \;\; id_2 \;\; \# \;\; id_3 \;\; \# \cdots$$

Analogously to [LR], we can define a function $N : \Delta^6 \rightarrow \mathcal{P}(\Delta^6)$ that verifies the matching of these strings. If σ and τ are infinite computations as given, then $\forall i (\tau_i, \ldots, \tau_{i+5}) \in N(\sigma_i, \ldots, \sigma_{i+5})$. The following lemma shows how we can use N to determine if A has an infinite computation.

Lemma 5.2 (LR) *If σ, τ are infinite strings over Δ such that:*

1. $\sigma \in \#^6\$((\neg\{\#, \$\}\$)^*\#^3\$)^\omega$
2. $\tau \in (\neg\$\$)^\omega$
3. $\forall i : (\tau_i, \ldots, \tau_{i+5}) \in N(\sigma_i, \ldots, \sigma_{i+5})$
4. $collapse(\sigma) = collapse(\tau)$

Then σ and τ are infinite computations.

We will construct a formula ψ_A, such that ψ_A is satisfiable with respect to $\mathcal{C}_{(nf,nl,sync)}$ if and only if A is recurrent. As in [LR], we will encode two infinite computations on each run. Again we partition runs into an infinite number of intervals by the propositional variable *tick*. Let ψ_1 be the formula:

$$E\Box((tick \rightarrow \Diamond\neg tick) \wedge (\neg tick \rightarrow \Diamond tick))$$

If $(r_0, i_0) \models \psi_1$ then by (uis, nl), *tick* alternates on all runs.

Since we will encode two strings on each run, we need to encode 2 elements of Δ per point. Therefore we introduce for each $c \in \Delta$ two propositional variables s_c and t_c. Let ψ_2 be the conjunction of the following formulas:

$$E\Box(\bigvee_{c\in\Delta}(s_c \wedge \neg \bigvee_{d\in\Delta, d\neq c} s_d)) \wedge E\Box(\bigvee_{c\in\Delta}(t_c \wedge \neg \bigvee_{d\in\Delta, d\neq c} t_d))$$

If $(r_0, i_0) \models \psi_2$ and $(r, i) \sim_k (r_0, i_0)$ $(k \in \{1, 2\})$ then each point on r after i encodes exactly 2 elements of Δ, say a point encodes s = a and t = b if exactly s_a and t_b hold. An interval $[r, i]_n$ encodes $s = a$ [resp. $t = b$] if each point in that interval encodes $s = a$ $[t = b]$. Now we can define the encoding of strings on a run: (r, i) encodes $s^\omega = \sigma$ $[t^\omega = \tau]$ if for all n : $[r, i]_n$ encodes $s = \sigma_n$ $[t = \tau_n]$.

The formula ψ_A that we will construct will force the existence of strings σ and τ fulfilling the conditions of lemma 5.2. Following [LR], we will encode *collapse*(σ) and *collapse*(τ) on the current run and σ and τ on other runs. We use propositional variable *coll*, constant on runs, to discriminate between the current run, where we want *coll* to hold, and the runs that encode the noncollapsed computations. The following formula ψ_3 will take care of this.

$$coll \wedge \neg K_1 coll \wedge E((coll \rightarrow \Box coll) \wedge (\neg coll \rightarrow \Box\neg coll))$$

As in [LR], we will enforce the following situation: if $(r_0, i_0) \models \psi_A$ then there exist strings σ and τ fulfilling conditions 1,2,3 and 4 of lemma 5.2 such that:

- if $(r_0, i_0) \sim_1 (r, i)$ and $(r, i) \models \neg coll$ then (r, i) encodes $s^\omega = \sigma$ and $t^\omega = \tau$
- (r_0, i_0) encodes $s^\omega = collapse(\sigma)$ and $t^\omega = collapse(\tau)$

If we have constructed ψ_A and $(r_0, i_0) \models \psi_A$, then by lemma 5.2, (r_0, i_0) encodes an infinite computation of A. We can then easily force this computation to be recurrent by adding the following conjunct ψ_{rec} to ψ_A:

$$\Box\Diamond \bigvee_{a\in\Gamma} s_{<s_0,a>}$$

We now turn to the construction of the formula ψ_A. First of all we have to make sure that if $(r_0, i_0) \sim_1 (r, i) \sim_1 (r', i')$ and $(r, i), (r', i') \models \neg coll$, then (r, i) and (r', i') encode the same strings. As a first step, we force synchrony for $\sim_1$, by the following formula ψ_4:

$$K_1\Box((tick \rightarrow K_1 tick) \wedge (\neg tick \rightarrow K_1\neg tick))$$

If $(r_0, i_0) \models \psi_1, \ldots, \psi_4$ and $(r, i) \sim_1 (r_0, i_0)$ then by (nl) for each $j_0 \geq i_0$ there exists some $j \geq i$ such that $(r, j) \sim_1 (r_0, j_0)$. By lemma 3.1, it follows that for all n : $[r, i]_n \sim_1 [r_0, i_0]_n$. We can now force all $\neg coll$ runs to encode the same strings, by formula ψ_5:

$$K_1\Box(\neg coll \wedge s_c \rightarrow K_1(\neg coll \rightarrow s_c)) \wedge K_1\Box(\neg coll \wedge t_c \rightarrow K_1(\neg coll \rightarrow t_c))$$

If $(r_0, i_0) \models \psi_1, \ldots, \psi_5$, $(r_0, i_0) \sim_1 (r, i) \sim_1 (r', i')$ and $(r, i), (r', i') \models \neg coll$ then, by ψ_4, $\forall n : [r, i]_n \sim_1 [r', i']_n$. By ψ_2 each point on r_0 and r encodes exactly two elements in Δ and therefore by ψ_5 $\forall n : [r, i]_n$ encodes $s = a$ $[t = b]$ if and only if $[r', i']_n$ encodes $s = a$ $[t = b]$.

We have to ensure that $\neg coll$ runs encode strings σ and τ fulfilling the conditions of lemma 5.2, i.e. $\sigma \in \#^6\$((\neg\{\#,\$\}\$)^*\#^3\$)^\omega$ and $\tau \in (\neg\$\$)^\omega$ such that $\forall i : (\tau_i, \ldots, \tau_{i+5}) \in N(\sigma_i, \ldots, \sigma_{i+5})$.

Following [LR], it can easily be seen that these conditions can be checked locally: we can construct a local condition such that if for all n this condition holds for $\sigma_n \ldots \sigma_{n+5}, \tau_n \ldots \tau_{n+5}$ (taking some extra care for the first seven symbols), then σ and τ are of the appropriate form. This is the reason why Ladner and Reif can force this situation using just one run. Obviously, one run won't suffice in our situation, since we don't have the nexttime operator. However, we can force the local condition for one interval at each run.

If $(r, i) \sim_1 (r_0, i_0)$, and $(r, i) \models \neg coll$ we use (r, i) to check the local condition for some interval $[r, i]_n$. In order to do this, we have to be able to distinguish the first 7 intervals of (r, i). We mark interval 0 to interval 6 of (r, i) by propositional variables $start_0$ to $start_6$, by the following formula ψ_6.

$$K_1(\neg coll \rightarrow start_0 \wedge \bigwedge_{k=0}^{5} \textit{1-int}(start_k, start_{k+1}) \wedge \textit{1-int}(start_6, up_{start}))$$

We can check the local condition for some interval by just looking at that interval and its 5 successors. We mark 6 consecutive intervals on each $\neg coll$ run by arg_0 to arg_5, using formula ψ_7:

$$K_1(\neg coll \rightarrow \bigwedge_{k=0}^{4} \textit{1-int}(arg_k, arg_{k+1}) \wedge (\textit{1-int}(arg_5, up_{arg}))$$

It is now easy to construct a formula ψ_8 such that: if $(r_0, i_0) \models \psi_1, \ldots, \psi_8$ and $(r_0, i_0) \sim_1 (r, i)$, $(r, i) \models \neg coll$ and $[r, i]_n \models arg_0$ then $[r, i]_n$ fulfills the local condition (we leave the construction of this formula to the reader).

By ψ_5 we know that for each $(r', i') \sim_1 (r_0, i_0)$ such that $(r', i') \models \neg coll$ the following holds: $\forall n : [r, i]_n$ encodes $s = a$ $[t = b]$ if and only if $[r', i']_n$ encodes $s = a$ $[t = b]$. Therefore $[r', i']_n$ fulfills the local conditions as well. We have to make sure that each interval is checked, i.e. for each n there must be some $(r, i) \sim_1 (r_0, i_0)$ such that $(r, i) \models \neg coll$ and $[r, i]_n \models arg_0$. The following formula ψ_9 provides for this:

$$\Box \neg K_1 \neg(\neg coll \wedge arg_0)$$

Suppose $(r_0, i_0) \models \psi_1, \ldots, \psi_9$. Choose some $(r_0, j_0) \in [r_0, i_0]_n$. By ψ_9 there exists some $(r, j) \sim_1 (r_0, j_0)$ such that $(r, j) \models \neg coll \wedge arg_0$. By (nf), there is some $i \leq j$ such $(r, i) \sim_1 (r_0, i_0)$. Then by lemma 3.1, $(r, j) \in [r, i]_n$ and $[r, i]_n \models arg_0$ as required.

We have proved that if $(r_0, i_0) \models \psi_1, \ldots, \psi_9$, there exist σ and τ fulfilling conditions 1,2 and 3 of lemma 5.2 such that: for all $(r, i) \sim_1 (r_0, i_0)$ with $(r, i) \models \neg coll : (r, i)$ encodes $s^\omega = \sigma$ and $t^\omega = \tau$.

In order to apply lemma 5.2, we have to ensure that condition 4 holds as well, i.e. $collapse(\sigma) = collapse(\tau)$. We will let (r_0, i_0) encode $s^\omega = collapse(\sigma)$ and $t^\omega = collapse(\tau)$ and force the two strings encoded by (r_0, i_0) to be equal. First we will force the condition for τ. Let ψ_{10} be the formula:

$$\Box(t_c \to K_1 t_c)$$

If $(r_0, i_0) \models \psi_1, \ldots, \psi_{10}$ then by ψ_3 there exists some $(r, i) \sim_1 (r_0, i_0)$ such that $(r, i) \models \neg coll$. By ψ_4, $\forall n : [r_0, i_0]_n \sim_1 [r, i]_n$. Since (r, i) encodes $t^\omega = \tau$ and each point on r_0 encodes exactly one value for t, (r_0, i_0) encodes $t^\omega = \tau = collapse(\tau)$.

We ensure that (r_0, i_0) encodes two equal strings by the following formula ψ_{11}:

$$\Box(t_c \leftrightarrow s_c)$$

If $(r_0, i_0) \models \psi_1, \ldots, \psi_{11}$ then (r_0, i_0) encodes $s^\omega = t^\omega = collapse(\tau)$.

Finally, we force (r_0, i_0) to encode $s^\omega = collapse(\sigma)$. As in [LR] we will use $\sim_2$ to simulate the collapse function for σ. Since $\sigma \neq collapse(\sigma)$, $\sim_2$ must behave differently from $\sim_1$. Therefore we partition the runs into different intervals, this time using our propositional variable $s_\$$. Let $[r, i]^\$_n$ be the n-th $s_\$$-interval of (r, i).

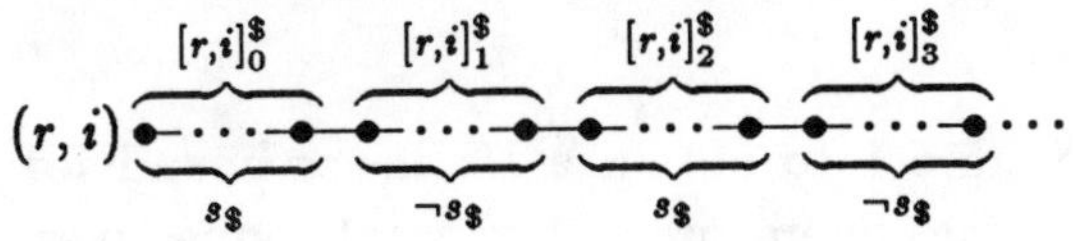

We can now force $\sim_2$ to be synchronous with respect to $s_\$$ intervals. Let ψ_{12} be the formula:

$$K_2\Box((s_\$ \to K_2 s_\$) \wedge (\neg s_\$ \to K_2 \neg s_\$))$$

If $(r_0, i_0) \models \psi_1, \ldots, \psi_{12}$ and $(r, i) \sim_2 (r_0, i_0)$ then by (nl) $\forall j_0 \geq i_0$ there exists some $j \geq i$ such that $(r, j) \sim_2 (r_0, j_0)$. By lemma 3.1, it follows that $\forall n : [r, i]^\$_n \sim_2 [r_0, i_0]^\$_n$. We want the n-th $s_\$$ intervals of (r_0, i_0) and (r, i) to encode the same value for s. The following formula ψ_{13} will take care of this.

$$K_2\Box(s_c \to K_2 s_c)$$

Suppose $(r_0, i_0) \models \psi_1, \ldots, \psi_{13}$, $(r_0, i_0) \sim_2 (r, i)$ and (r, i) encodes $s^\omega = \alpha$ and $collapse(\alpha) \in (\neg\$\$)^\omega$. Then $[r, i]^\$_n$ must encode $s = (collapse(\alpha))_n$, since the $s_\$$ intervals take adjacent identical s-symbols together. By ψ_{13}, $[r_0, i_0]^\$_n$ encodes $s = (collapse(\alpha))_n$ as well. Since we already know that (r_0, i_0) encodes $s^\omega = collapse(\tau) \in (\neg\$\$)^\omega$, the $s_\$$ and $tick$ intervals of (r_0, i_0) coincide. Thus, $[r_0, i_0]_n$ encodes $s = (collapse(\alpha))_n$ and therefore (r_0, i_0) encodes $s^\omega = collapse(\alpha)$. Since we want (r_0, i_0) to encode $collapse(\sigma)$, and $collapse(\sigma) \in (\neg\$\$)^\omega$, we just need to force the existence of some $(r, i) \sim_2 (r_0, i_0)$ such that (r, i) encodes $s^\omega = \sigma$. Let ψ_{14} be the formula:

$$\neg K_2 \neg(\neg coll \wedge arg_0 \wedge \textit{1-int}(start_0, start_1) \wedge \Box(arg_0 \to s_\#))$$

If $(r_0, i_0) \models \psi_1, \ldots, \psi_{14}$ then there exists some $(r, i) \sim_2 (r_0, i_0)$ such that $(r, i) \models \neg coll$ and $start_0$ holds exactly at $[r, i]_0$ and $[r, i]_0$ encodes $s = \#$. By (uis, nl), there must exist some j such that $(r, j) \sim_1 (r_0, i_0)$. By ψ_3, $(r, j) \models \neg coll$, and therefore (r, i) encodes $s^\omega = \sigma$ and $start_0$ holds exactly at $[r, j]_0$. But then (r, i) also encodes $s^\omega = \sigma$, and by ψ_{13} it follows that (r_0, i_0) encodes $s^\omega = collapse(\sigma)$.

Finally, let ψ_A be the conjunction of ψ_1 to ψ_{14}. If $(r_0, i_0) \models \psi_A$ then by lemma 5.2 (r_0, i_0) encodes $s^\omega = collapse(\sigma)$ and $collapse(\sigma)$ is an infinite computation of A. If (r_0, i_0) satisfies ψ_{rec} as well, then *collapse*(σ) is an infinite recurrent computation of A. Therefore, if $\psi_A \wedge \psi_{rec}$ is satisfiable with respect to $\mathcal{C}_{(nf,nl,uis)}$, then A is recurrent.

To conclude the proof of theorem 5.1 we have to check that $\psi_A \wedge \psi_{rec}$ is satisfiable with respect to $\mathcal{C}_{(nf,nl,uis)}$ if A is recurrent. Again, this is left to the reader.

Theorem 5.3 *The validity problem for* $\overline{KL}_{(\geq 2)}$ *and* $\overline{CKL}_{(\geq 2)}$ *is co-r.e.-complete with respect to* $\mathcal{C}_{(nl,uis)}$.

In the proof of theorem 4.5, we have mentioned that no learning enables us to force intervals to be synchronous with respect to finite prefixes of runs. Now we can add an extra conjunct to formula ψ_A of the previous proof to encode the halting problem. This gives us a r.e. lower bound for satisfiability and therefore a co-r.e. lower bound for validity. The corresponding upper bound follows from [HV89].

Two Dimensional Temporal Logic

We can apply the techniques of the proof of theorem 5.1 to obtain a Π^1_1 lower bound for two-dimensional temporal logic with only the two sometimes operators as temporal connectives. The models for two-dimensional temporal logic are two-dimensional grids, infinite to the right and upwards, i.e. each point is a pair (i,j) of natural numbers. Let $\overline{L}_2$ be the propositional language with operators $\Diamond_r$ (sometimes to the right) and $\Diamond_u$ (sometimes upwards) such that: $(M,i,j) \models \Diamond_r\varphi \Leftrightarrow \exists i' \geq i : (M,i',j) \models \varphi$, and $(M,i,j) \models \Diamond_u\varphi \Leftrightarrow \exists j' \geq j : (M,i,j') \models \varphi$.

Theorem 5.4 *The validity problem for* $\overline{L}_{(2)}$ *is* Π^1_1*-hard.*

We will briefly sketch how to construct a formula φ_A such that φ_A is satisfiable if and only if A is recurrent. First of all, note that if φ_A is satisfiable, then there exists a model M, such that $(M,0,0) \models \varphi_A$. Therefore, we will assume that the constructed formula is satisfiable in $(0,0)$. Introduce two propositional variables $tick_r$ and $tick_u$ such that $tick_r$ alternates on horizontal runs and is constant on vertical runs, and $tick_u$ alternates on vertical runs and is constant on horizontal runs. We will use two-dimensional intervals $[(n,m)]$ $(n,m \in \mathbb{N})$ to take over the role of points:

$$[(n,m)] := \{(i,j) : (i,0) \text{ in the } n\text{-th } tick_r \text{ interval of } (0,0) \text{ and } (0,j) \text{ in the } m\text{-th } tick_u \text{ interval of } (0,0)\}$$

Now we do have a gridlike structure: for all n and m, there exist i_1, i_2, j_1, j_2 such that $[(n,m)] := \{(i,j) | i_1 \leq i \leq i_2 \wedge j_1 \leq j \leq j_2\}$

Using the same trick as in the proof of theorem 5.1, we can force the existence of strings σ and τ fulfilling conditions 1,2 and 3 of lemma 5.2, such that each horizontal run encodes $s^\omega = \sigma$ and $t^\omega = \tau$ on its consecutive horizontal $tick_r$ intervals.

We want $(0,0)$ to encode the same strings *collapse*(σ) and *collapse*(τ) vertically, i.e. on its consecutive $tick_u$ intervals. We use two new sets of propositional variables $\{\hat{s}_c : c \in \Delta\}$ and $\{\hat{t}_c : c \in \Delta\}$ and force the values of $\hat{s}$ and $\hat{t}$ to be constant on horizontal runs. To ensure that $(0,0)$ encodes $\hat{t}^\omega =$ *collapse*(τ), we mark the diagonal with propositional variable D, i.e. $(i,j) \models D$ if and only $(i,j) \in [(n,n)]$ for some n. Now we can force points on the diagonal to encode the same values for t and $\hat{t}$. This ensures that $(0,0)$ encodes $\hat{t} =$ *collapse*(τ).

It is easy to ensure that the strings vertically encoded on $(0,0)$ are equal. To ensure that $(0,0)$ encodes $\hat{s} = collapse(\sigma)$, we partition horizontal runs into intervals with $s_\$$ and vertical runs into intervals with $\hat{s}_\$$. Since the value of $s_\$$ is constant on vertical runs, and the value of $\hat{s}_\$$ is constant on horizontal runs, this gives us again a two-dimensional gridlike structure. We can mark the diagonal in this structure with D_s, and force the points where D_s holds to encode the same values for s and $\hat{s}$. This ensures that $(0,0)$ encodes $\hat{s} = collapse(\sigma)$. By lemma 5.2, $(0,0)$ encodes an infinite computation of A, and it is trivial to add a conjunct that forces this computation to be recurrent.

6 A Generic Reduction from Linear to Branching Time

Intuitively, the validity problems for branching time languages are harder then the corresponding validity problems for linear time. We will show that we can uniformly reduce the validity problems for $CK\overline{L}_{(m)}$ and $K\overline{L}_{(m)}$ to the corresponding validity problem for $CK\overline{B}_{(m)}$ and $K\overline{B}_{(m)}$, thus corroborating our intuition.

There is an obvious way to associate a branching time model with each linear time model and vice versa: suppose $M = (R, \pi, \sim_1, \dots \sim_m)$ is a linear time model, then M is a branching time model as well; if $M = (F, \pi, \sim_1, \dots \sim_m)$ is a branching time model then we define the corresponding linear time model M_L as $(R_F, \pi, \sim_1, \dots \sim_m)$ (recall that R_F is the set of branches in F). Note that if $M \in \mathcal{D}$ where $\mathcal{D}$ is one of our sixteen classes of models, then $M_L \in \mathcal{D}$.

Theorem 6.1 *There exists a polynomial time bounded function f from $CK\overline{L}_{(m)}$ to $CK\overline{B}_{(m)}$ formulas such that:*

1. *for each linear time model M and all (r,i): $(M,r,i) \models \varphi \Rightarrow (M,r,i) \models f(\varphi)$*
2. *for each branching time model M and all (r,i): $(M,r,i) \models f(\varphi) \Rightarrow (M_L,r,i) \models \varphi$*

And if $\varphi \in K\overline{L}_{(m)}$ then $f(\varphi) \in K\overline{B}_{(m)}$.

As a first attempt, we take g to be the function that replaces all $\Diamond$ occurrences in a $CK\overline{L}_{(m)}$ formula by $\forall\Diamond$. Function g does not satisfy the conditions. The problem is that in branching time models $\exists\Diamond g(\psi)$ can hold, while $\forall\Diamond g(\psi)$ does not hold. Given a $CK\overline{L}_{(m)}$ formula φ, we will exclude this situation for all subformulas $\Diamond\psi$ of φ in all relevant points. Define a function *lin* from $CK\overline{L}_{(m)}$ to $CK\overline{B}_{(m)}$ formulas:

$$lin(p) = T;\ lin(\neg\varphi) = lin(\varphi);\ lin(\varphi \wedge \psi) = lin(\varphi) \wedge lin(\psi)$$
$$lin(K_k\varphi) = K_k lin(\varphi);\ lin(E\varphi) = E lin(\varphi);\ lin(C\varphi) = C lin(\varphi)$$
$$lin(\Diamond\varphi) = (\forall\Diamond g(\varphi) \leftrightarrow \exists\Diamond g(\varphi)) \wedge \forall\Box\, lin(\varphi)$$

By an easy induction on the structure of formula φ, we can prove the following lemma.

Lemma 6.2 *If $M = (F, \pi, \sim_1, \dots \sim_m)$ is a branching time model such that $(M,r,i) \models lin(\varphi)$ then $(M,r,i) \models g(\varphi) \Leftrightarrow (M_L,r,i) \models \varphi$.*

Let $f(\varphi) := g(\varphi) \wedge lin(\varphi)$; we will prove that f fulfills the conditions of theorem 6.1. Suppose M is a linear time model and $(M, r, i) \models \varphi$. If we view M as a branching time model, then for all points (r', i') in M and all branching time formulas ψ : $(M, r', i') \models \forall\Diamond\psi \leftrightarrow \exists\Diamond\psi$. Therefore, $(M, r, i) \models lin(\varphi)$ and by lemma 6.2, $(M, r, i) \models g(\varphi)$. But then $(M, r, i) \models f(\varphi)$ as required. If M is a branching time model and $(M, r, i) \models f(\varphi)$, then by lemma 6.2 $(M_L, r, i) \models \varphi$.

Corollary 6.3 *If $\mathcal{D}$ is one of our sixteen classes of models then there is a polynomial time reduction from the validity problem for $CK\overline{L}_{(m)}$ (resp. $K\overline{L}_{(m)}$) with respect to $\mathcal{D}$ to the validity problem for $CK\overline{B}_{(m)}$ (resp. $K\overline{B}_{(m)}$) with respect to $\mathcal{D}$.*

Corollary 6.4

- *The validity problem for $CK\overline{B}_{(\geq 2)}$ is Π_1^1-complete with respect to $\mathcal{C}_{(nf)}$, $\mathcal{C}_{(nf,uis)}$, $\mathcal{C}_{(nf,sync)}$, $\mathcal{C}_{(nf,nl)}$, $\mathcal{C}_{(nf,sync,uis)}$, $\mathcal{C}_{(nf,nl,sync)}$, $\mathcal{C}_{(nl,sync)}$ and $\mathcal{C}_{(nl)}$.*
- *The validity problem for $CK\overline{B}_{(\geq 2)}$ and $K\overline{B}_{(\geq 2)}$ is Π_1^1-complete with respect to $\mathcal{C}_{(nf,nl,uis)}$.*
- *The validity problem for $CK\overline{B}_{(\geq 2)}$ and $K\overline{B}_{(\geq 2)}$ is co-r.e.-complete with respect to $\mathcal{C}_{(nl,uis)}$.*

Lower bounds by theorems 4.1, 4.3, 4.5, 5.1 and 5.3. Upper bounds by [HV89].

Acknowledgements: I'd like to thank Otto Moerbeek and Michiel Smid for their help with LaTeX, Peter van Emde Boas for his helpful comments on various versions of this paper, and most of all, Rineke Verbrugge for the discussions and comments on every draft of this paper, and for all her support.

References

[Ha] D. Harel, Recurring dominoes: making the highly undecidable highly understandable, *Proc. of the Conference on Foundations of Computing Theory*, Springer Lecture Notes in Computer Science - Vol. 158, 1983, pp. 177-194.

[HPS] D. Harel, A. Pnueli, and J. Stavi, Propositional dynamic logic of nonregular programs, *J. Comput. System Sci.*, 26, 1983, pp. 222-243.

[HV86] J.Y. Halpern and M.Y. Vardi, The complexity of reasoning about knowledge and time: extended abstract, *Proceedings of the 18th Annual ACM Symposium on the Theory of Computing*, 1986, pp. 304-315.

[HV89] J.Y. Halpern and M.Y. Vardi, The complexity of reasoning about knowledge and time, I: Lower Bounds, *J. Comput. System Sci.*, 38, 1989, pp. 195-237.

[LR] R. Ladner and J.H. Reif, The logics of distributed protocols, *Theoretical Aspects of Reasoning About Knowledge: Proceedings of the 1986 Conference*, 1986, pp. 207-221.

[SC] A.P. Sistla and E.M. Clarke, The complexity of propositional linear temporal logics, *J. Assoc. Comput. Mach.*, 32, 1985, pp. 733-749.

KOLMOGOROV'S LOGIC OF PROBLEMS AND A PROVABILITY INTERPRETATION OF INTUITIONISTIC LOGIC

S.Artemov
Steklov Mathematical Institute,
Vavilov str.,42, Moscow GSP-1,
117966, USSR.

ABSTRACT

In 1932 A.N.Kolmogorov suggested an interpretation of intuitionistic logic **Int** as a "logic of problems". Then K.Gödel in 1933 offered a "provability" understanding of problems, thus, providing an abstract "provability" interpretation for **Int** via a modal logic **S4**. Later papers by J.C.C.McKinsey & A.Tarski, A.Grzegorczyk, R.Solovay, A.V.Kuznetsov & A.Yu.Muravitskii, R.Goldblatt, G.Boolos imply that this provability interpretation of **Int** is complete if one decodes Gödel modality $\Box$ for an "abstract provability" in the following way: $\Box Q = Q \wedge Pr[Q]$, where $Pr[Q]$ is the standard provability predicate for Peano arithmetic. The paper shows that the definition of $\Box Q$ as $Q \wedge Pr[Q]$ is (in a certain sense) the only possible one. The Uniform Completeness Theorem for provability logics is extended to **Int** and other logics having Gödelian provability interpretation. The first order logics having provability interpretation are considered.

1 INTRODUCTION

A.N.Kolmogorov in [Kol] suggested an informal interpretation of sentences of intuitionistic logic **Int** as statements about the possibility of solving certain general problems; propositional variables were supposed to denote "problems", logical connectives were given a natural interpretation as operators over "problems": a formula $A \wedge B$ denotes a problem "to solve both A and B", a formula $A \vee B$ denotes "to solve either A or B", an implication $A \rightarrow B$ is interpreted as a problem "to reduce a solution of B to any solution of A", $\neg A$ is $A \rightarrow \bot$ that means a problem "to demonstrate an unsolvability of A". Kolmogorov hadn't given a precise definition of "problems", just appealing to the common sense of a working mathematician but had conjectured that his interpretation of **Int** was complete.

In [Göd] K.Gödel offered an interpretation of **Int** close to that in [Kol], where intuitionistic propositions were treated as assertions about provability. More precisely, in [Göd] there was defined a translation tr(F) of an intuitionistic formula, F obtained by prefixing a new operator □ that stands for an abstract "provability" to each subformula of F.

We call the logical language with the modality □ the □-language and a modal formula in □-language a □-formula. In [Göd] some properties of □ were accepted as axioms and rules of a modal logic S4. A possible axiom system for S4 includes

all the tautologies (in a propositional □-language),
$\Box P \wedge \Box(P \to Q) \to \Box Q$, $\Box P \to P$,
$\Box P \to \Box\Box P$

for all sentences P,Q. The rules of inference of S4 are *modus ponens* $P, P \to Q \vdash Q$ and *necessitation* $P \vdash \Box P$.

We look at logics as sets of formulae and therefore for each logic L and each formula F, $L \vdash F \iff F \in L$.

Theorem 1.(K.Gödel [Göd], J.C.C.McKinsey & A.Tarski [McK&Tar])
For each propositional formula F

$$F \in Int \iff tr(F) \in S4. \qquad (*)$$

Later in [Grz] A.Grzegorczyk introduced a new modal logic Grz (a proper extension of S4):

$$Grz = S4 + \Box(\Box(A \to \Box A) \to A) \to A$$

and showed that for Grz the property (*) was also valid.

Theorem 2. (A.Grzegorczyk [Grz]) *For each propositional □-formula* F

$$F \in Int \iff tr(F) \in Grz.$$

2 THE ARITHMETICAL PROVABILITY PREDICATE AS A MODALITY

In [Göd] K.Gödel considered also another interpretation of a modality as an arithmetical provability predicate Pr(x); we denote this modal operator by Δ, Δ-language is the logical language with Δ; a Δ-formula is a formula in Δ-language. A complete axiomatization of Δ was given in [Sol] where R.Solovay introduced a decidable propositional Δ-logic S, that describes all valid laws of provability Δ, and its sublogic GL, that stands for all laws of provability Δ, which can be demonstrated by means of Peano Arithmetic PA.

The logic GL can be axiomatized by the axioms:
tautologies (in a Δ-language), $\Delta P \wedge \Delta(P \to Q) \to \Delta Q$,
$\Delta(\Delta P \to P) \to \Delta P$,

for all sentences P,Q and rules *modus ponens, necessitation.*

Logic S can be defined as $GL + \Delta P \to P$ but without a necessitation rule.

A *realization* is a function that assigns to each sentence letter a sentence of the language of **PA**. The *translation* **fA** of a propositional Δ-formula **A** under a realization **f** is defined inductively: $f\bot=\bot$, $fp=f(p)$ (for each sentence letter **p**), $f(A\rightarrow B)=fA\rightarrow fB$, $f\Delta A=Pr[fA]$. We have taken the propositional constant ⊥ (falsity) to be among the primitive logical symbols of **PA**; we understand **Pr[F]** as the result of substituting the numeral for the Gödel number of **F** for the free variable **x** in **Pr(x)**, and therefore the translation of any modal formula under any realization is a sentence of the language of **PA**.

The following theorem shows that the logic **S** is exactly the collection of all valid principles of modal logic of provability Δ and that the logic **GL** is the set of those principles of this logic which are provable in **PA**.

Theorem 3. (R.Solovay [Sol]) *For each* Δ*-formula* **Q**

$$Q\in S \iff fQ \text{ is true in the standard model of PA for each realization } f,$$

$$Q\in GL \iff \text{for each realization } f\ PA\vdash fQ.$$

The theorem implies also that

$$GL\vdash Q \iff S\vdash \Delta Q.$$

Several papers independently give a uniform version of the second part of the Solovay Completeness Theorem.

Theorem 4. (F.Montagna [Mon79], S.Artemov [Art79], A.Visser [Vis81], G.Boolos [Boo82]) *There exists a realization* **f** *such that for each* Δ*-formula* **Q**

$$Q\notin GL \iff PA\nvdash fQ.$$

The first part of the Solovay Theorem does not admit uniformization: for each realization **f** for a propositional variable **p** either **fp** or **¬fp** is true in the standard model of arithmetic, but neither **p**, nor **¬p** belongs to the logic **S**.

In [Art79],[Art80],[Vis84],[Art86a] a general notion of a logic of formal provability was developed. Let $\alpha(t)$ be a *r.e.* formula that binumerates some axiom system of an extension of **PA** (i.e. a theory in the language of **PA** containing **PA**). Following [Fef], we can call such a formula $\alpha(t)$ a *numeration*. We denote by $|\alpha|$ the set of axioms that is numerically expressed by the formula α

$$|\alpha|:=\{F \mid F \text{ is an arithmetic sentence and } \alpha(\ulcorner F\urcorner) \text{ is true}\}$$

and by $\|\alpha\|$ the extension of **PA** determined by the set of axioms $|\alpha|$. Let $Pr_\alpha(x)$ signify a standard arithmetical formula of provability based on α as a formula for Gödel numbers of axioms ([Fef]). For each numeration α and each realization **f** we set $f_\alpha(p)=fp$ for each propositional letter **p**. Let f_α commutes with the Boolean connectives and

$$f_\alpha(\Delta Q)=Pr_\alpha[f_\alpha Q].$$

Let **U** be a theory and α a numeration. We define

$$L_\alpha(U)=\{Q \mid Q \text{ is a } \Delta\text{-formula and } U\vdash f_\alpha Q \text{ for each realization } \alpha\}.$$

The modal logics $L_\alpha(U)$ describe the laws of the provability Pr_α that can be justified by means of the theory **U**.

We say that a logic **l** is *logic of formal provability* if $l=L_\alpha(U)$ for some numeration α and extension of arithmetic **U**.

Obviously, **GL** is the least logic of formal provability. the Solovay Theorem provides another example of such a logic: $S=L_\alpha(TA)$ where $\|\alpha\|=PA$ and **TA** is the set of all true arithmetic sentences.

There exists continually many logics of provability [Art79], [Art80]. A Classification Theorem for logics of provability was accomplished by L.Beklemishev in [Bek].

3 A DEFINITION FOR THE MODALITY OF INTUITIVE PROVABILITY

In [Kuz&Mur77], [Gol], [Kuz&Mur86], [Boo80], [Art86b], [Boo79] and other papers there was considered a translation of $\Box A$ as $A\wedge\Delta A$, that provides an arithmetical provability interpretation of $\Box$-language, therefore, **Int**-language. It turns out that logics **Int** and **Grz** are complete under this interpretation. More precisely, let B^Δ denote the decoding of $\Box P$ as $P\wedge\Delta P$ in all subformulas $\Box P$ of a formula **B**.

Theorem 5. i.(A.Grzegorczyk [Grz]) *For an* **Int**-*formula* **B**

$$Int\vdash B \iff Grz\vdash tr(B).$$

ii.(A.V.Kuznetsov & A.Yu.Muravitskii [Kuz&Mur77],86]; R.Goldblatt [Gol]) *For a* $\Box$-*formula* **B**

$$Grz\vdash B \iff GL\vdash B^\Delta,$$

iii.(G.Boolos [Boo80]) *For a* $\Box$-*formula* **B**

$$Grz\vdash B \iff S\vdash B^\Delta.$$

Are there any reasons for adopting the definition $\Box P := P \wedge \Delta P$? The modality $\Box$ doesn't have an explicit mathematical model; it had been introduced as a modality for an intuitive notion of mathematical provability. On the contrary the modality Δ has an exact mathematical definition as an operator of formal provability $Pr(.)$ on the set of arithmetical sentences. Thus there is no way to prove that $\Box P = P \wedge \Delta P$; one can only hope to find some arguments in order to declare a

Thesis: $\Box P := P \wedge \Delta P$ (**)

(like the Church Thesis for computable functions). Gödel himself in [Göd] tried the obvious idea to define $\Box Q$ as ΔQ but noticed that this definition led to a contradiction between his axioms and rules for $\Box$ and the already known Gödel Second Incompleteness Theorem. Can one nevertheless give a reasonable definition of $\Box$ via Δ? The most optimistic expectations are

to find a Δ-formula $B(p)$ which satisfies known properties of $\Box p$ (first of all axioms and rules of $S4$) and such that for each other Δ-formula $C(p)$ with these properties

$$GL \vdash B(p) \leftrightarrow C(p).$$

In this case we have the right to declare a definition $\Box Q := B(p)$ as a Thesis. It turns out that this situation holds with $p \wedge \Delta p$ as $B(p)$. The main ideas of the proof of the following theorem were taken from [Kuz&Mur86].

Theorem 6. *For a given Δ-formula $C(p)$ if*

1. all axioms and rules of $S4$ for $C(p)$ as $\Box p$ are arithmetically valid (derivable in S) and

2. $GL \vdash C(p) \rightarrow \Delta p$ (this principle says that any "real" mathematical proof can be finitely transformed into a formal proof)

then

$$GL \vdash C(p) \leftrightarrow (p \wedge \Delta p).$$

Proof. Let $\top$ denotes the propositional constant "truth" so $\top \in Int, S4, Grz, GL, S$. Obviously, $S4 \vdash \Box \top$ and by the conditions of Theorem 6

1) $S \vdash C(\top)$,

2) $S \vdash C(C(p) \rightarrow p)$ (because $S4 \vdash \Box(\Box p \rightarrow p)$),

3) for each Δ-formula F that contains modality symbols only in combinations of a type $C(.)$

$$S \vdash F \quad \Rightarrow \quad S \vdash C(F),$$

(because of the necessitation rule for $S4$: $S4 \vdash Q \;\Rightarrow\; S4 \vdash \Box Q$),

4) $GL\vdash C(p)\rightarrow\Delta p$ (condition *2.* of the theorem).
We will show that

$$GL\vdash C(p)\leftrightarrow(p\wedge\Delta p)$$

and thus this formula is deducible in all logics of formal provability. According to 2)

$$S\vdash C(C(p)\rightarrow p),$$

thus ($GL\subseteq S$, condition *2.* of the theorem)

$$GL\vdash\Delta(C(p)\rightarrow p)$$

and

$$GL\vdash C(p)\rightarrow p.$$

Together with 4) this gives

$$GL\vdash C(p)\rightarrow p\wedge\Delta p.$$

Lemma. *For each* Δ*-formula* $D(p)$

$$GL\vdash(p\wedge\Delta p)\rightarrow(D(p)\leftrightarrow D(\top)).$$

The proof is an induction on the complexity of **D**. The basis step and induction steps for Boolean connectives are trivial. Let $D(p)$ be $\Delta E(p)$. By the induction hypothesis

$$GL\vdash(p\wedge\Delta p)\rightarrow(E(p)\leftrightarrow E(\top)).$$

The necessitation rule for **GL** and the commutativity of Δ with $\rightarrow$ and $\wedge$ give

$$GL\vdash(\Delta p\wedge\Delta\Delta p)\rightarrow(\Delta E(p)\leftrightarrow\Delta E(\top)).$$

Together with $GL\vdash\Delta p\rightarrow\Delta\Delta p$ this implies

$$GL\vdash(p\wedge\Delta p)\rightarrow(D(p)\leftrightarrow D(\top)).$$

By 2) $S\vdash C(\top)$ and according to 3),4), $S\vdash C(C(\top))$, $S\vdash\Delta C(p)$ and $GL\vdash C(p)$. Because of the lemma we have

$$GL\vdash(p\wedge\Delta p)\rightarrow C(p),\quad\text{whence}\quad GL\vdash C(p)\leftrightarrow(p\wedge\Delta p).$$

Remark. Without condition *2.* of the theorem we lose the uniqueness of the definition (****): $C(p):=p$ also fits.

Below we assume the *Thesis* (****). Theorems 3 and 5 may now be considered as an affirmation of Kolmogorov's conjecture on the Completeness of **Int** with respect to his *problem's* semantics where one understands *a problem* as *a problem to prove* and a *provability* operator $\Box(.)$ as $(.)\wedge\Delta(.)$.

Since the *Thesis* provides a provability interpretation

for the **Int**-language we can extend the notion of provability logics to this language. We use the notation $\mathcal{L}$**Int** for the lattice of all logics containing **Int**, $\mathcal{L}$**Grz** for the lattice of all extensions of **Grz**, and $\mathcal{L}$**GL** for the lattice of extensions of **GL**.

Let us consider a mapping ρ ([Mak&Ryb]) from $\mathcal{L}$**Grz** to $\mathcal{L}$**Int** which is determined by the Gödel translation **tr**: for each logic **m** from $\mathcal{L}$**Grz** we put

$$\rho(\mathbf{m})=\{F \mid F \text{ is an } \mathbf{Int}\text{-formula and } \mathbf{m}\vdash \mathbf{tr}(F)\}.$$

We can also consider a mapping μ ([Kuz&Mur86]) from $\mathcal{L}$**GL** to $\mathcal{L}$**Grz**: for each logic $\mathbf{m}\in\mathcal{L}\mathbf{GL}$, we set

$$\mu(\mathbf{m})=\{F \mid F \text{ is a } \Box\text{-formula and } \mathbf{m}\vdash F^{\Delta}\}.$$

We say that a logic **l** in an **Int**-language has *a provability interpretation* iff there exists a numeration α and an extension of the arithmetic **U** such that

$$\mathbf{l}=\rho\circ\mu\circ L_{\alpha}(\mathbf{U}).$$

In this situation the logic **l** describes those laws of the provability $\mathbf{Pr}_{\alpha}$ that can be expressed on the **Int**-language and justified by means of the theory **U**.

By Theorems 3 and 5 the logic **Int** has a provability interpretation and **Int** is the least such logic in this language. There are continually many logics extending **Int** in the language of **Int**. Which of them have a provability interpretation?

The following theorem provides a Classification of all logics in **Int**-language that have a provability interpretation. We denote by $\mathbf{LP}_n, n\leq\omega$, a logic $\mathbf{Int}+Q_n$, where

$$Q_0=\bot,\quad Q_{n+1}=p_{n+1}\vee(p_{n+1}\to Q_n),$$

and $\mathbf{LP}_{\omega}=\mathbf{Int}$. Obviously

$$\mathbf{LP}_0\supset\mathbf{LP}_1\supset\ldots\supset\mathbf{LP}_{\omega}=\mathbf{Int}$$

In fact $\mathbf{LP}_n$, $n\in\omega$, are the smallest logics in *finite slices* $\mathbf{s}_n$ by Hosoi-Ono and each of these logics is decidable. We note that $\mathbf{LP}_0$ is inconsistent, $\mathbf{LP}_1$ is the classical logic and the logics $\mathbf{LP}_n$, $n\geq 1$, have properties close to those of the classical one.

Theorem 7. ([Art86b]) *Among logics in the language of* **Int** *only*

$$\mathbf{LP}_0,\mathbf{LP}_1,\ldots\mathbf{LP}_{\omega}=\mathbf{Int}$$

have a provability interpretation.

This theorem shows that classical propositional logic **Cl** also has a provability interpretation.

Corollary. *The logic*

$$l=\rho\circ\mu\circ L_{\alpha}(U).$$

is classical iff

$$U\supseteq PA+\{F\rightarrow Pr_{\alpha}[F] \mid F \textit{ is an arithmetical sentence}\}$$

Thus, the classical logic **Cl** corresponds to those theories in which *the completeness principle* "all statements that are true are provable" for **PA** is derivable. This consideration shows a reasonable correspondence of formal results with intuition in classical propositional logic.

4 UNIFORMIZATION THEOREM

The following theorem extends the Uniform Arithmetical Completeness for **GL** (Theorem 4) to simultaneous uniformization for **GL**,**S**,**Grz**,**Int** and all $LP_n, n\in\omega$. For simplicity we assume below that $\|\alpha\|=PA$ and thus $Pr(x)$ signifies a standard provability formula for **PA**. In [Art79], [Art80] it was pointed out that the logic **S** is arithmetically complete with respect to an extension of **PA** by the Local Reflection Principle:

$$PA'=PA+\{Pr[\phi]\rightarrow\phi \mid \phi\in St_{PA}\}.$$

Moreover if $S\nvdash Q_0$ then one can choose a realization **f** for which $PA'\nvdash fQ$ and $fQ\in\Sigma^0_2$.

A provability interpretation of logics $LP_n, n\in\omega$, assigns to each of these logics a theory $PA+Pr^n[\bot]$, i.e.

$$LP_n=\rho\circ\mu\circ L_{\alpha}(PA+Pr^n[\bot]).$$

Here $Pr^0[\phi]=\phi$, $Pr^{n+1}[\phi]=Pr[Pr^n[F]]$.

Theorem 8. *There exists a realization* **f** *such that for each* Δ-*formula* **B**

$$GL\vdash B \iff PA\vdash fB \quad \textit{and} \quad S\vdash B \iff PA'\vdash fB,$$

for each □-*formula* **B**

$$Grz\vdash B \iff PA\vdash f(B^{\Delta}),$$

for each **Int**-*formula* **B**

$$Int\vdash B \iff PA\vdash f([tr(B)]^{\Delta}),$$

$$LP_n\vdash B \iff PA+Pr^n[\bot]\vdash f([tr(B)]^{\Delta}).$$

Proof. We prove a unformization theorem for the logic **S** first and then show that this uniform realization also fits for all other logics mentioned in the Theorem.

Lemma. *There exists a realization* f *such that for each* Δ*-formula* B

$$S\vdash B \iff PA'\vdash fB.$$

Proof is based on an improved version of Montagna's method from [Mon79]. For a Δ-formula $R(p_0,\dots,p_n)$ and any arithmetic formulae $B_0,\dots,B_n$ let $R(B_0,\dots,B_n)$ denote fR with a realization f such that $fp_i=B_i$, $i=0,\dots,n$.

Let $H[x,y,z,]$ mean that the following 3 conditions hold:

1. x is the Gödel number of an arithmetical formula $B(t)$ with one free variable, say;
2. y is the Gödel number of a Δ-formula $Q(p_0,\dots,p_n)$, which is not a theorem of S;
3. z is the Gödel number of a proof of $Q(B(0),\dots,B(n))$ in PA' and non of natural $v<z$ is the Gödel number of a proof in PA' of any $R(B(0),\dots,B(k))$ with some $R\not\in S$.

Obviously $H[x,y,z]$ is recursive. Let $H(x,y,z)$ is its representation in PA. Usual properties of such representations give that if $H[x,y,z,]$ then

$$PA\vdash\forall x,y(H(k,x,y,)\leftrightarrow x=m\wedge y=n).$$

Consider a recursive procedure which for any Δ-formula R not deducible in S constructs a realization g such that $T_1\nvdash gR$.

For such R and g let p_i^R denote an arithmetical formula gp_i.

Let us also define a recursive function $F(x,y)$ as follows:

if x is a number of some formula $R(p_0,\dots,p_n)$ not deducible in S and $y\le n$, then $F(x,y)=\ulcorner p_y^R\urcorner$; in all other cases $F(x,y)=0$.

Let also the formula $G(x,y,z)$ represent a function $F(x,y)$ in PA. Then $F(m,n)=k$ implies

$$PA\vdash\forall z(G(m,n,z)\to z=k).$$

Let $U(x,y)$ denote the arithmetical formula

$$\forall z,v(H(x,v,z)\to\forall w(G(v,y,w)\to Tr_s(w))),$$

where $Tr_2(x)$ is a standard formula defining truth for all Σ_2^0-sentences of arithmetic, i.e.

$$PA\vdash E\leftrightarrow Tr_2(\ulcorner E\urcorner)$$

for each $E \in \Sigma^0_2$. By the fixed-point lemma for PA one can get an arithmetic formula B(y) such that

$$PA \vdash B(y) \leftrightarrow \forall v,z(H(\ulcorner B \urcorner,v,z) \rightarrow \forall w(G(v,y,w) \rightarrow Tr_2(w))).$$

We can show now that B(0),B(1),... is a desired Uniform realization for S and PA'.

Suppose now that for some Δ-formula Q(p,...,p), $S \nvdash Q$ and $PA' \vdash Q(B(0),...,B(n))$. Let k be the least number which is a number of some derivation in PA' of an arithmetical formula R(B(0),...,B(m)) such that $I \nvdash R$. Then $H[\ulcorner B \urcorner,\ulcorner R \urcorner,k]$ holds, therefore

$$PA \vdash \forall v,z(H(\ulcorner B \urcorner,v,z) \leftrightarrow v=\ulcorner R \urcorner \wedge z=k).$$

Thus for each i, $0 \leq i \leq m$,

$$PA \vdash B(i) \leftrightarrow \forall v,z(v=\ulcorner R \urcorner \wedge z=k \rightarrow \forall w(G(v,i,w) \rightarrow Tr_2(w))).$$

Therefore

$$PA \vdash B(i) \leftrightarrow \forall w(G(\ulcorner R \urcorner,i,w) \rightarrow Tr_2(w)).$$

As $F(\ulcorner R \urcorner,i)=\ulcorner p^R_i \urcorner$ we get

$$PA \vdash \forall w(G(\ulcorner R \urcorner,i,w) \leftrightarrow w=\ulcorner p^R_i \urcorner).$$

Thus

$$PA \vdash B(i) \leftrightarrow Tr_2(\ulcorner p^R_i \urcorner)$$

and

$$PA \vdash B(i) \leftrightarrow p^R_i.$$

So

$$PA \vdash R(B(0),...,B(m)) \leftrightarrow R(p^R_0,...,p^R_m)$$

and

$$S \vdash R(p^R_0,...,p^R_m).$$

This contradicts the definition of p^R_i.

The Lemma is thus proved.

Let f be a uniform realization for S and PA'. We can show that f is a uniform realization for GL and PA. As we have already noticed $S \vdash \Delta Q$ implies $GL \vdash Q$. Thus $PA \vdash fQ$ implies $PA \vdash Pr[fQ]$ and so $PA' \vdash Pr[fQ]$ i.e. $PA' \vdash f(\Delta Q)$. The realization f is uniform for S and PA' and so $S \vdash \Delta Q$; Therefore $GL \vdash Q$.

The realization f is obviously uniform for Grz and PA: as we already noticed above $Grz=\mu(GL)$. Thus

$$Grz \vdash B \iff GL \vdash B^{\Delta} \iff PA \vdash f(B^{\Delta}).$$

Let us show now that f is also a uniform realization for

logics $GL+\Delta^n\bot$ (without *necessitation*) and theories $PA+Pr^n[\bot]$. Here

$$\Delta^0F=F, \quad \Delta^{n+1}F=\Delta\Delta^nF.$$

So $PA+Pr^n[\bot]\vdash fQ$ gives $PA\vdash Pr^n[\bot]\to fQ$ and $PA\vdash f(\Delta^n\bot\to Q)$. The realization f is uniform for GL and PA. Thus $GL\vdash\Delta^n\bot\to Q$ and $GL+\Delta^n\bot\vdash Q$.

According to [Art86b] and [Art88]

$$LP_n=\rho\circ\mu(GL+\Delta^n\bot)$$

and thus f is a uniform realization for LP_n and $PA+Pr^n[\bot]$:

$$LP_n\vdash B \iff GL+\Delta^n\bot\vdash[tr(B)]^\Delta \iff PA+Pr^n[\bot]\vdash f([tr(B)]^\Delta).$$

Theorem 8 is thus proved.

5 PROVABILITY INTERPRETATION OF THE PREDICATE LANGUAGE

The Gödel translation tr can be easily extended to the first order language: for each predicate formula F let tr(F) be a result of prefixing an operator □ to each subformula of *F*.

The notion of an arithmetical *realization* of Δ-language has also a natural extension to the predicate language ([Mon84],[Art85], [Var]). We assume that the predicate Δ-language does not contain equality and function symbols. By *a realization* we mean now a mapping f that associates with every predicate formula an arithmetic formula with the same free variables and that commutes with the operation of substitution for free variables and with the Boolean connectives and the quantifiers- In addition, let

$$f\Delta R(x_1,\dots,x_n)=Pr[fR(x_1,\dots,x_n)].$$

Here, for any formula F of PA, Pr[F] is the formula of PA with the same free variables as F that expresses the PA-provability of the result of substituting for each variable free in F the numeral for the value of that variable. For the details of the construction of Pr[F], the reader may consult [Boo79], p.42.

Thus each predicate Δ-formula can be thought of as a "provability law", where the predicate letters are treated universally and the modality signifies the provability in PA.

Let U be an extension of PA. We set

$$QL(U)=\{P \mid P \text{ is a predicate } \Delta\text{-formula and } U\vdash fP \text{ for each realization } f\}.$$

The modal logic QL(U) describes the principles of the provability Pr that can be demonstrated by means of the theory **U**.

Unlike the propositional case the logic **QL(TA)** that describes all true laws of provability in **PA** is not arithmetical ([Art85]) and the logic **QL(PA)** that describes all **PA**-provable laws of provability is not enumerable ([Var]). These results can be easily extended to the □-language: $\mu \circ$**QL(TA)** is not arithmetical ([Art88]) and $\mu \circ$**QL(PA)** is not enumerable (recent observation by P.Naumov).

It seems very interesting to study what kind of provability semantics for the first order logic is provided via Gödel translation **tr**, decoding □F=F∧ΔF (see *Thesis* (**)) and a provability interpretation of the predicate Δ-language. Let us put

$$i(U)=\rho\circ\mu\circ QL(U).$$

Lemma. **i(PA)=i(TA)**.

Proof. For each first order formula **P**, **tr(P)** begins with a modality □ and so it is equal to □**Q** for some □-formula **Q**. An arithmetic formula $f([\Box Q]^{\Delta})$ thus looks like **R∧Pr[R]** for some **R**. If **R∧Pr[R]** is true then **PA⊢R**. Thus **PA⊢Pr[R]** and **PA⊢R∧Pr[R]**.

According to the provability interpretation, each first order formula can be considered as a predicate principle of "provability problems" where the Gödel provability operator □(.) is interpreted as "(.) is true and provable in arithmetic". The lemma shows that there exists a set of first order formulae which for every correct extension of the arithmetic **U** (i.e. **U⊆TA**) coincides with the set of provability principles demonstrated by means of **U**.

Thus we may define a Quantified Logic of the Provability Problems

I:=i(PA) (=i(TA)=i(U) for any U such that PA⊆U⊆TA).

The following theorem shows that the provability interpretation provides a correct semantics for **HPC**.

Logicians often say that it is still unclear what system is to be accepted as the right one for *Intuitionistic Predicate Logic.* The provability interpretation may be considered as an attempt to give an independent definition for an intuitionistic first order logic. As we have seen above, this approach gives the traditional intuitionistic system **Int** in the propositional case.

Theorem 9. HPC⊆I.

Proof is obtained by a routine testing of axioms and rules of **HPC** to have translations correct in arithmetic.

Recently N.Pankrat'ev proved that **HPC**$\neq$**I**. His result actually states that **HPC+P**$\subseteq$**I** and **HPC**$\nvdash$**P**, where

$$P=\forall u\exists v((Q(u)\to Q(v))\to Q(u))\to\forall uQ(u)$$

and **Q** is a monadic predicate letter. D.Skvortsov and P.Naumov noticed that the Gabbay's formula

$$G=\neg\neg\forall u(Q(u)\vee\neg Q(u))$$

also fits, i.e. **HPC+G**$\subseteq$**I** and **HPC**$\nvdash$**G**. Pankrat'ev has shown that **HPC+P**$\vdash$**G** and **HPC+G**$\nvdash$**P**. These examples provide a kind of "lower bound" for the logic **I**.

Theorem 9 and the Kripke completeness of **HPC** with respect to reflexive and transitive frames imply that each first order formula which is valid in all such Kripke models belongs to **I**. The following theorem shows however that the difference between **I** and **HPC** can not be discerned by the finite Kripke models.

Theorem 10. *If a first order formula* **F** *fails in some finite Kripke model (reflexive, transitive) than* **F**$\notin$**I**.

Proof. A Kripke model for **HPC** (**HPC**-model) is a system $\mathcal{K}=(K,\preccurlyeq,\{V_i\}_{i\in K},\Vdash)$ such that

1. K is a nonempty set (called "the set of worlds");
2. $\preccurlyeq$ is a transitive and reflexive relation on K; we can even assume that $\preccurlyeq$ is a partial ordering on K;
3. $\{V_i\}_{i\in K}$ are nonempty sets (called "the domains") indexed by elements of K such that if $i\preccurlyeq j$ then $V_i\subseteq V_j$.
4. $\Vdash$ is a (forcing) relation between worlds $i\in K$ and closed formulas with parameters in V_i: for each formula **F**

$$i\Vdash F \text{ and } i\preccurlyeq j \;\Rightarrow\; j\Vdash F$$

and $\Vdash$ deals with connectives and quantifiers in a usual intuitionistic way

$i\Vdash P\wedge Q \iff i\Vdash P$ and $i\Vdash Q$,
$i\Vdash P\vee Q \iff i\Vdash P$ or $i\Vdash Q$,
$i\Vdash P\to Q \iff$ for every j if $i\preccurlyeq j$ then $j\Vdash Q$ or $j\nVdash P$,
$i\nVdash\bot$,
$i\Vdash\forall xP(x) \iff$ for each j if $i\preccurlyeq j$ then for each $a\in V_j$ $j\Vdash P(a)$,
$i\Vdash\exists xP(x) \iff$ for some $a\in V_i$ $i\Vdash P(a)$.

A Kripke model for Δ-language (Δ-model) is a system $\mathcal{K}=(K,\prec,\{V_i\}_{i\in K},\Vdash)$ such that $\prec$ is a transitive and irreflexive relation on K and a forcing relation $\Vdash$ satisfies conditions

$i\nVdash\bot$,

$i\Vdash P \to Q$ iff $i\nVdash P$ or $i \Vdash Q$,
$i\Vdash \forall x P(x)$ iff $i\Vdash P(k)$ for all $k\in V_i$,
$i\Vdash \Delta P$ iff for every j if $i\prec j$ then $j\Vdash P$.

We say that a closed predicate formula Q is valid in the model $\mathcal{K}=(K,\prec,\{V_i\}_{i\in K},\Vdash)$ iff $i\Vdash Q$ for every $i\in K$.

There is an obvious way to transform a **HPC**-model $\mathcal{K}$ into a Δ-model $\mathcal{K}'$ just replacing $\preccurlyeq$ by $\prec$, where $i\prec j$ may be defined as "$i\preccurlyeq j$ but not $j\preccurlyeq i$". The following natural lemma holds:

Lemma. *For every first order sentence* **P**, **HPC**-*model* $\mathcal{K}$ *and* $i\in K$

$$i\Vdash P \text{ (in a model } \mathcal{K}) \iff i\Vdash'(\mathrm{tr}P)^{\Delta} \text{ (in a model } \mathcal{K}').$$

Proof is a routine induction on the complexity of **P**.

We call a model *finite* iff K and every $V_i, i\in K$, are finite. It is clear that a transformation of a finite **HPC**-model is a finite Δ-model.

In order to complete the proof of Theorem 10 let us consider a main result of the paper [Art&Dzh] (a detailed proof is to appear in the Journal of Symbolic Logic in the paper "Finite Kripke models and predicate logics of provability"):

If a closed predicate Δ-*formula* **R** *is not valid in some predicate finite* Δ-*model then there exists a realization* **f** *such that* $PA\nvdash fR$.

Thus if **F** fails in a finite **HPC**-model $\mathcal{K}$ then we transform $\mathcal{K}$ into a finite Δ-model $\mathcal{K}'$ where **F** also fails by the lemma. Therefore there exists a realization **f** such that $PA\nvdash f[(\mathrm{tr}F)^{\Delta}]$. This implies $F\notin I$.

This theorem provides a kind of "upper bounds" for **I**. Let **Gr** denote a Grzegorczyk's formula

$$\forall x(P(x)\vee q) \to \forall x P(x)\vee q$$

where **P** is a monadic letter and **q** is a propositional one. We consider also the Markov Principle **MP**

$$[\forall x(P(x)\vee\neg P(x))\wedge\neg\neg\exists x P(x)] \to \exists x P(x).$$

It is well known that both of these formulae **Gr** and **MP** fail in corresponding finite **HPC**-models.

Corollary. $Gr, MP\notin I$.

The main problem here: whether **I** is enumerable?

References.

S.N.Artemov. Extensions of arithmetic and connected with them modal theories. VI LMPS Congress, Gannover, Abstracts, Sec.1-4, pp.15-9 (1979)

S.N.Artemov. Arithmetically Complete Modal Theories. Semiotika i Informatika, VINITI, Moscow, v.14, pp.115-133 (1980) (Russian). English transl.: Amer.Math.Soc.Transl. (2), v.135, pp.39-54 (1987)

S.N.Artemov. Nonarithmeticity of truth predicate logics of provability. Dokl.Akad.Nauk SSSR, vol.284, pp.270-271 (1985); English transl.in Soviet Math.Dokl. vol.33,pp.403-405 (1986)

S.N.Artemov. Numerically correct provability logics. Dokl.Akad. Nauk SSSR v.290, No.6, pp.1289-92 (1986) English transl.:Soviet Math.Dokl.v.34, No.2,pp.384-387 (1987)

S.N.Artemov. Superintuitionistic logics having a provability interpretation. Dokl.Akad.Nauk SSSR v.291,No.6, pp.1289-91 (1986) English transl.:Soviet Math.Dokl.v.34, No.3,pp.596-598 (1987)

S.N.Artemov. On logics having a provability interpretation. in: S.I.Adian, ed., Voprosy Kibernet., Complexity of calculations and algorithms, Nauka, Moscow, pp.5-22 (Russian) (1988)

S.N.Artemov & G.K.Dzhaparidze. On effective predicate logics of provability, Dokl.Akad.Nauk SSSR, vol.297, No.3, pp.521-523 (Russian) (1987)

L.D.Beklemishev. On Classification of Provability Logics. Izvest. AN SSSR, ser.matemat. v.53, No.5 (Russian)(1989)

G.Boolos. The Unprovability of Consistency; An Essay in Modal Logic. Cambridge University Press, Cambridge (1979)

G.Boolos. On systems of modal logics with provability interpretations. Theoria, v.46, No.1, pp.7-18 (1980)

G.Boolos. Extremely undecidable sentences. Journ.Symb.Logic, v.47, No.1, pp.191-196 (1982).

S.Feferman. Arithmetization of metamathematics in a general setting. Fundamenta Mathematicae, v.49, pp.35-92 (1960)

K.Gödel, Eine Interpretation des intuitionistischen Aussagenkalkuls, Ergebnisse Math. Colloq. 4, 39-40 (1933)

R.Goldblatt. Arithmetical necessity, provability and intuitionistic logic. Theoria, v.44, No.1, pp.38-46 (1978)

A.Grzegorczyk. Some relational systems and the associated topological spaces. Fundamenta Mathematicae, v.60,pp.223-31 (1967)

A.Kolmogoroff. Zur Deutung der intuitionistischen Logik. Math. Ztschr.,35,S.58-65 (1932)

A.V.Kuznetsov & A.Yu.Muravitsky. Magari algebras. Fourteenth All-Union Algebra Conf., Abstracts, Part 2: Rings, Algebraic Structures, Novosibirsk Univ., Novosibirsk, pp.105-6. (Russian) (1977)

A.V.Kuznetsov & A.Yu.Muravitsky. On superintuitionistic logics as fragments of proof logic. Studia Logica, v.XLV, No.1,pp.76-99 (1986)

L.L.Maksimova & V.V.Rybakov. On the lattice on normal modal logics.Algebra i Logika,v.13,No.2,pp.188-216 (Russian) (1974)

J.C.C.McKinsey & A.Tarski. Some theorems about the sentential calculi of Lewis and Heyting. Journ.Symb.Logic, v.13, No.1, pp.1-15 (1948)

F.Montagna. On the diagonilizable algebra of Peano arithmetic. Boll.della Unione Math.Ital.,v.66-B, pp.795-812 (1979)

F.Montagna. The predicate modal logic of provability. Notre Dame Journal of Formal Logic, v.25, No.2, pp.179-189 (1984)

R.M.Solovay. Provability interpretations of modal logic. Israel Journal of Math.,v.25, pp.287-304 (1976)

V.A.Vardanyan. Arithmetic complexity of predicate logics of provability and their fragments. Dokl.Akad.Nauk SSSR, v.288, No.1, pp.11-14 (1986); English transl. in Soviet Math. Dokl., vol.33, pp.569-572 (1986)

A.Visser. Aspects of diagonalization and provability. Ph.D. Thesis, Utrecht, (1981)

A.Visser. The provability logics of recursively enumerable theories extending Peano arithmetic at arbitrary theories extending Peano arithmetic. Journal of Philosoph. Logic, v.13, pp.97-113 (1984)

BILATTICES AND MODAL OPERATORS

Matthew L. Ginsberg
Computer Science Department
Stanford University
Stanford, California 94306

ABSTRACT

A *bilattice* is a set equipped with two partial orders and a negation operation that inverts one of them while leaving the other unchanged; it has been suggested that the truth values used by inference systems should be chosen from such a structure instead of the two-point set $\{t, f\}$. Given such a choice, we redefine a modal operator to be a function on the bilattice selected, and show that this definition generalizes both Kripke's possible worlds approach and Moore's autoepistemic logic. Extensions to causal and temporal reasoning are also discussed.

1 Introduction

Modal operators are used in a variety of ways in AI, including reasoning about knowledge and belief, about time, and applications to nonmonotonic inference [6,10,8, and others]. The semantics assigned to a particular modal operator are usually determined using a scheme due to Kripke [7] that is based on the notion of possible worlds linked by an accessibility relation. Moore, however, needs to define his own semantics in [8] in order to establish the desired link between a modal operator of knowledge and existing ideas in nonmonotonic reasoning.

The purpose of this paper is to show that Moore's and Kripke's ideas can be unified into a single approach if we view modal operators not in terms of possible worlds, but as mappings on the truth values assigned to various sentences. Thus the modal operator L, where Lp means, "I know that p," simply assigns the truth value true to Lp if p is known to be true, and assigns Lp the value false if p is either known to be false or is not known to be true or false (i.e., if p is not known to be true).

The approach we are proposing is made possible by the fact that we will work with a formal system that explicitly allows us to label sentences with values other than the conventional ones of true and false. The description in the previous paragraph, for example, implicitly took advantage of a potential label for p that indicated that it was "unknown" in that it was not known to be either true or false.

In Section 2, we discuss the mathematical ideas underlying this approach, where truth values are taken not from the two-point set $\{t, f\}$ but instead from a larger set known as a *bilattice*. Section 3 extends these ideas as we have suggested, formally defining a modal operator to be a function on the elements of the bilattice of truth values.

Section 4 contains a variety of mathematical results. We show that our approach has analogs to the modal operators used by Kripke and by Moore, although the argument that we generalize their constructions is delayed until Sections 5 and 6. We also present some results regarding modal operators generally, showing that Moore's L operator cannot be expressed in terms of conventional logical connectives but that it, in combination with Kripke-style modal operators, can be used to generate all possible modal operators on any bilattice corresponding to monotonic reasoning. In Section 5, we set the stage for proving that we have generalized Kripke's and Moore's work by extending our definition of inference to truth functions that involve modal operators. Finally, in Section 6 we return our attention to Moore's construction, showing that his notion of groundedness can be translated naturally into our setting. Sections 5 and 6 also contain our fundamental unifying results, showing that first-order logic, Kripke's work and Moore's construction are all special cases of our general approach.

Concluding remarks and suggestions for future work are the topic of Section 7. One especially promising feature of the work that we will present is that it allows us to define modal operators that accept more than a single sentence as an argument. This may allow us to develop precise formalizations of notions such as causality; applications to temporal reasoning are also discussed.

Proofs of theorems will appear elsewhere.

2 Mathematical preliminaries

In [5], a mathematical structure called a *bilattice* was introduced. Essentially, a bilattice is a set equipped with two partial orders and a negation operation that inverts one of them while leaving the other unchanged:

Definition 2.1 *A* bilattice *is a sextuple* $(B, \wedge, \vee, \cdot, +, \neg)$ *such that:*

1. $(B, \wedge, \vee)$ *and* $(B, \cdot, +)$ *are both complete lattices, and*
2. $\neg : B \rightarrow B$ *is a mapping with:*
   (a) $\neg^2 = 1$, *and*
   (b) $\neg$ *is a lattice homomorphism from* $(B, \wedge, \vee)$ *to* $(B, \vee, \wedge)$ *and from* $(B, \cdot, +)$ *to itself.*

A bilattice will be called distributive *if the bilattice operations* $\wedge$, $\vee$, $\cdot$ *and* $+$ *distribute with respect to one another.*

It is suggested in [5] that bilattices are natural objects to use in artificial intelligence applications, since the elements of the bilattice can be thought of as "truth values" labelling the statements in a declarative database. The two partial orders represent how much confidence we have in the validity of a particular sentence, and how much information we have about it. These ideas are expanded on considerably in [5] and have recently been explored by Fitting as well [2].

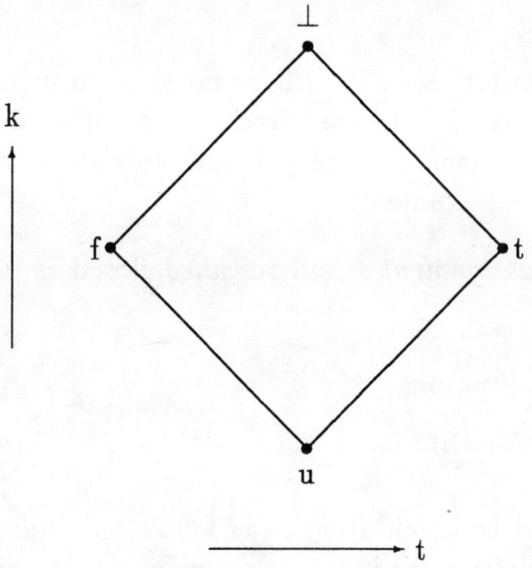

Figure 1: F, the smallest nontrivial bilattice

The two partial orders associated with a bilattice are denoted by $\leq_t$ and $\leq_k$. The partial order $\leq_t$ reflects how certain we are that some sentence is valid, and corresponds to the lattice operations $\wedge$ and $\vee$. The partial order $\leq_k$ is concerned with the amount of knowledge we have about a proposition, and is associated with the lattice operations $\cdot$ and $+$. The fact that negation inverts the t partial order is the representation of de Morgan's laws in our setting; negation leaves the k partial order unchanged because we know more about a sentence p than about a sentence q if and only if we know more about $\neg p$ than about $\neg q$.

Diagrammatically, we can draw a bilattice so that the partial order $\leq_t$ increases from left to right on the page, and the partial order $\leq_k$ from the bottom of the page to the top. Thus, for example, the simplest nontrivial bilattice is as depicted in Figure 1. This is the bilattice that corresponds most closely to conventional first-order reasoning. The four elements of this bilattice are used to label sentences that are known to be true (t) or false (f), about which nothing is known (u), or that are known to be true *and* false ($\perp$). (This last truth value indicates the presence of a contradiction in our declarative database.) Larger bilattices also contain the four distinguished elements t, f, $\perp$ and u, these being the maximal and minimal elements of the two partial orders $\leq_t$ and $\leq_k$.

In [5], bilattices are also discussed that correspond to assumption-based truth maintenance systems (ATMS's) and default reasoning; in [4], this work is extended to a bilattice that can often be used to determine whether or not a given sentence follows from the circumscription axiom.

In the setting suggested by this approach, a declarative database consists of a mapping ϕ from the set W of the well-formed sentences in our logical language into a fixed bilattice B:

Definition 2.2 *A* truth assignment *is a mapping* $\phi : W \rightarrow B$.

Given two truth assignments ϕ *and* ψ, *we will say that* ϕ *is an* extension *of* ψ, *writing* $\phi \geq_k \psi$, *if* $\phi(p) \geq_k \psi(p)$ *for every sentence* $p \in W$.

In practice, most of the sentences in W will be mapped to u (unknown).

Of course, these ideas are of little use without an associated notion of inference. The one we will present replaces the usual idea of a deductively closed set of sentences with that of a deductively closed truth assignment:

Definition 2.3 *A truth assignment ϕ will be called* closed *if:*

1. $\phi(\wedge_i p_i) \geq_k \wedge_i \phi(p_i)$,
2. $\phi(\neg p) = \neg\phi(p)$ *for all p, and*
3. *If $p \models q$, then $\phi(q) \geq_t \phi(p)$.*

The motivation behind this definition is as follows: Condition (1) says that we should know at least as much about a conjunction as we could conclude by conjoining the truth values assigned to the various conjuncts. (2) says that the two views of negation – as a syntactic operator on our language and as a bilattice function – are equivalent, and (3) says that if p entails q, then q should be "at least as true" as p is.

The reason that condition (1) does not read

$$\phi(\wedge_i p_i) = \wedge_i \phi(p_i) \tag{1}$$

can be seen by considering the sentence $p \wedge \neg p$, where the truth value assigned to p is u (unknown). Now condition (2) says that the truth value assigned to $\neg p$ should be u as well (since if we know nothing about p, then we also know nothing about its negation), and the constraint given by (1) would incorrectly lead us to assign u to $p \wedge \neg p$ as well.

The truth value assigned to $p \wedge \neg p$ is instead determined by conditions (2) and (3). Specifically, if q is any sentence with $\phi(q) = t$, then since $q \models \neg(p \wedge \neg p)$, we know from condition (3) that

$$\phi(\neg(p \wedge \neg p)) \geq_t t,$$

so that $\phi(\neg(p \wedge \neg p)) = t$, and therefore by condition (2) that $\phi(p \wedge \neg p) = f$.

To see that these notions generalize the conventional ones, we have:

Proposition 2.4 *A consistent set S of sentences is deductively closed if and only if there is some closed truth assignment ϕ such that $S = \phi^{-1}(t)$.*

3 Modal operators

Let us consider Definition 2.3 once again. What we would like to do at this point is to separate the third condition, which is the only one specifically involving entailment, from the first two.

As a preliminary, note that we can replace the second condition of the definition, that $\phi(\neg p) = \neg\phi(p)$, with the weaker constraint that

$$\phi(\neg p) \geq_k \neg\phi(p). \tag{2}$$

The reason for this is that the third condition gives us that $\phi(\neg\neg p) = \phi(p)$, so that (2), applied to $\neg p$, gives us

$$\phi(p) \geq_k \neg\phi(\neg p),$$

or

$$\neg\phi(p) \geq_k \phi(\neg p).$$

Combining this with (2), we conclude that $\phi(\neg p) = \neg\phi(p)$.

The point of this rewriting is that the first two conditions of Definition 2.3 are now of the same syntactic form. It is also not hard to see that Definition 2.3 is not altered if we include similar clauses involving other logical connectives. Disjunction is one of the functions describing the bilattice of truth values; implication can be described by taking

$$\supset (x, y) = \neg x \vee y.$$

Quantifiers can be handled similarly. We will view $\forall x.p(x)$ as shorthand for the set of all instantiations of $p(x)$, and take the associated bilattice function to be the infinitary version of $\wedge$ (recall that the t-lattice of any bilattice is complete). The quantifier $\exists$ is similarly related to $\vee$.

Lemma 3.1 *A truth assignment ϕ is closed if and only if it satisfies:*

1. $\phi(f(p_i)) \geq_k f(\phi(p_i))$ *for* $f \in \{\wedge, \vee, \neg, \supset, \exists, \forall\}$ *and*
2. *If* $p \models q$, *then* $\phi(q) \geq_t \phi(p)$.

Definition 3.2 *A truth assignment ϕ will be called* prestable *if*

$$\phi(f(p_i)) \geq_k f(\phi(p_i)) \tag{3}$$

for any $f \in \{\wedge, \vee, \neg, \supset, \exists, \forall\}$.

A consequence of this definition is that ϕ is closed if and only if it is prestable and satisfies the final clause of Definition 2.3.

What we have done in (2) and other expressions like it is to realize that negation plays two distinct roles in the approach we have proposed. The first role is as a unary function from our bilattice of truth values to itself; the second is as an operator on the set W of well-formed sentences in our language.

We will take the view that this is in fact a special case of a much more general phenomenon – bilattice operations can be viewed *in general* as establishing semantic meanings for their syntactic counterparts. These syntactic counterparts are generally referred to as *modal operators*; we define a modal operator to be instead the associated function on the underlying bilattice:

Definition 3.3 *A* modal operator *is any n-ary function from the bilattice B to itself. Given a set M of modal operators, we define the* extended language W_M *to be the smallest set satisfying the following properties:*

1. $W \subseteq W_M$.

2. For any modal operator $f \in M$ *and elements* $p_1, \ldots, p_n \in W_M$, $f(p_1, \ldots, p_n) \in W_M$.

If M *is the singleton set* $\{m\}$, *will denote* $W_{\{m\}}$ *simply by* W_m.

The definition of the extended language W_M matches the usual definition in which the set of well-formed formulae is extended in accordance with the introduction of one or more modal operators; when we say that $f(p_1, \ldots, p_n) \in W_M$, we mean only that W_M includes an element of this syntactic form, since the function f obviously cannot be applied directly to the various sentences p_i.

As we will see in Section 5, these notions lead to a natural generalization of Definition 3.2.

4 Examples and characterization results

4.1 Kripke-style modal operators

The usual description of modal operators is originally due to Kripke [7], and is based on the notion of *possible worlds.*

Roughly speaking, Kripke considers a set of possible worlds in which all of the sentences in the unextended language are assigned truth values of t or f. These possible worlds are related via an *accessibility relation* a, and Kripke defines a modal operator K_a by saying that $K_a(p)$ holds in a particular world w if and only if p holds in all worlds accessible from w.

One way to formalize this (although not the conventional one) is to introduce a function ϕ that takes a sentence p and a world w and returns the truth value of p in w. The condition defining the semantics of the modal operator K_a is now that

$$\phi(K_a p, w) = \bigwedge_{w'} \phi(p, w'), \tag{4}$$

where the conjunction is taken over the set of all w' with $a(w, w')$ (in other words, the set of all w' accessible from w). The semantics of the modal operator are determined by the requirement that the truth values assigned by ϕ satisfy (4) in addition to the usual restrictions associated with the classical logical connectives.

Of course, (4) bears a striking resemblance to our earlier equation (3) that was also intended to describe a semantics for modal operators. To make this observation precise, suppose that we denote by S the set of possible worlds appearing in the Kripke construction. F^S, the set of functions from S to F, now inherits a bilattice structure from the set F, where the bilattice operations are computed pointwise and the assignment of the function g to a sentence p means that the truth value taken by p at the world w is given by $g(w)$.

We can now capture the sense of (4) by fixing an accessibility relation a and defining the modal operator (i.e., bilattice function) given by:

$$K_a(g)(w) = \bigwedge_{w'} g(w'), \tag{5}$$

where the conjunction, as in (4), is taken over all worlds w' accessible from w.

4.2 Autoepistemic reasoning

Kripke is not the only author to consider modal operators. Moore, for example, formalizes in [8] a modal operator L, where Lp is intended to capture the notion of, "I know that p." This is related to the following unary mapping on the bilattice F:

$$L(x) = \begin{cases} t, & \text{if } x = t \text{ or } x = \bot; \\ f, & \text{otherwise.} \end{cases}$$

We know p if its truth value is either t of $\bot$ (if the latter, we know p to be both true *and* false), and do not know p if its truth value is either f or u.

In Section 5, we will see that once we have extended Definition 2.3 to deal with general modal operators, the redescriptions that we have given of Kripke's and Moore's definitions do indeed generalize this earlier work. Before doing so, however, we develop some general results concerning the form of modal operators on distributive bilattices.

4.3 Characterization results

The principal result of this section is Theorem 4.8, where we show that every modal operator on a distributive bilattice can be expressed in terms of conventional logical connectives, Moore's L operator, and a set of operators that we will call *projections*.

As a preliminary, we have the following:

Proposition 4.1 *The L operator on the bilattice F cannot be written in terms of the existing bilattice functions $\wedge$, $\vee$, $\cdot$, $+$ and $\neg$ defined on F.*

In other words, the L operator is legitimately distinct from those that have already been defined on the bilattice F. This explains why the semantics of autoepistemic logic cannot be captured by the existing methods of first-order reasoning.

Proposition 4.2 *Every modal operator on the bilattice F can be written as a combination of the operators $\wedge$, $\neg$, $+$, L, and the constant function u.*

As the upshot of the previous proposition was that the L operator cannot be written in terms of the existing logical connectives, the upshot of Proposition 4.2 is that no additional operators are needed, at least on the bilattice F.

For larger bilattices, there are additional possibilities. On the bilattice F^S, for example, there is a modal operator that assigns to the world j the truth values corresponding to the world i (corresponding to the accessibility relation a_{ij} where world i is accessible from world j and no other worlds are accessible at all). In terms of (5), we have

$$K_{a_{ij}}(g)(w) = \begin{cases} g(i), & \text{if } w = j; \\ t, & \text{otherwise.} \end{cases}$$

It will be more convenient if rewrite this as

$$K_{a_{ij}}(g) = \pi_{ij}(g) + c_j,$$

where c_j is given by

$$c_j(g)(w) = \begin{cases} u, & \text{if } w = j; \\ t, & \text{otherwise} \end{cases}$$

and

$$\pi_{ij}(g)(k) = \begin{cases} g(i), & \text{if } k = j; \\ u, & \text{otherwise.} \end{cases} \qquad (6)$$

Roughly speaking, πij projects the world i onto the world j, and c_j indicates that no world at all is accessible from any world other than j.

We also make the following definition:

Definition 4.3 *Let B be an arbitrary bilattice. We define a modal operator L on B by taking*

$$L(x) = \bigwedge\{y | y \geq_k (x \vee u) \text{ and } y \cdot \neg y = u\} \qquad (7)$$

Lemma 4.4 *L and L^S coincide on F^S.*

Lemma 4.5 *Any modal operator on F^S can be written in terms of $\wedge$, $\neg$, $+$, L, constant functions and the various π_{ij} appearing in (6) for $i, j \in S$.*

In general, of course, the bilattice being used in a particular application may not be of the form F^S for any set S. To deal with these situations, we need to generalize the modal operators π_{ij} appearing in (6).

Definition 4.6 *Let B be a bilattice. A* projection *on B is a bilattice homomorphism that factors through F.*

In other words, π is a projection if an only if there exist bilattice homomorphisms $s : B \to F$ and $i : F \to B$ such that $\pi = is$.

Lemma 4.7 *The various π_{jk} appearing in (6) are projections.*

Theorem 4.8 *Any modal operator on any distributive bilattice can be written in terms of $\wedge$, $\neg$, $+$, L, constant functions and projections.*

It is shown in [5] that a reasoning system is monotonic if and only if the associated bilattice is distributive. Theorem 4.8 therefore can be used to characterize all modal operators for monotonic inference systems.

5 Inference

In order to demonstrate that the description of modal operators that we have presented does in fact generalize earlier work, we need to extend Definition 2.3 to deal with inference in a wider setting.

Note first that Kripke and Moore view inference very differently. For example, autoepistemic reasoning is nonmonotonic: $\neg Lp$ is a consequence of the empty set $\emptyset$, but not of $\{p\}$. The reason for this is that the truth values assigned to sentences such as Lp or $\neg Lp$ are determined simply by evaluating the results of applying the modal operator L to the truth value of p.

In Kripke's case, things are not so simple. His approach requires that we consider the models of our base theory, and determine *from them* what truth values should be assigned to modal expressions. Thus if K is a modal operator corresponding to an accessibility relation that considers only one possible world W, and such that W is accessible from itself, we can prove

$$Kp \equiv p$$

so that it is possible to conclude p from Kp and $\neg p$ from $\neg Kp$. The analogous conclusions are not sanctioned in Moore's approach – from $\neg Lp$ we cannot conclude that p is actually false, even though p is false in the only model where $\neg Lp$ holds.

To formalize this distinction, we will split the set of modal operators on a particular bilattice B into *deductive* and *nondeductive* subsets. The intention is that we treat the deductive modal operators as Kripke does, determining their truth values by examining models, but treat the nondeductive modal operators simply as defining the truth values of their results.

Definition 5.1 *A modal operator on a bilattice B will be called* deductive *if and only if it commutes with $+$ and $\cdot$. All other modal operators will be called* nondeductive.

Proposition 5.2 *The L operator is nondeductive.*

Proposition 5.3 *Any modal operator on a distributive bilattice B that can be written in terms of $\wedge$, $\neg$, $+$, constant functions and projections is deductive. If B is either finite or isomorphic to F^S for some set S, then every deductive modal operator can be written in this fashion.*

We now need to extend the idea of a model to the bilattice setting. To do this, consider first the four-point bilattice F. It is fairly clear that a truth assignment corresponds to a model if and only if it assigns either t or f to every sentence in W. For larger bilattices such as F^2 corresponding to multiple copies of the four-point bilattice, we want to say that a "model" should label a sentence as being true or false in each *copy* of F. Thus for the bilattice F^2, we require

$$\phi(p) \in \{(t,t),(t,f),(f,t),(f,f)\}. \tag{8}$$

What characterizes the four bilattice points appearing in (8) is that they cannot be extended in the k direction without introducing some element of contradiction into the truth value that they represent. We formalize this as follows:

Definition 5.4 *An element x of a bilattice will be called* complete *if $x \cdot \neg x = u$ but for any element $y >_k x$, $y \cdot \neg y \neq u$.*

We are now in a position to give a definition of a model. Recalling our observation that the truth values assigned to sentences generated by nondeductive modal operators should *not* be determined by appealing to the truth values taken on models, we begin with the following:

Definition 5.5 *A truth assignment ϕ will be called* prestable *if*

$$\phi(f(p_1, \ldots, p_n)) \geq_k f(\phi(p_1), \ldots, \phi(p_n))$$

for every deductive modal operator f.

This leads to:

Definition 5.6 *A prestable truth assignment ϕ will be called a* model *if $\phi(p)$ is complete for every sentence p.*

If $\phi(q) \geq_t \phi(p)$ for every model ϕ, we will say that p entails *q and write $p \models q$.*

Definition 5.7 *A truth assignment ϕ will be called* stable *if and only if it satisfies the following conditions:*

1. *ϕ is prestable, so that*

   $$\phi(f(p_1, \ldots, p_n)) \geq_k f(\phi(p_1), \ldots, \phi(p_n))$$

   for any deductive modal operator f.

2. *If $p \models q$, then $\phi(q) \geq_t \phi(p)$.*

3. *For any nondeductive modal operator f,*

   $$\phi(f(p_1, \ldots, p_n)) = f(\phi(p_1), \ldots, \phi(p_n)).$$

The first two conditions describe the semantics of deductive modal operators, generalizing the notions appearing in Definition 2.3. The final condition makes precise the observation we made at the beginning of this section that the truth values assigned to sentences of the form $f(p_1, \ldots, p_n)$ for nondeductive f be determined simply by evaluating the result of applying the modal operator f to the truth values of the p_i.

To see that Definition 5.7 generalizes both first-order reasoning and Kripke's work, let K be a collection of modal operators of the form defined by Kripke. We now have:

Theorem 5.8 *A consistent set of sentences $S \subseteq W_K$ is deductively closed if and only if there is some stable truth assignment ϕ such that $S = \phi^{-1}(t) \cap W_K$.*

To draw a connection between this approach and the work on autoepistemic reasoning we need the following definition, repeated from [8], where Moore credits Stalnaker [11] with the idea:

Definition 5.9 *A set of sentences $S \subseteq W_L$ will be called a* stable set *if and only if it satisfies the following conditions:*

1. *S is deductively closed,*
2. *If $p \in S$, then $Lp \in S$ as well, and*
3. *If $p \notin S$, then $\neg Lp \in S$.*

Proposition 5.10 *A consistent set of sentences $S \subseteq W_L$ is a stable set if and only if there is some stable truth assignment ϕ such that $S = \phi^{-1}(t) \cap W_L$.*

Note the close resemblance between this result and Theorems 2.4 and 5.8.

6 Groundedness conditions

Unfortunately, as discussed in [8], the closure of an autoepistemic theory is not given by the intersection of the stable sets containing it. As an example, consider Moore's example

$$\neg Lb \supset \neg b, \tag{9}$$

which might be interpreted as, "If I don't know that I have a brother, then I don't have a brother."

If we denote this sentence by p, then there are two minimal stable sets containing p. In the first (the intended one), we have $\neg Lb$, $\neg b$, $L\neg b$, and so on. Here, $\neg Lb$ holds, so that we don't believe that we have a brother, and $\neg b$ holds as a result.

The other minimal stable set containing p contains Lb, and therefore contains b (if it did not, it would contain $\neg Lb$ by virtue of Definition 5.9). In this counterintuitive situation, we know that we have a brother, and conclude from this that we have a brother in order to close our beliefs under the L operator.

In order to distinguish between the two stable sets in this example, Moore makes the following definition:

Definition 6.1 *A set of sentences T will be called an* autoepistemic expansion *of a base theory S if and only if T satisfies the following equation:*

$$T = \mathrm{cl}(S \cup LT \cup \neg L\overline{T}), \tag{10}$$

where $\overline{T}$ is the complement of T in W_L.

Clearly any autoepistemic expansion of a set S is stable.

The appearance of S in (10) allows us to conclude from p in (9) that we do not have a brother. Specifically, if T is to be an autoepistemic expansion of the set $\{p\}$, then T cannot contain Lb unless it contains b. But there is no way for b to be a consequence of sentences in S, LT and $\neg L\overline{T}$.

The bilattice analog to this definition is the following:

Definition 6.2 *Let ϕ be a truth assignment and ψ a stable extension of ϕ. We will say that ψ is* grounded *if*

$$\psi \leq_k \phi + \sum_f \psi_f, \tag{11}$$

where the sum is over all nondeductive modal operators f.

Proposition 6.3 *Let $S \subseteq W_L$ be a set of sentences, and set*

$$\phi_S(p) = \begin{cases} t, & \text{if } p \in S; \\ u, & \text{otherwise.} \end{cases}$$

Then the grounded stable extensions of ϕ_S are in natural correspondence with the autoepistemic expansions of S.

In addition, Theorem 5.8 continues to hold because the sum in (11) is over nondeductive modal operators only, and the Kripke operators are excluded.

An immediate outgrowth of these results is that we can use our description to simultaneously provide a semantics for Kripke-style and autoepistemic modal operators.

7 Conclusion and future work

The purpose of this paper has been to argue that modal operators are best thought of not in terms of Kripke's possible-worlds construction, but as functions on the bilattice of truth values being used in any particular application. The technical content of the paper has been to show that this approach generalizes both the possible worlds work and Moore's autoepistemic logic.

7.1 Causality

The real value of our ideas, however, is not in their ability to combine existing notions under a single formal framework, but to extend them. As an immediate example, we have already noted that the work in Sections 4.1 and 4.2 will allow us to define modal operators that combine the features of Kripke's and of Moore's.

More interesting, however, is the fact that our construction does not inherit the possible-worlds construction's limitation to *unary* modal operators. If we write $p > q$ for "p causes

q," this suggests that it may be possible to interpret $>$ as a binary modal operator on its arguments.

This idea is lent support by recent work of Gärdenfors [3], where it is suggested that causal and explanatory reasoning can be understood in terms of probabilistic manipulations on the truth values assigned to the sentences whose causal relationship is being investigated. In [9], it is argued that the power of Gärdenfors's approach lies not in the probabilistic reasoning it uses, but in the idea that the causal relationship between p and q can be determined by examining the sets of assumptions needed to guarantee the truth of these two sentences. These assumptions can be recorded in a bilattice-based truth value[1] and the Gärdenfors construction then reduces to a modal operator of the sort we have discussed.

More specifically, suppose that we say that a causes b provided that a and b are both true, and that in the nearest world where a fails, b would fail as well.[2] In order to formalize this, we will suppose that we have identified some set C of ATMS contexts, and that for a given sentence p, we know the truth value of p in each of these contexts, so that our bilattice is in fact given by F^C. We will also assume the existence of a map n that accepts as arguments a set S of contexts and a particular context c and returns the context in S that is nearest to c.[3]

It is now reasonable to say that p causes q in a context c if $\phi(p)(c) = t = \phi(q)(c)$ (i.e., both p and q hold in c), and if q fails in $n(c, \phi(p)^{-1}(f))$, so that q fails in the context nearest to c among those in which p is false. In other words,

$$\phi(p > q)(c) = \phi(p)(c) \wedge \phi(q)(c) \wedge \neg\phi(q)[n(c, \phi(p)^{-1}(f))].$$

In modal terms, we have

$$x > y = \{x \wedge y \wedge \neg y[n(\cdot, x^{-1}(f))]\}.$$

In the framework we have developed, this expression immediately assigns a semantics to causality operator $>$.

7.2 Temporal reasoning

Finally, we will sketch a possible application of our ideas to temporal reasoning problems. As with the discussion of causality in the previous section, this work should be viewed as preliminary.

One of the conventional approaches to temporal reasoning involves reifying the sentences in our language, so that in order to say that some sentence p holds at a time t, we actually

---

[1]The close relationship of this bilattice to de Kleer's work on assumption-based truth maintenance [1] has led to this being called the ATMS bilattice in [5].

[2]My intention here is not to argue either in favor of or against this definition, but simply to show that it can be captured within the modal framework we have been discussing. Suffice it to say that definitions such as this are the topic of considerable discussion in the philosophical community.

[3]Once again, we sidestep philosophical issues such as whether or not this nearest context is unique. This is a paper about modal operators, not causality.

write

$$\texttt{holds}(p, t). \tag{12}$$

The term *reification* refers to the fact that we have had to make the sentence p an object of our language in order to include it under the scope of the holds relation.

It seems more natural instead to treat holds as a modal operator, although this raises the problem that we need to deal with the temporal variable appearing in (12) in some way. We will do this by replacing the bilattice B with which we are working with B^T, where T is the set of time points in our temporal language. Thus we label a sentence not with an element of B, but with a *function* that gives its truth value as a function of time. Sentences with no temporal component are labelled by constant functions from T to B.

Having taken this view, how are we to express a causal rule such as

$$\texttt{holds}(\texttt{clear}(b), t) \wedge \texttt{occurs}(\texttt{move}(b, l), t) \supset \texttt{holds}(\texttt{loc}(b, l), t + 1), \tag{13}$$

saying that we can relocate a block that is clear in the blocks world by moving it? The difficulty arises because the conclusion of the above rule is temporally delayed relative to the premises.

In order to describe this in our setting, we need to introduce a modal operator that corresponds to temporal delay. Here it is:

$$\Delta(f)(t) = f(t + 1).$$

Δ is a modal operator that takes any truth value (i.e., function from T into B) and delays it by one time unit. We can now rewrite (13) in the compact form:

$$\texttt{clear}(b) \wedge \texttt{move}(b, l) \supset \Delta\texttt{loc}(b, l). \tag{14}$$

Note that Δ is deductive.

There are some difficulties with this approach; for example, it is somewhat awkward to describe situations in which the amount of delay varies depending upon features of the situation at time t. It remains to be seen whether these difficulties are offset by the advantages of the simplicity of (14) and the flexibility resulting from the fact that reification is not needed by this approach.

7.3 Further work

This paper has only begun to investigate the ideas suggested by the approach we have presented. Indeed, this has been our intention – to describe the approach itself, to show that it generalizes a variety of existing notions including Kripke's and Moore's constructions, to suggest novel ways in which it can be used to describe causal and temporal reasoning, and then to leave the hard work for others.

Acknowledgement

This work has been supported by the Rockwell Palo Alto Laboratory, by General Dynamics, and by NSF under grant number DCR-8620059. I would like to thank Ken Fertig, Vladimir Lifschitz, David Smith, and especially Fred Linton for many enlightening discussions.

References

[1] J. de Kleer. An assumption-based truth maintenance system. *Artificial Intelligence*, 28:127–162, 1986.

[2] M. C. Fitting. Logic programming on a topological bilattice. *Fundamenta Informatica*, 11:209–218, 1988.

[3] P. Gardenfors. *Knowledge in Flux: Modeling the Dynamics of Epistemic States.* MIT Press, 1988.

[4] M. L. Ginsberg. A circumscriptive theorem prover. *Artificial Intelligence*, 39:209–230, 1989.

[5] M. L. Ginsberg. Multivalued logics: A uniform approach to reasoning in artificial intelligence. *Computational Intelligence*, 4:265–316, 1988.

[6] J. Y. Halpern and Y. Moses. A guide to the modal logics of knowledge and belief: Preliminary draft. In *Proceedings of the Ninth International Joint Conference on Artificial Intelligence*, pages 480–490, 1985.

[7] S. A. Kripke. Semantical considerations on modal logic. In L. Linsky, editor, *Reference and Modality*, pages 63–72, Oxford University Press, London, 1971.

[8] R. Moore. Semantical considerations on nonmonotonic logic. *Artificial Intelligence*, 25:75–94, 1985.

[9] E. Paek and M. L. Ginsberg. A justification-based theory of explanation. 1989. Unpublished manuscript.

[10] Y. Shoham. *Reasoning about Change: Time and Causation from the Standpoint of Artificial Intelligence.* MIT Press, Cambridge, MA, 1988.

[11] R. Stalnaker. A note on non-monotonic modal logic. Unpublished manuscript.

A Link Between Knowledge and Communication in Faulty Distributed Systems (Preliminary Report)

Murray S. Mazer
Department of Computer Science
University of Toronto
Toronto, Ontario
Canada M5S 1A4[1]

ABSTRACT

We identify new circumstances under which processes in faulty distributed systems must communicate for one process to gain knowledge about another. Our main result says that, in systems with process crash failures, message loss, or asynchronous processes, if a proposition of a certain type about a process p does not hold, and later another process q knows that the proposition holds, then there was a message chain from p to q. Systems in which processes vote, bid, or transmit private values are often ones in which processes gain knowledge of propositions of the sort described in our result. One can use this result as a new tool in showing message lower bounds and impossibility results and in designing protocols. We demonstrate this by showing a new impossibility result for commitment problems: if a round-based commitment protocol is resilient to process failures and recovery and such that a message may be received only in the round in which it is sent, then the protocol may run forever.

1 INTRODUCTION

We identify new circumstances under which processes in faulty distributed systems must communicate for one process to gain knowledge about another. This yields a new tool for showing message lower bounds and impossibility results and for designing protocols. The first step is to analyze the specification of a given problem to determine the knowledge each process needs to solve the problem. Then our knowledge gain result prescribes communication between processes so that the processes can gain the required knowledge; this yields the necessary underlying communication structure of any protocol to solve the given problem. One can then use this communication structure for impossibility results and protocol design.

Informally, our result says that, if at some time a proposition ϕ about process p is false and at some later time another process q knows that ϕ is true, then q received a message through some chain of message passing which originated at p, given one of the following conditions:

- processes can crash-fail and ϕ cannot become true while p is failed;
- messages can be lost and ϕ is never forced to become true; or
- processes are asynchronous.

We call this result the *Message Chain Theorem.*

[1]The author's current address is Digital Equipment Corporation, 550 King Street LKG1-2/A19, Littleton, MA 01460, U.S.A. Electronic address: mazer@crl.dec.com.

There are related results in the literature. Halpern and Moses (1990) showed that processes cannot attain common knowledge of certain propositions in systems with unguaranteed communication, asynchronous processes, or asynchronous communication. Chandy and Misra (1986) showed for asynchronous systems that if a process q "gains the knowledge" that another process p knows some proposition, then q must receive a message through some chain of message passing which originates at p. Further, if p later loses its knowledge, then there must be a message chain from q to p. Hadzilacos (1989) showed, in systems with process crash failures or message loss, that a receive event is the only event by which a process may acquire knowledge about certain eventual states of other processes.

Unlike the results of Halpern and Moses (1990), our result addresses knowledge weaker than common knowledge, in systems different from the ones which they considered. We can use the Message Chain Theorem to reason about both finite and infinite knowledge levels and about incremental gains in a process's knowledge through communication. We extend the knowledge gain result of Chandy and Misra (1990) to systems with failures, regardless of process synchrony. Unlike Hadzilacos, we make explicit the first and last processes in the message chain, and we consider more general conditions.

We have used our knowledge gain result extensively for lower bounds, impossibility results, and protocol design for the problem of negotiated commitment [Maze89], a problem closely related but incomparable to atomic commitment. We believe, however, that the result is more generally applicable; systems in which processes vote, bid, or transmit private values are often ones in which processes gain knowledge of propositions of the sort described in the Message Chain Theorem. Furthermore, although some of the impossibility results already have combinatorial proofs (at least for atomic commitment) which depend upon the communication inherent in the problem solution, the knowledge-theoretic proofs using message chains give semantic reasons, based on the problem specification, for the inherent communication. That is, a knowledge analysis of a problem determines, from the specification, the knowledge each process needs to solve the problem, without reference to particular protocols. The Message Chain Theorem provides a tool to link directly the communication required of any protocol for the problem to the knowledge gains needed to solve the problem. One cannot always easily determine how a combinatorial proof reflects the problem being solved.

The paper proceeds as follows. We define, in Sections 2 and 3 respectively, the types of distributed systems we address and the knowledge of processes in such systems. Then, in Section 4, we give the Message Chain Theorem. In Section 5, we define the negotiated commitment problem, followed in Section 6 by a new impossibility result about commitment protocols, based on a knowledge analysis of the problem specification and the resultant communication requirements.

2 MODEL OF DISTRIBUTED SYSTEMS

2.1 Executions

Adapting [Hadz89], we consider a distributed system to consist of two types of elements: ① processes, which execute events (let Π represent the set of n processes); and ② a communication system, $\mathcal{N}$, which contains a set of message packets (of the form $\langle p, \underline{\mathrm{m}}, q, i \rangle$, representing the message $\underline{\mathrm{m}}$ sent from p to q at time i). The events are of two kinds: communicative and noncommunicative. The communicative events are $\mathsf{SEND}(\underline{\mathrm{m}}, q)$ (the executing process sends message $\underline{\mathrm{m}}$ to process q, where $\underline{\mathrm{m}} \in \underline{\mathrm{M}}$, a message vocabulary) and $\mathsf{RECV}(\underline{\mathrm{m}}, q)$ (the executing process receives message $\underline{m}$ from process q). $\underline{m}$ may be the null message λ or a message from $\underline{M}$. These are the only two events by which a process may communicate externally; all other events are local and have no effect on the communication system.

A possible joint behaviour over time of the processes and the communication system is modelled by an *execution* (or *run*). Each execution e is a function mapping time to a global state tuple of the form $\langle time, history_{p1}, history_{p2}, \ldots, history_{pn}, packets\rangle$. *time* represents the time at which the system is observed; $history_{pi}$ represents the finite sequence of events executed by process p_i in execution e up to the observation instant; and *packets* is the set of message packets in transit at that instant. The *points* of an execution set $\mathcal{E}$, $\mathbf{Pts}(\mathcal{E})$, are $\{(e,f) \mid e \in \mathcal{E}$ and $f \in N\}$.

For $p \in \Pi$, we write $e(f,p)$ for $history_p$, p's history element in the tuple at point (e,f); similarly, we write $e(f,\mathcal{N})$ for *packets*, the set of message packets in the communication system at point (e,f). $d \dashv e(f,p)$ asserts that d is the last event in the sequence $history_p$ at point (e,f); $d \in e(f,p)$ indicates that event d appears in the sequence; $\mid e(f,p) \mid$ indicates the number of events in the sequence; and $e(f,p)\cdot d$ indicates the concatenation of event d to the sequence. We write $d \sqsubset (e,f+1,p)$ to say that process p has just executed event d at point $(e,f+1)$, i.e., $d \sqsubset (e,f+1,p)$ iff $e(f+1,p) = e(f,p)\cdot d$. $e(f+1,p) \geq e(f,p)$ denotes that p's event sequence up to time $f+1$ in e has, as a prefix, p's event sequence up to f in e.

For each $p \in \Pi$, we define a relation $=_p$ on the points in system $\mathcal{E}$ which captures when p has the same event sequence in two points. For $(e,f),(e',g) \in \mathbf{Pts}(\mathcal{E})$, we write $(e,f) =_p (e',g)$ iff $e(f,p) = e'(g,p)$. For process set $P \subseteq \Pi$, $(e,f) =_P (e',g)$ iff $(e,f) =_p (e',g)$ for all $p \in P$. Similarly, the communication system is the same in both points, written $(e,f) =_{\mathcal{N}} (e',g)$, iff $e(f,\mathcal{N}) = e'(g,\mathcal{N})$.

We define an *historical equivalence* relation on points as follows: given two executions $e', e \in \mathcal{E}$ and instant $f \in N$, $(e',f) \equiv (e,f)$ iff, for all $0 \leq g \leq f$, $(e',g) =_\Pi (e,g)$ and $(e',g) =_{\mathcal{N}} (e,g)$. This says that two points are historically equivalent if the two executions are indistinguishable over all preceding and current observation instants. A point (e',g) *extends* (e,f), written $(e',g) \geq (e,f)$, iff $(e',f) \equiv (e,f)$ and $g \geq f$. An execution e' *extends* a point (e,f) iff $(e',f) \equiv (e,f)$.

Executions conform to the following informal operational behaviour. At the beginning of time, time 0, the communication system is empty, and no process has executed any events. Each process executes at most one event between successive observation instants. A message is removed from the communication system if it is received or lost. Only messages which were sent but not yet removed may appear in the communication system. We describe this behaviour axiomatically in [Maze89].

2.2 Systems of Executions

Informally speaking, we characterize the behaviours of a distributed protocol by a set of executions $\mathcal{E}$ over Π and $\mathcal{N}$. An execution set must exhibit some closure properties which ensure that if the set represents certain behaviours, then it represents certain other behaviours; these properties capture the ways in which one process's event sequence and the behaviour of the communication system affect another process's event sequence. We call such a closed execution set a *system*. Intuitively, the ability of a process to execute some event should not depend on the events executed so far by other processes or on the behaviour of the communication system, unless the event is a receive — a process can execute a RECV event only if there is an appropriate message in the communication system, and such a message must have been sent by some process.

For $P,Q \subseteq \Pi$, $e(f,\mathcal{N})[P,Q] \stackrel{\text{def}}{=} \{\langle p,\underline{m},q,i\rangle \in e(f,\mathcal{N}) \mid p \in P \text{ and } q \in Q\}$. That is, $e(f,\mathcal{N})[P,Q]$ is the set of messages in transit from processes in P to processes in Q at instant f of execution e. $\overline{P} \stackrel{\text{def}}{=} \Pi \setminus P$.

Given a set of executions $\mathcal{E}$, points $(e',g),(e,f) \in\mathbf{Pts}(\mathcal{E})$, and process set $P \subseteq \Pi$, **replace**$((e',g),P,(e,f))$ is the set of executions $e'' \in\mathcal{E}$ which extend (e',g) such that
① in e'', each member of $\overline{P}$ executes the same event at $(e'',g+1)$ as it did at $(e',g+1)$,
② in e'', the event executed by each member of P at $(e',g+1)$ is *replaced* by the event it executed at $(e,f+1)$, and
③ the messages from P to Π are the messages not sent or received in e' between g and $g+1$, plus any messages received in e' at $g+1$ by $p \in P$ but not in e by p at $f+1$, plus any messages newly sent by P; and the messages from $\overline{P}$ to Π are whatever was in e' at $g+1$, plus whatever P received in e' at $g+1$, minus whatever P received in e at $f+1$ or was lost in transit to P in e at $f+1$ [Hadz89].

The progress-closure properties we require here are these:[2]

S1 (Nonreceive Progress): The ability of a process to perform a nonRECV event depends on the process's behaviour only.

Let $(e,f),(e',g) \in\mathbf{Pts}(\mathcal{E})$ and $p \in \Pi$ be such that

- $(e,f) =_p (e',g)$,
- $\mathsf{RECV}(\underline{m},q) \not\sqsubset (e,f+1,p)$, for any message $\underline{m}$, $q \in \Pi$

Then **replace**$((e',g),\{p\},(e,f)) \neq \emptyset$.

Sλ (Null Receive Progress): A process' ability to receive a null message from another process depends on the state of the former process, the messages sent to the recipient by the latter process, and the behaviour of the communication system.

Let $e,e' \in\mathcal{E}$, $g \in N$, and $q,p \in \Pi$ be such that

- $(e,g) =_p (e',g)$,
- $e'(g,\mathcal{N})[\{q\},\{p\}] \subseteq e(g,\mathcal{N})[\{q\},\{p\}]$,
  (There are no different messages in the communication system from q to p up to time g in e' than in e), and
- $\mathsf{RECV}(\lambda,q) \sqsubset (e,g+1,p)$.

Then **replace**$((e',g),\{p\},(e,g)) \neq \emptyset$.

S3 (Available Receive Progress): Once a process p has sent a message to another process q, q's ability to receive the message cannot depend on p's subsequent behaviour; q's ability to receive the message does depend on the communication system.

Let $e,e' \in\mathcal{E}$, $f,g \in N$, and $q,p \in \Pi$ be such that

- $(e,g) =_p (e',g)$
- $\mathsf{RECV}(\underline{m},q) \sqsubset (e,g+1,p)$,

[2] These closure properties correspond to a natural set of assumptions on the protocols which "produce" the behaviours in the execution sets [Maze89].

- $\langle q, \underline{m}, p, f\rangle \in e'(g, \mathcal{N})$ (the message is still available in e' at g, as in e)
- let $\eta = \{\langle q, \underline{m}, p, i\rangle \mid \langle q, \underline{m}, p, i\rangle \in e'(g, \mathcal{N})$ and $0 \leq i \leq f\}$;
  $\eta \subseteq e(g, \mathcal{N})[\{q\}, \{p\}]$ (The set of messages available at (e', g), sent before $f+1$, and from q to p are a subset of those available at (e, g).)

Then $\mathbf{replace}((e', g), \{p\}, (e, g)) \neq \emptyset$.

2.3 System Characteristics

A system $\mathcal{E}$ is *weakly terminating* if every point of $\mathcal{E}$ can be extended to a point beyond which no process executes any more events in any extension [KoTo88].

Definition 1 A system $\mathcal{E}$ is *weakly terminating* if, for each point $(e, f) \in \mathbf{Pts}(\mathcal{E})$, there is (e', g) extending (e, f) such that, for all $p \in \Pi$ and all $(e'', h) \in \mathbf{Pts}(\mathcal{E})$ extending (e', g), $e''(h, p) = e'(g, p)$.

(e', g) is a *terminating extension* of (e, f) and a *terminating point* of $\mathcal{E}$. ⊠

We capture process crash failures and message loss by another set of closure properties. Informally, a system is *subject to process failures* if any process subset may fail at any time. A failure of process p is modelled by a FAIL event in an event sequence for p. We collect into $\mathbf{fail}(e, f, P)$ each execution e' in an execution set $\mathcal{E}$ such that ① e' extends $(e, f-1)$; ② processes other than those in P execute the same events at (e', f) as at (e, f); ③ each nonterminated member of P is failed; and ④ any message that $p \in P$ sends at (e, f) does not appear in $e'(f, \mathcal{N})$, and any message that $p \in P$ receives at (e, f) appears in $e'(f, \mathcal{N})$.

Definition 2 A system $\mathcal{E}$ is *subject to process failures* if, for any $(e, f) \in \mathbf{Pts}(\mathcal{E})$:
(any process subset may fail) for any $P \subseteq \Pi$, $\mathbf{fail}(e, f, P) \neq \emptyset$. ⊠

Let *Failed*(e, f) represent the set of failed processes at point (e, f):

$$Failed(e, f) = \{p \mid p \in \Pi \text{ and FAIL} \dashv e(f, p)\}.$$

A system is *subject to process failures and recovery* if, at any time, any process subset may fail, and any subset of failed processes may recover.

Definition 3 A system $\mathcal{E}$ is *subject to process failures and recovery* if, for any $(e, f) \in \mathbf{Pts}(\mathcal{E})$:

(any process subset may fail) for any $P \subseteq \Pi$, $\mathbf{fail}(e, f, P) \neq \emptyset$.

(any subset of failed processes may recover) for each nonempty $P \subseteq Failed(e, f)$, there is $(e', g) \in \mathbf{Pts}(\mathcal{E})$ properly extending (e, f) such that FAIL $\not\dashv e'(g, p)$, for all $p \in P$. ⊠

A system is *subject to communication failures* if any subset of messages in transit at any time may be lost. Let M be a subset of the messages in transit at point (e, f): $M \subseteq e(f, \mathcal{N})$. We collect into the set $\mathbf{lose}(e, f, M)$ the set of executions $e' \in \mathcal{E}$ such that e' extends $(e, f-1)$, $(e', f) =_{\Pi} (e, f)$, and $e'(f, \mathcal{N}) = e(f, \mathcal{N}) \setminus M$.

Definition 4 A system $\mathcal{E}$ is *subject to communication failures* if, for any $(e, f) \in \mathbf{Pts}(\mathcal{E})$ and any $M \subseteq e(f, \mathcal{N})$: $\mathbf{lose}(e, f, M) \neq \emptyset$. ⊠

We also model systems in which a message has a maximum lifetime in transit. A system is *k-transit bounded* if any message sent disappears from the communication system at most k time units after being sent.

Definition 5 A system $\mathcal{E}$ is *k-transit bounded* (for some finite $k \geq 0$) if, for any $\underline{m} \in \underline{M}$, $q,p \in \Pi$, $e \in \mathcal{E}$: if $\mathsf{SEND}(\underline{m}, q) \sqsubset (e, f, p)$, then $\langle p, \underline{m}, q, f \rangle \notin e(f+k, \mathcal{N})$. ⊠

Round-based protocols typically assume k-transit bounded systems.

A system has *asynchronous processes* if, at any point, any process may execute no event in the next time step.

Definition 6 A system $\mathcal{E}$ has *asynchronous processes* if, for any $e \in \mathcal{E}$, $f > 0$, $p \in \Pi$, there is $e' \in \mathcal{E}$ extending $(e, f-1)$ such that

- $(e', f) =_p (e, f-1)$ (p executes no event),
- $(e', f) =_{\Pi \setminus \{p\}} (e, f)$ (the others do as they did in e), and
- $e'(f, \mathcal{N}) = (e(f, \mathcal{N}) \cup A) \setminus B$ (the communication system is adjusted), where A contains the message packet for any message p receives at (e, f) and B contains the message packet for any message p sends at (e, f).

3 KNOWLEDGE LOGIC

We use the knowledge logic of Halpern and Moses (1990), including process knowledge and collective knowledge within process sets. The language of the logic has the following symbols: a set Φ of primitive propositions; a finite set Π of process names; $\{\neg, \vee, \Box, (,)\}$; $\{K_x \mid x \in \Pi\}$; and $\{K_X \mid X \subseteq \Pi, X \neq \emptyset\}$. The set of well-formed formulae (or *wffs*) $\mathcal{L}_\Pi(\Phi)$ is the smallest set such that (1) every member of Φ is a well-formed formula, and (2) if ϕ and ψ are well-formed formulae, then so are $(\neg\phi)$, $(\phi \vee \psi)$, $\Box\phi$, $K_x\phi$, $K_X\phi$. We abbreviate $(\neg((\neg\phi) \vee (\neg\psi)))$ by $(\phi \wedge \psi)$ and $((\neg\phi) \vee \psi)$ by $(\phi \supset \psi)$[3].

We interpret wffs via possible worlds semantics relative to an *interpreted system* (or *model*), a structure $\mathbf{M} = (\mathcal{E}, \mathcal{A})$ in which $\mathcal{E}$ is a system over Π and $\mathcal{N}$, and $\mathcal{A}: \Phi \rightarrow 2^{\mathbf{Pts}(\mathcal{E})}$ is an interpretation mapping each primitive proposition to the set of points in $\mathcal{E}$ in which the proposition holds. The points of the system are the possible worlds. Knowledge is based on a complete history interpretation [HaMo90].

Given a model $\mathbf{M}$, we write $(\mathbf{M}, e, f) \models \phi$ to express that wff ϕ holds in point (e, f) of the model. (If $\mathbf{M}$ is understood from context, we write $(e, f) \models \phi$.) We define $\models$ as follows (assume $\phi, \psi \in \mathcal{L}_\Pi(\Phi)$):

[Primitives] For $\phi \in \Phi$, $(\mathbf{M}, e, f) \models \phi$ iff $(e, f) \in \mathcal{A}(\phi)$.

[Negation] $(\mathbf{M}, e, f) \models (\neg\phi)$ iff $(\mathbf{M}, e, f) \models \phi$ does not hold.

[Disjunction] $(\mathbf{M}, e, f) \models (\phi \vee \psi)$ iff $(\mathbf{M}, e, f) \models \phi$ or $(\mathbf{M}, e, f) \models \psi$ (inclusively).

[Henceforth] $(\mathbf{M}, e, f) \models \Box\phi$ iff, for all $e' \in \mathcal{E}$ such that $(e, f) \equiv (e', f)$, $(\mathbf{M}, e', g) \models \phi$ for all $g \geq f$. ("henceforth ϕ" holds in point (e, f) iff ϕ holds now and in any possible extension of (e, f).)

[Process Knowledge] For $p \in \Pi$, $(\mathbf{M}, e, f) \models K_p\phi$ iff $(\mathbf{M}, e', g) \models \phi$, for all $(e', g) \in \mathbf{Pts}(\mathcal{E})$ such that $(e, f) =_p (e', g)$. ("p knows ϕ" iff ϕ is true in all points which look to p similar to the current one.)

[Collective Knowledge] For $P \subseteq \Pi$, $(\mathbf{M}, e, f) \models K_P\phi$ iff $(\mathbf{M}, e', g) \models \phi$,

[3] In the sequel, we elide the parentheses "(" and ")" in the usual way in formulae in which no ambiguity results. Furthermore, for clarity, we sometimes use "[" for "(" and "]" for ")".

for all $(e',g) \in\mathbf{Pts}(\mathcal{E})$ such that $(e,f) =_P (e',g)$. ("the members of P collectively know ϕ" iff ϕ holds in all points which the members of P collectively think possible.)

A wff ϕ is *valid in structure* $\mathbf{M}$, written $\mathbf{M} \models \phi$, iff $(\mathbf{M}, e, f) \models \phi$ for all points $(e, f) \in\mathbf{Pts}(\mathcal{E})$. Processes in this logic have the *introspection* property: for any wff ϕ, $P \subseteq \Pi$, and model $\mathbf{M}$, $\mathbf{M} \models K_P\phi \supset K_P K_P\phi$ and $\mathbf{M} \models \neg K_P\phi \supset K_P\neg K_P\phi$.

We now identify a set of useful and important properties of formulae in interpreted systems. Then we relate these concepts to each other.

Stable: A wff ϕ is *stable* (in $\mathbf{M}$) if the following property holds: $\mathbf{M} \models \phi \supset \Box\phi$. A stable wff stays true forever after it becomes true [ChLa85]. Stability is useful for expressing immutable choices and decisions, such as the choice to accept a contract or commit a transaction.

Local: A formula ϕ is *local to P* (in $\mathbf{M}$), for $P \subseteq \Pi$, if $\mathbf{M} \models K_P\phi \vee K_P\neg\phi$. That is, P always knows the truth value of ϕ [ChMi86]. Local formulae are intended to model predicates whose value is controlled by or locally testable by the actions of the processes to which the formulae are local. If $P = \{p\}$, we write that ϕ is local to p instead of $\{p\}$.

P-failure-dissociated: A formula ϕ is called *P-failure-dissociated* (in $\mathbf{M}$), for $P \subseteq \Pi$, if, whenever ϕ is false, ϕ remains false as long as a process in P is failed [Hadz89]. That is, for any $(e, f) \in\mathbf{Pts}(\mathcal{E})$, if $(e, f) \models \neg\phi$ and $\mathsf{FAIL} \dashv e(f+1,p)$, for any $p \in P$, then $(e, f+1) \models \neg\phi$. If $P = \{p\}$, we write that ϕ is p-failure-dissociated instead of $\{p\}$-failure-dissociated.

P-receive-dependent: A formula ϕ is called *P-receive-dependent* (in $\mathbf{M}$) if, when it is false, it can become true only if some process in P receives a nonnull message from a process not in P [Hadz89]. That is, for any $(e, f) \in\mathbf{Pts}(\mathcal{E})$, if $(e, f) \models \neg\phi$ and $(e, f+1) \models \phi$, then $\mathsf{RECV}(\underline{m}, q) \sqsubset (e, f+1, p)$, for some $p \in P$, $\underline{m} \neq \lambda$, and $q \in \overline{P}$. If $P = \{p\}$, we write that ϕ is p-receive-dependent instead of $\{p\}$-receive-dependent.

Pointwise nontrivial: A formula ϕ is called *pointwise nontrivial* (in $\mathbf{M}$) iff, whenever it is false, it may remain false in the next time instant; i.e., for any $(e, f) \in\mathbf{Pts}(\mathcal{E})$, if $(e, f) \models \neg\phi$, then there is $e' \in\mathcal{E}$ such that e' extends (e, f) and $(e', f+1) \models \neg\phi$.

Intuitively, locality means that the proposition is "about" the process set to which the proposition is local. For example, if we were modelling the outcome of a coin toss by process p and wff ϕ represents the proposition "p has flipped a heads", then we expect ϕ to be local to p. Furthermore, we do not expect ϕ to become true while p is failed, so ϕ is p-failure-dissociated. Finally, we expect the outcome of p's coin toss to be fair and not forced to be either heads or tails, so ϕ is pointwise nontrivial.

As the following lemma shows, these concepts are strongly related.

Lemma 7 Given any model $\mathbf{M}$, wff ϕ, and $P \subseteq \Pi$, ϕ is pointwise nontrivial in $\mathbf{M}$ if any of the following holds:

- $\mathbf{M}$ is subject to process failures and ϕ is P-failure-dissociated.
- $\mathbf{M}$ is subject to communication failures and ϕ is P-receive-dependent.
- $\mathbf{M}$ has asynchronous processes and ϕ is local to P.

Further, if $\mathbf{M}$ is subject to process failures and ϕ is P-receive-dependent, then ϕ is P-failure-dissociated. ◻

4 MESSAGE CHAINS

Given an execution e, a *message chain from process p to process q in interval* (e,f) *to* (e,g) is a sequence of send/receive pairs such that ($f \leq f_1$; $f_i < f_{i+1}$, for $1 \leq i < 2n$; $f_{2n} \leq g$):

$\mathsf{SEND}(\underline{m}_1, p_1) \sqsubset (e, f_1, p)$; $\mathsf{RECV}(\underline{m}_1, p) \sqsubset (e, f_2, p_1)$; $\mathsf{SEND}(\underline{m}_2, p_2) \sqsubset (e, f_3, p_1)$; $\mathsf{RECV}(\underline{m}_2, p_1) \sqsubset (e, f_4, p_2)$; ... $\mathsf{SEND}(\underline{m}_n, q) \sqsubset (e, f_{2n-1}, p_{n-1})$; $\mathsf{RECV}(\underline{m}_n, p_{n-1}) \sqsubset (e, f_{2n}, q)$.

The abbreviation $P \xrightarrow{+} Q$ indicates a message chain of length at least one from P to Q (execution and interval will be clear from context). We abbreviate $\{p\} \xrightarrow{+} \{q\}$ as $p \xrightarrow{+} q$.

For any model $\mathbf{M}$, $e \in \mathcal{E}$, nonempty process sets $P \subset \Pi$ and $Q \subset \Pi$ such that $P \cap Q = \emptyset$, and wff ϕ local to P, a *ϕ-message chain* from P to Q in interval (e,f) to (e,i) is a message chain from some $p \in P$ to some $q \in Q$ in an interval (e,j) to (e,i) such that $f < j$, $(\mathbf{M}, e, j-1) \models \neg\phi$, $(\mathbf{M}, e, j) \models \phi$, and $(\mathbf{M}, e, i) \models K_Q\phi$.

Finally, we can give our knowledge gain result. Recall that, informally, our result says that, if at some time a proposition ϕ about process p is false and at some later time another process q knows that ϕ is true, then q received a message through some chain of message passing which originated at p, given one of the following conditions: processes can crash-fail and ϕ cannot become true while p is failed; messages can be lost and ϕ is never forced to become true; or processes are asynchronous.

Theorem 8 (The Message Chain Theorem)
Assume any model $\mathbf{M}$, nonempty $P \subset \Pi$ and $Q \subset \Pi$ such that $P \cap Q = \emptyset$, wff ϕ local to P, point (e,f) in $\mathcal{E}$, and $i > f$ such that

- $(\mathbf{M}, e, f) \models \neg\phi$ and $(\mathbf{M}, e, i) \models K_Q\phi$, and
- one of
  - $\mathbf{M}$ is subject to process failures and ϕ is P-failure-dissociated in $\mathbf{M}$, or
  - $\mathbf{M}$ is subject to communication failures and ϕ is pointwise nontrivial in $\mathbf{M}$, or
  - $\mathbf{M}$ has asynchronous processes.

There is a ϕ-message chain from P to Q in (e,f) to (e,i). ◻

We can give an intuitive explanation of the Message Chain Theorem in terms of potential causality between events, using Lamport's "happened before", or *affects*, relation (Lamport 1978). One way to view the claim in the Message Chain Theorem is that there must be ① an event d_p in the event sequence of some process in P between times j (at which ϕ starts to hold) and i in e, and ② an event d_q in the event sequence of some process in Q in the same interval, such that d_p affects d_q. Because $p \neq q$, there must be a message chain between the two processes. If no such events exist, then the events of P in the interval of interest do not affect the events of Q in that interval, so there is another execution possible in which the processes in Q do as in (e,j) to (e,i) and those in P execute other events which ensure that ϕ is false when q comes to "know" ϕ, yielding a contradiction.

The proof of this result is long and detailed; see [Maze89]. The proof follows a common structure for each of the three conditions, to wit:

1. Use pointwise nontriviality to identify an execution $e' \in \mathcal{E}$ which extends $(e, j-1)$ such that $(e', j) \models \neg\phi$.

2. Identify $e'' \in \mathcal{E}$ extending $(e', j-1)$ such that $(e'', i) =_Q (e, i)$ and $(e'', i) \models \neg\phi$, which yields the contradiction $(e'', i) \models \phi \wedge \neg\phi$. Do this by inductively identifying a sequence of intermediate executions $e^0, e^1, \ldots, e^k$, for $k = i - j$, in which
   (a) Q's event sequence from e is exactly preserved up to time i, by using the progress-closure properties (otherwise, we could not guarantee that $(e'', i) \models \phi$!)
   (b) P's event sequence is *not* preserved (otherwise $(e'', i) \models \phi$!) We invoke the relevant conditions on $\mathbf{M}$ and ϕ for any member of P to prevent any messages from P sent at or after (e', j) from reaching any other process. We do this by having the members of P fail instead of sending such a message, having the message lost when sent, or having the members of P freeze just before sending the message.
   (c) for each $q' \in \Pi \setminus (Q \cup P)$, q''s event sequence from e is maintained via the progress-closure properties as long as possible, to support Q's event sequence (to ensure any message sent by q' to Q, which message is not part of a chain from P to Q in (e, j) to (e, i), can still be received by Q). The event sequence from e for q' is preserved unless q' receives a message which is along a message chain from P beginning at or after (e, j). For any such q', we change its event sequence, again invoking the relevant conditions on $\mathbf{M}$ and ϕ to prevent messages from q' from entering the communication system. Informally speaking, this cannot affect Q's ability to execute the same events as in e, because we assume that there is no chain from P to Q in e, so in particular there is none through q', so there is no chain from q' to Q from the instant q''s sequence changes.

We note that, as a corollary of the Message Chain Theorem, if ϕ in the statement of the theorem is initially false in $\mathbf{M}$, then ϕ requires a ϕ-message chain $P \xrightarrow{+} Q$ to become known to Q in $\mathbf{M}$. Further, if ϕ requires $P \xrightarrow{+} Q$ to become known to Q in $\mathbf{M}$, then $K_Q\phi$ is Q-receive-dependent in $\mathbf{M}$. Finally, using the asynchronous processes case of the Message Chain Theorem, one can easily show the knowledge gain and loss results of [ChMi86] mentioned in Section 1 [Maze89].

5 NEGOTIATED COMMITMENT

We now introduce the negotiated commitment problem and illustrate the use of the Message Chain Theorem, by analyzing negotiated commitment. The problem of negotiated commitment is to ensure that the processes in a distributed negotiation commit consistently to the outcome, even in the face of failures. Negotiated commitment is related, but incomparable, to the problem of atomic commitment in distributed transaction systems, differing as follows. First, in negotiated commitment, a distinguished process, historically called the *manager*, coordinates the commitment; in atomic commitment, there need not be a single coordinator. Second, in negotiated commitment, commitment may be established among subsets of the participating processes; in atomic commitment, a commitment must include all processes. The specifications of these two problems reflect these differences. Our lower bound and impossibility results for negotiated commitment convert easily to apply to atomic commitment.

For negotiated commitment, we divide the processes in the system into two disjoint sets: the manager, $\{m\}$, and the *contractors*, or bidders, C. Each of the contractors chooses whether to bid or not on an announced contract. The manager selects from among the bidding contractors to establish a *dependency set*, representing those contractors which the manager wants to commit to performing the announced task; contractors not in the dependency set must not carry out the task. We represent contractor c's choice to bid by a primitive proposition BID_c; we represent its choice not to bid by $NO\text{-}BID_c$. We represent the manager's possible dependency set choices by the primitive propositions $DEPEND_m^x$ for each nonempty $x \subseteq \mathcal{C}$. For each $c \in \mathcal{C}$, we define the allowed dependencies set $\mathcal{D}_c \subseteq \{x \mid x \in 2^{\mathcal{C}} \text{ and } c \in x\}$. The manager records locally a decision outcome for each contractor, either $AWARD_m^c$, representing that m expects c to carry out the task, or $REJECT_m^c$, representing that m expects c not to carry out the task. Similarly, each contractor records locally a decision outcome, either $ACCEPT_c$, representing that c will carry out the contract, or $REFUSE_c$, that c will not carry out the contract. Informally, the processes reach consistent commitment if, for each $c \in \mathcal{C}$, the manager decides $AWARD_m^c$ and c decides $ACCEPT_c$, or m decides $REJECT_m^c$ and c decides $REFUSE_c$. Each BID_c, $NO\text{-}BID_c$, $ACCEPT_c$, and $REFUSE_c$ proposition is stable and local to c; BID_c is also c-failure-dissociated. Each $DEPEND_m^x$, $AWARD_m^c$, and $REJECT_m^c$ proposition is stable and local to m; $DEPEND_m^x$ is also m-failure-dissociated. All of these propositions are initially false.

A *C-system* is an interpreted system which satisfies the specification of negotiated commitment under process or communication failures. The potential for failures in the system makes consistent negotiated commitment nontrivial to achieve. The C-system properties fit into four general categories: necessity, exclusivity, freedom of choice, and decision completion. Five necessity properties tell which propositions must hold when others hold. Eleven exclusivity properties proscribe two propositions from holding simultaneously. Five nontriviality properties capture the notion that a proposition (which may intuitively represent a choice to be made by a process) is not forced to hold at any time. Two decision completion properties describe situations and combinations in which processes must decide. Below, we list the properties relevant to our discussion.

Dependent Acceptance: For all $c \in \mathcal{C}$, $\mathbf{M} \models ACCEPT_c \supset \vee_{x \in \mathcal{D}_c} DEPEND_m^x$.
(An accepted contractor must be a codependent.)

Dependent Award: For all $c \in \mathcal{C}$, $\mathbf{M} \models AWARD_m^c \supset \vee_{x \in \mathcal{D}_c} DEPEND_m^x$.
(An awarded contractor must be a codependent.)

No Unilateral Dependencies: For all $c \in \mathcal{C}$, $\mathbf{M} \models \vee_{x \in \mathcal{D}_c} DEPEND_m^x \supset BID_c$.
(A codependent must have bid.)

Nonintersecting Dependencies:
For each $c \in \mathcal{C}$, for each pair $x, y \in \mathcal{D}_c$ such that $x \neq y$,
$\mathbf{M} \models \neg(DEPEND_m^x \wedge DEPEND_m^y)$.
(c may be involved in at most one dependency set in any one negotiation.)

Decision Harmony: For all $c \in \mathcal{C}$,

$\mathbf{M} \models \neg(AWARD_m^c \wedge REFUSE_c)$ $\quad$ $\mathbf{M} \models \neg(REJECT_m^c \wedge ACCEPT_c)$
(The manager and each contractor can never decide inconsistently.)

$\mathbf{M} \models \neg(AWARD_m^c \wedge REJECT_m^c)$ $\quad$ $\mathbf{M} \models \neg(ACCEPT_c \wedge REFUSE_c)$.
(Only one of two possible decisions is allowed for each process.)

Four other properties state that if contractors c and d are both in the dependency set x, then m cannot decide for them inconsistently, c and d cannot decide inconsistently with each other,

m cannot award to c while a codependent d refuses, and m cannot reject c while a codependent d accept.

It is straightforward to show the following simple knowledge requirements.

Lemma 9 For any C-system $\mathbf{M}$, $c \in \mathcal{C}$, $p \in \Pi$,

- $\mathbf{M} \models K_p(\vee_{x \in \mathcal{D}_c} DEPEND^x_m) \supset K_p BID_c$.
- $\mathbf{M} \models K_p AWARD^c_m \supset K_p(\vee_{x \in \mathcal{D}_c} DEPEND^x_m)$.
- $\mathbf{M} \models K_p AWARD^c_m \supset K_p BID_c$.
- $\mathbf{M} \models K_p ACCEPT_c \supset K_p(\vee_{x \in \mathcal{D}_c} DEPEND^x_m)$.
- $\mathbf{M} \models K_p ACCEPT_c \supset K_p BID_c$. ◻

Lemma 9 gives us some of the knowledge a contractor needs to accept or a manager needs to award. We can now use the Message Chain Theorem to derive communication requirements from the knowledge requirements. Using Lemma 9 and the Message Chain Theorem, it is easy to show, for systems with process crash failures, message loss, or asynchronous processes, that, for a contractor c to accept, there must be one message chain from c to m, so that m knows that c bid, and a subsequent message chain from m to c, so that c knows that m selected c as a codependent. This matches our intuition about the problem; the important point is that we are able to formalize and validate that intuition directly. As we shall see in Section 6, the knowledge requirements and the corresponding communication requirements are not always so simple.

We have used the Message Chain Theorem to establish a message lower bound and several impossibility results for negotiated commitment. All but one of these results was known in some form for atomic commitment, but we have shown them using knowledge theory and, in particular, the Message Chain Theorem, sometimes providing a more general result. For example, the message lower bound follows from the argument above that, for each contractor which has accepted, two messages must be sent and received in the system. This is a different, and perhaps more direct, proof strategy than that given combinatorially by Dwork and Skeen (1983) and knowledge-theoretically by Hadzilacos (1989) for atomic commitment.

6 THE IMPOSSIBILITY RESULT

The result we give below states that there is no protocol for negotiated commitment which guarantees weak termination in a system in which processes may fail and recover and in which messages may spend a bounded amount of time in transit. All of the impossibility results have the same form: ① determine the knowledge required for the desired commitment behaviour in the specific type of system; ② determine the communication, in terms of message chains, required to establish that knowledge in any protocol; and ③ argue that the communication is unattainable.

To obtain our result, we will prove that, in weakly terminating C-systems which are k-transit bounded and subject to process failures and recovery, ① an accepting contractor c must have arbitrarily deeply nested knowledge about the manager's knowledge about c's knowledge that m made c a codependent, and ② an awarding manager must have arbitrarily deeply nested knowledge about c's knowledge that m made c a codependent. We show this, in Lemma 16, by induction on the knowledge nesting level. Then the Message Chain Theorem allows us to show that the required knowledge cannot be gained in finite time (Theorem 18), by showing that arbitrarily many consecutive message chains are needed to gain the required knowledge (Lemma 17). In order to show Lemma 16, we must show ① how m's award to c depends on c's acceptance knowledge and c's acceptance depends on m's award knowledge (Lemma 14), and ② that each of the nested levels of knowledge in Lemma 16 can be attained only by message receipt (Lemma 15). Lemma 14 shows that ① if c must know c-receive-dependent proposition ϕ in order to accept, then an awarding m must know that c knows ϕ, and ② if m must know m-receive-dependent proposition ϕ in order to award, then, in order to accept, c must know that m knows ϕ. Lemma 14 and Lemma 15 allow us to show the interleaved knowledge requirement in Lemma 16, using, as a basis, the fact that an accepting c must know that it is a codependent (Lemma 9).

Lemma 10 and Theorem 11 give some preliminary results about termination and decision. Lemma 10 states that, at any terminating point of a C-system subject to process failures and recovery, all processes have decided and no process is failed.

Lemma 10 In a C-system subject to process failures and recovery, if (e, f) is a terminating point, then $(e, f) \models \bigwedge_{c\in\mathcal{C}}(ACCEPT_c \vee REFUSE_c) \wedge \bigwedge_{c\in\mathcal{C}}(AWARD^c_m \vee REJECT^c_m)$ and $Failed(e, f) = \emptyset$. ◪

Theorem 11 states that, in any weakly terminating system which is k-transit bounded and subject to process failures, every point can be extended to a terminating point without any process receiving any further messages. (Koo and Toueg (1988) showed this for weakly terminating systems subject to communication failures; instead of communication failures, we use the combination of k-transit boundedness and process failures to ensure that messages may disappear without being received.)

Theorem 11 Given a weakly terminating model $\mathbf{M} = (\mathcal{E}, \mathcal{A})$ which is k-transit bounded and subject to process failures, for all $(e, f) \in \mathbf{Pts}(\mathcal{E})$, there is a terminating extension (e', g) such that no process receives a nonnull message after (e', f). ◪

Lemma 12 states that m's dependency set choices cannot start to hold while m is failed and are not forced to hold.

Lemma 12 For any C-system $\mathbf{M}$ and $c \in \mathcal{C}$, $\bigvee_{x\in\mathcal{D}_c} DEPEND^x_m$ is m-failure-dissociated and pointwise nontrivial.

Based on the Message Chain Theorem and Lemma 12, Lemma 13 asserts that, if a contractor c knows that m made c a codependent, there must be a message chain from m to c.

Lemma 13 For any C-system $\mathbf{M}$, $c \in \mathcal{C}$, and $(e, f) \in \mathbf{Pts}(\mathcal{E})$, if $(e, f) \models K_c \bigvee_{x\in\mathcal{D}_c} DEPEND^x_m$, then there is a $\bigvee_{x\in\mathcal{D}_c} DEPEND^x_m$-message chain $m \xrightarrow{+} c$ in $(e, 0)$ to (e, f). ◪

Therefore, $K_c \bigvee_{x\in\mathcal{D}_c} DEPEND^x_m$ is c-receive-dependent.

The first part of Lemma 14 below says intuitively that, in order for m to award to c at some point, m must be sure that c has received enough information to accept. This is because otherwise the system may terminate without any more messages being received (by Theorem 11), so that c cannot gain the knowledge it needs to accept and must therefore refuse (by

Lemma 10), violating the **Decision Harmony** property.[4] The second part of Lemma 14 has the corresponding assertion needed for c to accept.

Lemma 14 In any weakly terminating C-system **M** which is k-transit bounded and subject to process failures and recovery, for any $c \in \mathcal{C}$,

- if $K_c\phi$ is c-receive-dependent and $\mathbf{M} \models ACCEPT_c \supset K_c\phi$, then $\mathbf{M} \models AWARD^c_m \supset K_m K_c\phi$.
- if $K_m\phi$ is m-receive-dependent and $\mathbf{M} \models AWARD^c_m \supset K_m\phi$, then $\mathbf{M} \models ACCEPT_c \supset K_c K_m\phi$.

Proof: We prove the first; the second follows analogously. We use the following claim: $\mathbf{M} \models AWARD^c_m \supset K_c\phi$.

Proof of claim: Assume, by way of contradiction, that there is $(e,f) \in \mathbf{Pts}(\mathcal{E})$ such that $(e,f) \models AWARD^c_m \wedge \neg K_c\phi$. Therefore, $(e,f) \models \neg ACCEPT_c$. By Theorem 11, there is $(e',h) \in \mathbf{Pts}(\mathcal{E})$ which is a terminating extension of (e,f) such that no process receives a nonnull message after (e',f). By Lemma 10, $(e',h) \models ACCEPT_c \vee REFUSE_c$, and by $K_c\phi$ being c-receive-dependent, $(e',h) \models REFUSE_c$. Therefore, $(e',h) \models AWARD^c_m \wedge REFUSE_c$, violating **Decision Harmony**. □Claim

Because $AWARD^c_m$ is local to m, whenever $AWARD^c_m$ holds in a particular point, it holds in all points which m considers similar. Therefore, $K_c\phi$ also holds in those points, so $\mathbf{M} \models AWARD^c_m \supset K_m K_c\phi$. □

We will call the first part of Lemma 14 the Award Knowledge Rule and the second part the Accept Knowledge Rule.

Below, we abbreviate $\vee_{x \in \mathcal{D}_c} DEPEND^x_m$ by $DEPEND^x_m$. Lemma 15 shows that, in a C-system subject to process failures, ① c must receive a message for the knowledge level $(K_cK_m)^j K_c DEPEND^x_m$ to hold; and ② m must receive a message for $(K_mK_c)^i DEPEND^x_m$ to hold.[5]

Lemma 15 In a C-system **M** subject to process failures, for any $c \in \mathcal{C}$,

- $(K_cK_m)^j K_c DEPEND^x_m$ is c-receive-dependent and initially false, for all $j \geq 0$; and
- $(K_mK_c)^i DEPEND^x_m$ is m-receive-dependent and initially false, for all $i \geq 1$.

Proof: We prove the first by induction on the knowledge nesting level j; the second follows similarly by induction on the knowledge nesting level i.

Base case: $j = 0$. We claim that $K_c DEPEND^x_m$ is c-receive-dependent. This holds from the requirement of a $DEPEND^x_m$-message chain (Lemma 13). $K_c DEPEND^x_m$ is initially false because $DEPEND^x_m$ is so.

---

[4] Unlike agreement problems, in which the post-failure decisions of faulty processes are irrelevant, commitment problems impose the same consistency requirements on all processes, whether they decide before or after failures. This motivates m, when it awards to c, to know that c has received enough information to decide consistently; otherwise, for example, c might fail and not recover until there are no more messages for it to receive, which guarantees that c cannot decide consistently.

[5] For any $p, q \in \Pi$, $j \geq 0$, we abbreviate $\underbrace{K_pK_q}_{1}\underbrace{K_pK_q}_{2}\ldots\underbrace{K_pK_q}_{j}\phi$ by $(K_pK_q)^j\phi$. We also abbreviate $p \xrightarrow{+} q \underbrace{\xrightarrow{+} p \xrightarrow{+} q}_{1} \underbrace{\xrightarrow{+} p \xrightarrow{+} q}_{2} \ldots \underbrace{\xrightarrow{+} p \xrightarrow{+} q}_{j}$ by $p \xrightarrow{+} q(\xrightarrow{+} p \xrightarrow{+} q)^j$.

Inductive step: $j > 0$. Assume the inductive hypothesis holds for $j-1$.
Therefore, $(K_cK_m)^{j-1}K_cDEPEND^x_m$ is c-receive-dependent and initially false. We now claim $K_cK_m(K_cK_m)^{j-1}K_cDEPEND^x_m$ is c-receive-dependent. By Lemma 7, introspection, and the Message Chain Theorem, $K_m(K_cK_m)^{j-1}K_cDEPEND^x_m$ is m-receive-dependent. Further, $K_m(K_cK_m)^{j-1}K_cDEPEND^x_m$ is initially false, because $DEPEND^x_m$ is. Therefore, by Lemma 7, introspection, and the Message Chain Theorem, $K_cK_m(K_cK_m)^{j-1}K_cDEPEND^x_m$ is c-receive-dependent; further, $K_cK_m(K_cK_m)^{j-1}K_cDEPEND^x_m$ is initially false, because $DEPEND^x_m$ is. ☒

Lemma 16 shows that ① $(K_cK_m)^jK_cDEPEND^x_m$ must hold for arbitrarily deep nesting in order for c to accept, and ② $(K_mK_c)^iDEPEND^x_m$ must hold for arbitrarily deep nesting for m to award to c.

Lemma 16 For any weakly terminating C-system **M** which is k-transit bounded and subject to process failures and recovery,

- $\mathbf{M} \models ACCEPT_c \supset (K_cK_m)^jK_cDEPEND^x_m$, for any $c \in C$, and for all $j \geq 0$.
- $\mathbf{M} \models AWARD^c_m \supset (K_mK_c)^iDEPEND^x_m$, for any $c \in C$, and for all $i \geq 1$.

Proof: We show the first; the second follows immediately. We prove this by induction on j.

Base case: $j = 0$. The claim that $\mathbf{M} \models ACCEPT_c \supset K_cDEPEND^x_m$ holds by Lemma 9.

Inductive hypothesis: $j > 0$. Assume the inductive hypothesis holds for $j-1$. Therefore, $\mathbf{M} \models ACCEPT_c \supset (K_cK_m)^{j-1}K_cDEPEND^x_m$. We now claim that $\mathbf{M} \models ACCEPT_c \supset K_cK_m(K_cK_m)^{j-1}K_cDEPEND^x_m$. This holds immediately from
(a) an application of the Award Knowledge Rule on $(K_cK_m)^{j-1}K_cDEPEND^x_m$ (which is c-receive-dependent by Lemma 15), and
(b) an application of the Accept Knowledge Rule on the result of application (a) (which is m-receive-dependent, also by Lemma 15).☒

Lemma 16 gave knowledge levels required for commitment; Lemma 17 now establishes the accompanying communication requirement of arbitrarily many consecutive message chains.

Lemma 17 In a C-system **M** subject to process failures,

- for all $j \geq 0$, if, for some $(e,f) \in \mathbf{Pts}(\mathcal{E})$ and $c \in C$, $(e,f) \models (K_cK_m)^jK_cDEPEND^x_m$, then there is a sequence of consecutive message chains $m \xrightarrow{+} c(\xrightarrow{+} m \xrightarrow{+} c)^j$ in $(e,0)$ to (e,f); and
- for all $i \geq 0$, if, for some $(e,f) \in \mathbf{Pts}(\mathcal{E})$ and $c \in C$, $(e,f) \models (K_mK_c)^iDEPEND^x_m$, then there is a sequence of consecutive message chains $c \xrightarrow{+} m(\xrightarrow{+} c \xrightarrow{+} m)^i$ in $(e,0)$ to (e,f).

Proof: We prove the first by induction on the length of the sequence of chains, j; the second follows analogously by induction on i.

Base case: $j = 0$. The claim is that, for any $(e,f) \in \mathbf{Pts}(\mathcal{E})$, if $(e,f) \models K_cDEPEND^x_m$, then there is a $DEPEND^x_m$-message chain from m to c in interval $(e,0)$ to (e,f). This holds by Lemma 13.

Inductive step: $j > 0$. Assume the inductive hypothesis holds for $j-1$. Now we claim that $K_cK_m(K_cK_m)^{j-1}K_c DEPEND^x_m$ requires a sequence of message chains $m \xrightarrow{+} c(\xrightarrow{+} m \xrightarrow{+} c)^j$. That is, if $(e,f) \models K_cK_m(K_cK_m)^{j-1}K_c DEPEND^x_m$, then there is a sequence of consecutive message chains $m \xrightarrow{+} c(\xrightarrow{+} m \xrightarrow{+} c)^j$ in interval $(e,0)$ to (e,f). From the inductive hypothesis, we can assert the existence of the chain sequence $m \xrightarrow{+} c(\xrightarrow{+} m \xrightarrow{+} c)^{j-1}$, required to establish $(K_cK_m)^{j-1}K_c DEPEND^x_m$. By Lemma 15, $(K_cK_m)^{j-1}K_c DEPEND^x_m$ is *c*-receive-dependent in M. Therefore, by Lemma 7, $(K_cK_m)^{j-1}K_c DEPEND^x_m$ is *c*-failure-dissociated in M. By Lemma 15, $(K_cK_m)^{j-1}K_c DEPEND^x_m$ is initially false. By process introspection, $(K_cK_m)^{j-1}K_c DEPEND^x_m$ is local to *c*. Therefore, by the Message Chain Theorem, there is a $(K_cK_m)^{j-1}K_c DEPEND^x_m$-message chain $c \xrightarrow{+} m$ in $(e,0)$ to (e,f), to establish $K_m(K_cK_m)^{j-1}K_c DEPEND^x_m$. Now this chain must strictly follow $m \xrightarrow{+} c(\xrightarrow{+} m \xrightarrow{+} c)^{j-1}$, because $(K_cK_m)^{j-1}K_c DEPEND^x_m$ must hold at the start of the new $c \xrightarrow{+} m$, and $(K_cK_m)^{j-1}K_c DEPEND^x_m$ cannot hold any earlier than the end of $m \xrightarrow{+} c(\xrightarrow{+} m \xrightarrow{+} c)^{j-1}$. From this, we conclude the existence of $m \xrightarrow{+} c(\xrightarrow{+} m \xrightarrow{+} c)^{j-1} \xrightarrow{+} m$. By similar reasoning, there is a $K_m(K_cK_m)^{j-1}K_c DEPEND^x_m$-message chain, to establish $K_cK_m(K_cK_m)^{j-1}K_c DEPEND^x_m$. We can conclude the existence of $m \xrightarrow{+} c(\xrightarrow{+} m \xrightarrow{+} c)^{j-1} \xrightarrow{+} m \xrightarrow{+} c$, or $m \xrightarrow{+} c(\xrightarrow{+} m \xrightarrow{+} c)^j$. ◻

From the fact that commitment between *c* and *m* requires infinitely long sequences of message chains between *c* and *m* and the fact that commitment must be possible in any C-system, we conclude our impossibility result.

Theorem 18 There is no weakly terminating C-system which is *k*-transit bounded and subject to process failures and recovery. ◻

The analogue of this result for atomic commitment tells us the following: if a round-based atomic commitment protocol is resilient to process failures and recovery and such that a message may be received only in the round in which it is sent, then the protocol may run forever.

From the knowledge levels in Lemma 16, one might think that one can prove Theorem 18 using common knowledge. Indeed, another way to prove this theorem would be to show that commitment in the given systems requires common knowledge among $\{x\}$ and *m* of $DEPEND^x_m$, which, as a direct corollary of the Message Chain Theorem, is impossible. The current results on attaining common knowledge do not address systems with process failures (although this extension should not be difficult). The Message Chain Theorem allows us to reason about both finite and infinite knowledge levels in several kinds of systems, including systems in which one cannot attain common knowledge. Further, we can reason about incremental gains in a process's knowledge through communication. Finally, the Message Chain Theorem applies to a broad class of problems.

We note that commitment under other system assumptions may require a variant of common knowledge of some proposition; for example, [Hadz88] shows the impossibility of nonblocking atomic commitment under permanent communication failures or weak termination and communication failures by showing ① the need for eventual common knowledge of a particular proposition, and ② the impossibility of attaining that common knowledge in the given systems. Our proof technique using nested knowledge levels and consecutive message chains may also be used directly in this example [Maze89].

7 SUMMARY

Our contribution in this paper is twofold. First, the Message Chain Theorem gives new, general situations in which message chains are required for knowledge gain. This can be used as a tool in examining knowledge and communication requirements for problems in distributed systems, without the need to repeat the lengthy combinatorial proof of the Message Chain Theorem. We note that, with minor changes to the proof, one can show similar message chain results for systems with other behaviours, such as asynchronous communication. Second, we illustrate the use of the Message Chain Theorem in showing impossibility results, by giving a new result for commitment problems, based on a knowledge and communication analysis of the problem specification.

Acknowledgements

Many discussions with Vassos Hadzilacos greatly influenced the work reported here. Questions from Joe Halpern and from Mark Tuttle led to some important clarifications and improvements in presentation. This research has been partially supported by the Natural Sciences and Engineering Research Council of Canada under grant A3356 and the University of Toronto under a Graduate Fellowship.

References

[ChLa85] K.M. Chandy and L. Lamport. "Distributed Snapshots: Determining Global States of Distributed Systems." *ACM Trans. on Computer Systems*, **3**, 1 (February 1985), 63-75.

[ChMi86] K.M. Chandy and J. Misra. "How Processes Learn." *Distributed Computing*, **1**, 1 (1986), 40-52.

[Hadz88] V. Hadzilacos. Class notes, CSC2221F (Topics in Distributed Systems), Department of Computer Science, University of Toronto, Toronto ON, Fall Term 1988.

[Hadz89] V. Hadzilacos. "A Knowledge Theoretic Analysis of Atomic Commitment." Submitted for publication.

[HaMo90] J. Halpern and Y. Moses. "Knowledge and Common Knowledge in a Distributed Environment." To appear in *Journal ACM*. (A preliminary version appears in *Proc. Third ACM Symp. Principles of Distributed Computing*, 1984, 50-61; revised versions appears as Research Report RJ4421, IBM Research Laboratory, San Jose CA, 1986, 1988.)

[KoTo88] R. Koo and S. Toueg. "Effects of Message Loss on the Termination of Distributed Protocols." *Information Processing Letters*, **27**, 4 (1988), 181-88.

[Lamp78] L. Lamport. "Time, Clocks and the Ordering of Events in a Distributed System." *CACM*, **21**, 7 (July 1978), 558-65.

[Maze89] M.S. Mazer. *A Knowledge-Theoretic Account of Negotiated Commitment*, Ph.D. Thesis, Department of Computer Science, University of Toronto, 1989 (available at Technical Report CSRI-237, Computer Systems Research Institute, University of Toronto, 1990).

AUTHOR INDEX